George Kazantzidis
Lucretius on Disease

Trends in Classics – Supplementary Volumes

Edited by
Franco Montanari and Antonios Rengakos

Associate Editors
Stavros Frangoulidis · Fausto Montana · Lara Pagani
Serena Perrone · Evina Sistakou · Christos Tsagalis

Scientific Committee
Alberto Bernabé · Margarethe Billerbeck
Claude Calame · Jonas Grethlein · Philip R. Hardie
Stephen J. Harrison · Stephen Hinds · Richard Hunter
Christina Kraus · Giuseppe Mastromarco
Gregory Nagy · Theodore D. Papanghelis
Giusto Picone · Alessandro Schiesaro
Tim Whitmarsh · Bernhard Zimmermann

Volume 117

George Kazantzidis

Lucretius on Disease

The Poetics of Morbidity in *De rerum natura*

DE GRUYTER

ISBN 978-3-11-111664-8
e-ISBN (PDF) 978-3-11-072276-5
e-ISBN (EPUB) 978-3-11-072292-5
ISSN 1868-4785

Library of Congress Control Number: 2021932591

Bibliographic information published by the Deutsche Nationalbibliothek
The Deutsche Nationalbibliothek lists this publication in the Deutsche Nationalbibliografie;
detailed bibliographic data are available on the Internet at http://dnb.dnb.de.

© 2022 Walter de Gruyter GmbH, Berlin/Boston
This volume is text- and page-identical with the hardback published in 2021.
Editorial Office: Alessia Ferreccio and Katerina Zianna
Logo: Christopher Schneider, Laufen
Printing and binding: CPI books GmbH, Leck

www.degruyter.com

Contents

Acknowledgments —— VII

Introduction —— 1

1   Disease and the (Un)Making of the World —— 11
1.1   Disease as an Architect —— 13
1.2   Re-reading the *clinamen* —— 20
1.3   Conclusion —— 33

2   Disease, Closure and the Sense of an Ending —— 37
2.1   What's in a Disease? —— 41
2.2   Sex Can Kill —— 51
2.3   The End of it All —— 60
2.4   Plague and the Suffering Body —— 67
2.5   Conclusion —— 74

3   Disease and the Marvellous. Epilepsy in Book 3 and 6 —— 76
3.1   Epilepsy and the Hippocratic Tradition —— 78
3.2   Epilepsy Re-considered —— 89
3.3   Epilepsy, Earthquakes and Volcanic Eruptions. Reinstating the Wondrous in a World of Sickness —— 99
3.4   Epilepsy and the Female in the Paradoxographical Tradition —— 108
3.5   Conclusion —— 120

4   From Callimachean Aesthetics to the Sublime. The Plague in Book 6 —— 122
4.1   Lucretius and Callimachean Aesthetics —— 123
4.2   Lucretius' Plague and Callimachus —— 136
4.3   Lucretius' Plague and the Sublime —— 147
4.4   Conclusion —— 160
4.5   Appendix —— 165

5   Afterword —— 173

Bibliography —— 175
Index Rerum et Nominum —— 197
Index Locorum —— 203

Acknowledgments

I am grateful to all those people who have read parts of the book or the entire manuscript and helped me with their feedback: Gordon Campbell, Philip Hardie, Katerina Oikonomopoulou, Theodore Papanghelis, Sotiris Paraschas, Chiara Thumiger. I have benefited tremendously from the friendship of my colleagues at the Department of Philology in Patras: special thanks are due to Aristoula and Katerina. The book would not have been written without the support and patience of Antonios Rengakos: I owe him a lot.

Chapter 2 is a revised and extended version of "Disease, Closure and Lucretius' Sense of an Ending", which was first published in A.N. Michalopoulos, S. Papaioannou and A. Zissos (eds.) (2017), *Dicite, Pierides: Classical Studies in Honour of Stratis Kyriakidis*, Cambridge, Cambridge Scholars Publishing. Some of the material discussed in Chapter 4 has already appeared in G. Kazantzidis (2018), "Intratextuality and Closure: The End of Lucretius' *De rerum natura*", in S.J. Harrison, S. Frangoulidis and T.D. Papanghelis (eds.), *Intratextuality and Latin Literature*, Berlin/Boston, De Gruyter.

The book is dedicated to the people I love; they know who they are, so no need of lists of names here. Meropi, Savvas, Olga and Marilia are a league of their own: a *concilium* to treasure like no other.

Patras, October 2020

Introduction

Towards the end of Book 1 Lucretius sets out to explain why he chose poetry to communicate his philosophical message. The passage, which contains one of the most celebrated similes in the *DRN*, runs as follows (1.926–50):

> avia Pieridum peragro loca nullius ante
> trita solo. iuvat integros accedere fontis
> atque haurire, iuvatque novos decerpere flores
> insignemque meo capiti petere inde coronam
> unde prius nulli velarint tempora Musae:
> primum quod magnis doceo de rebus et artis
> religionum animum nodis exsolvere pergo,
> deinde quod obscura de re tam lucida pango
> carmina, musaeo contingens cuncta lepore.
> id quoque enim non ab nulla ratione videtur;
> sed veluti pueris absinthia taetra medentes
> cum dare conantur, prius oras pocula circum
> contingunt mellis dulci flavoque liquore,
> ut puerorum aetas inprovida ludificetur
> labrorum tenus, interea perpotet amarum
> absinthi laticem deceptaque non capiatur,
> sed potius tali pacto recreata valescat,
> sic ego nunc, quoniam haec ratio plerumque videtur
> tristior esse quibus non est tractata, retroque
> volgus abhorret ab hac, volui tibi suaviloquenti
> carmine Pierio rationem exponere nostram
> et quasi musaeo dulci contingere melle,
> si tibi forte animum tali ratione tenere
> versibus in nostris possem, dum perspicis omnem
> naturam rerum qua constet compta figura.

I traverse pathless tracks of the Pierides never yet trodden by any foot. I love to approach virgin springs and there to drink; I love to pluck new flowers, and to seek an illustrious chaplet for my head from fields whence before this the Muses have crowned the brows of none: first because my teaching is of high matters, and I proceed to unloose the mind from the close knots of superstition; next because the subject is so dark and the lines I write so clear, as I touch all with the Muses' grace. For even this seems not to be out of place; but as with children, when physicians try to administer rank wormwood, they first touch the rims about the cups with the sweet yellow fluid of honey, that unthinking childhood be deluded as far as the lips, and meanwhile may drink up the bitter juice of wormwood, and though beguiled be not betrayed, but rather by such means be restored and regain health, so now do I: since this doctrine commonly seems somewhat harsh to those who have not used it, and the people shrink back from it, I have chosen to set forth my doctrine to you in sweet-speaking Pierian song, and as it were to touch it with the Muses' delicious honey, if by chance in such a way I might engage your mind in my verses, while you are learning to see in what shape is framed the whole nature of things.¹

The meaning in these lines seems fairly straightforward:² just as doctors smear honey around the rim of the cup to make children drink their bitter medicine,³ so does Lucretius sweeten his apparently harsh doctrine by applying the soothing medium of hexameter poetry; this is not a deception meant to do harm but a necessary step to be taken for the patient's own sake.⁴ Intrinsic to the simile is Lucretius' emerging role as a doctor. The idea that philosophy steps in to fill a gap for the treatment of the soul, since conventional medicine is predominantly focused on the body, can be traced back to classical sources (especially Plato),⁵ and becomes particularly prominent during the Hellenistic period. Indeed, despite their different views and strong disagreements on a number of important matters, both Epicurean and Stoic ethics appear to agree at least on the fact that what is principally at stake is the *remedy* of people's soul by means of curing it of false assumptions and of the attendant affections or "passions" (*pathē*).⁶ Chrysippus is reported by Galen to have claimed that since there is an art (*technē*) which we call

---

1 Translations of Lucretius are adapted from Rouse/Smith whose 1992 Loeb text I have used unless otherwise noted. 1.926–50 is repeated, with a few minor alterations, in 4.1–25.
2 Bibliography on this passage is rather extensive. For some illuminating discussions, see Classen 1968; Mitsis 1993; Gale 1994, 138ff.; Volk 2002, 96–99; Clay 2003; Nethercut 2019; Gellar-Goad 2020, 103–105.
3 In ancient botany and pharmacology the bitter and unpleasant taste of a plant was believed to make it suitable to be used as a drug; see Theophr. *Caus. pl.* 6.4.5–6. In this respect, Lucretius' choice of wormwood — the bitter herb *par excellence* — is not incidental; for the plant's medicinal properties, see Dioscorides, *De materia medica* 3.23, with Totelin 2018, 60–61.
4 Reasonable and resourceful as Lucretius' didactic choice at this point appears to be, later writers respond to it in a critical way. Persius proposes a kind of poetry which can be efficient only as long as it retains its "acerbity"; for the satirist's "poetics of discomfort" and his opposition to Lucretius' method of deceptive sweetness, see Freudenburg 2001, 182; Bartsch 2014, 246. Quintilian also revisits the Lucretian image with a certain touch of irony (*Inst.* 3.1.3–4, on the author's "apology" for the relative absence of *voluptas* in the pages to follow, which deal with the history of rhetoric): "I have tried to add some touch of elegance ... to lure young people into learning what I regarded as necessary for their studies, in the hope that they might be attracted by some pleasure in reading ... This is the reason Lucretius gives for writing philosophy in verse ... [citation of Lucretius 1.936–38 = 4.11–13] ... But I fear this book may appear to have too little honey and too much wormwood, and be more healthy for the student than agreeable" (... *sed nos ueremur ne parum hic liber mellis et absinthii multum habere uideatur, sitque salubrior studiis quam dulcior*); translation by Russell in Hunter/Russell 2011, 70. Cf. Sen. *Ep.* 75.5–7.
5 For the so-called "medical analogy", according to which philosophy treats the mind/soul just as medicine treats the body, see Holmes 2010a; 2013.
6 Nussbaum 1994 remains the most comprehensive and illuminating treatment on the subject.

medicine and which deals with the diseased body, it would be a mistake to think that there is no corresponding art for the diseased soul, namely philosophy: "nor is it true that the latter is inferior to the former, in its theoretical grasp and therapeutic treatment of individual cases" (*SVF* 3.471).[7] Similarly, according to Epicurus, philosophical discourse is "empty", *kenos* (a word used to signify the void), if it fails to "cure" human suffering: "for just as there is no use in medical expertise if it does not give therapy for bodily diseases, so too there is no use in philosophy if it does not expel the suffering of the soul" (fr. 221 Usener).[8]

Lucretius' simile could be appropriately placed in this context. Similes, however, operate on slippery ground; they can be revealing and instructive, but they can also harbor obscure and ambivalent meanings.[9] This is not the only place where Lucretius speaks of taste and honey in the same context. In Book 4, the poet says clearly that taste can be a relative matter; it is a sensible quality that is determined by the state of the perceiver rather than an intrinsic property of the substance that is consumed.[10] In Margaret Graver's words, according to Lucretius,

---

7 Galen, *PHP* 5.2.22, 5.437 K.: τί δὲ Χρύσιππος ἐν τῷ περὶ παθῶν ἠθικῷ γράφει ταυτί; "οὔτε γὰρ περὶ τὸ νοσοῦν σῶμά ἐστί τις τέχνη ἣν προσαγορεύομεν ἰατρικήν, οὐχὶ δὲ καὶ περὶ τὴν νοσοῦσαν ψυχήν ἐστί τις τέχνη οὔτ' ἐν τῇ κατὰ μέρος θεωρίᾳ τε καὶ θεραπείᾳ δεῖ λείπεσθαι ταύτην ἐκείνης". For a discussion of this text, see Nussbaum 1994, 316ff.

8 Porphyry, *Ad Marcellam* 31 (quoting Epicurus): κενὸς ἐκείνου φιλοσόφου λόγος, ὑφ' οὗ μηδὲν πάθος ἀνθρώπου θεραπεύεται· ὥσπερ γὰρ ἰατρικῆς οὐδὲν ὄφελος <εἰ> μὴ τὰς νόσους τῶν σωμάτων θεραπεύει, οὕτως οὐδὲ φιλοσοφίας, εἰ μὴ τὸ τῆς ψυχῆς ἐκβάλλει πάθος. Translation in Long/Sedley 1987, 155. For the analogy between philosophy and medicine in Epicureanism, see further: Epic. *Men.* 122, *SV* 64, Cic. *Fin.* 1.59, Diog. Oen. frs. 1–3 Smith. For bibliography on the subject, see Gigante 1975; Nussbaum 1986; 1994, 102–39; Tsouna 2009.

9 See, e.g., Mitsis 1993 who, based on Lucretius' self-image as a doctor who is deceiving children into drinking their bitter medicine, develops the argument about the poet's not entirely good-natured "didactic coercion"; according to Mitsis, Memmius, the poem's principal addresse, is treated throughout with a certain degree of condescension and becomes the didactic fool (*nēpios*) who is struggling to understand what the speaker is trying to teach. Bartsch 2015, 208, on the other hand, draws attention to the ambivalent meaning of *contingere* in these lines: "When Lucretius allows metaphors into *De rerum natura*, he offers a concessive nod to the danger of his undertaking: the very same verb he uses for the honey touching the cup, *contingere*, is used for how humans contaminate the invisible atomic world with the qualities of the world of the senses [see 2.755]–presumably using metaphor to do this as well". Finally, Clay 2007, 28 focuses his attention on Lucretius' ambiguous view of poetry as a "coating": "Lucretius' simile, if it is taken seriously, has an important consequence. Poetry is something external to, and fundamentally unlike, the substance of Lucretius' argument" (p. 28 n. 11).

10 See, especially, 4.633–35: *Nunc aliis alius qui sit cibus ut videamus / expediam, quareve, aliis quod triste et amarumst, / hoc tamen esse aliis possit perdulce videri*, "Next I will explain and enable us to see how different food is suited to different creatures, and why what is sour and bitter for some may yet seem very delicious to others".

"all things, perceiving subjects as well as the objects they perceive, consist of mixtures of differently shaped atoms ... Thus, if a substance contains both the smooth, round atoms which evoke sweetness and the barbed atoms of biterness, it is possible that a perceiver might be so configured as to admit only one or the other".[11] This explains why the same thing is sweet to some and bitter to others, fragrant or foul-smelling,[12] and so on. What is more, considering that the atomic arrangement of our bodies does not stay the same but changes constantly (as, for instance, when afflicted by a disease) the way we perceive and sense things varies accordingly (4.663–72):

> Nunc facile est ex his rebus cognoscere quaeque.
> quippe ubi cui febris bili superante coorta est
> aut alia ratione aliquast vis excita morbi,
> perturbatur ibi iam totum corpus, et omnes
> commutantur ibi positurae principiorum;
> fit prius ad sensum ut quae corpora conveniebant
> nunc non conveniant, et cetera sint magis apta,
> quae penetrata queunt sensum progignere acerbum;
> utraque enim sunt in mellis commixta sapore–
> id quod iam supera tibi saepe ostendimus ante.

> It is easy now from these explanations to understand every separate case. For when fever arises in anyone, from overflow of bile, or when the energy of some disease is excited in another way, then the whole body is thrown into a riot and all the positions of the first-beginnings are changed about; it follows that the bodies which once were suitable to cause sensation are so no longer, and the other things are more apt, which in penetrating can engender a bitter sensation; indeed, both these are commingled in the savour of honey–a matter which I have explained to you often before.[13]

---

[11] Graver 1990, 94.
[12] For subjective variations in the perception of smell, see 4.677–80. Significantly, Lucretius' example in this case involves the scent of honey to which bees are attracted; vultures, on the other hand, prefer the scent (and taste) of corpses. Although not spelled out, the point here seems to be that as bees find corpses appalling, so vultures remain indifferent to the sweetness of honey.
[13] The last line of the quoted passage, *id quod iam supera tibi saepe ostendimus ante* (4.672), is problematic since Lucretius has not, in fact, made this particular point about honey before. We can think of passages such as 2.398–407 and 3.191–95 but in neither of them is it stated explicitly that honey contains both smooth and rough particles; see Furley 1993, 85. As always in these cases, the theory is invoked that the poem did not receive a final revision.

Disease changes the way we see[14] and sense the world; it can even make honey taste bitter. Lucretius does not make the point explicitly, but this is what can be inferred and is an idea confirmed by several other sources, e.g. Seneca, *Ep.* 109.7: *sunt enim quidam quibus morbi vitio mel amarum videatur*, "for there are those to whom, because they have been affected by disease, honey looks bitter".[15] Sextus Empiricus, a philosopher and a doctor, makes the same claim in more detail: "Honey, which persuades many healthy people that it is sweet, but does not persuade the one person who has jaundice, we truly call sweet. But this is silly. For when we are inquiring about truth, we should not look to the number of people who agree but to their conditions. The sick person is in one condition, and all the healthy people are in one state. This condition, then, is no more to be relied on than that one, since if it is supposed, conversely, that many people are embittered by the honey (people in a fever, for example), and that the one person who is healthy is sweetened, it will certainly follow that we call the honey bitter — which is absurd".[16] This type of "perceptual relativity"[17] ultimately derives from Democritus — to whom Sextus attributes the thesis that "honey is neither sweet nor bitter"[18] — and is succinctly encapsulated in Plutarch's statement that, according to Epicurus, none of the flavours has a fixed quality (αὐτοτελῆ ποιότητα)

---

14 Literally so; in 4.332–36, for example, Lucretius states that patients who suffer from jaundice see everything a greenish-yellow (*lurida ...tuentur*), because many seeds of this colour "stream out from their bodies to meet the images of things, and besides many are mingled in their own eyes which by their contact paint everything with lurid hues".
15 See Bartsch 2015, 139–40.
16 *Against the Logicians* 2.53–54; translation in Bett 2005, 98–99.
17 I borrow the term from Graver 1990.
18 Sextus Empiricus, *Outlines of Scepticism* 1.213: "The philosophy of Democritus is also said to have something in common with Scepticism, since it is thought to make use of the same materials as we do. For from the fact that honey appears sweat to some and bitter to others, they say that Democritus deduces that it is neither sweet nor bitter, and for this reason utters the phrase 'No more', which is Sceptical" (translation in Annas/Barnes 2000, 54–55); see also 2.63, and cf. Theophr. *Sens.* 63–67 with Lee 2005, 217–42; Burnyeat 2012, 276. Furley 1993, 86 is right to observe that whereas taste is not explained in a systematically different way from the other senses, Lucretius nonetheless raises the issue of subjective experience in this case more intensely: "Lucretius goes on to talk about smells, and seems to be more confident about their ontology than he is about tastes. Taste is a matter of contact on particular occasions, and it cannot easily be given a durable identity, except as experienced. But smells are explained by Lucretius in much the same way as vision ... Without explicitly making the point, Lucretius appears to make smells, like colours, properties of the object. The impact of a smell touches the nostrils (*naris adiectus odoris / tangat*, 4.673–74)" (1993, 86). But with taste things are different, since in that case the atoms are said to *generate* it (*progignere*, 4.670) *in* the sense organ. Cf. Graver 1990, 94 and see also O'Keefe 2005, 74–75; Rudolph 2018, 49–54.

or power (δύναμιν) of its own but acquires different properties as it blends with different bodies (*Adv. Colot.* 1110b12–c2).¹⁹ Considering that Lucretius' programmatic statement in 1.926–50 can only make sense if we assume that he is addressing a *sick* audience in need of a cure, we then start to wonder if honey is really enough to cover up the wormwood that lies beneath — or if it has the opposite effect: that of accentuating the harsh taste it was supposed to eliminate.²⁰

Lucretius' references to disease are not always as straightforward as they seem. The standard view in scholarship is that disease in the *DRN* is simply a problem to be solved and then dispensed with. And yet, as we can see from 1.936–42, even in a formal statement that sets out to establish the poet's role as a doctor of the soul, things turn out to be more layered and complex than they appear at first sight: just as *morbus* causes a radical rearrangement of atoms in the body and makes the patient engage with alternative and up to that point unknown dimensions of the sensible world,²¹ so does disease as a theme generate a multiplicity of meanings in the text. The present book argues for a reconsideration of *morbus* in the poem along those lines: it invites the reader to revisit the topic of disease and reflect on the various, and often contrasting, discourses that unfold around it. More specifically, I wish to focus my attention on how, apart from calling for therapy and from being conceived as a problem that has to be eliminated, disease, due to its dominant presence in the narrative, transforms at the same time into a concept that is integral both to the poem's philosophical agenda but also to its wider aesthetic concerns as a literary product.

The first chapter — "Disease and the (Un)Making of the World" — discusses in detail the poet's striking reference to disease as an "architect of death" (3.472: *leti fabricator*) and explores how *morbus* effectively substitutes, throughout the

---

19 See Rudolph 2018, 52, with Castagnoli 2013. For the ontological status of sensible qualities in Democritus and Epicurus, see the detailed discussion in O' Keefe 1997.

20 See Totelin 2018, 68; for the fundamental similarities between honey and wormwood throughout the poem, see Nethercut 2019. Indeed, we can think of many cases in the *DRN* in which the "honey of poetry" is used to create unsettling images of extreme violence and to produce graphic descriptions of death and disease. In other words, we should remain aware of the fact that what we usually refer to as "purple passages" in Lucretius do not concern only passages in the poem which seem to be governed by a positive spirit (such as the opening hymn to Venus in Book 1) but include also grim and gloomy scenes, such as the plague at the end of Book 6, with their own powerful literary qualities. For Lucretius' fascination with images of violence in the *DRN*, see the recent discussion in Gale 2018.

21 Cf. Thumiger 2019, 102: "Bodily, or mental suffering is not simply a matter of being a patient afflicted by a named disease, and/or cured by a certain therapy, to finally recover (or not), but the intrusion of a new world, the beginning of an entirely different mode of life that commands the renegotiation of one's existence on all levels".

narrative, the absent gods by importing its own kind of order and design into a world that is otherwise conceived as the result of randomly clashing atoms. In this context, I examine how the *clinamen*, and its explanation as a *deviation* from an ordered chaos, is conceptually aligned with disease which in its turn is understood by the poet to break and disrupt an established arrangement of atoms in the body. My intention here is to illustrate how images of birth and creation blend with ideas of dissolution and decay to the extent that they become almost indistinguishable, and how disease emerges as a crucial catalyst that allows for the never-ending recycling of matter into newly fixed atomic compounds. In the second chapter — "Disease, Closure and the Sense of an Ending" — I move on to examine how the theme of disease is intimately linked to the poem's structure. One of the main devices employed by Lucretius to tie up the *DRN* into a unified whole, I argue, is the presence of disease in the closing sections of Book 3, 4 and 6, which gradually transforms from an affection of the soul — from a πάθος in the conventional philosophical sense of the term — to a physical ailment that is affecting the body, thereby foreshadowing the poem's impending end, the plague. Narrative cohesion is thus maintained through sections of the text which anticipate, in some form or another, the horrific scene of death, which brings the poem to a close. Significantly, this closural script calls for a reconsideration of the plague in at least one important respect: the increasing emphasis placed on physical pain and the threat of material dissolution as we move towards the poem's conclusion puts the body on centre stage. While it has now become an established view in scholarship that the plague should be read metaphorically, as a symbol of the mind's anxieties and the suffering caused by the lack of *ataraxia* in people's lives, I suggest that the importance of the body should by no means be underestimated, and that it is mainly from its association with the conclusiveness of biological death that the poem's final disease derives its meaning. In the third chapter — "Disease and the Marvellous. Epilepsy in Book 3 and 6" — I proceed to explore what happens when Lucretius' descriptions of disease are mixed with that "honey of poetry" which he has mentioned in 1.938. Taking as my case study the presentation of epilepsy in Book 3 (3.487–509), I focus on the similes, metaphors and analogies employed by Lucretius in order to show how this figurative language undermines the clinical and detached idiom by which the disease is originally introduced in the text. The cause of the disease is said to hide within the deep recesses of our bodies — and not, as is regularly the case, to invade us from without — and to attack us at will as though it were an animate force of its own. With this image the poet invites us to think of the body's capacity to transform, through illness, into something foreign to us: it is at this critical point, when we suddenly lose touch with what we thought to be intimately acquainted, that the marvellous (*mirum*), in the sense of the extraordinary and the bizarre, becomes reinstated in the narrative. Significantly, epilepsy becomes itself a metaphor for the earth's shaking and convulsing body in the course of Book 6. This is a wondrous terrain inhabited by forces which, even when they have been explained by the poet, retain, to a substantial degree, their marvellous properties, their power to captivate our imagination with mixed feelings of fascination and fear. The fact that earthquakes and volcanic eruptions become throughout assimilated to epileptic seizures, I suggest, should not necessarily be seen as diminishing our wonder for these phenomena — by means, that is, of associating them with the familiar reality of sickness; it can also have the opposite effect, that of exposing us as individuals to inconceivably grand proportions of pain and suffering and ultimately of estranging us from our very own bodies. That the (shaking) earth is throughout conceptualized as a woman's body only helps put epilepsy into dialogue with another persisting paradox in the poem, that of the female's bizarre and mystifying nature, something which Lucretius not only refrains from dismissing explicitly but reproduces eagerly at various points in the *DRN*. In the fourth and final chapter — "From Callimachean Aesthetics to the Sublime. The Plague in Book 6" — I explore further the intricate dialogue developed between disease and the discourse of wonder in the poem, this time by focusing my attention on the ways in which *morbus* becomes aestheticized and helps to produce magnificent spectacles of destruction that equal in beauty and intensity images of birth and creation in the narrative. Substantial attention has been recently drawn to the topic of the sublime in Lucretius, especially with regard to the celestial and earthly marvels in Book 6, but no due emphasis has been placed on the plague in this context. In this chapter I argue that instead of simply trying to decipher the exact meaning and function of the plague in philosophical terms, we should also take a moment to look at it as a piece of poetry and appreciate its powerful literary qualities. The poem's final scene, as I will attempt to illustrate, revolves around images of filth, excess and impurity, which reflect, among other things, Lucretius' uncomfortable relationship with Callimachus throughout the *DRN*. At the same time, it is precisely out of the messy and disordered world of disease that the poet aspires to create a spectacle that is exciting and appalling at the same time, horrifying and yet deeply fascinating. The feeling of dread that emerges as a response to the plague, I suggest, does not present itself as an exclusively negative emotion but forms part of a complicated aesthetic script which is ultimately designed to stir the poem's readers, for one last time, with the thrill of the sublime.

To argue for the salience of disease as a topic which does not only call for the poet's therapeutic intervention but which continues to appeal to his imagination both philosophically and aesthetically should by no means be misunderstood as an attempt to reinstate the old "anti-Lucretius within Lucretius" agenda. It should rather be seen as an invitation to explore the multiple voices which unfold around disease in the poem and to listen to the dialogue among them by remaining sensitive to the polyphony[22] of the text and to the tensions that might sometimes inevitably arise. In the introduction to a recent collection of essays devoted to Lucretius, Alison Sharrock aptly observes that

> the willingness among literary critics to read 'multiple voices' in the text of Lucretius is substantially less than it is in the text of Virgil. The surprising outcome of this situation is that Lucretius and Virgil have almost changed places in the way various aspects of their texts are read against themselves. Whereas once Lucretius was read 'against himself', even by those who were not quite convinced by the full force of Patin's anti-Lucrèce, and Virgil was read according to the monolithic canons of Augustanism (I exaggerate slightly for effect), the situation is now almost reversed. Lucretius is read, at least by some readers, as if no problem should be allowed to trouble the peaceful surface of his Epicurean *ataraxia*, whereas the rumblings under the Augustan surface of Virgil's poem are regularly encouraged to shoot out their flares.[23]

The idea that tensions inevitably lead to annoying inconsistencies and problematic self-contradictions, as Sharrock suggests, has made people, in some cases at least, turn a blind eye to the multiplicity of meanings generated by the *DRN*. Don Fowler, in a review of Lucretian scholarship, which was published back in 1991, makes the same point, but in a more provocative way, when observing that "[t]he stress (over the last 30 years) has been on the *control* of apparently disturbing elements. But recent literary theory has made this concept of "control" problematic: what keeps these elements in their place? Why can't one flip the *DRN* as well as the *Aeneid*? What about a dark "two-voices" view of Lucretius for a change?"[24] As I pointed out above, my discussion of disease in the *DRN* is not meant to bring out the poem's "dark" aspects. In a universe in which the primary constituents of matter never really perish and in which decomposed bodies are seen literally to breed new forms of life,[25] disease becomes more and more a natural, dynamic

---

22 For the "polyphony" of the *DRN*, see Segal 1990, 46–47. Cf. O'Hara 2007, 64–67.
23 Sharrock 2013, 11. Cf. Gillespie/Hardie 2007, 7.
24 Fowler 1991, 237.
25 See e.g. 3.719–21: *unde cadavera rancenti iam viscere vermes / expirant, atque unde animantum copia tanta / exos et exanguis tumidos perfluctuat artus?*, "[if the soul is immortal and exits intact from the dying body] how do corpses exhale worms from flesh already grown putrid, whence comes all the great mass of living creatures, boneless and bloodless, that surge through the swelling limbs?" Compare how worms and maggots are said to appear from mother earth in warm and moist conditions in 5.795–98; cf. 2.871–72, with Kennedy 2007, 392.

process which involves not only the idea of an ending but that of a new beginning as well. It is at this crucial intersection between endings and new beginnings where *morbus*, the "architect of death", comes into play as a profoundly ambivalent force whose dissolving effect produces the conditions which are required for new forms of life to emerge.[26] "Morbidity", appearing in the title of this book, is thus not meant as a hint at Lucretian pessimism but serves instead to underscore the crucial role played by disease in shaping Lucretius' worldview as a philosopher and a poet.

---

26 See 1.262–64 (discussed below): "no visible object utterly passes away, since nature makes up again one thing from another, and does not permit anything to be born unless aided by another's death".

1 Disease and the (Un)Making of the World

> I can do nothing about the vortex that brought my birth, and whose unfolding will bring my death. The science of time, that of things and of the world, teaches me that existence is disorder and disordered destruction.
>
> Michel Serres, *The Birth of Physics*

> Disease was a perverse, a dissolute form of life. And life? Life itself? Was it perhaps only an infection, a sickening of matter? Was that which one might call the original procreation of matter only a disease?
>
> Thomas Mann, *The Magic Mountain*

In the course of Book 3 Lucretius adduces a number of arguments in order to prove that the soul[1] is mortal; this helps him to establish that there is no existence after death and therefore neither should there be any fear for what happens to us once we die. One of those arguments is grounded on the observation that in bodily diseases (*morbis in corporis*) the mind can become infected. Given that disease transcends the narrow limits of the *corpus* and "contaminates" the *animus*,[2] it follows that the latter is subject to dissolution; "for both pain and disease are *makers of death*" (3.463–73):

---

1 Throughout Book 3, Lucretius uses *animus*, "mind", and *anima*, "spirit", to refer to two distinguishable parts of the *psuchē*. These two parts are conjoined in "one nature" (3.136–37: *nunc animum atque animam dico coniuncta teneri / inter se atque unam naturam conficere ex se*) and correspond to the "rational" and "irrational" part of the soul respectively. "That, however", as Kenney 2014, 91 observes, leaves Lucretius "with no one word for that whole corresponding with ψυχή. Thus he is forced either to couple the two or for the sake of brevity to use one or the other for the whole"; cf. Everson 1999, 544–45 and Taylor 2007, 81–83.

2 I do not mean, of course, to suggest here a mind-body dualism. In 3.96–97, Lucretius has explained that the *animus* is a "part of man", no less than the hands, the feet or the eyes, *esse hominis partem nilo minus ac manus et pes / atque oculi partes animantis totius extant*. He then, however, proceeds to qualify this claim by stressing that, though corporeal in nature, the mind consists of atoms which have an exceptionally refined quality (3.179–80). The idea of "contamination" in 3.471 (*penetrant in eum contagia morbi*) should be set in this context. The fact that the *animus* is described as "catching" the disease underlines its intrinsic affinity to the rest of the body, while at the same time stressing its special status as something cleaner and purer than the stuff which surrounds it. Cf. 6.1236, describing how the plague spreads across *different* bodies: *ex aliis alios* avidi *contagia morbi*. For Lucretius' adaptation of images — in the course of Book 3 — which are originally linked to a dualist conception of the relation between mind/soul and body, see Schrijvers 2007, 282–83.

> Quin etiam morbis in corporis avius errat
> saepe animus; dementit enim deliraque fatur,
> interdumque gravi lethargo fertur in altum
> aeternumque soporem oculis nutuque cadenti,
> unde neque exaudit voces nec noscere voltus
> illorum potis est, ad vitam qui revocantes
> circumstant lacrimis rorantes ora genasque.
> quare animum quoque dissolui fateare necessest,
> quandoquidem penetrant in eum contagia morbi;
> nam dolor ac morbus leti fabricator uterquest,
> multorum exitio perdocti quod sumus ante.

Moreover, in bodily diseases the mind often wanders astray; for it is demented and talks deliriously, and at times is carried by heavy lethargy into the deep everlasting sleep with eyes drooping and dejected head, from which it can neither catch the voices nor recognize the looks of those who stand round calling it back to life, their faces and cheeks bedewed with tears. Therefore you must confess that the mind also is dissolved, since the contagion of disease penetrates within it; for both pain and disease are makers of death, as we have been well taught by the perishing of many before now.

In his brief note on 3.472, *morbus leti fabricator,* Edward Kenney speaks of a "striking metaphor … since disease is generally thought of as a destroyer".[3] Charles Segal draws attention to the fact that the phrasing at this point reveals Lucretius' conception of disease as "a quasi-personified force": *morbus* is presented not simply as a condition from which the individual is suffering in a passive way but as an active force at work which, even under circumstances of extreme physical and mental pain, continues to devise and produce new results.[4] Indeed, if we consider that in Lucretius' atomic universe dissolution is a necessary requirement for (re)generation, the application of *fabricator* to disease implies not just the immediate product of death but also that of a new life emerging through death. As we are told in 1.262–64, due to the fact that atoms are indivisible, solid and, therefore, indestructible,[5] "no visible object utterly passes away, since nature makes up again one thing from another, and does not permit anything to be born unless aided by another's death" (*haud igitur penitus pereunt quaecumque videntur, / quando alid ex alio reficit natura, nec ullam / rem gigni*

---

3 Kenney 2014, 139.
4 Segal 1990, 63–64. Cf. Waszink 1966, 250 n. 2 and 253–56; Michels 1955, 161–63. Compare how disease and pain are described by medical authors as "settling in" / "becoming established" within the body, e.g. in [Hipp.] *Coac.* 309 (5.652 L.): πόνος ἐς στῆθος ἱδρυνθείς.
5 Cf. 1.485–86: *sed quae sunt rerum primordia, nulla potest vis / stinguere,* "but those which are the first-beginnings of things no power can quench".

*patitur **nisi morte adiuta aliena***). In the constant flow and transformation of matter, life becomes dependent on dissolution, and disease is naturally assuming the role of a crucial catalyst: as an "architect of death", it releases the atoms from the structures to which they currently belong and allows them consequently to provide the material for newly fixed atomic compounds.[6]

1.1 Disease as an Architect

And yet the implications of *fabricator* in 3.472 (the noun is attested only once in the poem)[7] run deeper than that. As I will proceed to argue, this striking and unprecedented metaphor flags Lucretius' sustained engagement with disease as a concept which effectively comes to play the role of the absent gods, in the sense of importing and imposing its own peculiar kind of order and design[8] into a world

---

[6] See Fitzgerald 1984, 83.
[7] The verb is used in 3.728, significantly in a context of rotting and decay. Lucretius dismisses at this point the possibility that the worms which come out of a corpse have spirits of their own; rather, they draw their life from the soul particles which remain trapped in, and dissolve along with the rest of the rotting body (3.722–29): "Now if you believe by any chance that spirits can creep into the worms from without ... here is a question that it seems worthwhile to ask and to bring under examination, whether in fact the spirits go a-hunting for all the seeds of little worms and themselves make them a habitation, or whether they creep as it were into bodies already formed", ... *utrum tandem animae venentur semina quaeque / vermiculorum ipsaeque sibi **fabricentur** ubi sint, / an quasi corporibus perfectis insinuentur.*
[8] *Fabricator* implies skillfull craftsmanship as well as the execution of a predetermined plan; see e.g. Vitr. 1.1.1. Schrijvers 2007, 283–4 draws attention to Lucretius' choice to avoid the "traditional dualist representation of the body as dwelling place of the soul. The absence of this metaphor from the *De rerum natura*", he argues, "is probably to be explained by the fact that the image of the house is very popular with thinkers whose world view is theological and teleological, and that Lucretius judged *the use of analogies taken from the realm of artefacts* (emphasis added) too hazardous because, owing to their teleological implications, they ran the risk of being exploited by the opponents of Epicureanism"; cf. Husner 1924, 60–66. But note how the image of the *collapsing* building is regularly used throughout the poem in contexts of death, e.g. in 3.584–86; 4.867–68, 942–43. Although metaphors which play out the notions of design and purposeful action are by no means restricted to images of destruction (see e.g. Kennedy 2007, 388–91 on the personification of Nature in the *DRN*), it appears that they become particularly relevant when the *unmaking* of things comes to the fore. This applies also to (*ruet moles et*) *machina mundi* in 5.96. The phrase, as Berryman 2009, 39 observes, does not involve any concrete allusions to technology, and its meaning "could be little more than a vague sense of an arrangement of system, perhaps in contrast to mere undifferentiated mass"; nonetheless, its exceptional appearance in the poem, in a context which speaks of the ultimate disbanding of the world, is significant. One would be tempted to think that Lucretius' engagement with the concept of design

that is said to have been produced as the result of randomly clashing atoms and in which chance continues to occupy a prominent position.⁹

We should start by stressing that this is the first occurrence of *fabricator* in Latin poetry; it subsequently occurs in Vergil, Ovid and Manilius,¹⁰ and remains relatively rare elsewhere in classical Latin. Cicero's use of the word in his translation of Plato's *Timaeus*¹¹ betrays its philosophical significance and, more crucially, establishes its fundamental link with Plato's ideas about the *creation* of the world (*Timaeus* 6):

> Atque illum quidem quasi parentem huius universitatis invenire difficile et, cum iam inveneris, indicare in vulgus nefas. Rursus igitur videndum, ille fabricator huius tanti operis utrum sit imitatus exemplar, idne, quod semper unum et idem et sui simile, an id, quod generatum ortumque dicimus.

The corresponding Greek text runs as follows (*Ti.* 28c–29a):

> Τὸν μὲν οὖν ποιητὴν καὶ πατέρα τοῦδε τοῦ παντὸς εὑρεῖν τε ἔργον καὶ εὑρόντα εἰς πάντας ἀδύνατον λέγειν· τόδε δ' οὖν πάλιν ἐπισκεπτέον περὶ αὐτοῦ, πρὸς πότερον τῶν παραδειγμάτων ὁ **τεκταινόμενος** αὐτὸν ἀπηργάζετο, πότερον πρὸς τὸ κατὰ ταὐτὰ καὶ ὡσαύτως ἔχον ἢ πρὸς τὸ γεγονός.

> But it would be a hard task to discover the maker and father of this universe of ours, and even if we did find him, it would be impossible to speak of him to everyone. So what we

---

intensifies precisely at points in the narrative which focus on the ending of life, be it through disease or through destructions of larger proportions.

9 As Kennedy 2007, 381 points out, "[t]he desired goal of the *DRN*, ridding our minds of the notion of divine causation, entails abandoning the notion of design. Our world is a chance occurrence, not created for us; and we are chance inhabitants of it, not the culmination of a process of creation. If the world happens to fulfil our needs and pleasures, that is pure chance; for many other species, it has not been so, and they have perished".

10 Verg. *Aen.* 2.264; Ov. *Met.* 1.57; *Tr.* 5.12.47; Man. 5.31. Vergil's use is the one which lies closer to Lucretius' text. Unlike Manilius, for example, who applies the word to the divine demiurge (5.30–31: *has stellis proprias vires et tempora rerum / constituit magni quondam fabricator Olympi*; see Hübner 2010, 27 and, for the Platonic echoes in this passage, MacGregor 2005, 47–48), Vergil uses it for Epeos, the one who devised the "fraud", i.e. the Trojan horse, that will bring about pain and death to the enemies of the Greeks: *et ipse **doli fabricator** Epeos. Dolus*, as Paschalis 1997, 105 observes, echoes Hom. *Od.* 8.493–94 (τὸν Ἐπειὸς ἐποίησεν ... δόλον); at the same time, it could be taken as an acoustic allusion to the Lucretian ***dolor** ac morbus leti fabricator*.

11 Cicero's translation, which is believed to have been produced at some point between 45 and 43 BCE, covers the section 27d–47b of the Greek text. For some discussions of this translation, see Lévy 2003; Sedley 2013; Hoenig 2018, 44ff.; cf. Reydams-Schils 2013.

have to ask is, again, which of those two kinds of model the creator was using as he constructed the universe. Was he looking at what is consistent and permanent or at what has been created?[12]

Cicero is focusing at this point on Plato's divine "craftsman", an entity that is believed to have intelligently designed the world in the best possible way; *fabricator deus* likewise appears in Apuleius as distinctly reminiscent of the language applied to the cosmos' delicate construction in Plato's *Timaeus*.[13] The extent to which Lucretius could have been familiar with this particular meaning of the word remains open to speculation. The fact that its first occurrence in a context which explicitly reveals its Platonic associations is attested in Cicero by no means entails that *fabricator* could not have already been used by the poet with a view to the same philosophical background. Several passages in the *DRN* contain extended allusions to Plato's dialogues.[14] While Lucretius is not always hostile,[15] his overall tendency is to engage critically with Plato's views, often by indulging in what scholarship has identified as a consistent and pervasive "anti-Timaean polemic" throughout the poem.[16] In 2.67–70, for example, Lucretius states that the matter of the visible world is not "stuck together": *nam certe **non inter se stipata cohaeret** / **materies**, quoniam minui rem quamque videmus / et quasi longinquo*

---

12 Translation in Waterfield 2008, 17. For Plato's divine craftsman, see Broadie 2012, 7–26.
13 See e.g. Apul. *De dogmate Platonis* 1.8: *Idcirco autem perfectissimo et pulcherrimo mundo instar pulchrae et perfectae sphaerae **a fabricatore deo** quaesitum est, ut sit nihil indigens, sed operiens omnia coercensque contineat, pulcher et admirabilis, sui similis sibique respondens*. For a discussion, see Hoenig 2018, 145.
14 For some illuminating discussions, see De Lacy 1983; Sedley 1998, 62–69, 75–81; Reinhardt 2004; Warren 2006, 248–49; Park 2012. Cf. Solmsen 1951.
15 Especially when it comes to the use of metaphors; compare, for instance, the idea that it is futile to store up pleasures into a "leaky vessel" in 3.936–37 with Pl. *Grg.* 493a–494c; see Görler 1997 and Warren 2014, 92–93. With Lucretius' connection between the fears of the unenlightened and those which possess small children in the dark (2.55–61 = 6.35–41), compare Pl. *Soph.* 234b; *Rep.* 598c; *Phd.* 77e; see Fowler 2002, 136; cf. Gale 1994, 48–49; Marcović 2008, 30.
16 This becomes particularly evident in Book 5, where Lucretius' anti-evolutionary model of creation is heavily inspired by the high drive to oppose the teleology of Plato's *Timaeus*; see Campbell 2003, 1–8; cf. Campbell 2000. There can be little doubt that this polemic ultimately derives from Lucretius' Greek model. As Sedley 1998, 152 observes, "one can imagine that Epicurus, in developing his own account of the world's origin in *On nature* xi–xii, felt the need to respond point by point to the *Timaeus*". Cf. Cic. *N. D.* 1.18, at which point the Epicurean Velleius joins the discussion with the following acerbic remark: *"Audite" inquit, "non futtilis commenticiasque sententias, non opificem aedificatoremque mundi, Platonis de Timaeo deum…"*, "I am not going to expound to you doctrines that are mere baseless figments of the imagination, such as the artisan deity and world-builder of Plato's *Timaeus*" (translation in Rackham 1933, 21).

fluere omnia cernimus aevo / ex oculisque vetustatem subducere nostris, "for certainly matter is not one packed and coherent mass, since we see each thing decreasing, and we perceive all things as it were ebbing through length of time, and age withdrawing them from our eyes". The lines harbor an implicit critique of the idea that the world's *materies* has been appropriately arranged by a superior divine agent. In *Timaeus* 15 Cicero uses the phrase *apte cohaeret* to translate Plato's εἰς ταὐτὸν αὑτῷ συνελθόν (*Ti.* 32c), adding that matter cannot be dissolved unless by divine will (... *ita apte cohaeret, ut dissolvi nullo modo queat nisi ab eodem, a quo est conligatus*).[17] Indeed Plato leaves enough space for the suggestion that the whole world is indestructible and thus eternal, at least as long as the demiurge is willing to maintain it in this state (*Ti.* 41a–b).[18] By contrast, at the beginning of Book 5 Lucretius explains how the bond between earth, water and air, the three elements which have combined to create the world as we know it, will one day collapse (5.94–96): *tris species tam dissimilis, tria talia texta, / una dies dabit exitio, multosque per annos / sustentata ruet moles et **machina mundi**,*[19] "these three forms so different [i.e. sea, earth and sky], these three textures so interwoven, one day shall consign to destruction; the mighty and complex system of the world, upheld through many years, shall crash into ruins". Some scholars have read these lines as a critique of Stoicism's idea of a providentially designed universe that holds fast because there is a bond, δεσμός, between its parts which prevents them from separating;[20] yet, given that the Stoics concede that the world

---

17 The corresponding Greek text (32b–c) reads as follows (on the four elements which the demiurge has used to create the world): καὶ διὰ ταῦτα ἔκ τε δὴ τούτων τοιούτων καὶ τὸν ἀριθμὸν τεττάρων τὸ τοῦ κόσμου σῶμα ἐγεννήθη δι' ἀναλογίας ὁμολογῆσαν, φιλίαν τε ἔσχεν ἐκ τούτων, **ὥστε εἰς ταὐτὸν αὑτῷ συνελθὸν ἄλυτον ὑπό του ἄλλου πλὴν ὑπὸ τοῦ συνδήσαντος γενέσθαι.**
18 See Rubenstein 2014, 23–24.
19 The expression *machina mundi* occurs here for the first time in Latin. Marcović 2008, 52 connects it to Plato's Timaean conception of the world as a structure of a remarkably complex design. The reception of the phrase in later Latin literature reveals its systematic reemployment in contexts of destruction; rather than point to any form of endurance, *machina* — as Lucretius was the first to establish — is suggestive of a fragile arrangement. See e.g. Man. 2.807: *dissociata fluat resoluto machina mundo*; Luc. 1.79–80: *totaque discors / machina divolsi turbabit foedera mundi*.
20 The concept of δεσμός is attributed to Chrysippus; see *SVF* 2.719: δεσμὸς ὢν τῶν ἁπάντων, ὡς εἴρηται, καὶ συνέχει τὰ μέρη πάντα καὶ σφίγγει, κωλύων αὐτὰ διαλύεσθαι. Cf. *SVF* 1.106, 2.458, 802. As the Stoic Balbus, in Cic. *N.D.* 2.115, confirms: *maxime autem corpora inter se iuncta permanent, cum quasi quodam **vinculo** circumdato colligantur*, "moreover bodies conjoined maintain their union most permanently when they have some bond encompassing them to bind them together" (translation in Rackham 1933, 233).

will at one point perish in a cosmic "conflagration" (*ekpurōsis*),²¹ it is likelier that Lucretius' attack at this point is directed against the Timaean concept of an eternally holding structure²² (this crucial difference between Plato and the Stoics with regard to the world's presumed eternity is appropriately underlined by the Epicurean Velleius in Cic. *N.D.* 1.20).²³ The hypothesis of an "anti-Timaean" polemic is further confirmed by other passages in the *DRN*. In Book 5, Lucretius has made it abundantly clear that, during the early stages of the world, there was no pre-existing pattern for the forms of life that sprang from the earth: animals were created randomly, some without eyes (5.841: *sine voltu caeca*), some without feet (5.840: *orba pedum*), others without hands (5.840: *manuum viduata*) or mouths (5.841: *muta sine ore*). Certain creatures managed to adapt, while others became extinct because of their incompleteness. The image drawn here could not be any more different from the Timaean view, according to which "all species", as Gordon Campbell points out, "come into being to fulfill the purpose of the demiurge and so complete the perfect match of this world with the original".²⁴ In *Timaeus* 31a–b, Plato speaks of a uniquely beautiful world that "cannot have a double" (μεθ' ἑτέρου δεύτερον οὐκ ἄν ποτ' εἴη); in a statement which is clearly aimed to dismiss earlier atomic theories, we read that the divine craftsman did not make "two or an infinite plurality of worlds" (οὔτε δύο οὔτ' ἀπείρους ἐποίησεν ὁ ποιῶν

---

21 See Long 1985; Algra 2003, 173–74.
22 This is Sedley's (1998, 75–76) reading of Lucr. 5.156–234, a text which is foreshadowed by 5.94–96 and deconstructs in detail the view that the world was created by the gods for men's sake and that it will therefore last forever. "To say further that for men's sake (*hominum causa*) they had the will to prepare the glorious structure of the world, and that therefore it is fitting to praise it as an admirable work of the gods; and to think that it will be everlasting and immortal (*aeternumque putare atque immortale futurum*) ... to feign this, and other such conceits, one upon another, Memmius, is the act of a fool" (5.156–65). As Sedley 1998, 76 observes, while the *Timaeus* "does not supply the specific thesis, so characteristic of Stoicism, that the world was created for the sake of mankind ... it remains entirely possible that [it] was being read in this way by Epicurus' day". See also Sedley 2007, 139–50.
23 Cic. *N.D.* 1.20 (Velleius addressing the Stoic Balbus): *Pronoea vero si vestra est, Lucili, eadem, requiro quae paulo ante, ministros machinas omnem totius operis dissignationem atque apparatum; sin alia est,* **cur mortalem fecerit mundum, non, quem ad modum Platonicus deus, sempiternum,** "While as for your Stoic Providence, Lucilius, if it is the same thing as Plato's creator, I repeat my previous questions, what were its agents and instruments, and how was the entire undertaking planned out and carried through? If on the contrary it is something different, I ask why it made the world mortal, and not everlasting as did Plato's divine creator?" (translation in Rackham 1933, 23).
24 Campbell 2000, 161. For the roots of "optimality reasoning" (we attempt to understand the way things are by appealing to some idea of an optimal design at work) in Plato's *Timaeus* and its reception in Aristotle's natural teleology, see Henry 2013.

κόσμους),²⁵ but, instead, the world we inhabit "is and will continue to be a unique creation" (ἀλλ' εἷς ὅδε μονογενὴς οὐρανὸς γεγονὼς ἔστιν καὶ ἔτ' ἔσται).²⁶ Lucretius' polemic emerges as a response to this critical treatment of atomism, and reinstates a world of imperfectness and randomness in the place of what had been proposed by Plato to be a singularly conceived and brilliantly executed design.

The hypothesis that *fabricator* had been transposed by Lucretius from the divine realm — in which one would have expected it to feature in a Platonic context — to that of death and disease, which have a far more potent presence in his poem, could be seen as forming part of the same revisionist critique of the *Timaeus*.²⁷ To appreciate fully Lucretius' subversive attitude at this point, let us return to 3.472 in light of Cicero, *Timaeus* 16–17:

> Earum autem quattuor rerum, quas supra dixi, sic in omni mundo partes omnes conlocatae sunt, ut nulla pars huiusce generis excederet extra, atque ut in hoc universo inessent genera illa universa, id ob eas causas, primum ut mundus animans posset ex perfectis partibus esse perfectus, deinde ut unus esset nulla parte, unde alter gigneretur, relicta, postremo ne qui morbus eum posset aut senectus attingere. Omnis enim coagmentatio corporis vel caloris vel frigoris <vi> vel aliqua inpulsione vehementi labefactatur et frangitur et ad morbos senectutemque conpellitur. Hanc igitur habuit rationem effector mundi et molitor deus, ut unum opus totum atque perfectum ex omnibus et totis atque perfectis absolveret, quod **omni morbo** et senio vacaret.

> Of the four things which I mentioned all parts have been placed in all the universe in such a way that no part of this kind should move outside, and that the latter kinds of things [the elements] should exist entire in the former [the universe], also entire; this has been done for these reasons, firstly so that the universe should be a perfect creature made from perfect parts, then so that it should be one, with no part left from which another universe could be produced, and finally so that no disease or old age could touch it. For every composition of a body is loosened and broken by the force of heat or cold or some strong impact, and driven

---

25 As, for example, Democritus had maintained. For the idea of "innumerable worlds" in ancient atomism, see Warren 2004a.
26 As Rubenstein 2014, 24 observes, "the argument here is that the universe must be singular in order to resemble its model most perfectly".
27 At the same time, of course, it could also be targeting the Stoics who also believe strongly in the "fabric" of the world as the result of an intelligent design; see e.g. Cic. *Luc.* 119: *nec magis adprobabit nunc lucere quam, quoniam Stoicus est, hunc mundum esse sapientem, habere mentem quae **et se et ipsum fabricata sit** et omnia moderetur moveat regat*, "so he will approve the claim that it is light now no more firmly than, e.g. — since we're dealing with a Stoic — the doctrines that the world is wise, and that it has a mind that constructed itself and the world and orders, moves, and governs everything" (translation in Brittain 2006, 69). Cf. Cic. *N.D.* 1.4; 2.133.

to diseases and old age. So this was the reason of the god who fashioned and built the universe, to complete one whole and perfect work from elements that were all whole and perfect, which would be free from all disease and age.²⁸

The idea that the world ultimately derives from a divinely inspired design and continues to be maintained by a supreme, guarding agent is crucially linked in Plato with the *absence* of disease on a cosmic level. This is a point to which, as we can see, Cicero pays due attention in his translation of the Greek original.²⁹ If we are willing then to accept that Lucretius' *fabricator* alludes, in some way or another, to Plato's *Timaeus*, it transpires that its application to *morbus* has been designed to overturn Plato's "healthy" world: in an Epicurean universe with which the gods do not interfere (since they enjoy an ideal habitat of their own, protected from pain, *dolor*, and other ills),³⁰ disease has been left to roam free, being produced by the earth and the sky in "immeasurable quantities"³¹ and sweeping everything in its path, from the bodies of human beings to the entire fabric of the world;³² in fact, its very presence in our lives could be seen as proof

---

28 Translation in Hutchinson 2013, 195.
29 For the corresponding Greek passage, see Pl. *Ti.* 32c–33d: τῶν δὲ δὴ τεττάρων ἓν ὅλον ἕκαστον εἴληφεν ἡ τοῦ κόσμου σύστασις. ἐκ γὰρ πυρὸς παντὸς ὕδατός τε καὶ ἀέρος καὶ γῆς συνέστησεν αὐτὸν ὁ συνιστάς, μέρος οὐδὲν οὐδενὸς οὐδὲ δύναμιν ἔξωθεν ὑπολιπών, τάδε διανοηθείς, πρῶτον μὲν ἵνα ὅλον ὅτι μάλιστα ζῷον τέλεον ἐκ τελέων τῶν μερῶν εἴη, πρὸς δὲ τούτοις ἕν, ἅτε οὐχ ὑπολελειμμένων ἐξ ὧν ἄλλο τοιοῦτον γένοιτ' ἄν, ἔτι δὲ ἵν' ἀγήρων καὶ **ἄνοσον** ᾖ, κατανοῶν ὡς συστάτῳ σώματι θερμὰ καὶ ψυχρὰ καὶ πάνθ' ὅσα δυνάμεις ἰσχυρὰς ἔχει περιιστάμενα ἔξωθεν καὶ προσπίπτοντα ἀκαίρως λύει καὶ **νόσους** γήρας τε ἐπάγοντα φθίνειν ποιεῖ. διὰ δὴ τὴν αἰτίαν καὶ τὸν λογισμὸν τόνδε ἕνα ὅλον ὅλων ἐξ ἁπάντων τέλεον καὶ ἀγήρων καὶ **ἄνοσον** αὐτὸν ἐτεκτήνατο. See Hutchinson 2013, 194–96. On a human level disease is of course present (*Ti.* 81e–82a), but Plato presents it as unnatural and unnecessary; see Grams 2009, 165–66 and van der Eijk 2017, 221–25.
30 See 2.646–51 (*divom natura ... / privata dolore omni, privata periclis*) and 3.18–22.
31 6.663–64: *et satis haec tellus morbi caelumque mali fert, / unde queat vis* **immensi procrescere morbi**, "and this earth and sky produce enough noxious disease that from it may grow forth an immeasurable quanity of disease".
32 See Segal 1990, 97: "In the argument for the mortality of the world in book 5, Lucretius describes its subjection to "diseases" (*morbis*) in exactly the same terms as he does the human body. In both cases "some harsher cause" will bring not just sickness but total destruction (cf. 5.346–47, *ibi si tristior incubuisset / causa*, "if some grimmer cause had pressed upon things"; 3.485–86, *paulo si durior insinuarit / causa*, "if a somewhat harsher cause slipped within"). The "diseases" of the world, moreover, include natural disasters like conflagrations, torrential floods and earthquakes, which themselves involve death for "generations of men" and cities and towns (5.339–42), so that here, too, there is both analogy and continuity between death of the world and the deaths of men". Cf. Clay 1983, 260.

that our world is too faulty to be considered a divine product.[33] However, instead of functioning as a blind, obliterating force, disease is seen to perform a function that would have otherwise been attributed to divine agency, imposing its own design on the coming-to-be and consequent dissolution of things. Lucretius' world is by no means perfect and it follows no predetermined plan; on the contrary, it exists as the result of random and unpredictable collisions of atoms. Generation, as the poet emphasizes time and again, is contingent on destruction (1.263–64): *nec ullam / rem gigni patitur nisi morte adiuta aliena*. In this kind of reality, disease, as an "architect of death", does not lead to conclusive ends but instead allows for the recycling of matter — its transition from composite bodies which dissolve to new forms of existence.

1.2 Re-reading the *clinamen*

In fact, the language of disease can even be said to permeate the very moment of the beginning of creation. Here is how Lucretius describes the *clinamen*, the "swerve", in 2.216–24:[34]

> Illud in his quoque te rebus cognoscere avemus,
> corpora cum deorsum rectum per inane feruntur
> ponderibus propriis, incerto tempore ferme
> incertisque locis spatio depellere paulum,
> tantum quod momen mutatum dicere possis.
> quod nisi declinare solerent, omnia deorsum,
> imbris uti guttae, caderent per inane profundum,
> nec foret offensus natus nec plaga creata
> principiis: ita nil umquam natura creasset.

> One further point in this matter I desire you to understand: that while the first bodies are being carried downwards by their own weight in a straight line through the void, at times quite uncertain and uncertain places, they swerve a little from their course, just so much as you might call a change of motion. For if they were not apt to incline, all would fall downwards like raindrops through the profound void, no collision would take place and no blow would be caused amongst the first-beginnings: thus nature would never have produced anything.

---

[33] As Lucretius rhetorically asks in 5.220–21, in the context of refuting the world's divine origin: *cur anni tempora **morbos** / **adportant**? quare mors inmatura vagatur?*, "why do the seasons of the year bring disease? Why does untimely death stalk abroad?"
[34] For a thorough discussion of the *clinamen* in 2.216–24, see O'Keefe 2005, 110–122; cf. Fowler 2002, 407–27 (on the question of *clinamen* and free will), with further references to secondary literature on the subject. Furley 1967, 169–237 remains essential reading.

Don Fowler, in his note on 2.223, observes that "there is an air of paradox about *offensus* (with connotations perhaps of destruction) being born; it is the central paradox of Epicurean physics, the creation of worlds from endless atomic strife".[35] Even more intriguing, in this respect, is the use of *plaga* in the same line. The word describes the actual moment of impact between two different atoms, implying that the bonding of the first elements — leading eventually to the formation of composite bodies — requires their having been "wounded" before. Conceptually, this lies extremely close to Lucretius' description of sexual desire and intercourse at the end of Book 4. In 4.1068–72 we are told that the only way to avoid obsession with a single object of desire is by replacing old and festering "wounds" with new ones; for when desire is left to linger in the body, the disease becomes chronic and is more difficult to cure:

> ulcus enim vivescit et inveterascit alendo,
> inque dies gliscit furor atque aerumna gravescit,
> si non prima novis conturbes volnera **plagis**
> volgivagaque vagus Venere ante recentia cures
> aut alio possis animi traducere motus.

> For feeding the sore increases its strength and makes it inveterate; day by day the madness takes on and the misery becomes worse, unless you confuse the old wounds with new blows and cure them in time while fresh by wandering with some random-roaming Venus, or turn your thoughts in some other direction.

When Lucretius proceeds in the following lines to describe intercourse, he conveys it in a language which reminds us of a violent collision of atoms. What defines the intimate encounter between the two partners is a kind of erratic, "uncertain" movement (similar to that generated by the random clash of atoms during their downward fall in the void) as the lovers, immersed in frenzied desire, find themselves unable to follow a regular course of sensing and touching what lies at hand (see 4.1104 below: *errantes incerti*; cf. 2.218–9 above: *incerto tempore... incertisque locis*), and swerve their bodies in random and unpredictable ways.[36] More importantly, when these two bodies finally come together they continue to inflict injuries upon each other and thus to *breed* the sickness instead of

---

35 Fowler 2002, 313.
36 There are several points in the poem, which invite us to think of the bonds formed between atoms in terms parallel to those underlying human relationships, especially with regard to sex. See e.g. how Venus compels lovers to join together (randomly) in the early stages of the development of civilization in 5.960–65: *quod cuique obtulerat praedae fortuna, ferebat / **sponte sua** sibi quisque valere et vivere doctus. / Et Venus in silvis iungebat corpora amantum; / **conciliabat***

curing it. Procreation naturally follows — and Lucretius gives us an extended account of it in the last section of Book 4 — but there is also a profound sense of frustration in the whole scene. However hard they try, the two craving bodies fail to fuse into a single substance (4.1101–11):

> sic in amore Venus simulacris ludit amantis,
> nec satiare queunt spectando corpora coram,
> nec manibus quicquam teneris abradere membris
> possunt **errantes incerti** corpore toto.
> denique cum membris conlatis flore fruuntur
> aetatis, iam cum praesagit gaudia corpus
> atque in eost Venus ut muliebria conserat arva,
> adfigunt avide corpus iunguntque salivas
> oris et inspirant pressantes dentibus ora,
> nequiquam, quoniam nil inde abradere possunt
> nec penetrare et abire in corpus corpore toto.

So in love Venus mocks lovers with images, nor can bodies even in real presence satisfy lovers with looking, nor can they rub off something from tender limbs with hands wandering aimless all over the body. Lastly, when clasped body to body they enjoy the flower of their age, at the moment when the body foretastes its joy and Venus is on the point of sowing the woman's field, they cling greedily close together and join their watering mouths and draw deep breaths pressing teeth on lips; but all is vanity, for they can rub nothing off, nor can they penetrate and be absorbed body in body.

The idea of a failed fusion (4.1111) could be reminiscent of Plato, *Symposium* 191a5–8: ἐπειδὴ οὖν ἡ φύσις δίχα ἐτμήθη, ποθοῦν ἕκαστον τὸ ἥμισυ τὸ αὑτοῦ συνῄει, καὶ περιβάλλοντες τὰς χεῖρας καὶ συμπλεκόμενοι ἀλλήλοις, ἐπιθυμοῦντες συμφῦναι, "Now, since their natural form had been cut in two, each one longed

---

enim vel mutua quamque cupido / vel violenta viri vis atque inpensa libido / vel pretium, "whatever prize fortune gave to each, that he carried off, every man taught to live and be strong for himself at his own will. And Venus joined the bodies of lovers in the woods; for either the woman was attracted by mutual desire, or caught by the man's violent force and vehement lust or by a bribe". Compare these lines with 2.1058–63: *et ipsa / **sponte sua** forte offensando semina rerum / multimodis temere incassum frustraque coacta / tandem coluerunt ea quae coniecta repente / magnarum rerum fierent exordia semper, / terrai maris et caeli generisque animantum*, "and the seeds of things themselves of their own accord, knocking together by chance, clashed in all sorts of ways, heedless, without aim, without intention, until at length those combined which, suddenly thrown together, could become in each case the beginnings of mighty things, of earth and sea and sky and the generation of living creatures". As Shearin 2015, 79 observes, *sua sponte* in 2.1059 is "grouped with a stream of adverbs (*forte, multimodis, temere, incassum, frustra*) that together emphatically present the (initially) undesigned state of atomic creation, a state hardly far-removed from the chaotic coupling of humans" described in 5.960–65.

for its own other half, and so they would throw their arms about each other, weaving themselves together, wanting to grow together".[37] However, the image in 4.1111, *nec penetrare et abire in corpus corpore toto*, can also be appropriately placed in Lucretius' atomic universe. Although atoms can coexist and form all sorts of bonds with each other, they always retain their autonomy as indivisible particles. In a way, atomic creation follows the pattern outlined in the erotic scene in 4.1105–1111:[38] given that the prime stuff of matter is so concretely fixed as to be literally "uncuttable" (*individuum*),[39] its mixing with other particles will always be imperfect — in the sense that it cannot produce an absolute merging of bodies — and thus subject to fragmentation and collapse. The imagery of disease in Book 4 (desire is conceptualized as a wound which intercourse only helps to exacerbate; in its turn, intercourse maintains an illusory sense of merging which in effect consumes one's vital forces almost to the point of death)[40] helps in essence to foreshadow the eventual dissolution of things: just as in 4.1068 what is said to acquire a life of its own is not the offspring that results from sex but the wound itself (*ulcus enim vivescit et inveterascit*),[41] so does the *plaga* — which is

---

37 Translation by Nehamas/Woodruff in Cooper 1997. According to Aristophanes, the speaker in this passage, at some distant point in the past, humans used to be complete wholes but Zeus split them in two halves; these halves consequently try to recover their joined form and fuse back to the single body to which they originally belonged, but to no avail; see Hunter 2004, 60–71; and for the connection of this passage with Lucretius, Nussbaum 1994, 173 n. 57.
38 Cf. Cicero's erotic language in his description of the *clinamen* in *Fin*. 1.19: *deinde ibidem homo acutus, cum illud occurreret, si omnia deorsus e regione ferrentur et, ut dixi, ad lineam, numquam fore ut atomus altera alteram posset attingere itaque attulit rem commenticiam: declinare dixit atomum perpaulum, quo nihil posset fieri minus; ita effici* **complexiones et copulationes et adhaesiones atomorum inter se**, *ex quo efficeretur mundus omnesque partes mundi, quaeque in eo essent*, "At the same time our brilliant man [i.e. Epicurus] now encounters the problem that if everything moves downwards in perpendicular fashion — in a straight line, as I said — then it will never be the case that one atom can come into contact with another. His solution is a novel one. He claims that the atoms swerve ever so slightly, to the absolutely smallest extent possible. This is how it comes about that the atoms combine and couple and adhere to one another. As a result, the world and all its parts and the objects within it are created" (translation in Annas/Woolf 2001, 9). For the discussion of clinamen in Cicero's writings, see Maso 2005.
39 The term appears in Cic. *Fin*. 1.17: *corpus individuum*.
40 See, especially, 4.1113–14: *usque adeo cupide in Veneris compagibus haerent, / membra voluptatis dum vi* **labefacta liquescunt**, "so eagerly do they cling in the couplings of Venus, while their limbs slacken and melt under the power of delight". For the combined use of *labefacta/liquisse* in a text with describes a near-death experience, see 3.592–98.
41 The bodies of the two lovers in 4.1101–11 bring to mind the erotic couple of Venus and Mars in 1.31–36: "For you alone, Venus, can delight mortals with quiet peace, since Mars mightly in battle rules the sagave works of war, who often casts himself upon your lap wholly vanquished

the first thing that is said to be born (*creata*) from the swerve in 2.223 — indicate that creation bears in it the seeds of its own unmaking and destruction.[42]

As its very name implies, the *clinamen* is conceptualized as a deviant form of movement, an aberration which signals a departure from an established norm (we can imagine this norm taking the form of atoms falling downwards in the void in perfect parallel lines, never touching or sticking to each other).[43] However imperceptible this departure may be — as Lucretius tells us, an atom need only make a sideways jump of one minimum unit of space (2.220) — it suffices to cause a profound change on the state of things. Notoriously, there is no explicit reference to the doctrine of "swerve" in Epicurus' extant writings;[44] later Greek sources, however, agree in using the term παρέγκλισις to refer to the concept (e.g. Philodemus, *De signis* col. 36. 12–13: τὰς ἐπ' ἐλάχι- / στον παρενκλίσεις τῶν ἀτό- μων).[45]

---

by the ever-living wound of love (*vulnere amoris*), and thus looking upward, with shapely neck thrown back, feeds his eager eyes with love, gaping upon you, goddess (*pascit amore avidos inhians in te, dea, visus*)". Venus is described here as putting a spell on Mars (compare Hera's seduction of Zeus in Hom. *Il.* 14.153–351), so that she be left free to assume her positive role as the creative force she is presented to be in the proem to Book 1. Book 4, in this respect, presents us with something of an unpleasant surprise: even when the goddess has been left to operate on her own, wounding and suffering are still present, and poignantly so; rather that abandon Mars, Venus in Book 4 has subsumed the god of war. Cf. Singer 2009, 131 (with reference to Lucr. 1.1– 49): "In following Empedocles, Lucretius sees no possibility of love without strife. Worshipping Venus, he worships both principles at once. In their unitary structure they constitute a single world order and underlie the mechanical nature of everything. Indeed, they *are* that mechanism. Lucretius would not worship them otherwise". For the "Empedoclean opening" of Lucretius Book 1, see Sedley 1998, 1–34.

42 *Plaga* is elsewhere used in the poem to describe the assaults which composite bodies suffer before they dissolve back to their primary constituents. Everything that exists in nature as a combination of atoms and void, and is therefore not entirely solid, is liable to perish at some point by a blowing force; see e.g. 5.351–68: the atoms can suffer blows but they can reject them (*respuere ictus*), since they allow nothing to penetrate and break them into smaller parts; the void is unaffected by blows because it cannot be touched by them (*plagarum quia sunt expertia*); but virtually everything else that has been produced as a mixture of void and atoms (*admixtumst in rebus inane*) is bound to disintegrate (*valida dissolvere plaga*); cf. 3.806–18.

43 Cf. Fowler 2002, 311 on *rectum per inane*: "there is a paradoxical air about the notion of emptiness being ruled straight, though the sense — that it naturally obliges objects to move in straight lines — is obvious. Perhaps we should think of the break with the determinist rules of the universe that the *clinamen* represents".

44 See O'Keefe 2005, 118.

45 For Philodemus and other Greek passages which make mention of παρέγκλισις, see Fowler 2002, 302–303. See, especially, the title of a lost work by Zeno of Sidon — the eminent Epicurean

It has long escaped attention that apart from its occurrence in Epicurean sources, a second, equally concrete, *technical* meaning of παρέγκλισις in ancient Greek is documented in medical texts. The word is regularly used in that case to describe an unnatural "flexion" of the womb, which indicates a pathological condition[46] and often results in failed procreation. For instance, in ps.-Galen, *Definitiones medicae* 19.453–54 K. we read that, "according to some", teratogenesis occurs κατὰ παρέγκλισιν τῆς μήτρας, "due to a swerving of the womb", since the sperm cannot follow a straight course and is poured inside the misplaced reproductive organ "in an anomalous way" (παρεγχεόμενον ἀνωμάλως).[47] Ps.-Galen could be alluding here to Soranus of Ephesus, a Methodist doctor who was active in Rome during the first half of the 2nd century CE. Soranus appears to be the first physician to have made systematic use of the concept of παρέγκλισις in a pathological context. In one of the chapters of his surviving gynaecological treatise, subtitled 'Περὶ παρεγκλίσεως καὶ ἀποστροφῆς καὶ ἀναδρομῆς μήτρας', we read (*Gynaecia* 3.50):

> Τοῖς ἀγκυλωθεῖσι δακτύλοις παραπλησίως τὸ στόμιον τῆς ὑστέρας καὶ ὁ τράχηλος ἀποστροφὰς καὶ **παρεγκλίσεις** ὑπομένει, ποτὲ μὲν εἰς τὰ πλάγια, ποτὲ δὲ εἰς τὰ ἔμπροσθεν, ποτὲ δὲ εἰς τὰ ὀπίσω καὶ ποτὲ μὲν ἄνω, ποτὲ δὲ κάτω, ποτὲ δὲ προσαναφεύγει. καὶ γίνεται ταῦτα φανερὰ τῇ τε καθέσει τῶν δακτύλων (καταλαμβάνεται γὰρ διὰ τῆς ἁφῆς, εἰς ὃ μέρος γέγονεν ἡ διαστροφή) καὶ τοῖς παρακολουθοῦσι σημείοις. τῇ μὲν γὰρ εἰς τὰ πλάγια **παρεγκλίσει** τοῦ καταλλήλου μηροῦ γίνεται τάσις καὶ πόνος καὶ νάρκη, ποτὲ δὲ καὶ ἀτροφία καὶ κατάψυξις καὶ παραποδισμὸς τοῦ περιπατεῖν ἢ καὶ ἵστασθαι.

> Similar to fingers that have become ankylosed, the orifice of the uterus and its neck suffer bending and flexion, sometimes laterally, forward, or backward and sometimes upward or downward, and sometimes entirely dislocated. These conditions become manifest upon insertion of the fingers (for the direction in which the distortion has taken place is perceived by touch) and through the accompanying signs. For with lateral flexion, tension, pain, and numbness arise in the corresponding leg, sometimes also atrophy, coldness, and hindrance to walking or even standing.[48]

---

whose lectures Cicero attended in Athens — transmitted as Περὶ παρεγκλίσεως καὶ τῆς τοῦ ἀθρόου προκαταρχῆς.
46 See e.g. Galen, *Ad Glauconem de methodo medendi* 1.15 (11.47–48 K.): καὶ ὑστερικῆς πνίξεως ἁπάσης λειποθυμία προηγεῖται· καὶ ταῖς ἀναδρομαῖς τῶν ὑστέρων ἕπεται καὶ ταῖς παρεγκλίσεσι δὲ καὶ ταῖς φλεγμοναῖς αὐτῶν πολλάκις ἀκολουθεῖ.
47 The full text reads as follows: Τέρατα γίνεται, ὡς μέν τινες λέγουσι, κατὰ παρέγκλισιν τῆς μήτρας· τὸ γὰρ σπέρμα παρεγχεόμενον ἀνωμάλως ποιεῖ τὰ τέρατα, ὃν τρόπον καὶ τὸν μόλιβδον θερμὸν ὄντα, ἐπειδὰν καταχυθῇ ἀνωμάλως, ἀνώμαλον ποιεῖ τὸ δημιούργημα.
48 Translation in Temkin 1956, 173. See Lloyd 1983, 196–97.

What is intriguing about παρέγκλισις, both in the passage cited above and on other occasions in Soranus' treatise,[49] is the fact that it appears as a technical term in a medical school of thought (Methodism)[50] whose origins can be ultimately traced back to atomism. Asclepiades of Bithynia (late 2nd/early 1st cent. BCE), commonly acknowledged as a figure of major influence for the Methodists,[51] is known to have introduced a corpuscular theory of the body in direct analogy to Epicurean physics. In Asclepiades' system, the body, like all perceptible objects, consists of imperceptible particles (ὄγκοι) and void.[52] What presents itself as a key requirement for health is not so much the idea of a quantitative equilibrium between different bodily substances (such as, for example, the humours in Hippocratic medicine), but the free and balanced motion of the particles through imperceptible pores in the body[53] — these pores, as Galen emphasizes time and again, should be treated as equivalent to Epicurean void spaces.[54] Accordingly, disease is caused by blockages and rebounds which arise from the differences in the sizes and shapes of the particles and the pores. Overall, it is crucial to bear in mind that health for Asclepiades is premised on the *unobstructed* flow of atom-like entities inside the body and that anything that disrupts this flow can cause serious harm.

Given that none of Asclepiades' writings have survived, the terminology he employed to lay out his medical doctrines is mostly a matter of reconstruction

---

49 See also Soranus, *Gyn.* 1.8, 2.5, 3.7, 3.9, 3.18, 4.8, 4.10.
50 For Soranus and Methodism, see Hanson/Green 1994 and Flemming 2000, 228–46; cf. Frede 1983.
51 See Vallance 1990, 131–43. For Asclepiades' practice in Rome and his reputation as a remarkably skillful and successful doctor, see Rawson 1982.
52 For the close correspondence between Asclepiades' medical doctrine and Epicurean physics, see Leith 2009; 2012. According to Leith, Asclepiades' ὄγκοι share the same basic characteristics with Epicurean atoms, except for the fact that they are physically divisible. As for the "pores" through which these ὄγκοι move inside the human body, they are similar to the void interstices between atoms within solid objects in Epicurus' theory. For a more skeptical view regarding Asclepiades' debt to Epicurus, see Polito 2006; 2013.
53 See Allen 2001, 94.
54 See e.g. Galen, *Ther. Pis.* 11 (14.250 K.): εἰ μὲν γὰρ ἐξ ἀτόμου καὶ τοῦ κενοῦ κατὰ τὸν Ἐπικούρου τε καὶ Δημοκρίτου λόγον συνεστήκει τὰ πάντα, ἢ ἔκ τινων ὄγκων καὶ πόρων κατὰ τὸν ἰατρὸν Ἀσκληπιάδην· καὶ γὰρ οὕτως ἀλλάξας τὰ ὀνόματα μόνον καὶ ἀντὶ μὲν τῶν ἀτόμων τοὺς ὄγκους, ἀντὶ δὲ τοῦ κενοῦ τοὺς πόρους λέγων τὴν αὐτὴν ἐκείνοις τῶν ὄντων οὐσίαν εἶναι βουλόμενος, "for if everything is constituted out of atom and void according to the theory of Epicurus and Democritus, or out of certain *onkoi* and pores according to the physician Asclepiades — for in this way he changed only the names, speaking of *onkoi* instead of atoms, and pores instead of void, and wanting the substance of what exists to be the same as they (did)" (translation in Leith 2012, 167).

from later sources and testimonies. One thing that can be inferred from them is that in some cases the language that had been used by the Greek atomists to describe the process of creation was, surprisingly, re-appropriated by Asclepiades in a pathological context. For instance, ἄθροισμα — a word used by Epicurus to describe aggregates of invisible atoms forming into macroscopic, compound bodies[55] — seems to have been linked by Asclepiades with the idea of a pathological blockage resulting from the excessive accumulation of particles at the entrance of the body's pores.[56] As Caelius Aurelianus informs us, according to "the followers of Asclepiades", the so-called *cardiaca passio* is an inflammation caused by the *"piling together* of little corpuscles" around the area of the heart, *corpusculorum* **coacervatione**.[57] The language is strikingly similar to what we find in the ps.-Plutarchan, *Placita Philosophorum* 884d3–8, which groups together Empedocles, Epicurus and other philosophers who speak of the world as the result of "the assemblage of small particles", κατὰ **συναθροισμὸν** τῶν λεπτομερῶν σωμάτων.

Whether παρέγκλισις, or a similar term, featured in the same (subversive) context in Asclepiades' work can only remain a speculation — if this had been the case, it would have provided a fitting background for Lucretius' treatment of *clinamen* as by nature a deviant form of movement, ambiguously placed at the crossroads between creation and destruction (the hypothesis sounds all the more appealing considering that Lucretius is believed to have had a first-hand knowledge of the Greek physician's work and to keep a close eye on his theories, e.g. in 4.649–57 which speaks of atoms moving through "passages" and "interstices" of various sizes and shapes within the body).[58] Be that as it may, the well-documented occurrence of παρέγκλισις in medical sources helps to establish that the swerve is conceptually embedded in a language which is pregnant with pathological associations. As a notion which can be variously interpreted along the lines of twisting, bending and straying, the swerve can account not only for orderly existence, but also, quite appropriately, for its violent disruption.

Lucretius' text systematically confounds the boundaries between order and disorder. As Michel Serres points out, the turbulence caused by the *clinamen* in 2.216–24

---

55 See O' Keefe 2005, 68–69 and Bronowski 2019, 56 with n. 98. Cf. von Staden 2000, 81–82.
56 In the ancient testimonies, Asclepiades' "blockage model" of disease is conveyed by such terms as ἔμφραξις, ἔνστασις — and in Latin sources — *statio, coacervatio*; see Vallance 1990, 7.
57 *De morbis acutis* 2.31.163; see Harris 1973, 474. See also *concursus atomorum* — used in Cic. *N.D.* 1.91; 2.94 to describe the fortuitous production of the world in Epicurean terms — and compare it with Cael. Aurel. *De morbis acutis* 3.19.188: *concursus corpusculorum* is once again linked there to Asclepiades and appears in a pathological context.
58 See Leith 2012, 185–86. Cf. Pigeaud 1980, 176.

contains a paradox. Laminar flow, the figure of chaos, is at first sight a model of order. The atoms pour out in parallel, without mixing or sticking to each other. The preliminary rows are already a taxonomy, as the word itself indicates. Turbulence seems to introduce a disorder into this arrangement.[59]

On Serres' reading, the swerve marks a critical moment of deviation from an ordered chaos. As such, it is "productive and destructive… formative and declining" at the same time;[60] "it is the slope that begins with a loss of equilibrium, with a difference in relation to this pre-equilibrium that is homogenous",[61] so that it "grants being" even while "it leads back to phenomenal non-being".[62] By signaling the entry of chance[63] into an ordered rain of atoms, the *clinamen*, occurring unexpectedly at no specific place and time, gives birth to a world which is by constitution riddled with flaws.[64] In the context of refuting the theories of the

---

[59] Serres 2000, 27.
[60] Serres 2000, 92.
[61] Serres 2000, 33.
[62] Serres 2000, 59. For some illuminating discussion of Lucretius' reception in Serres' work, see Berressem 2005; Webb 2006; Holmes 2016.
[63] See e.g. Plutarch, *De soll. an.* 964c: "an atom swerves to the very smallest extent (ἄτομον παρεγκλῖναι μίαν ἐπὶ τοὐλάχιστον) in order that the heavy bodies, living things and chance may come into existence (τύχη παρεισέλθῃ) and that what is in our power may not perish" (translation in Rist 1972, 52). As Rist 1972, 52 points out, "there is no reason to distrust Plutarch's suggestion that Epicurus associated 'chance' with swerves… In the letter to Menoeceus Epicurus is at pains to point out that the existence of chance does not militate against the achievement of the good life. There is a random element, an element of chance in nature" and it is very likely that "Epicurus attributed it to the swerve of atoms"; cf. Guyau 1878, 85–91; Bailey 1928, 326; Solmsen 1951, 19 and De Lacy 1969, 108 who accepts an element of sheer contingency in the Epicurean explanation of natural phenomena. Cf. Philodemus, *De signis* col. 36 11–17: "It is not enough to accept the minimal swerves of the atoms on account of chance (διὰ τὸ τυχηρὸν) and free will; one must also show that no other clear perception conflicts with this view" (translation in Fowler 2002, 302–303). The fact that certain things evidently happen by chance is interpreted by Philodemus in this passage as an effect – and a confirmation of the existence – of the swerve. See Bobzien 2000, 330 n. 91. Contra: Long 1977 who draws attention to the emphasis placed on the regularity of phenomena in the Epicurean system, and restricts the effects of *clinamen* within a created world to animate *voluntas*.
[64] Lucretius' argument against the view that the gods designed the world is that nature is full of defects and shortcomings (2.180–81): *nequaquam nobis divinitus esse creatam / naturam mundi: tanta stat praedita culpa*, "the nature of the universe has by no means been made for us through divine power: so great are the faults it stands endowed with". There can be little doubt that when the concept of the swerve is introduced a few lines below (2.216–24), a contrast is built between the idea of randomness on the one hand and that of a perfectly executed divine design on the other; at the same time, the random collisions behind the world's beginning can help to explain that not everything in nature is perfect. See Wilson 2008, 87.

early atomists (*Phys.* 197a18–33), Aristotle observes that chance, τύχη, is "a thing beyond reason/unaccountable" (εἶναί τι παράλογον); not only is it indefinite (καὶ ἡ τύχη ἀόριστον), it is also "unstable as none of the things which result from it can hold always or for the most part" (ἡ γὰρ τύχη ἀβέβαιος· οὔτε γὰρ ἀεὶ οὔθ' ὡς ἐπὶ τὸ πολὺ οἷόν τ' εἶναι τῶν ἀπὸ τύχης οὐθέν).[65] While Aristotle sees chance as posing a threat to the idea that there is a purposeful design in nature, atomism allows space for it in its system precisely so that it breaks free from such determinist notions of design. True, there are fixed natural laws, *foedera naturae*, according to which the phenomenal world can be understood as a causal system of things conforming to predictable patterns and not happening randomly and inexplicably.[66] But as Gordon Campbell aptly observes, atomism's chaotic potential is never laid to rest: "At the heart of the problem is the need for atomism to explain that creation by random chaotic collisions at the atomic level can account for both the variety of nature and for the stability and order of nature at the phenomenal level: always lurking in the background is the spectre of ontological chaos, threatening to throw the cosmos into disorder".[67] Because of its fundamental link with chance, the swerve contracts a "positive" and a "negative" outcome

---

[65] Simplicius, *in Phys.* 331.16ff. identifies Democritus as the target of this passage. See Dudley 2012, 148–50; Allen 2015, 66–67.

[66] See Fowler 2002, 308: "The *clinamen* has a possible cosmogonic function but none within a formed world except in the psychological sphere ... Within normal compounds the effect of some atoms swerving is swamped by the regular movements of the others; only within the finest molecules of the soul can the behaviour of the whole compound be affected"; cf. Bobzien 2000, 330: "the function of the swerve is ... to provide an explanation of the possibility of chance events and volitions *without* undermining the atomistic explanation of the order in the universe". But see note below.

[67] Campbell 2007, 61. In Campbell's understanding, the sense of indeterminacy conferred by the swerve brings the behavior of atoms close to that of subatomic particles in quantum physics. According to Jacques Monod, cited by Campbell, mutations "belong in the realm of microscopic physics — in the realm of events that by their very nature cannot be individually predicted and cannot be individually controlled". Campbell assumes a similar unpredictability in the Lucretian universe: "To allow the atomic theory to account for the variety of nature we must appeal to its powerfully metamorphic creative capabilities, but how far do these capabilities extend, and can atomic physics really provide guiding limits to prevent species mutations from getting out of hand?" (2007, 62). See also O' Keefe 2005, 120 who draws attention to the fact that the atoms in the *clinamen* passage, and more specifically in 2.221, are said to "be *accustomed* to turn aside" (*declinare **solerent***): "On the standard interpretation of Lucretius' argument, the conclusion ought to be, strictly speaking, not that the atoms do swerve, but that they did swerve — after all, this is all that is needed to get collisions started. Under my interpretation, however, Lucretius would be justified in concluding that the atoms do swerve now, since the type of *archê* that the

in the same conceptual space. In fact, considering that the swerve has no a priori structure of determination and is without a cause,[68] the unhappy or fortunate results it delivers converge insofar as they are both identically produced as chance events. This is exactly what Jacques Derrida has in mind when, in a discussion of the *clinamen*, he notes that "bad luck is when one is out of luck … however, it is at the same time in a very significant way a phenomenon of luck or chance".[69]

The chance element which pervades the process of creation is best brought out in 2.1058–63: *et ipsa / sponte sua forte offensando semina rerum / multimodis temere incassum frustraque coacta / tandem coluerunt ea quae coniecta repente / magnarum rerum fierent exordia semper, / terrai magis et caeli generisque animantum*, "and the seeds of things themselves of their own accord, knocking together by chance, clashed in all sorts of ways, heedless, without aim, without intention, until at length those combined which, suddenly thrown together, could become in each case the beginning of mighty things, of earth and sea and sky and the generation of living creatures".[70] There is nothing in this process that can guarantee a good, viable and functional result,[71] except for the statistical possibility

---

swerve provides is not a temporal *archê*, but an explanatory *archê*, one that refers to the nature of the atoms and their motion".

68 See Cic. *Fin.* 1.19: *nam et ipsa declinatio ad libidinem fingitur — ait enim declinare atomum sine causa; quo nihil turpius physico, quam fieri quicquam sine causa dicere*, "the swerving is itself an arbitrary fiction; for Epicurus says the atoms swerve without a cause, — yet this is the capital offence in a natural philosopher, to speak of something taking place uncaused" (translation in Rackham 1931, 21). Cf. Cic. *Fat.* 22. See Sharples 1991–3, 188: "Swerves happen, for no reason; that is the essential thing about them"; cf. Mitsis 1988, 159–60 n. 73 and Hankinson 1998, 227 who criticizes Sedley 1988 according to whom the swerve need not necessarily be uncaused.

69 Derrida' essay, entitled "My Chances/Mes Chances: A Rendezvous with Some Epicurean Stereophonics", is reprinted in Smith/Kerrigan 1984 (for the quoted passage, see p. 6 of the volume). Cf. Johnson 1993, 139–41.

70 Cf. 5.416–31, where the world is said to have been created by random collisions of atoms, without any pre-existing pattern or organizing principle. See especially 5.422–31: "but because many first-beginnings of things in many ways, struck with blows and carried along by their own weight from infinite time up to the present, have been accustomed to move and to meet in all manners of ways, and to try all combinations (*omnia pertemptare*), whatsoever they could produce by coming together, for this reason it comes to pass that being spread abroad through a vast time, by attempting every sort of combination and motion (*omne genus coetus et motus experiundo*), at length those come together which, being suddenly brought together, often become the beginnings of great things, of earth and sea and sky and the generation of living creatures".

71 As Campbell 2003, 106–107 points out with reference to 5.416–31 (cited in the note above), the process through which the first life is said to have been produced (5.430–31) accounts, in exactly the same way, also for the creation of maladapted, monstrous creatures which could not

that, given the infinite time and space and the ensuing infinite number of atomic combinations, we are bound eventually, *tandem*, to see a world like ours coming to existence. But based on the same reasoning, other, more unwelcome things can emerge in the process. This is how Lucretius introduces his account of the plague in 6.1090–97:

> Nunc ratio quae sit morbis, aut unde **repente**
> mortiferam possit cladem conflare **coorta**
> morbida vis hominum generi pecudumque catervis,
> expediam. primum multarum semina rerum
> esse supra docui quae sint vitalia nobis,
> et contra quae sint morbo mortique necessest
> multa volare. ea cum casu sunt forte coorta
> et **perturbarunt** caelum, fit morbidus aer.
>
> Now I will explain the reason of diseases, and from what place the force of disease can suddenly gather together, and blow together a storm of deadly destruction for mankind and for flocks and herds. Firstly, I have shown above that there are many seeds of things which support our life, and on the other hand there must be many flying about which make for disease and death. When these by chance or accident have gathered together, and thrown the heavens in turmoil, the air becomes diseased.

Just as chance (*forte*) combinations in 2.1058–63 can "suddenly", *repente*, produce a fortunate event, as for example a habitable world, so they are inevitably destined to result in unfortunate occurrences (see, especially, 6.1096: *cum casu ... forte*).[72] For Lucretius, disease is brought to existence, *coorta*, through a combi-

---

make it in the end; "the creatures we see today are the descendants of the original animals 'correctly' assembled by chance" (p. 106). As an idea, this goes back to Empedocles' zoogony (creatures, in that case, are formed by the random combination of disparate limbs; if it so happens that the "appropriate" limbs come together, then the creature survives; if not, it perishes instantly) which is criticized by Aristotle (*Phys.* 198b–199b) precisely because it relies so much on the element of chance and coincidence (ἀπὸ τοῦ αὐτομάτου / ἀπὸ συμπτώματος) without appealing to any sort of design and purposefulness (ἕνεκά του εἶναι) in nature; see Bolton 2015, 141.

72 The idea that diseases can be the result of chance is an old one. As Holmes observes, "the unstable identity of the foodstuff or the humour – beneficial or harmful – haunts the body as a complex system" in Hippocratic medicine. Insofar as there are things in the body that happen of their own accord, that is in scenarios where τύχη and *to automaton* come into play, "the physical body and, more specifically, the cavity, *is conceptualized as a terrain of unruly forces only contingently aligned with health* (emphasis added)". See e.g. [Hipp.] *Loc.* 33 (6.326 L.) which speaks of bile breaking out spontaneously, forced by a power which has its origin in the body: χολὴ ἐπὴν

nation of the appropriate seeds, *semina rerum*; it is built into a concrete body before it accomplishes the unmaking of other composite bodies, seamlessly orchestrating, *conflare*, their dissolution.⁷³ The language of creation and destruction here become conflated, indistinguishable from each other. The fact that the disease is described as throwing the sky in turmoil (*perturbarunt*) is also significant. It ultimately derives from the idea that — similar to the way in which the swerve operates — the most distinctive characteristic of *morbus* is that of causing a violent *rearrangement* of atoms. This is what we read e.g. in 4.664–67: *quippe ubi cui febris bili superante coorta est / aut alia ratione aliquast vis excita morbi, / **perturbatur** ibi iam totum corpus, et omnes / **commutantur ibi positurae principiorum***, "For when fever arises in anyone, from overflow of bile, or when the energy of some disease is excited in another way, then the whole body is thrown into a riot and all the positions of the first beginnings are changed about". As elsewhere in the poem, so here the change of places threatens an established order of things (cf. 2.947: *dissoluuntur enim positurae principiorum*; 4.943–44: *conturbantur enim positurae principiorum / corporis atque animi*). Assuming that an order, though of a different form and nature, is already traceable in the perfectly executed, straight fall of atoms through the void,⁷⁴ we might begin to reconsider *clinamen*'s violent interference as equally disturbing: a force in and of itself, the swerve challenges a fixed state of atomic rain, yielding results which can hardly be predicted.⁷⁵

αὐτομάτη ῥαγῇ ἢ κάτω ἢ ἄνω, χαλεπωτέρη παύειν· **ἡ γὰρ αὐτομάτη ὑπὸ βίης γινομένης** τῷ σώματι βιῆται.

73 *Conflare* in 6.1091 (*mortiferam possit cladem conflare*) brings out well Lucretius' tendency to conceptualize disease as a force which *creates* death by putting together elements which can harmoniously work with each other before they unleash turmoil. The verb has been used in Book 3 to describe the synthesis of body and mind required for sensation (3.333–36): *nec sibi quaeque sine alterius vi posse videtur / corporis atque animi seorsum sentire potestas, / sed communibus inter eas **conflatur** utrimque / montibus accensus nobis per viscera sensus*, "and we see that neither body nor mind has the power to feel singly without the other's help, but by common motions proceeding from both conjointly sensation is kindled for us in our flesh". Cf. Cic. *N.D.* 2.100: *ut una ex duabus naturis conflata videatur* (a text which describes how beautifully and effortlessly the sea and the earth blend with each other on a shore, and fuse into a single phusis).

74 See Cic. *Fat.* 22: *gravitate feruntur ad perpendiculum corpora individua **rectis lineis***. For the implicit presence of order here, cf. Caes. *Gal.* 7.23.5: *rectis lineis suos ordines servant*.

75 Such as James Joyce's disordered opening sentence in *Finnegans Wake*: "riverrun, past Eve and Adam's, from swerve of shore to bend of bay, brings us by a commodious vicus of recirculation back to Howth Castle and Environs". Without the *clinamen*, Joyce seems to imply, there would be no principle of creation in the universe, and no text for us to read. But while acting as a generative force, the "swerve" mentioned in the opening sentence serves also as a warning for

1.3 Conclusion

But just as the swerve has a chaotic potential,[76] so does disease, by virtue of its intrinsic association with the swerve, hold in store the seeds for new forms of life. To understand the paradox, we only have to recall what the poet himself tells us in 2.1002–6: *nec sic interemit mors res ut materiai / corpora conficiat, sed coetum dissupat ollis; /* **inde aliis aliud coniungit, et efficit** *omnes / res ita convertant formas mutentque colores / et capiant sensus et puncto tempore reddant,* "nor does death so destroy things as to annihilate the bodies of matter, but it disperses their combination abroad; then it conjoins others with others, and brings it about that thus all things alter their shapes and change their colours and receive sensation and in a moment of time yield it up again". This is a radical worldview, since it actually posits that we should see death not as a destructive but instead as a transformative force: *mors* — the grammatical subject of *coniungit* and *efficit* — is virtually said to be the efficient cause of (re)generation, breathing new life into bodies of matter by fixing them into new forms and shapes.[77] Even though death can defeat us on an individual level, it nonetheless fails to subdue the indestructible atoms from which we are made;[78] what is more, by releasing them from the fixed compounds in which they have been arranged, it instantly increases the possibility of new forms of creation, which are bound to take place sooner or later. "Birth, growth, decay and death" thus become, according to Alessandro Schiesaro, "little more than metaphorical descriptions for a series of phenomena that in the context of Lucretian physics can be explained in purely quantitative terms. What we actually mean by these words, Lucretius says, are various stages of aggregation and disaggregation of matter".[79]

---

the reader: it highlights the collapse of the established distinction between meaning and nonsense in what is to follow. See Brown 2013, 261.

76 For an evenly balanced distribution of life and death, attributed to the same motions and forces operating on an atomic level, see 2.62–66: *nunc age, quo motu genitalia materiai / corpora res varias gignant genitasque resolvant, / et qua vi facere id cogantur ... / expediam*, "listen now, and I will set forth by what motion the generative bodies of matter beget the various things and dissolve them once begotten, and by what force they are compelled to do it". For the connection between these lines and Lucretius' subsequent discussion of *clinamen* in Book 2, see Owen 1968, 409–10.

77 For these lines, see Garani 2007, 185; Rzepka 2012, 125–26.

78 See 1.485–86: *sed quae sunt rerum primordia, nulla potest vis / stinguere; nam solido* **vincunt** *ea corpore demum*, "but those which are the first-beginnings of things no power can quench; they conquer everything, by virtue of their solid body". This is an obvious reversal of the motif that death is "invincible".

79 Schiesaro 1994, 90.

The plague at the end of the poem has been read as a scene which presents the destruction of a human society in a fashion comparable to the dissolution of an atomic *concilium*.[80] Such dissolution, as is made abundantly clear in 6.1096, is the result of pure chance: the disease is brought to life through an accidental coming together of noxious seeds,[81] and then swerves its way from far-distant Egypt to Athens before it strikes its population and dismantles the civic body.[82] But is dissolution all that we get from the poem's final scene? On a human level the plague has some surprisingly liberating — one might in fact say, "positive" — side effects, first and foremost the realization, on the patients' part, that the gods have no interest, or for that matter power to intervene, in human affairs (6.1276–77): *nec iam religio divom nec numina magni / pendebantur enim: praesens dolor exsuperabat*, "for indeed now neither the worship of the gods nor their power was much regarded: the present pain exceeded everything else". *Exsuperare* brings to mind the military language and imagery used by Lucretius to describe in other sections of the poem Epicurus' triumph over the evil foe represented by *religio*:[83] it is as though the excruciating, overpowering pain, *dolor*, in the poem's final scene offers a clearer vision and a better perception of reality, forcing people — with the effectiveness that no rational argument would ever have hoped to achieve — to see human life for what it actually is: that is, devoid of any divine

---

80 See Cabisius 1985, 118; Shearin 2015, 79. Cf. Penwill 1996, 154: the fact that the plague affects the *intima pars* of the body, thereby transposing suffering to an invisible level, suggests that "these are *corpora caeca* at work". For the anthropomorphization of atoms and the atomization of humans in Lucretius, see Shearin 2015, 74–82 with Fowler 2007, 427–28 and Kennedy 2002, 78–85.
81 Cf. 5.366–69: *neque autem corpora desunt, / ex infinito quae possint **forte coorta** / corruere hanc rerum violento turbine summam / aut aliam quamvis cladem inportare pericli*, "nor again are bodies lacking that can by chance gather out of the infinite, and overwhelm this sum of things in a violent hurricane or bring in any other disaster and danger".
82 For the plague as a "radical manifestation of the Lucretian *clinamen*", see Demastes 1998, 169, who observes: "Actual 'cruelty' notwithstanding on the discrete individual level (where death is seen as an end to be avoided) the plague works well on a collective, social level (where death is part of a process of continuation), as a call for the human necessity of acceding to natural processes".
83 See Buchheit 2007, 111–12. For *exsuperare* with the meaning of overpowering an enemy, see e.g. 5.380–84 (on the war between different elemental forces in the world): *denique tantopere inter se cum maxima mundi / **pugnent** membra, pio nequaquam concita bello, / nonne vides aliquam longi **certaminis** ollis / posse dari finem? vel cum sol et vapor omnis / omnibus epotis umoribus **exsuperarint***, "again, since the greatest members of the world fight so hard together, stirred by most unrighteous war, do you not see that some end may be given to their long strife? Either when sun and all heat shall prevail, having drunk up all the waters…"

presence and meaning.⁸⁴ At the same time, as we watch the patients being gradually reduced to lifeless bodies of matter (6.1268: *semanimo cum corpore*), there is a lingering impression that new generative forces might already be at work. As we read in 6.1278–81: *nec mos ille sepulturae remanebat in urbe, / quo prius hic **populus** semper consuerat humari; / perturbatus enim totus trepidabat, et **unus** / **quisque** suum pro re et pro tempore maestus humabat*, "nor did that custom of sepulture remain in the city, with which this nation in the past had been always accustomed to be buried; for the whole nation was in trepidation and dismay, and each man in his sorrow buried his own dead as time and circumstances allowed". Freed from observance to common customs and established laws, each citizen is now seen to do things separately. These lines could be an allusion to the absence of social bonds during the early man's life in Book 5, implying as it were that disease entails a return to a pre-cultural, savage state of things;⁸⁵ however, on an atomic level acting of one's own accord (*sponte sua*)⁸⁶ is by no means a negative concept. On the contrary, this is precisely the kind of language applied to the free and spontaneous atomic movement which is required for the eventual creation of new, composite bodies (e.g. 2.1058–63, 3.31–34, 4.45–48).⁸⁷ Lucretius' commitment to the principle that matter is dissolved and recycled but can never

---

84 See Penwill 1996, 150. We can compare here instances, especially from Greek tragedy, where pain and suffering, rather than serve as a reminder of divine presence, they lead instead to the realization that the gods are actually absent: Euripides' Bellerophon would be a prime example; see Riedweg 1990.

85 See Cabisius 1985, 119.

86 For the connection between the fragmented, selfish action of the plague's victims, marked by *unus quisque* in 6.1280–81 (cf. 6.1231) and the spontaneous action of atoms in 2.1059, see Shearin 2015, 78–79. Compare how humans are described to behave in the early stages of the development of civilization in 5.958–61: *nec commune bonum poterant spectare, neque ullis / moribus inter se scibant nec legibus uti. / quod cuique obtulerat praedae fortuna, ferebat / **sponte sua sibi quisque** valere et vivere doctus*, "they could not look to the common good, they did not know how to govern their intercourse by custom and law. Whatever prize fortune gave to each, that he carried off, every man taught to live and be strong for himself at his own will". That things during the plague are happening *sponte sua* is confirmed by Ovid's adaptation of the Lucretian scene (*Met.* 7.541): *sponte sua lanaeque cadunt et corpora tabent*.

87 For the combined sense of emancipation and creativity that is pregnant in *sponte sua*, see especially 2.1090–92: *quae bene cognita si teneas, natura videtur / libera continuo, dominis privata superbis, / ipsa sua per se sponte omnia dis agere expers*, "if you hold fast to these convictions, nature is seen to be free at once and rid of proud masters, herself doing all by herself of her own accord, without the help of the gods". For a detailed discussion of *sponte sua* as a vital concept for Lucretius' Epicurean physics, biology, psychology, ethics and politics, see Johnson 2013.

become extinguished does not allow us to see death as something final and conclusive.⁸⁸ The wailing of the plague's victims (6.1245) and that of their relatives (6.1248: *lacrimis lassi luctuque redibant*) brings to mind an earlier scene in Book 5, which combines helplessness, lament and an utter sense of desperation with the arrival of a new life (5.223–26): *nudus humi iacet, infans, indigus omni / vitali auxilio, cum primum in luminis oras / nixibus ex alvo matris natura profudit, / vagituque locum **lugubri** complet*, "[the newborn child] lies naked upon the ground, speechless, in need of every kind of vital support, as soon as nature has split him forth with throes from his mother's womb into the regions of light, and he fills all around with doleful wailings".⁸⁹ The plague thus brings life to an end but not without implying that a new life lies ahead; to comprehend fully the metaphor of disease as *fabricator leti*, it is essential to keep in mind that the execution of the design does not involve only endings but new beginnings as well.

---

88 The idea goes back to Empedocles; see Long 2019, 25: "Empedocles is not denying the reality of death — he very often refers to 'mortal' creatures ... But he denies its finality or its being an 'end'.... When a creature dies, its constituent parts are subject to 'change': they are transferred and available for reuse in the development of new creatures".

89 For additional similarities, compare *nudus humi iacet* with 6.1173: *nudum iacientes corpus in undas* and 6.1264–65: *multa siti prostrata ... / corpora silanos ad aquarum strata iacebant*. The phrase *indigus omni vitali auxilio* applies perfectly to the situation in which the plague's victims find themselves. Cf. 2.576–77: *miscetur funere vagor / quem pueri tollunt visentes luminis oras*, "with the funeral dirge is mingled the wail that children raise when they first see the borders of light".

2 Disease, Closure and the Sense of an Ending

> It is frequently easier to say where the beginning ends than where the end begins.
> Don Fowler, *Second Thoughts on Closure*[1]

> All plots tend to move deathward.
> Don DeLillo, *White Noise*

While it is often claimed that individual sections of Lucretius' *DRN* seem to be missing the poet's final touch,[2] or even that Lucretius died without making extensive planned revisions,[3] the poem's architecture has long been received as the result of imaginative designing that was carried out (almost) down to the last detail.[4] Lucretius' six-book epic falls as neatly into three distinct parts (1–2 + 3–4 + 5–6) as it can be divided into two halves (1–3 + 4–6).[5] According to the first division, the poem makes a start with an investigation into the basic constituents of the universe (1–2), moves on to examine the material nature of the soul (3–4) and expands on the natural world and its wonders (5–6). The second model, which

---

[1] Fowler 1997, 21.
[2] The plague at the end of Book 6 presents us with one such tricky passage; see e.g. Volk 2002, 82 with n. 41: although the poem "can, and should, be interpreted as a meaningful and unified whole... there are signs to point to the fact that [it] was left unfinished"; cf. Kenney 1977, 22–23; 2007, 110 and Sedley 1998, 160–65. Contra: Fowler 1989, 85 (according to whom "there can be little doubt that the work originally ended with the lines 1247–51"); Penwill 1996 and P. Fowler 1983, 564–67; 2007, 202–206. Lucretius promises in 5.155 that he shall discuss the abodes of the gods in more detail below - a promise which is never fulfilled in the poem as we have it; Rozelaar 1943, 116–36 and Bignone 1945, 318–22 believe that this discussion would have concluded the poem, had Lucretius the time to finish it; cf. Bailey 1947, 1724–25. For further discussion, see Gale 2009, 123–24.
[3] Sedley 1998, 163: "In the case of the plague, as of much else in the second half of the poem, the reworking simply had not yet taken place when [Lucretius] died". It should be stressed, however, that what we take as inconsistencies, ambiguities, dissonances — and therefore as signs of incomplete revision — in the poem can be a very subjective and arbitrary thing; see O'Hara 2007, 69–74 (criticizing some of Sedley's arguments).
[4] See the important discussion in Farrell 2007. Not surprisingly, the hypothesis of a tightly woven structure (based on intricate symmetries, analogies, parallelisms between different parts of the narrative etc.) goes hand in hand with the conclusion that the poem, as we have it, is "substantially complete" (Farrell 2007, 78 n. 12). For Lucretius' preconceived plan (and the signposting throughout the poem that this plan is being meticulously followed), see Fowler 1995, 10; cf. Kyriakidis 2004, 27–28.
[5] For this structure, see Bailey 1947, 31–37; Boyancé 1963, 69–83; Sedley 1998, 144–45. For Lucretius' structural models (with emphasis on the six-book division) in earlier Greek and Latin poetry, see Farrell 2008.

suggests a structural arrangement that is simultaneously conceived with and in effect complements the first, is based in its turn on a transition from the basic principles of atomism (1–3) to its ethical and psychological implications (4–6). At the same time each book is designed as an independent unit, with a formal beginning and a recognizable end.[6] The overall result is that of a progressive development of the argument from the simple (even though unseen) principles of atoms and void to the most complex (yet visible) natural phenomena, which allows Lucretius to impart his lessons one at a time and to communicate his message to the widest audience possible.[7]

In this chapter I shall concentrate on one specific aspect of the poem's architecture, looking at how disease is exploited as a theme that adds unity to the narrative. I argue that one of the central structural devices employed in the poem to tie it up into a unified whole reveals itself, somewhat insistently, as a process of foreshadowing, and gradual realisation, of the poem's approaching end; narrative cohesion is thus to a great extent maintained through sections of the text which prefigure, in some form or another, the horrific scene of disease and death that brings this text to a close.[8] Long before we reach the plague in Book 6 (6.1138–1286) Lucretius provides us with signs of the looming end in the closing section of Book 3 (3.1053–75), which then return and take on significance at the end of Book 4 (4.1030–1287).[9] What all three sections have in common — along with the books to which they serve as conclusions — is an intense preoccupation with disease (*morbus*),[10] in itself a sign of deterioration and decline towards an

---

[6] See Kenney 1977, 18; cf. van Sickle 1980, 12.

[7] For the explanatory nature of Lucretius' work, which is aimed at "a wide audience of educated Latin readers", see Warren 2007, 19–20; for Lucretius' didactic poetics, see Mitsis 1993 and Volk 2002, 69–118. Classen 1968 remains essential reading.

[8] For the meaning assigned to any story through its ending, see Brooks 1984, 94: "We might say that we are able to read present moments — in literature and, by extension, in life — as endowed with narrative meaning only because we read them in anticipation of the structuring power of those endings that will retrospectively give them the order and significance of the plot".

[9] This is not to say, of course, that closural signs pointing to the end of the poem cannot be traced in the closing sections of Book 1, 2 and 5, or in other parts of the narrative; see e.g. P. Fowler 2007, 209–14. It must be pointed out, however, that disease is not explicitly discussed as a theme in the first two books and, apart from incidental references, it remains of little relevance to the contents of Book 5. See the influential hypothesis of Mussehl 1912, according to whom Books 1, 2 and 5 were written first; this would seem to imply an increased emphasis on disease in the three books of the poem that were written last (3, 4 and 6). Cf. Townend 1978.

[10] This is especially evident in the case of Book 3 and 6, where one finds by far the highest concentration of the words *morbus* / *morbidus* in the narrative, 13 and 27 times respectively, out of a total of 46 times in the entire poem (in the first two books, *morbus* occurs only once, in 1.133).

end but also a manufacturing force which implies that some sort of design is at play (3.472: *morbus leti fabricator*).[11] I shall argue that, as we move from one closing section to the next, disease gradually loses its metaphorical meaning and acquires a literal value instead. This change of meaning, which rests essentially on a shift of focus from "affections of the soul" (broadly understood in philosophical discourse as manifestations of psychological and moral weakness, which involve illness in — what may be termed — a "metaphorical" sense)[12] to physical pain and illness affecting the body, is combined in the text with an increasing appeal to medical literature and the use of a clinical idiom that helps to establish disease

---

In Book 4 disease appears at crucial points of the narrative, even before we reach its final section: in 4.663–72, for example, it concludes an important argument about the relativity of taste (4.615–72); at the same time, Lucretius' tendency to discuss the senses in terms of emitted particles which literally penetrate and often hurt our bodies establishes a clear line of connection with the imagery of the "blowing force" of disease in Book 3; see, especially, the violent language used in the section on sight in 4.706–21.

11 For death as a closural device in Latin literature, see e.g. Barchiesi 1997a, 189; Hardie 1997, 143; 153–54; Armstrong 2004, 293; P. Fowler 2007.

12 By "metaphorical" I do not mean to suggest, of course, that these affections of the soul lack a concrete identity or that they cannot be as serious and hard to treat as a severe bodily disease. As Nussbaum 1994, 14 observes: "Philosophy heals human diseases, diseases produced by false beliefs. Its arguments are to the soul as the doctor's remedies are to the body. They can heal, and they are to be evaluated in terms of their power to heal. As the medical art makes progress on behalf of the suffering body, so philosophy for the soul in distress ... [T]he medical analogy is not simply a *decorative metaphor* (emphasis added); it is an important tool both of discovery and of justification. Once one has in a general way understood that philosophy's task is like the doctor's task, one can then rely on that general understanding ... to find out, more concretely and in greater detail, how the philosopher ought to proceed in a variety of circumstances". Emphasis is placed here by Nussbaum on the serious implications which the medical analogy has for philosophy's therapeutic role. However, precisely because this role is construed by means of an analogy, the "metaphorical" element is not excluded from the picture. For metaphor by analogy (κατὰ τὸ ἀνάλογον), see Arist. *Poet.*1457b, with Gibbs 1994, 210ff. Cicero (*Tusc.* 3.7), as we shall see below, remains wary of using *morbus* as a translation for πάθος in a philosophical context; fear, desire and other emotions, to his mind, look like "illnesses" but they are not exactly so in the strict, medical sense of the term. For the "metaphorical sense" in which strong emotions and moral vices are viewed as illnesses in Greek and Roman philosophical discourse, see Hershkowitz 1998, 7. And for the distinction between proper mental illnesses (such as mania and melancholy) in medical texts and πάθη *qua* "affections of the soul" in Stoicism, see Graver 2003. Significantly, as Devinant 2018, 202 observes, at a later stage, "Galen consistently refrains from using the phrase πάθη τῆς ψυχῆς to designate conditions such as *phrenitis* or melancholy. Although he could very well have done so, he reserves the term for emotions". This differentiation between πάθη ψυχῆς in an ethical context — that is, with the broad meaning of emotions — and specifically medical psychic ailments is also noted by Singer (forthcoming).

as a tangible, inevitable reality.¹³ This process helps to underline the transition from spiritual to biological death and, through it, marks a descent towards the end of the poem itself.

Hellenistic philosophy presents itself as a medicine for the mind and the soul. Philosophers use the treatment of the body, for which doctors are responsible, as a firm point of reference on the basis of which their curing strategies and restorative practices are subsequently formulated.¹⁴ This new method of healing is thus appending itself to an established model of medical practice, and aspires to extend its therapeutic grasp beyond the narrow limits of the body, reaching to more elusive entities. During this process, the body often becomes downgraded:¹⁵ what is said to really matter is the mental ability to stay calm and unaffected by external circumstances — even when these circumstances involve terrible illnesses and excruciating physical pain.¹⁶ Lucretius is no exception to the rule. The medical analogy he employs in Book 1 designates clearly the reader's tranquillity as the poet's prime concern (1.936–50). But the body, as I wish to stress in this chapter, does not recede to the background. On the contrary, Lucretius' increasing emphasis on physical suffering as we move towards the poem's conclusion reveals an intense concern with the material conditions which define our existence — that fragile "vessel" within which we reside and which, as is repeatedly claimed throughout the *DRN*, is destined by its nature to dissolve at some point. By using this dissolution as a pathway which guides us through the narrative and

---

13 One could object that in Lucretius' materialist philosophy, where the mind and soul also consist of atoms, every kind of pain and illness are ultimately of a bodily nature. True as this may be, Lucretius maintains a fine distinction throughout the poem between two types of pathology: "affections of the soul", such as intense emotions of fear and desire, are regularly indicated by the use of *aeger/aegrescere* (e.g. in 3.521; 3.824–27; 3.933–34; 3.1070). On the other hand, *morbus* is almost exclusively applied to the *corpus*, indicating a physical disease; see 3.41; 3.463; 3.472; 4.665; 5.220; 6.657; 6.793; 6.1095–98. The intrinsic link between *corpus* and *morbus* — on the basis of which the analogy is built with pathological conditions that affect the mind/soul — is underlined in 3.459–61: *huc accedit uti videamus,* **corpus ut ipsum** */ suscipere inmanis morbos durumque dolorem, / sic animum curas acris luctumque metumque*, "add to this that, just as the body itself is liable to awful diseases and harsh pain, so we see the mind liable to carking care and grief and fear". I discuss this distinction in more detail below.
14 See Nussbaum 1994.
15 So, for instance, in Plato the care of the soul is often highlighted in contexts which betray a hostile attitude towards conventional medicine because of the latter's excessive emphasis on the body; see e.g. Pl. *Resp.* 407b4–c6. The difference between body and soul highlighted through the medical analogy — as Holmes 2010a, 353–56 points out — can be understood in terms of a hierarchy: the soul is most dear, among others reasons because it can take care of the body (while the reverse is not possible); see Pl. *Prt.* 313a6–7; *Ap.* 30a7–b2. Cf. Holmes 2013, 21.
16 See e.g. Diog. Laert. 10.22 = fr. 52 Arrighetti, on Epicurus' deathbed letter (discussed below).

finally shows us the exit, Lucretius makes a factual statement: however compelling his arguments may be to help us ease the pain and enjoy our short lives, there is nothing his healing art can do to make this last forever.

2.1 What's in a Disease?

Lucr. 3.1053–75 is found at the climax of the poet's diatribe against the fear of death (3.830–1094)[17] and is drawn as a concise portrait of a life burdened with discontent, restlessness and unresolved suffering; this is life as most (unenlightened) people live it and — to Lucretius' mind at least — there seems to be nothing to distinguish it from death itself (cf. *mortua vita* in 3.1046):[18]

> Si possent homines, proinde ac sentire videntur
> pondus inesse animo quod se gravitate fatiget,
> e quibus id fiat causis quoque noscere et unde
> tanta mali tamquam moles in pectore constet,
> haud ita vitam agerent, ut nunc plerumque videmus
> quid sibi quisque velit nescire et quaerere semper
> commutare locum, quasi onus deponere possit.
> exit saepe foras magnis ex aedibus ille,
> esse domi quem pertaesumst, subitoque revertit,
> quippe foris nilo melius qui sentiat esse.
> currit agens mannos ad villam praecipitanter,
> auxilium tectis quasi ferre ardentibus instans;
> oscitat extemplo, tetigit cum limina villae,
> aut abit in somnum gravis atque oblivia quaerit,
> aut etiam properans urbem petit atque revisit.
> hoc se quisque modo fugit, at quem scilicet, ut fit,
> effugere haud potis est, ingratis haeret et odit,
> propterea morbi quia causam non tenet aeger;
> quam bene si videat, iam rebus quisque relictis
> naturam primum studeat cognoscere rerum,
> temporis aeterni quoniam, non unius horae,
> ambigitur status, in quo sit mortalibus omnis
> aetas, post mortem quae restat cumque, manenda.

---

17 See Wallach 1976.
18 The section which follows our text as the existing conclusion to the book, 3.1076–94, has long been contested as repetitive and somewhat redundant. Bailey 1947, 1173 finds in it "a series of disconnected points" which fail to maintain a sense of formal ending; cf. Brown 1997, 221. Giussani 1897, 143 suggests that Book 3 was originally intended to end in 3.1075.

> Just as men evidently feel that there is a weight on their minds which wearies with its oppression, if so they could also recognize from what causes it comes, and what makes so great a mountain of misery to lie on their hearts, they would not so live their lives as now we generally seem them do, each ignorant what he wants, each seeking always to change his place as if he could drop his burden. The man who has been bored to death at home often goes forth from his great mansion, and then suddenly returns because he feels himself no better abroad. Off he courses, driving his Gallic ponies to his country house in headlong haste, as if he were bringing urgent help to a house on fire. The moment he has reached the threshold of the house, he yawns, or falls into heavy sleep and seeks oblivion, or even makes haste to get back and see the city again. Thus each man tries to flee from himself, but to that self, from which of course he can never escape, he clings against his will, and hates it, because he is a sick man who does not know the cause of his complaint; for could he see that well, at once each would throw his business aside and first study to learn the nature of things, since the matter in doubt is not his state for one hour, but for eternity, in what state mortals must expect all time to be passed which remains after death.

Lucretius speaks in these lines of nothing less than a discontent with life itself,[19] an overwhelming feeling of disgust and satiety that makes its presence felt as a burdening weight (3.1054: *pondus*, 3.1056: *moles*, 3.1059: *onus*) constantly pressing on people's minds and depriving them of all sense of fulfilment and satisfaction. The poet identifies this condition as a "disease" (3.1070: *morbus*) whose cause remains elusive to the patient (3.1053–56: *si possent... e quibus id fiat causis... noscere et unde... constet*); in fact, not knowing the cause is what is most distinctive about this peculiar condition — perhaps even what makes it a disease in the first place (3.1070: *morbi quia causam non tenet aeger*). This sense of elusiveness implicates the audience as well: although this section forms part of the diatribe that has commenced in 3.830 we still cannot be certain that fear of death is its subject;[20] the narrative at this point appears to disengage itself from the immediate context and could easily stand as a self-contained excursus on life's anxieties and unfulfilled desires.[21] Equally suggestive in this respect is the fact that Lucretius does not quite tell us in the end how this disease can be healed. His

---

19 See 3.1061: *pertaesumst*, with Kaster 2005, 128 and 200 n. 94. For the same feeling, see Sen. *Tranq.* 2.15; *Ep.* 24.26; 89.18.
20 See Bailey 1947, 1170. Kenney 2014, 224 objects, but with caution: "Lucretius does not make the identification [i.e. between fear of death and the discontent depicted in 3.1053–75] in so many words, but it can be felt in the opening lines of the section". It should be mentioned that Lucretius' Ennian intertext (a chorus of soldiers in *Iphigenia* pronounce that when someone spends his life in leisure, "the mind doesn't know what it wants", *otioso in otio animus nescit quid velit*) has nothing to do with death; see Skutsch 1968, 157–65.
21 Cf. Sen. *Ep.* 28; *Tranq.* 2.13–15: both Senecan passages thrive with allusions to Lucr. 3.1053–75 but none of them speaks of death directly; being dissatisfied with life does not necessarily imply an anxiety about our state as mortal beings; see Montiglio 2006, 563–64.

final advice, that one should strive to understand the "nature of things" (3.1072), is premised on the condition that the cause of the disease has been in the meantime identified (3.1071: *quam bene si videat* [i.e. *causam*]); but how this is to be done exactly remains without an explanation.[22]

The text thus speaks of a disease while concealing it at the same time. Part of this confusion extends to the question of how one should understand its most significant symptom, namely its manifestation as a pressing "weight" (*pondus*). One line of interpretation would be to take this weight literally,[23] as an actual feeling of heaviness, which affects the mind and the chest at the same time: considering that the mind consists of atoms and is assigned with a fixed place in the body (3.140: *media regione in pectoris*), it is natural to suppose that something pressing on it takes the form of an embodied experience. According to Charles Segal, "metaphors of weight are very much alive for Lucretius and need to be taken seriously. They exemplify the somatic sensitivity to emotions, and especially emotions of fear, worry, and anxiety ... Even the metaphorical heaviness or the constriction of anxiety has ... the status of a strong, physical sensation."[24] A solid parallel to this thought is provided by Hippocratic writings which tend to speak of emotional distress in terms of a sensation of heaviness that is specifically located in the chest (βάρος ἐν τοῖσι στήθεσιν) or in the head.[25] In fact, closer examination of the phrasing in 3.1053–54, *sentire videntur / pondus inesse animo* [=*pectore*], reveals significant correspondences with a patient's experience of bodily pain in a medical context and, in particular, with the difficulties involved in communicating that pain to others: note, especially, Lucretius' use of *inesse*, indicating something that lies inside the affected body and can be felt but cannot be seen, and compare it, for instance, with the Hippocratic *De morbis* 3.7 (7.124 L.), which describes a swelling in the lungs as it is felt from within, thus allowing

---

22 As noted by Klingner 1956, 191; Perelli 1969, 38; Bonelli 1984, 102.
23 See Pigeaud 1981, 205–206.
24 Segal 1990, 164; Cf. Hampe 2017, 9.
25 Βάρος ἐν τοῖσι στήθεσιν: [Hipp.] *Morb.* 3.15 (7.136 L.); *Dieb. iudic.* 10 (9.306 L.), where the phrase occurs in close association with extreme mental discomfort: καὶ βάρος ἐν τοῖσι στήθεσιν καὶ παραφροσύναι. For βάρος in the head, see [Hipp.] *Epid.* 3.17, case 14 (3.140 L.): κεφαλῆς... βάρος μετ' ὀδύνης· ἄγρυπνος ἐξ ἀρχῆς, σιγῶσα δὲ καὶ σκυθρωπή. For psychological symptoms of fear and anxiety combined with a sensation of heaviness in the inward parts of the body, βάρος ἐπὶ τοῖσι σπλάγχνοισι, see [Hipp.] *Morb.* 2.72–3 (7.108–112 L.), with Langholf 1990, 54. Βάρος in medical texts has a strong physical feel to it, e.g. in [Hipp.] *Morb.*1.13 (6.160L.): ὁκόταν δὲ ὁ χρόνος προΐῃ, τρηχύνεταί τε ὁ πλεύμων, καὶ ἑλκοῦται ἔνδοθεν ὑπὸ τοῦ φλέγματος ἐνισταμένου καὶ ἐνσηπομένου, καὶ βάρος τε παρέχει τοῖσι στήθεσι καὶ ὀδύνην ὀξέην, "as time goes on, the lung becomes rough and ulcerates internally because of the phlegm standing and putrefying in it, and this produces heaviness in the chest and sharp pain" (translation in Potter 1988, 125).

us some insight into the patient's own perception of what is affecting him: καὶ τὰ στήθεα αὐτῷ ἀείδειν **δοκέει καὶ βάρος ἐνεῖναι**, διὸ χωρέειν οὐ δύναται τὰ στήθεα, "and it seems to him that a hissing sound is coming out of his chest and that there is a heaviness in it that prevents it from moving".[26] Although βάρος in medical writings is not altogether free from metaphorical associations, it always remains rooted in the nature of the body, and cannot be fully understood unless we approach it as a physically grounded experience.

At the same time, *pondus* in Lucretius' text recalls Greek expressions of emotional discomfort, which seem to involve weight in a more figurative sense (e.g. βαρέως φέρειν/βαρέως ἔχειν).[27] One passage in particular deserves special attention. It comes in a fragment from Menander's *Phasma* and contains the dialogue between a lecturing slave (some believe him to be a tutor) and his master. Although many of the dialogue's details are missing, enough of the text survives to allow for the scene's reconstruction as some form of informal debate on whether boredom and restlessness can actually qualify as mental illnesses in the medical sense of the term: thus, while the master appears to be convinced that he is suffering from some kind of mental disease (νόσος/ἀρρώστημα), which makes him feel "weighed down", the slave keeps on refuting this condition as trivial, nonexistent even — in his view, nothing that a simple change of attitude in life cannot cure. I should stress in advance that I take several of that dialogue's details to lie particularly close to Lucr.3.1053–75; whether this convergence is a matter of coincidence or the product of a closer engagement with the comedian's text (perhaps through the medium of a Roman adaptation) remains of course open to speculation. It is worth remembering, at any rate, that comic motifs are abundantly attested throughout the *DRN* — often in the context of sustained references to individual texts and authors[28] — and that Lucretius' moralising discourse at the end of Book 3 draws on a tradition of Roman satire that is interacting closely with Plautus and Terence.[29]

---

[26] For the use of δοκεῖ as a way by which the patient's own perspective is signposted in medical narratives, see Thumiger 2016, 118–20; 2018, 287; cf. Holmes 2010b, 74–75.

[27] For βαρέως φέρειν, identified by Biles/Olson 2015, 123 as a late 5th/4th cent. BCE prose idiom, see Hdt. 5.19; Isoc. 9.54. The phrase is especially favourite to Aristophanes: *Eccl.* 174–5; *Ran.* 26. 803; *Thesm.* 385, 474; *Vesp.* 114, 158.

[28] See Domenicucci 1981 and Brown 1987, 135–36. For links between the *DRN* and Plautine comedy, see Snyder 1980, 72–73, 78–79; Hanses 2015, 90–107. For the "Lucretius-*Ego* as comic speaker", see Gellar-Goad 2020, 128ff.

[29] For Lucilius' satire and Roman comedy, see Muecke 2005, 36–37, 42; Pezzini 2018, 162–63; cf. Keane 2006, 13–15. For the importance of Menander in Roman satire, see Hor. *Sat.* 2.3.11–12, with Freudenburg 1993, 107–108; cf. Gowers 2012, 152–53.

Menander's text runs as follows:[30]

(?ΠΑΙΔΑΓΩΓΟΣ) αἴσθου σαυτὸν ὄντα, [Φειδία,
ἄνθρωπον, ἄνθρωπον δὲ καὶ [τὸν ἐνδεῆ,
ἵνα μὴ 'πιθυμῇς τῶν ὑπὲρ σ[ὲ πραγμάτων.
ὅταν δ' ἀγρυπνεῖν εἴπῃς, τίς ὁ [βίος σοῦ σκοπῶν
τὴν αἰτίαν γνώσει· περιπατεῖς [
εἰσῆλθες εὐθύς, ἂν κοπιάσῃς τ[ὰ σκέλη·
μαλακῶς ἐλούσω· πάλιν ἀναστ[ὰς ἐνέφαγες
πρὸς ἡδονήν· ὕπνος αὐτὸς ὁ βί[ος ἐστί σου.
τὸ πέρας· κακὸν ἔχεις οὐδέν, ἡ ν[όσος δέ σου
ἔσθ' ἣν διῆλθες.
      [...]
...τἀληθῆ λέγω, νὴ τοὺς θεούς·
τοῦτ' ἐστὶ τἀρρώστημα.
(Φε.)   καὶ μὴ[ν οὐ κρατῶ
ἀτόπως ἐμαυτοῦ καὶ <u>βαρέως</u> [ἔχω πάνυ.
[?Πα.] <u>ἀσθενικόν ἐστι τἀνόητο[ν</u>
(Φε.) εἶέν· πάνυ γὰρ ταυτὶ λελο[γισμένως λέγεις.
τί μοι παραινεῖς;
(?Πα.)   ὅ τι παρ[αινῶ;
εἰ μέν τι κακὸν ἀληθὲς εἶχες, Φειδία,
ζητεῖν ἀληθὲς φάρμακον τούτου σ' ἔδει·
νῦν δ' οὐκ ἔχεις· <u>κενὸν εὑρὲ καὶ τὸ φάρμακον</u>
<u>πρὸς τὸ κενόν</u>, οἰήθητι δ' ὠφελεῖν τί σε.
                                    (*Phasma* 31–53)

[Tutor] Think, Pheidias, you're human; but a poor man's human too. You must not set your sights on what's beyond your powers. And when you say you cannot sleep, you will find out the cause if you just think what your own life is like. You stroll around at leisure; when your legs are tired, at once you go back home. You bath luxuriously; then up you get and eat again to please yourself. Your very life is just a sleep! In short, you have no illness; no, your sickness is what you have just described... By god, I speak the truth. That's what your illness is.
[Pheidias] But still, it's strange — I cannot control myself; I'm very down.
[Tutor] It's your foolishness that makes you feel ill.
[Pheidias] Oh well, your words are logical enough. Then what do you advise?
[Tutor] You ask me for advice? Well, if you really suffered from some illness, you should now be looking for the proper cure for that. But you have none. So for a fancied illness you must find a fancied cure and then imagine that it does some good.[31]

---

30 For the text I follow Sandbach's 1990 OCT edition.
31 Translation in Balme 2001 (modified at points).

Three aspects of this dialogue need to be highlighted: first, as lines 34 (ὅταν δ' ἀγρυπνεῖν εἴπῃς) and 39–40 (ἡ ν[όσος³² δέ σου / ἔσθ' ἣν διῆλθες) indicate, in an earlier scene Pheidias must have been talking about his "disease" in detail,³³ in all likelihood describing himself as finding no satisfaction in life while revealing at the same time that the exact cause of his troubles escapes him: the slave's remark that some introspection is all that it would take for this cause to be revealed (35: τὴν αἰτίαν γνώσει) could be responding to one of his master's expressed complaints. Furthermore, considering that no actual treatment is proposed at any point in the dialogue (the slave's final advice is to use a placebo, a fitting medicine to an imaginary, "empty",³⁴ condition; 50–53), it seems safe to assume that finding this cause would also mean the end of the disease. Second, both Lucretius and the Greek comedian make the interesting point that mental distress in its pathological form (or in what might be confused as one) can be socially conditioned: Lucretius' unfailing emphasis on signs of wealth and luxury in 3.1060–65 falls in line with the slave's explicit critique in Menander, according to which Pheidias' supposed illness is ultimately linked to his excessive desires (33) and unlimited leisure in life (35–38). A third and final point relates to the emphasis placed on wandering and fatigue in both texts: lines 35–37 in Menander (περιπατεῖς³⁵ ... εἰσῆλθες εὐθύς... πάλιν ἀναστ[ὰς) — one of the first attempts to tackle with the elusive notion of boredom in Greek literature — are re-enacted in

---

32 The reading νόσος is adopted both in Sandbach's OCT and Arnott's 2000 Loeb edition. It was first suggested by Wilamowitz 1876, 506; see also Turner 1969, 312–13, 318–19 and Arnott 1998, 43.
33 See Turner 1969, 313.
34 See the emphatic repetition of κενόν in the Greek text's concluding lines. Compare Lucretius' use of *inanis* as a way of indicating that people's fear and anxieties are actually empty; see e.g. 3.982: *sed magis in vita divom metus urget inanis*.
35 As Thomas 1979, 184 points out, "the verb περιπατεῖν [in New Comedy and especially in Menander]... could, with no additional explanation, refer to the frustrated antics of the comic lover"; if we add to this that in line 34 the idea of insomnia crops up, it can then be concluded that the slave is "mistaking for mere petulance what are, in fact, the unmistakable symptoms of frustrated love" (p. 196). Although I believe that the present dialogue extends to something more than a (misunderstood) case of lovesickness, it is possible that Menander could be blurring at this point two different strands of moralizing discourse: one directed against misguided desire in general, and another one implicating sexual desire specifically. In Lucr. 3.1053–75 there is nothing to point in the direction of an erotic burden; but see Catul. 76.13: *difficilest longum subito deponere amorem*, and 76.25: *ipse valere opto et taetrum hunc deponere morbum*; cf. Lucr. 3.1059: *onus deponere*. For the "Lucretian vividness" in Catullus' imagery of disease in poem 76, see Booth 1997, 165.

full detail in Lucretius 3.1060–67, where attention is likewise drawn to the endless movement between private and public space.[36] At the same time, the slave's striking claim that a life deprived of meaning is no different from sleep, ὕπνος αὐτὸς ὁ βί[ος ἐστί σου (38), is also echoed in Lucretius: *abit in somnum gravis* in 3.1066 looks back at *mortua vita* (3.1046) a few lines above, explained by the poet as the kind of life which is being wasted on sleep and dreams, the latter figuring in the text both in a literal and in a metaphorical sense (3.1046–48): *mortua cui vita est prope iam vivo atque videnti, / qui somno partem maiorem conteris aevi / et vigilans stertis nec somnia cernere cessas*, "You whose life is now all but dead though you live and see, you who waste the greater part of your time in sleep, who snore open-eyed and never cease to see dreams".[37]

On the whole the slave's viewpoint is that Pheidias' condition should not be a cause for alarm; in fact what he is actually suggesting is that there is no sickness at all.[38] A similar attitude can be traced in Lucretius' text: although the presence of *morbus* is in that case incontestable, the poet's implicit claim that finding its cause should be enough to eliminate it (3.1053–57) ultimately downgrades its significance and makes it look less grave than it appears at first sight. One wonders then how Lucretius' possible engagement with a comic text (or, more broadly, with a comic tradition) which in essence disputes the idea that diseases of the mind can be viewed as fixed medical categories would have worked at this point. I would suggest that Lucretius' comic intertext, evolving as it does into a subtle debate on when and how the word νόσος should be used, signposts the poet's own preoccupation with the elusive identity of disease in 3.1053–75.

---

36 See the supplement κ[ατ' ἀγοράν at the end of line 35 (following περιπατεῖς), which is adopted in Arnott's 2000 Loeb edition. Instead of πάλιν ἀναστ[ὰς ἐνέφαγες in line 37, Arnott proposes: πάλιν ἀναστ[ὰς περιπατεῖς.
37 For *somnia* with the meaning of "delusions/false beliefs", cf. Cic. *N.D.* 1.42, with Harris 2009, 140–41 n. 104.
38 Another fragment of the play speaks of someone with a "slight touch of melancholia" (line 57: ὑπεμελαγχόλη[σε); although we cannot be certain, scholars have identified this patient with Pheidias; see Turner 1969, 318–19; Webster 1974, 174; Traill 2008, 66. Greek μελαγχολία is typically discussed by medical writers and philosophers as manifesting itself with fits of groundless depression; it assumes the form of a sadness which has "no evident cause", ἄλογος, e.g. in [Arist.] *Pr.* XXX.i 954b35. The profile of a melancholic patient who is feeling unwell without knowing why would seem to fit well with Pheidias' complaint in the fragment cited above (see especially line 46: ἀτόπως ἐμαυτοῦ καὶ βαρέως [ἔχω πάνυ) — but it would also suggest that the lecturing slave is not entirely right when observing that there is absolutely nothing wrong with the young master.

Evidence from the time of Lucretius reveals a cautious linguistic approach as to what exactly qualifies as *morbus animi* in Latin. While Cicero accepts that *morbus* could be proposed as equivalent to Greek πάθος — a word used by philosophers to designate the state of an "ailing" mind or soul —[39] his suggestion is that the term should better be left for mental illness in a strictly medical context,[40] without being stretched, that is, to describe instances where sickness is implicated in a metaphorical sense (*Tusc.* 3.7): *formidines libidines iracundiae ... fere sunt eius modi, quae Graeci πάθη appellant; ego poteram 'morbos', et id verbum esset e verbo, sed in consuetudinem nostram non caderet. nam misereri, invidere, gestire, laetari, haec omnia morbos Graeci appellant, motus animi rationi non obtemperantis, nos autem hos eosdem motus concitati animi recte, ut opinor, perturbationes dixerimus,* **morbos autem non satis usitate**, "terror, desire, anger ... all such things the Greeks call them πάθη. A literal translation for πάθη would be 'sicknesses', but that would run counter to normal usage. For pity, envy, elation, gladness, and so forth are all called by the Greeks 'sicknesses', as being movements of the mind not obedient to reason. But I think I was right to refer to these same movements of the mind as 'disorders', since 'sicknesses' would sound peculiar".[41] These observations subsequently lead Cicero to the important distinction between *insania* and *furor* (3.11): the first carries with it the meaning of insanity in a figurative sense since it applies to everyone who has not yet reached a perfect state of wisdom;[42] the latter refers to madness in a clinical context. The difference between the two is that *insania* has an extended, wider application (*patet latius*) because of its association with folly, *stultitia*;[43] *furor*, on the other

---

39 For the Stoic theory of πάθη of the soul, with which Cicero engages at this point, see Inwood 1985, 127–81; Frede 1986; Graver 2008.
40 For the Stoic distinction between affections of the soul (such as wrong judgments and emotional states which are obstructive to reason) and mental illnesses in the strict, medical sense, see Graver 2003.
41 Translation in Graver 2002, 5–6 (slightly modified). For the same point, see Cic. *Fin.* 3.35. For a similar distinction in Seneca, between *adfectus* and *morbus*, the first being used as a more fitting translation for πάθη, see Sen. *Ep.* 75.11; 83.10. But Seneca also uses *morbus* to describe a condition of the soul that has fallen prey to passions; see Armisen-Marchetti 1989, 132–38; Borgo 1998, 134–36; Setaioli 2014, 240.
42 See Cic. *Parad.* 4: ὅτι πᾶς ἄφρων μαίνεται. As Hor. *Sat.* 2.3 brilliantly demonstrates, if understood literally, this Stoic maxim sounds absurd since it fails to maintain a semantic distinction between insanity *qua* moral weakness and mental illness in the proper sense of the term.
43 Cicero puts it as follows (*Tusc.* 3.11): *eos enim sanos quoniam intellegi necesse est, quorum mens motu* **quasi morbo** *perturbata nullo sit, qui contra adfecti sint, hos insanos appellari necesse est ... Graeci autem* μανίαν *unde appellent, non facile dixerim; eam tamen ipsam distinguimus nos melius quam illi. hanc enim insaniam,* **quae iuncta stultitiae patet latius**, *a furore disiungimus,*

hand, is more narrowly delineated: to cure it one has to seek the help of a proper doctor, not a philosopher.[44]

A quick look at Lucretius' use of *morbus* reveals a tendency on the poet's part to associate it almost exclusively with the *corpus / membra corporis*,[45] and to indicate with it primarily bodily illnesses, including fevers (4.664–65), swellings in the feet (6.658), diseases of the eyes (6.659) and the skin (6.660–61), or the plague (6.1095–98); when Lucretius wishes to speak of an "affection of the soul" in — what Cicero would have described as — an extended, loose sense, he switches to the use of *aeger / aegrescere* (3.521: *animus ...aegrescit*; 3.824–27; 3.933–34; 3.1070).[46] The *anima*, as we read in 3.731–32, is impossible to be affected by *morbus* when it has left the body: *neque enim, **sine corpore cum sunt**, / sollicitae* [i.e. *animae*] *volitant **morbis** alguque fameque*, "for as long as the spirits are without bodies, they are not plagued with disease as they fly about, or with cold and hunger".[47] In other cases,

---

"since the word 'sane' has to refer to those whose minds are not disturbed by any movement or, as it were, sickness, those who are in the opposite condition must be termed 'insane' ... Why the Greeks call this state 'mania' I really cannot say. Our language makes clearer distinctions: we discriminate between insania, which has a wide application because of its link with folly, and furor or 'frenzy'" (translation in Graver 2002, 6–7).
44 For a detailed discussion, see Kazantzidis 2013.
45 The same applies to *dolor*; see e.g. the definition provided in 2.963–96: *dolor est, ubi materiai / corpora vi quadam per viscera viva per artus / sollicitata suis trepidant in sedibus intus, / inque locum quando remigrant, fit blanda voluptas*, "there is pain when the bodies of matter, attacked by some force through the living flesh and limbs, tremble in their secret habitations within, and when they move back to their place comes a soothing delight". Cf. 3.110: *pes cum dolet*; 3.147–48: *cum caput aut oculus temptante dolore / laeditur in nobis*; 3.459–60: *corpus ut ipsum / suscipere inmanis morbos durumque dolorem*; 3.495–96: *membra dolore / adficiuntur*; 6.1202–3: *multus capitis cum saepe dolore / corruptus sanguis expletis naribus ibat*. For the intrinsic link between *dolor* and *corpus* in a passage which distinguishes *corpus* from *mens*, see 2.16–19: *nonne videre / nil aliud sibi naturam latrare, nisi utqui / **corpore seiunctus dolor absit**, mensque fruatur / iucundo sensu cura semota metuque?*, "[how pitiful it is] not to see that all nature barks for is this, that pain be removed away out of the body, and that the mind, kept away from care and fear, enjoy a feeling of delight". There are only a few cases (see e.g. 3.905 and 4.1067) where Lucretius uses *dolor* to describe mental or emotional pain (*privata dolore omni* in 1.47 could be read as referring to the fact that the gods do not experience physical pain). Contrast the rather common use of *dolor animi* in Cicero, e.g. *Clu.* 16, 168; *Dom.* 97; *Fam.* 2.16.1, 4.6.1, 13.77.3; *Fin.* 1.43, 1.55; 2.107; *Mur.* 86; *Phil.* 2.40, 2.64; *Ver.* 2.5.158.
46 But these words can also be used for the body; see e.g. 3.106 (*corpus ... aegret*); 3.510 (*corpus ... aegrum*).
47 The lines echo Empedocles' view that incarnation is a sort of defilement, a degenerative process accelerated, among others, through sickness. At the moment of birth, the souls enter (B 121 D–K): ἀτερπέα χῶρον, / ἔνθα φόνος τε κότος τε καὶ ἄλλων ἔθνεα κηρῶν / αὐχμηραί τε νόσοι καὶ σήψιες ἔργα τε ῥευστά / Ἄτης ἂν λειμῶνα κατὰ σκότος ἠλάσκουσιν, "a joyless place where there

morbus can be actually seen as affecting the mind,[48] but the way in which this is described, as a process of "contamination", ultimately points to the fact that the disease is primarily associated with *corpus*: it can "penetrate" the mind but it remains extrinsic to it, in the same way that our bodies are liable to be penetrated by things that lie outside them.[49] It could thus be said that the closing section of Book 3 presents us with a deviation from the poet's linguistic norms: it experiments with the possibility of a *morbus* that does not simply affect the *animus* directly, but essentially originates from it. The result is that the metaphoric and the literal become blurred: bordering on the line between a heaviness that is actually felt on the chest and an elusive one that is pressing on the mind, *morbus* in 3.1053–75 remains in the end impalpable and vague[50] precisely because its exact *corporeal* nature is not explicitly identified.

As Charles Segal observes, "the move towards the psychological "constriction" and "weight" at the end of book 3 tends to shift the emphasis from the physical (and often fatal) sufferings given in the proofs of mortality of the soul in the first half to more figurative and more inward sufferings. This shift of emphasis also reinforces the point of the proem ... that Epicurus' relief of emotional suffering is more important to human happiness than healing the body's physical ills".[51] And yet, as I propose to show, it is precisely with these physical ills that Lucretius becomes increasingly preoccupied as we move from the closing section

---

are slaughter and hatred and hordes of other violent deaths and parching fevers and consumptions and dropsy, and they wander in darkness over the field of Ate" (translation in Wright 1981, 278).

48 When it eventually does so, it results in clinical conditions such as those designated by Cicero as proper *morbi animi*, e.g. *furor*; see Lucr. 3.462–71.

49 See e.g. 3.470–71: *quare animum quoque dissolvi fateare necessest, / quandoquidem* **penetrant** *in eum* [i.e. *animum*] *contagia morbi*, "therefore you must confess that the mind also is dissolved, since the contagion of the disease penetrates within it"; for the application of *penetrare* to an external force which invades a compound object and shatters it, see e.g. 1.221–24. The idea of contamination in Lucr. 3.470–71 brings to mind the Platonic dichotomy between body and soul, e.g. in Pl. *Phd.* 67a: καὶ ἐν ᾧ ἂν ζῶμεν, οὕτως ... ἐγγυτάτω ἐσόμεθα τοῦ εἰδέναι, ἐὰν ὅτι μάλιστα μηδὲν ὁμιλῶμεν τῷ σώματι μηδὲ κοινωνῶμεν, ὅτι μὴ πᾶσα ἀνάγκη, μηδὲ **ἀναπιμπλώμεθα** τῆς τούτου φύσεως, ἀλλὰ **καθαρεύωμεν ἀπ' αὐτοῦ**. For the idea of (embodied) life as a disease in Plato, see Nehamas 1998, 161–62.

50 Cf. Serenus' self-diagnosis in Sen. *Tranq.* 1.2: *in statu ut non pessimo, ita maxime querulo et moroso positus sum:* **nec aegroto nec ualeo**. Seneca replies that his friend's condition — an intense form of discontent with life itself — is not exactly like a disease (2.1ff.), although it requires some form of intervention. Not incidentally, in Seneca's understanding, Serenus suffers precisely from the symptoms outlined by Lucretius in 3.1053–75; see e.g. *Tranq.* 14.1: *Ut ait Lucretius, hoc se quisque modo semper fugit.*

51 Segal 1990, 168.

of Book 3 to the ends of Book 4 and 6. What paves the way to the poem's conclusion is a progressive abandonment of figurative models of suffering, and a shift that puts the main emphasis on the biological realities of the body. During this process, disease acquires a more concrete, tangible identity; at the same time, death is more and more presented in terms of a material dissolution, imposing a sense of finality that is deeply rooted in our frail corporeal existence.

2.2 Sex Can Kill

The dialogue between the closing section of Book 3 and Lucretius' diatribe against love and sex at the end of Book 4 is a complex one which operates on different levels. The association between the two endings is primarily maintained through an antithesis: while the first of the two scenes revolves around the individual's failing attempt to almost split himself into two halves and get rid of the part that is weighing on him (3.1068–69), the latter is about two craving bodies which fail to merge with each other and to reach complete fusion (4.1108–1111): *adfigunt avide corpus iunguntque salivas / oris et inspirant pressantes dentibus ora — / nequiquam, quoniam nil inde abradere possunt /* **nec penetrare et abire corpus in corpore toto**, "they cling greedily close together and join their watering mouths and draw deep breaths pressing teeth on lips; but all is vanity, for they can rub nothing off, nor can they penetrate and be absorbed body in body". Images of self-alienation, loss of interest in life and disgust thus come to be substituted with contrasting feelings of strong and passionate (though equally vain and misguided) desire.[52]

The tension between the two sections brings to mind Lucretius' implicit distinction between *lethargus* and *furor* as this can be found in 3.464–65 and then, more directly, in 3.828–29.[53] Sleep in 3.1066 (*aut abit in somnus gravis atque*

---

[52] Disgust with life is predominant as a notion throughout 3.1053–75. Lucretius' lovers at the end of Book 4 experience no such feeling, but the way sexual intercourse is described seems designed to elicit a strong response of disgust from the readers; see Fowler 1996, 814–15: "the principal tactic that Lucretius employs in Book 4–the deromanticization of love–coupled with the continual engendering of the didactic narratee as male produces a disturbing counter-text [the author refers here to Nussbaum's argument that the poet is presenting us with a positive image of the relationship between the two sexes; 1994, 140–91]. The temptation is to use disgust as a weapon in this deromanticization, and it is a temptation Lucretius does not avoid".

[53] See, especially, 3.828–29: **adde furorem** *animi proprium atque oblivia rerum, /* **adde** *quod in nigras* **lethargi** *mergitur undas*, "add madness, which is peculiar to the mind, and forgetfulness of all things, add that it is drowned in the black waters of lethargy". For the distinction between lethargy and madness in ancient medical sources, see Drabkin 1955, 226; Gourevitch 1983, 18;

oblivia quaerit) has been presented in terms which designate it clearly as a pathological condition:[54] the adjective *gravis* fits well with the section's emphasis on *pondus* but it could also have been meant as an allusion to lethargy as the kind of illness which induces a feeling of heaviness and makes one "sink" under its grip (3.465: **gravi lethargo** *fertur in altum*);[55] likewise the "oblivion" mentioned in 3.1066 recalls the lethargic patient's incapacity in 3.467–68 to recognize the faces of those around him as he is struggling with the disease. Lethargy is said by Lucretius to resemble a "deep, everlasting sleep" (3.465–66: *altum / aeternumque soporem*). This is precisely the image we find in 3.1047–48 (*qui somno partem maiorem conteris aevi / et vigilans stertis nec somnia cernere cessas*): sleep functions in that case as a metaphor for a meaningless life burdened by false beliefs and a loss of orientation, for which 3.1053–75 stands as a prime example. Love and sex, on the other hand, create a far more animated scene at the end of Book 4. It suffices to note that *furor* — an otherwise rare word in the poem[56] — occurs not once but twice:[57] first, in the poet's striking image of desire as a sore which grows and thickens from within (4.1068–69): *ulcus enim vivescit et inveterascit alendo, / inque dies gliscit **furor** atque aerumna gravescit*; and then in close association with *rabies*, by way of describing the mad passion which cannot be extinguished (4.1116–17): *parva fit ardoris violenti pausa parumper. / inde redit rabies eadem et **furor** ille revisit*, "there is a short pause for a while in the furious burning. Then the same frenzy returns, and once more the madness comes". Insatiable desire

---

and, specifically for Latin medical texts, see Cels. 3.20.1: *Alter quoque morbus est aliter **phrenetico contrarius**. In eo difficilior somnus, prompta ad omnem audaciam mens est: in hoc marcor et inexpugnabilis paene dormiendi necessitas. Lethargum Graeci nominarunt*, "there is also another disease, a contrast in a different way to the phrenetic. In the latter sleep is got with great difficulty, and the mind is disposed to any foolhardiness; in this disease there is a pining away, and an almost insurmountable need of sleep" (translation in Spencer 1935, 309). In Latin literature, a distinction between frenzy and lethargy seems to be already at play in Pl. *Men.* 889–91 (the one who speaks these lines is a doctor): *quid esse illi morbi dixeras? narra, senex. / **num** laruatust aut cerritus? fac sciam. / **num** eum veternus aut aqua intercus tenet?*, "what illness did you say he has? Tell me, old man. Is he possessed by evil spirits or by Ceres? Inform me. Does lethargy or dropsy hold him in its grip?" (translation in de Melo 2011, 517); for a discussion of these lines, see Stok 1996, 2312–13.

54 Cf. 4.907–53 where sleep, even under normal circumstances, is assimilated to disease. See, especially, 4.943–44: *conturbantur enim positurae principiorum / corporis atque animi* and compare it with 4.666–67 (on the effects of disease): *perturbatur ibi iam totum corpus, et omnes / commutantur ibi positurae principiorum*.
55 Cf. Hor. *Sat.* 2.3.145: *lethargo grandi est oppressus*.
56 The noun occurs overall five times in the *DRN*: 2.621, 3.828, 4.1069, 4.1117 and 6.49.
57 Viewing love as madness has an incredibly rich tradition in Greek literature; for an overview of the concept — focusing on material from Greek tragedy — see Thumiger 2013.

and a mad craving for union are typical of metaphorical descriptions of love as an illness;[58] in Lucretius, they take on additional meaning by being juxtaposed to the image of the lonely individual at the end of Book 3, whose problem seems to be exactly the opposite: that of a complete loss of interest in life and a self-isolating mode of existence, which renders any human contact redundant.

Once we set the two closing sections side by side more points of contrast emerge. One of them is related to the idea of wandering (*errare*), which appears in both texts as a manifestation of discontent and lack of fulfilment: while in 3.1058 erratic movement is attributed to the absence of a specific object of desire (*quid sibi quisque velit nescire*), in 4.1076–78 it emerges as a response to the possession of that object: *etenim potiundi tempore in ipso / fluctuat **incertis erroribus** ardor amantum, / nec constat quid primum oculis manibusque fruantur*, "indeed, in the very time of possession, lovers' ardour is storm-tossed, uncertain in its course, hesitating what first to enjoy with eye or hand". In this context, it is worth observing that Lucretius' advised solution of promiscuous sex as the only way to avoid infatuation is presented in terms of an erotic restlessness (note, especially, 4.1071–72: *volgivaga vagus*[59] *Venere ante recentia cures / aut alio possis animi traducere motus*, "[the wounds of love become worse] unless you cure them in time while fresh by wandering with some random-roaming Venus, or turn your thoughts in some other direction"): instead of being thought as detrimental to one's peace of mind, constant move and change are recommended on this occasion as the only effective cure for erotic obsession.[60]

Equally important is the shared idea of ignorance between the two texts. As I have pointed out above, what makes the disease in 3.1053–75 painful and hard to cure is the fact that its cause remains elusive; that the exact nature of the affection eschews a concrete definition (3.1050): **nec reperire** *potes tibi quid saepe mali*. A similar lack of knowledge is highlighted in 4.1119–20 (***nec reperire*** *malum id possunt quae machina vincat: / usque adeo incerti tabescunt volnere caeco*, "they

---

58 For love as illness in a Roman context, see Caston 2006.
59 Cf. 3.1052: *animi incerto fluitans errore vagaris*.
60 See also 4.1063–64. As Fitzgerald 1984, 77 observes, "this is curious advice coming from a philosopher who is supposed to uphold the supreme value of *ataraxia*". The problem seems to be solved if we think that, when applied to the physical world, words such as *error* and *vagari* abandon their negative meaning; in that case, it is the constant "wandering" of atoms through the void, which allows them to conjoin motions and to form composite bodies. According to Fitzgerald, Lucretius' emphasis on the pleasures of "a wandering Venus" is nothing less than an invitation to stop thinking of ourselves as uniquely privileged individuals (a thought which feeds single-minded obsession with an object of desire) and to fuse with the jostling vitality of a constantly shifting atomic universe (see, especially, pp. 83–84); cf. Anderson 1960, 3.

can find no device to master the trouble: in such uncertainty they pine with their secret wound"), only this time ignorance is contained within the text and it affects only its characters; for we, as readers, have been provided with a fairly detailed account of both the original cause of the disease (4.1037–57) and its appropriate treatment (4.1058–72) – in other words, what we are missing as information at the end of Book 3. One would have thought that this advanced knowledge would have made the disease easier to treat; as we shall see, however, getting a grip on the precise identity of *morbus* usually has in Lucretius the opposite effect: the more insight we gain into the nature and cause of illness, the more imposing its presence, and that of death, become in the poem.[61]

To a large extent, this advanced insight is owing to the fact that love and desire are treated in physical terms. Before stressing its association with *furor*, Lucretius first describes love as an expanding, suppurating sore which, having infected the body, leads eventually to a mental breakdown (4.1068–69; cited above). As Robert Brown points out, "so perfectly is it made to fit Lucretius' theoretical analysis and so deeply is it woven into the poetic fabric, that the "wound" of love almost ceases to be a metaphor and approaches a pathological fact".[62] Indeed, considering Lucretius' reductionist attribution of desire to a single harmful substance (one of the words used in the text to describe semen is *umor* (e.g. in 4.1056), applied elsewhere in the poem to the humoural cause of disease)[63] and his subsequent presentation of post-coital exhaustion in terms of a near-death

---

[61] The individual in 3.1053–75 is doomed to live his life in a never-ending loop of boredom, experiencing what is primarily a mental type of discomfort. Sexual intercourse, by contrast, threatens the body in an actual, physical sense; see 4.1121–22: *adde quod absumunt viris pereuntque labore, / adde quod alterius sub nutu degitur aetas*, "add this also, that they consume their strength and kill themselves with the labour; add this, that one lives at the beck of another". Cf. Cels. 1.1.4: (*concubitus*) *rarus corpus excitat, frequens solvit.*

[62] Brown 1987, 134.

[63] E.g. in 3.503 and 4.664–65: *quippe ubi cui febris* **bili superante** *coorta est / aut alia ratione aliquast vis excita morbi*. With the overflow of bile in these lines compare the collection of semen in the genitals in 4.1040–44: *ex homine humanum semen ciet una hominis vis. / quod simul atque suis eiectum sedibus exit, / per membra atque artus decedit corpore toto / in loca conveniens nervorum certa, cietque / continuo partis genitalis corporis ipsas*, "but only the power of man can draw forth human seed from a man. As soon as the seed comes forth, driven from its retreats, it is withdrawn from the whole body through all the limbs and members, gathering in fixed parts in the loins, and arouses at once the body's genital parts themselves". The idea of semen coming out of its retreats (*suis eiectum sedibus exit*) evokes the image of the noxious humour in 3.502–3, which comes out of its "lair" to inflict harm and then hides again: *inde ubi iam morbi reflexit causa, reditque / in latebras acer corrupti corporis umor*. See also 4.1034: *loca* **turg**ida *semine multo* and compare it with e.g. the list of medical conditions listed in 6.655–61, among which podagra makes its appearance in the following terms: *op**turg**escit enim subito pes.*

experience,[64] it might be argued that little room is left in the end for a metaphorical reading:[65] sexual desire is no more suggested to be approximately the same with disease but literally turns into one.[66]

This tendency naturally generates a complex network of medical allusions in the text, aimed to reinforce the poet's implicit claim that desire should be counted as no different from, and no less threatening than, other serious medical conditions.[67] Lucretius' appeal to medicine materialises on two levels: on the one hand, through a series of sustained allusions to Greek medical theories, in parts of the narrative, which either precede or follow his central discussion of sexual intercourse; on the other hand, through the use of a language which, though not conclusively technical, bears a striking resemblance to the idiom of medical Latin (especially Celsus). Both the account of dreams in 4.1011–36 (concluding with a section on wet dreams,[68] which serves as a transition to the topic of sexual desire) and the poet's section on heredity in 4.1209–32 (which follows upon the observa-

---

[64] See, especially, 4.1114: *membra voluptatis dum vi labefacta liquescunt* ("while their limbs slacken and melt under the power of desire") and compare it with 3.593–98: *saepe aliqua tamen e causa labefacta videtur / ire anima ac toto solvi de corpore velle, / et quasi supremo languescere tempore voltus, / molliaque exsangui cadere omnia corpore membra. / quod genus est, animo male factum cum perhibetur / aut animam liquisse*, "nevertheless, when weakened by some cause or other, it often appears that the spirit wishes to depart and to be released from the whole body, and the countenance appears to grow languid as at the last hour, and all the limbs to relax and droop from the bloodless body. This is what happens when the phrase is used 'the mind fails' or 'the spirit faints'".

[65] On the "literalisation of the metaphor" of love in the case of Ovid's Narcissus and its connections with Lucretius' account of desire in Book 4, see Hardie 2002, 160.

[66] The literalisation of the metaphor of love is especially favourite among Hellenistic poets. See e.g. Theoc. *Id.* 11.15: ἔχθιστον ἔχων ὑποκάρδιον ἕλκος (=*ulcer*) and 30.2: τετόρταιος ἔχει παῖδος ἔρος μῆνά με δεύτερον. In *Id.* 11.70–1, Polyphemus' "throbbing πόδες", a cause of pain and discomfort, may be related to the implication that too much semen has been collected in that area; see Liapis 2009. Cf. Ap. Rhod. *Argon.* 3.761–5 with Erbse 1953, 189–90 and Solmsen 1961, 195–97. For a general discussion, see Toohey 2004, 59–103.

[67] Similar claims are abundantly attested in medical sources. See e.g. Sor. *Gyn.* 1.30 (coupling the harmful effect of desire with that of ejaculation): κάμνει τὰ σώματα διὰ τὰς ἐπιθυμίας... τῶν ἐρώντων ὠχρὸν καὶ ἄτονον καὶ ἰσχνὸν τὸ σῶμα βλέπομεν... ἔπειτα πᾶσα σπέρματος ἔκκρισις ἐπιβλαβὴς ὡς ἐπὶ τῶν ἀρρένων οὕτως καὶ ἐπὶ τῶν θηλειῶν, "the body is made ill by desire... we see the bodies of lovers pale, weak and thin... furthermore, all excretion of seed is harmful in females as in males" (translation in Temkin 1956, 27); see Pinault 1992. Cf. Arist. *Gen. an.* 725b4–8, 726b1–13: loss of semen usually weakens the body, because it is "a separation of pure and natural heat [from the body]"; see also [Arist.] *Pr.* 880a22–29.

[68] See Brown 1994.

tion that women experience real pleasure during sex; 4.1192–1208) build on Hippocratic theories and intertexts: in the first case, it has been observed that Lucretius' distinction between dreams arising from psychological reasons and those attributed to a physical disturbance in the body has a lot in common with [Hipp.] *Vict.* 4.86–93 (6.640–62 L.), which also describes dreams as either reflecting daytime activities[69] or indicating the presence of sickness in the body.[70] Likewise, the transition from female excitement in sex (4.1192–1208) to complex theories of conception and reproduction has been read by many as somewhat abrupt; it can nonetheless be explained by the fact that in Hippocratic medicine the female's pleasure during intercourse is taken as evidence that she too produces semen, which consequently determines the child's sex and distinctive characteristics.[71]

Lucretius' discussion of desire as illness is thus placed in a medically informed context. To stress the pathology of infatuation the poet also switches to the use of technical language. The lines which describe the infectious spread of disease in 4.1068–70 are particularly important in this respect: *ulcus enim vive**scit** et invetera**scit** alendo, / inque dies gli**scit** furor atque aerumna grave**scit**, / si non prima novis conturbes volnera plagis*, "for feeding the sore increases its strength and makes it inveterate; day by day the madness takes on and the misery becomes worse, unless you confuse the old wounds with new blows". The concentration of verbs ending with – *scit*, the choice of *inverascit* to denote the setting in of a chronic condition[72] and the use of *plagis* with the implicit meaning of a surgical incision are designed to mimic the dry and factual style of a medical diagnosis. Scholars have aptly pointed out the linguistic affinities displayed at this point with Celsus' medical prose, leaving the possibility open that, though not yet fully developed, some kind of medical idiom already existed in Latin during the 1st century BCE.[73] As it is, Lucretius' tendency to conceive of sexual desire as

---

69 Roughly equivalent to those outlined in Lucr. 4.962–83.
70 See Brown 1987, 171–72. For the Hippocratic text, see the discussion in Harris 2009, 243–49.
71 See [Hipp.] *Genit.* 4–5 (7.474–6 L.). The same idea can be found in Democritus, Aristotle and Diocles of Carystus; it is however important to notice that Lucr. 4.1209–32 (expanding on theories of prevalence of female over male and male over female seed) has striking similarities with chapters 6–9 of the Hippocratic treatise. See Lonie 1981, 120–121 and the recent discussion in Pope 2019.
72 Cf. Cic. *Tusc.* 4.24: *permanat in venas et inhaeret in visceribus illud malum, existitque* **morbus** *et aegrotatio, quae evelli* **inveterata** *non possunt.*
73 For the medical flavour of Lucr. 4.1068–70, see Brown 1987, 209–14 and Landolfi 2006, 96–99; cf. Langslow 1991, 118–20 and Traina 1981. According to Langslow 2000, 34: "the language used by Lucretius in medical images and metaphors [such as the one we find in 4.1068ff.]... was intended to echo a contemporary or earlier Latin medical idiom, whether spoken or written". See, further, Langslow 1999, 202–205 and 2000, 30–33. Cf. Nutton's positive claim that "there

an actual wound can also be supported with a view to his literary intertexts at this point. Thus, while ἕλκος features prominently as a metaphor in previous erotic poetry, the phrasing in 4.1068–70 brings to mind one particular patient who is experiencing his pain primarily in bodily terms, Sophocles' Philoctetes: the flaring-up of infection, designated by the use of *vivescit*, echoes the tragic hero's understanding of disease as an almost animate force with a life of its own, which "flourishes" and becomes stronger day by day (*Phil.* 259–60): ἡ δ' ἐμὴ νόσος / ἀεὶ **τέθηλε** κἀπὶ μεῖζον ἔρχεται. Accordingly, a fitting way to understand Lucretius' arresting statement that the infatuated patient is "nourishing" (*alendo*) his own disease is by associating it with Philoctetes' similar claim when, deprived as he is of any means that would help him ease the pain, he acknowledges that he is spending his time "feeding the devouring illness", βόσκων τὴν ἀδηφάγον νόσον (313). Philoctetes' festering wound, ἕλκος, is as real as it gets; Lucretius' allusion to it is meant to suggest that equally real is the purulent inflammation that is caused by — and continues to feed — sexual desire. The intensity conveyed by 4.1068–70 relies precisely on the implication that the wound of love is no more seen as a metaphor; rather, it has turned into an actual bodily infection.

Another literary intertext which comes to mind is Sappho fr.31 Voigt.[74] An allusion to it can be traced in Lucr. 4.1061–62 where, much in line with the Greek text, vision and sound are singled out as the two principal senses through which desire materializes into a concrete embodied experience (the difference seems to be that whereas in Sappho it is presumably an encounter with the object of desire, which gives rise to tension,[75] in Lucretius it is the absence of that object which activates sight and hearing so that it can be restored — as though it were present — in the person's imagination): *nam si abest quod ames, praesto simulacra tamen sunt / illius, et nomen dulce obversatur ad auris*, "for if what you love is absent, yet its images are there, and the sweet name sounds in your ear".[76] On the face of it, these two lines have no explicit pathological significance. It can however be said that the text at this point reminds us of a previous allusion to Sappho, in 3.152–58,[77] where a medical angle seems to be more actively at play:

---

already existed a substantial, sophisticated and wide-ranging technical vocabulary of medicine in Latin in the late third century BC" (2004, 158); see also Adams 1995, 642; 2003, 341.
74 For a recent discussion of Sappho fr.31, see D'Angour 2013.
75 See lines 11–12 in the Greek text: ὀππάτεσσι δ' οὐδὲν ὄρημμ', ἐπιβρό- / μεισι δ' ἄκουαι, "I cannot see anything with my eyes and my ears are buzzing".
76 A powerful inversion of Epicurus' claim that without the presence of the beloved love wanes; see *Sent. Vat.* 18: "if sight, association and physical contact are removed the passion of love (τὸ ἐρωτικὸν πάθος) will come to an end".
77 A text which explores the effects of *terror animi*.

> verum ubi vementi magis est commota metu mens,
> consentire animam totam per membra videmus
> sudoresque ita palloremque existere toto
> corpore et infringi linguam vocemque aboriri,
> caligare oculos, sonere auris, succidere artus,
> denique concidere ex animi terrore videmus
> saepe homines.

> But when the intelligence is moved by more vehement fear, we see the whole spirit throughout the frame share in the feeling: sweating and pallor hence arise over the whole body, the speech falters, the voice dies away, blackness comes before the eyes, a sounding is in the ears, the limbs give way beneath; in a word we often see men fall to the ground for mental terror.

Two aspects of the passage need to be highlighted: on the one hand, while Lucretius' text corresponds closely with Sappho fr. 31,[78] it clearly aims to recall the Greek original by enhancing its pathological overtones: the three short cola in 3.156, *caligare oculos, sonere auris, succidere artus*, imitate the simple and objective recording of symptoms in Hippocratic medicine.[79] On the other hand, Lucretius' (eroticized) description of the bodily effects of *terror animi* has a lot in common with his detailed account of epilepsy a few hundred lines below, in 3.487–509. What is interesting in the latter case is that several of the symptoms which help to diagnose an epileptic fit are loaded with sexual innuendos, effectively blurring the image of the suffering patient with that of a person who is reaching climax during intercourse (3.489–91): *concidit et spumas agit, ingemit et tremit artus, / desipit, extentat nervos, torquetur, anhelat / inconstanter, et in iactando membra fatigat*, "he falls to the ground, foams at the mouth, groans and shudders, raves, grows rigid, twists, pants irregularly, outwearies himself with contortions". In this context, one might compare especially the "seeds of voice", *semina vocis*, which are "forced out", *eiiciuntur*, from the epileptic's mouth in 3.495–97 with the language that is subsequently used by the poet to describe the process of ejaculation (*semen ... eiectum*) in 4.1037–57 as an almost involuntary, reactive

---

[78] See Segal 1990, 84–85, with Sappho fr.31. 9–16: ἀλλὰ †καμ† μὲν γλῶσσα †ἔαγε†, λέπτον / δ' αὔτικα χρῶι πῦρ ὑπαδεδρόμακεν, / ὀππάτεσσι δ' οὐδὲν ὄρημμ', ἐπιβρό- / μεισι δ' ἄκουαι, / †ἔκαδε† μ' ἴδρως κακχέεται, τρόμος δὲ / παῖσαν ἄγρει, χλωροτέρα δὲ ποίας / ἔμμι, τεθνάκην δ' ὀλίγω 'πιδεύης / φαίνομ' ἔμ' αὔται.

[79] See Fowler 2000, 151. For the medical flavour of Sappho's passage, to which Lucretius responds appropriately, see Di Benedetto 1985, 145–51; Bonanno 1990, 151–54; Acosta-Hughes 2010, 24. The emphasis placed by the poet on (a) obstructed vision (~ 6.1146), (b) buzzing ears (~ 6.1185) and (c) the faltering tongue (~ 6.1147–50), foreshadow the signs of approaching death in the case of the plague.

release of bodily fluid. The allusive presence of sexual language in the case of epilepsy[80] foreshadows the appearance of *furor* in 4.1069 and reveals the poet's tendency to conceptualize desire as an actual seizure that takes hold of the patient and makes him lose control over his body and mind.

Long before we reach the end of Book 4 Lucretius thus invites us to see desire as being conceptually indistinguishable from disease; though mentally motivated, infatuation is revealed in the end to be reduced to an excess of fluids in the body, which are almost automatically released once an appropriate stimulus has been presented, "just like the blood is spurting out from a wound and taints the person nearby who has inflicted it" (4.1049–51).[81] This emphasis on the body — underlined by the transition from a richly metaphorical and, at least on the face of it, more benevolent Venus in the proem to Book 1 to the crude physiology of sex in Book 4 —[82]

---

80 Cf. Macr. 2.8.16: "Hippocrates, a man of godlike understanding, thought that sexual intercourse has something in common with the utterly repulsive illness (*partem esse quandam morbi taeterrimi*) we call the 'comitial disease': his words, as they have been handed down, are: 'Intercourse is a small epileptic seizure'", τὴν συνουσίαν εἶναι μικρὰν ἐπιληψίαν (translation in Kaster 2011, 387; slightly modified). The idea, absent from the Hippocratic Corpus, is otherwise attributed to Democritus (Clem. Alex. *Paedagogue* 1.94, Stob. 3.6.28). See also Galen, *De usu partium* 14.10 (4.187 K.): πηλίκην γὰρ δύναμιν εἰς τὴν τῶν περιεχομένων ἔκκρισιν ὁ οἷον σπασμὸς τῶν μορίων τοῖς ἀφροδισίοις ἐπόμενος, ἔνεστί σοι μαθεῖν ἔκ τε τῶν ἐπιληψιῶν τῶν μεγάλων.

81 For these lines, see Bartsch 2006, 74 who observes that the wound of love has a figural as well as a physiological meaning in it. The particles emitted by the love object literally pierce into the eyes of the person falling in love, consequently setting up "a corresponding reaction by which the wounded lover shoots back with his own bodily fluid". Cf. Aesch. *Ag.* 1389–92 where Clytemnestra perversely turns the blood spurting from her husband's wound into a symbol of rebirth by assimilating it to a rain shower sent by Zeus to give new life to the fields. Whereas the Greek tragedian invites us to see blood turning into semen, Lucretius' wound imagery is built around the reverse process.

82 Venus in the proem to Book 1 is a metaphor for birth and growth; in Book 4, she is primarily discussed along the lines of an embodied experience; see 4.1058 (following upon the explanation of the cause of sexual desire): *haec Venus est nobis*, "this is all that our revered goddess of love amounts to" — namely, a physiological process that revolves around the collection and ejection of bodily fluids; cf. Gale 1994, 40. For feminine personifications in Lucretius, such as that of Mother Earth, devolving at several points in the poem into (inanimate) corporeal substances, see Nugent 1994; Keith 2000, 38–39. For the poet's reductionist approach toward sexual desire and love, built around the wordplay — and implicit identification — between *amor* and *umor*, see West 1969, 95–96; Betensky 1980; Brown 1987, 200; Papanghelis 1987, 45 and Fowler 1996, 815: "Approaching sex via bed-wetting and wet dreams is to make a natural process of it"; Clay 1983, 82–110, 226–34 is essential reading. For a different interpretation, one that posits that psychology plays a crucial role in Lucretius' discussion of desire, see Nussbaum 1994, 140–91. A reductionist approach toward (female) sexual desire can already be traced in the Hippocratic Corpus, see Dean-Jones 1992.

is still missing from the end of Book 3,[83] but becomes further accentuated during the plague at the end of the poem. In that case, as we shall see, metaphors are still crucial for the interpretation of the text; what dominates the scene, however, and what ultimately makes it different from all other closing scenes in the poem is the attention it pays to terminal *physical* suffering, caused by an illness whose treatment is impossible to find.

2.3 The End of it All

The plague in Book 6 (6.1138–1286) combines death and disease (6.1144: *morbo mortique*) with a force that has no precedent in the poem. The narrative's closing scene has long been read as an elaborate adaptation of Thucydides 2.47–54, which, though closely modelled on the Greek original, departs from it in a number of significant ways. One crucial aspect of Lucretius' revision concerns the enrichment of the Greek text with additional medical references, drawn from a wide range of scientific texts which span from the Hippocratic Corpus to Hellenistic medicine to the work of Asclepiades of Bithynia (1st cent. BCE).[84] A second noticeable twist is related to Lucretius' "psychologising" attitude: although Thucydides' account of the plague already reveals an intense preoccupation with the psychological and moral side-effects of the disease,[85] Lucretius stresses its links with mental distress even further: by treating clinical phenomena as emotionally motivated actions and by intertwining medical data with an ethical kind of commentary the poet manages to extend the plague's symbolic potential, presenting it eventually as an image of a life burdened with anxiety and the fear of death.[86]

In what follows I will attempt to demonstrate that reading the plague in light of the closing sections in Book 3 and 4 helps to put into a new perspective both aspects of Lucretius' revising strategy: on the one hand, the poet's systematic use

---

83 See, especially, 4.1048: *idque petit corpus, mens unde est saucia amore* – a line which affords prime agency to the body rather than the person; contrast 3.1067: *aut etiam properans urbem petit* (referring to the suffering individual).
84 See Notaro 2002 and Filippetti 2007. For some illuminating discussions of Thucydides' plague, see Page 1953; Parry 1969; Erbse 1981; Woodman 1988, 32–40; Craik 2001; Thomas 2006; 2017.
85 See e.g. Thuc. 2.51.4: δεινότατον δὲ παντὸς ἦν τοῦ κακοῦ ἥ τε ἀθυμία ὁπότε τις αἴσθοιτο κάμνων (cf. Lucr. 6.1230–34); 2.52.4: νόμοι τε πάντες ξυνεταράχθησαν οἷς ἐχρῶντο πρότερον περὶ τὰς ταφάς, ἔθαπτον δὲ ὡς ἕκαστος ἐδύνατο (cf. Lucr. 6.1272–81).
86 See, especially, Commager 1957; cf. Segal 1990, 228–37. For discussions of Lucretius' plague, see Bright 1971; Clay 1983, 257–66; Gale 1994, 223–8; Penwill 1996; Stoddard 1996; Stover 1999; Fowler 2007; Foster 2009; Hutchinson 2013, 210–19; Gardner 2019, 79–112.

of medical language in 6.1138–1286 will be discussed as completing what I have identified at the beginning of this chapter as a progressive transition from metaphors of disease to clinical realities of the sick body. On the other hand, this transition, with its increasing emphasis on physical pain and the threat of material dissolution, puts the body on centre stage. Although it is indeed possible to read the plague as a metaphor of mental blindness and confusion, sickness — I will argue — serves as a fitting conclusion to the poem primarily because it is there to remind us that nothing can be compared to the finality of biological death.

A good point to start is with the plague's most distinctive symptom: a burning sensation that consumes the interior of the bodies and gives rise to a thirst that cannot be extinguished (6.1163–77):

> Nec nimio cuiquam posses ardore tueri
> corporis in summo summam fervescere partem,
> sed potius tepidum manibus proponere tactum
> et simul ulceribus quasi inustis omne rubere
> corpus, ut est per membra sacer dum diditur ignis.
> intima pars hominum vero flagrabat ad ossa,
> flagrabat stomacho flamma ut fornacibus intus.
> nil adeo posses cuiquam leve tenveque membris
> vertere in utilitatem, at ventum et frigora semper.
> in fluvios partim gelidos ardentia morbo
> membra dabant nudum iacientes corpus in undas.
> multi praecipites lymphis putealibus alte
> inciderunt, ipso venientes ore patente:
> insedabiliter sitis arida, corpora mersans,
> aequabat multum parvis umoribus imbrem.

Yet you could not perceive the outermost part of the body of anyone to be burning with excessive heat on the surface, but rather to give forth a sensation of warmth to the hand, and at the same time to be red all over with ulcers as it were burnt into it, like when the sacred fire spreads abroad over the limbs. But the inward parts in men burnt to the bones; a flame burnt in the stomach as in a furnace. There was nothing so light or thin that you could turn it into use for their bodies; only wind and cold always. Some cast their frame burning with the plague into cool streams, throwing the body naked into the waters. Many fell headlong from a height into wells of water, which they struck first with gaping mouth as they came. Dry thirst beyond all quenching drenched their bodies, and made a flood of water no more than a drop.

Fire and thirst, it should be remembered, are both essential for Lucretius' account of erotic desire at the end of Book 4.[87] Unsatisfied desire has been paralleled in that case with a dream in which someone's thirst cannot become extinguished because there is no access to real water, only to its evasive *simulacrum* (4.1097–1100): *ut bibere in somnis sitiens quom quaerit, et umor / non datur, ardorem qui membris stinguere possit, / sed laticum simulacra petit frustraque laborat / in medioque sitit torrenti flumine potans*, "as when in dreams a thirsty man seeks to drink, and no water is forthcoming to quench the burning in his frame, but he seeks the image of water, striving in vain, and in the midst of a rushing river thirsts while he drinks". The plague is fairly similar in this respect: although water is eventually reached by the victims of the disease and is consumed in great quantities, it remains in the end equally unsatisfying, with large amounts of liquid being reduced, because of the illness, to a single drop (6.1176–77: *insedabiliter sitis arida, corpora mersans, / aequabat multum parvis umoribus imbrem*;[88] cf. Thuc. 2.49.5). What we first encounter in the poem as a dreamy illusion turns at the end of it into a nightmarish reality.[89] Likewise, the flame of desire in Book 4, though designated in terms which stress its presence in the body as an almost physical entity, has not entirely abandoned its metaphorical associations. In the poem's final scene, that flame becomes real. This is already evident in Thucydides' account, where a number of expressions are used to indicate varying degrees

---

87 See, especially, 6.1168: *intima pars hominum vero flagrabat ad ossa* and compare it with the conventional idea that the flame of love is lodged in the bones or marrow; cf. Eur. *Hipp*. 255; Theoc. 3.17; Catull. 45.16; Verg. *Aen*. 4.66; Hor. *Carm*. 1.13.8; Ov. *Met*. 1.473. Lucretius' line retains at the same time a strong medical flavour; see e.g. [Hipp.] *Morb*. 1.29 (6.198 L.): τὰ μὲν ἔνδον καίονται, [Hipp.] *Morb*. 2.41 (7.58 L.): ἔσωθεν δὲ καίεται. Thucydides uses a similar expression (τὰ δὲ ἐντός ... ἐκάετο, 2.49.5) but the phrase "to the bone" is a Lucretian addition, designed among others to allude to the element of desire in this scene.

88 These lines look simultaneously back at Book 3. *Insedabiliter sitis arida* "echoes and climaxes the mourners' insatiable weeping (*insatiabiliter*) at the dead man's pyre (3.907) and the *sitis arida* of the banqueters at 3.917, whose drinking cups are as inadequate as the *multus imber*, the 'flood of water', was for the plague sufferers" (Galloway 1986, 59).

89 See also the dream in 4.1024–25, mentioned just before Lucretius turns to the topic of wet dreams and, through them, to sexual desire: *flumen item sitiens aut fontem propter amoenum / adsidet et totum prope faucibus occupat amnem*, "again, one athirst often sits beside a stream or a pleasant spring, and all but swallows the whole river". Compare these lines with one the plague's final scenes (6.1264–66): *multa siti prostrata viam per proque voluta / corpora silanos ad aquarum strata iacebant / interclusa anima nimia ab dulcedine aquarum*, "many bodies, thrown down by thirst and rolling over the road, lay stretched by the water-spouts, cut off from the breath of life by the too great sweetness of water".

of heat and burning⁹⁰ and is further accentuated by Lucretius' poignant reference to *sacer ignis* (6.1167),⁹¹ an infection known by medical writers to cause redness and blisters in the skin combined with an excessive sensation of heat.⁹² This transition from the metaphorical to the literal is combined in Lucretius' text with a shift from invisible to visible categories of pain and suffering: the wound of love has been identified in 4.1068 as a "sore" (*ulcer*) which remains hidden from the eye (4.1120: *volnere caeco*) and thus, one might add, elusive as to the whether it really exists or not; the sores caused by the plague, by contrast, are located on the surface of the body (6.1166–67: *et simul ulceribus quasi inustis omne rubere / corpus*) and can be seen and touched (6.1165: *manibus...tactum*) by everyone.⁹³

The end of Book 3 is equally important for understanding the poem's final scene. *Oblivia* in 3.1066 (the forgetfulness which one seeks in sleep) has been discussed above as aiming to recall the dreadful effects of lethargy, described in detail in 3.465–69. The disease at the end of Book 6 reactivates the original clinical meaning of the word — that of an actual loss of memory and consciousness — but

---

90 E.g. θέρμαι ἰσχυραί, φλόγωσις (2.49.1), τὰ δὲ ἐντὸς οὕτως ἐκάετο (2.49.5), ὑπὸ τοῦ ἐντὸς καύματος (2.49.6).
91 Cf. Verg. *G.* 3.566: *contactos artus **sacer ignis** edebat*, the line which concludes the account of the Noric plague and which imitates closely Soph. *Trach.* 1051–54: καθῆψεν ὤμοις τοῖς ἐμοῖς Ἐρινύων / ὑφαντὸν ἀμφίβληστρον, ᾧ διόλλυμαι. / πλευραῖσι γὰρ προσμαχθὲν ἐκ μὲν ἐσχάτας / **βέβρωκε σάρκας**, "[she] has fastened upon my shoulders, a woven, encircling net of the Furies, by which I am utterly destroyed. It clings to my sides, it has eaten away my inmost flesh" (translation by Jameson in Griffith / Most 2013). The poison with which the robe of Heracles has been anointed is misunderstood by Deianeira as a love charm, inviting us to view the hero's agonizing pain as some sort of twisted erotic — or even sexual — suffering; see Wender 1974, 12. Vergil's tragic intertext at this point reveals an interest in exploring the plague as a reperformance and an accentuation of the illness of desire — an association which can be ultimately traced back to Lucretius. For the "parallel movement between the account of the disastrous effects of uncontrollable *amor* on livestock (3.242–83) and that of the catastrophe of the plague (3.440–566)" in *Georgics* 3, see Thomas 1988 vol. 1, 13. For more detailed discussions, see Gale 2000, 48 with n.90 and Thomas 2008, 57–61; cf. Ross 1987, 164–67 and 181–83.
92 Lucretius must be referring here to ἐρυσίπελας. See e.g. [Hipp.] *Progn.* 23 (2.176–8 L.): "When throat and neck are both red, the illness is more protracted, and recovery is most likely should neck and chest be red and the erysipelas does not turn back inwards. Should, however, the erysipelas disappear neither on the critical days nor with the formation of an abscess on the exterior, and if the patient should not cough up pus easily and without pain, it is a sign of death or of a relapse of the redness. The most hopeful sign is for the redness to be determined as much as possible outwards" (ἀσφαλέστατον δὲ τὸ ἐρύθημα ὡς μάλιστα ἔξω τρέπεσθαι), translation in Jones 1923, 47. Cf. Lucr. 6.1147–53, in which case the disease turns inwards, with lethal effects. For ἐρυσίπελας, see Grmek 1991, 203.
93 Cf. 6.1150: the patients' tongue was *aspera tactu*, "rough to the touch".

not without the mediation of 3.1066. Thus, while 6.1213–14 (*atque etiam quosdam cepere **oblivia rerum** / cunctarum, neque se possent cognoscere ut ipsi*, "and there were others who fell into oblivion of all things, so that they could not even tell who they were") is primarily meant as an allusion to 3.465–69 and 3.828–29 (***oblivia rerum** / ...lethargi*), it can also be read, in combination with 6.1248–49 (*lacrimis lassi luctuque redibant; / inde bonam partem in lectum maerore dabantur*, "weary with weeping and mourning they returned, then for the greater part took to their beds with grief"), as a morbid reminiscence of 3.1065–66: *oscitat extemplo, tegitit cum limina*[94] *villae, / aut abit in somnum gravis atque **oblivia** quaerit.*[95] At the same time, what in the closing section of Book 3 has been figuratively presented as a "dead life", *mortua vita* (3.1046), acquires in Book 6 a concretely biological meaning: *semanimo cum corpore* in 6.1268 (*languida semanimo cum corpore membra videres*, "you could see bodies half-dead with fainting limbs") is also about a state on the verge between life and death,[96] only this time applied to the body and taken in a literal sense. As Hunter Gardner points out, "the vulnerability of the body" in the course of the plague "is not only demonstrated through rot and decay, but also through the increasing confusion between life and death. The poet puts a border (*limen*) between them only to show repeatedly how it is crossed".[97] One can in fact detect here a subversive attitude towards Epicurus, for whom death should not be feared since its presence coincides with our absence.[98] Lucretius' conclusion to the poem entertains the possibility of an

---

94 For threshold imagery in the plague, see 6.1156–57: *omne / languebat corpus **leti iam limine in ipso***, "the whole body grew faint, being already on the very threshold of death".

95 Apart from these three occurrences of the noun (3.828, 3.1066 and 6.1213), one finds it again in the poem only in 4.826: *quod ne miremur sopor atque oblivia curant*, "but sleep and oblivion see to it that we do not wonder" at the strange things we witness and experience in our dreams.

96 *Semanimus* is used only here in the poem. Cf. Thuc. 2.52.2: ἐκαλινδοῦντο καὶ περὶ τὰς κρήνας ἁπάσας **ἡμιθνῆτες** τοῦ ὕδατος ἐπιθυμίᾳ. But see also Ennius, *Ann.* 483–4 Skutsch (for the first attested use of the adjective in Latin): *oscitat in campis caput a ceruice reuolsum / **semianimes**que micant oculi lucemque requirunt.* Ennius' striking image of a chopped head whose eyes continue to seek out the light of day is echoed in Lucr. 3.654–56: *et caput abscisum calido viventeque trunco / servat humi voltum vitalem oculisque patentis, / donec reliquias animai reddidit omnes*, "even the head shorn off from the hot and living trunk retains on the ground the look of life and its open eyes, until it has rendered up all that is left of the spirit"; cf. Verg. *Aen.* 10.394–96. For Ennius' passage, see Elliott 2013, 101–102.

97 Gardner 2019, 86. For the plague turning the patients into "lifeless ghosts", cf. Ap. Rhod. 4.1278–82: ἐν δ' ἄρα πᾶσιν / παχνώθη κραδίη, χύτο δὲ χλόος ἀμφὶ παρειάς. / οἷον δ' **ἀψύχοισιν** ἐοικότες **εἰδώλοισιν**/ ἀνέρες εἰλίσσονται ἀνὰ πτόλιν, ἢ πολέμοιο / ἢ **λοιμοῖο τέλος ποτιδέγμενοι**.

98 As Epicurus stresses in his epistle to Menoeceus (§ 125): τὸ φρικωδέστατον οὖν τῶν κακῶν ὁ θάνατος οὐθὲν πρὸς ἡμᾶς, ἐπειδήπερ ὅταν μὲν ἡμεῖς ὦμεν, ὁ θάνατος οὐ πάρεστιν, ὅταν δὲ ὁ

unsettling co-existence, at a liminal point when death is experienced as a certainty and when half of our life force has already departed.[99]

Both 3.1053–75 and 4.1037–1120 draw our attention to the fact that disease is by its nature something that tests the limits of our knowledge. What is missing as information in 3.1050 is the exact cause and nature of the disease: **nec reperire potes** *tibi quid saepe mali*. This subsequently gives its place in 4.1119 to a lack of knowledge as to how the illness might be cured: **nec reperire** *malum id* **possunt** *quae machina vincat*. The plague poses a different, more difficult kind of problem: what "cannot be found" this time is someone who has been left untouched by the disease (6.1250–51): *nec* **poterat** *quisquam* **reperiri**, *quem neque morbus / nec mors nec luctus temptaret tempore tali*, "nor could anyone be found whom neither disease had assailed nor death nor mourning at such a time". The sense of utter loss and helplessness conveyed by this observation emerges crucially at a point in the text (for some, the poem's final lines)[100] when the disease has been already exhaustively discussed and its so-called *ratio* (6.1138) has become transparent. In this respect, the arresting image of a muttering and silent medicine in 6.1179 (*mussabat tacito medicina timore*), applied to doctors at the time of the plague, creates a contrast with the poet's own loquaciousness and the sheer clinical confidence by which medical details are being imparted to the audience.

Lucretius' authoritative tone reaches its peak in the section of the text which discusses the signs of approaching death (an addition to Thucydides' original account, where no such information is included). 6.1182–96 reads as follows:

> multaque praeterea mortis tum signa dabantur:
> perturbata animi mens in maerore metuque,
> triste supercilium, furiosus voltus et acer,
> sollicitae porro plenaeque sonoribus aures,
> creber spiritus aut ingens raroque coortus,
> sudorisque madens per collum splendidus umor,
> tenvia sputa minuta, croci contacta colore
> salsaque, per fauces rauca vix edita tussi.

θάνατος παρῇ, τόθ' ἡμεῖς οὐκ ἐσμέν. οὔτε οὖν πρὸς τοὺς ζῶντάς ἐστιν οὔτε πρὸς τοὺς τετελευτηκότας, ἐπειδή περ περὶ οὓς μὲν οὐκ ἔστιν, οἳ δ' οὐκέτι εἰσίν, "so death, the most frightening of bad things, is nothing to us; since when we exist, death is not yet present, and when death is present, then we do not exist. Therefore, it is relevant neither to the living nor to the dead, since it does not affect the former, and the latter do not exist" (translation in Inwood/Gerson 1994, 29).
99 Cf. Lucr. 5.990–93, describing someone as witnessing his own death while he is being devoured by a wild animal.
100 For the transposition of 6.1247–51 after 6.1286, the last line of the poem as we have it, see Fowler 1989, 85; P. Fowler 2007, 201–206; cf. Bright 1971, 622–23; Schiesaro 1994, 92.

in manibus vero nervi trahere et tremere artus
a pedibusque minutatim succedere frigus
non dubitabat. item ad supremum denique tempus
conpressae nares, nasi primoris acumen
tenve, cavati oculi, cava tempora, frigida pellis
duraque, in ore iacens rictum, frons tenta manebat.
nec nimio rigida post artus morte iacebant.

And many another sign of death was then to be seen: a mind disordered in all this sorrow and fear, a gloomy brow, a mad and fierce look, ears also troubled and full of droning, quick pants or deep breaths rising at long intervals, dank sweat streaming and shining over the neck, fine thin spittle, salt and yellow in colour, expelled with an effort through the throat by hoarse coughing. Relentlessly the sinews in the hands twitched, the limbs trembled, from the feet cold crept up by inches. At the latter end also the nostrils were compressed, the tip of the nose grew sharp, the eyes were sunken, the temples hollow, the skin cold and hard, the mouth agape and grinning, the forehead remaining tense. No long time after the limbs lay stiff in death.

6.1193–95 follows almost word by word the series of symptoms mentioned in [Hipp.] *Progn.* 2 (2.114 L.) as signs of a terminal condition: ῥὶς ὀξεῖα, ὀφθαλμοὶ κοῖλοι, κρόταφοι συμπεπτωκότες, ὦτα ψυχρὰ καὶ συνεσταλμένα καὶ οἱ λοβοὶ τῶν ὤτων ἀπεστραμμένοι καὶ τὸ δέρμα τὸ περὶ τὸ πρόσωπον σκληρὸν καὶ περιτεταμένον καὶ καρφαλέον ἐόν.[101] The medical author proceeds to add at the end of the same paragraph that "when the lips are loose and hanging" this is another sign of impending death (θανατῶδες δὲ καὶ χείλεα ἀπολυόμενα καὶ κρεμάμενα), which seems to explain the addition of (the otherwise problematic) *in ore iacens rictum* in 6.1195.[102] Lucretius' engagement with the Hippocratic treatise yields further points of contact: *croci contacta colore* in 6.1188 certainly has something to do with the observation that when (in cases of a persisting pain in the lungs or the ribs) the saliva is yellow (ξανθὸν πτύελον), the diagnosis is not good (ch.14 = 2.144 L.). Likewise, Lucretius' choice to locate the "dripping sweat" in the upper part of the body (6.1187: *sudorisque madens **per collum** splendidus umor*), and even though the burning sensation has been earlier described as spreading through all its parts, echoes the idea that "worst are the cold sweats which break out only around the head and neck; for these with acute fever indicate death",[103] κάκιστοι δὲ [ἱδρῶτες] οἱ ψυχροὶ καὶ μοῦνον περὶ τὴν κεφαλὴν γιγνόμενοι καὶ τὸν αὐχένα. οὗτοι γὰρ σὺν μὲν ὀξεῖ πυρετῷ θάνατον σημαίνουσιν (ch. 6 = 2.124 L.).

---

101 For the close resemblance between the two passages, see Langslow 1999, 209. Fowler 2000, 151–52 argues that Lucretius has been directly influenced by the medical text.
102 For a discussion of this difficult phrase, see Sinclair 1981; cf. Filippetti 2007, 130.
103 Translation in Jones 1923, 15.

Finally, the reference to quick pants alternating with deep and slow breathing (6.1186: *creber spiritus aut ingens raroque coortus*) evokes the two types of respiration discussed alongside by the medical author in ch. 5 (2.122 L.): πνεῦμα πυκνὸν is mentioned in that case as an indication of pain and inflammation in the area above the diaphragm; deep and slow respiration, on the other hand, μέγα δὲ ἀναπνεόμενον καὶ διὰ πολλοῦ χρόνου [πνεῦμα], is taken to be a sign of παραφροσύνη (cf. 6.1184: *furiosus voltus et acer*).[104]

It is intriguing that the point where Lucretius decides to depart from Thucydides' original and to contribute his own scientific insight to the discussion is heavily influenced by a medical text which is specifically focused on the effects of disease at a stage when death looks inevitable. Unlike, or even in calculated contrast with Thucydides, Lucretius seems to emphasize the fact that recovery from the plague has been made this time almost impossible. Bleak as it may be, the Greek historian's narrative allows considerable space for hope (2.51.6): ἐπὶ πλέον δ' ὅμως οἱ διαπεφευγότες τόν τε θνήσκοντα καὶ τὸν πονούμενον ᾠκτίζοντο διὰ τὸ προειδέναι τε καὶ αὐτοὶ ἤδη ἐν τῷ θαρσαλέῳ εἶναι· δὶς γὰρ τὸν αὐτόν, ὥστε καὶ κτείνειν, οὐκ ἐπελάμβανεν, "yet it was those who had survived the disease that showed most compassion for the sufferers, both because they knew from experience what it was like and because they were now feeling more confident about themselves — since the plague did not strike the same person twice, at least not fatally".[105] By contrast, in Lucretius' plague even the "best of men" (6.1243–46), who show compassion and help the sick, suffer in the end a terrible death.[106] There is a strong sense of finality here which suggests that the plague is no accidental ending.

2.4 Plague and the Suffering Body

In a seminal article published in 1957, Steele Commager pointed out that several details in Lucretius' account of the plague, and especially his tendency to highlight the psychological impact of the disease on the patients, diverge from the

---

[104] For further references to other medical texts in 6.1182–96, see the discussion by Filippetti 2007. Compare, e.g. Lucr. 6.1185 with [Hipp.] *Coac.* 189 (5.624 L.): βόμβος δὲ καὶ ἦχος ἐν ὠσὶ, θανάσιμον.
[105] Translation in Mynott 2013, 121.
[106] See Foster 2009, 390–91. Cf. Penwill 1996, 164 n. 10: "Lucretius is editing out whatever vestiges of hope there are in Thucydides' bleak narrative of the same event".

Greek historian's text where most of the emphasis is placed on the body.[107] In the author's view:

> [T]he alterations from Thucydides point to, and look at Lucretius' account as at least tending towards metaphorical statement [...] Lucretius' habit of conceiving mental sicknesses in terms of physical disease might have encouraged him to see in the physical plague the emblem of a mental one. Several other elements in Thucydides' account might have similarly appealed to Lucretius' imagination as being the physical actuality for terms he himself had used as metaphors for fear and desire; as being the objective equivalent of mental or psychological truths. Situations which for Thucydides represented historical fact might for Lucretius embody a depth of moral significance and possess a symbolic resonance gained from his own handling of them as figures in nonphysical contexts. His discovery, in Thucydides' factual account, of particular situations which held for him a wealth of symbolic reference, might also have influenced him, consciously or unconsciously, to treat the whole plague as, in a sense, a metaphor for life.[108]

Several other interpretations have been advanced ever since: some have seen the plague as a kind of ultimate test for the reader; as a challenge posed by Lucretius for all of us "to contemplate with a mind that has found its peace the scene of

---

107 For an intriguing example which illustrates well how Lucretius is shifting attention from the body to the mind, see 6.1151–53: *inde ubi per fauces pectus complerat et ipsum / morbida vis in cor maestum* confluxerat aegris, / omnia tum vero vitai claustra lababant, "after that, when passing through the throat the fell disease had filled the chest and had flooded into the sorrowful mind of the sufferer, then indeed all the barriers of life did totter". *Cor maestum* is reminiscent of Thuc. 2.49.3: καὶ ἐν οὐ πολλῷ χρόνῳ κατέβαινεν ἐς τὰ στήθη ὁ πόνος μετὰ βηχὸς ἰσχυροῦ. καὶ ὁπότε **ἐς τὴν καρδίαν** στηρίξειεν, ἀνέστρεφέ τε αὐτήν. While the historian, however, is using καρδία at this point to indicate specifically a part of the body ("apparently a point *en route* to the lower abdominal cavity", Craik 2001, 106), Lucretius mentions *cor* as the seat of a person's intelligence: what matters to him, so Commager 1957, 105–6 argues, is not the plague per se but the emotional response to it and how it is processed by the mind.
108 Commager 1957, 111; see also Schrijvers 1970, 314–20; Segal 1990, 228–37; Schiesaro 1994, 55–58. For plague and disease as Epicurean metaphors for false opinion, see Diog. Oin. 3.IV.3–V.8: "Since as I have said most men suffer alike from false opinions as if in a plague (καθάπερ ἐν λοιμῷ), and the number of sufferers increases, since by copying one another they catch the disease like sheep (ἄλλος ἐξ ἄλλου λαμβάνει τὴν νόσον ὡς [τ]ὰ πρόβατα) and it is right to give help to future generations, for they are ours even if they are yet unborn, having regard further to the love of mankind and the duty of giving help to strangers who are at hand, forasmuch as the benefits of the written word are spread abroad I decided to use this colonnade and set forth in it the means of safety (τὰ τῆς σωτηρίας φάρμακα) for all to see" (translation in Commager 1957, 110).

dissolution of the highest form of human society".¹⁰⁹ Others have read the scene as being designed to generate a new reading of the *DRN*: the striking presence of death at the finale of the poem can only be counterbalanced, according to this interpretation, by the emphasis placed on birth and creation in the proem to Book 1, the Hymn to Venus (1.1–49); it is there that one is consequently driven to seek comfort, thus beginning the poem all over again.¹¹⁰ All these interpretations evidently share the assumption that the poem was not left unfinished; that the end in its present state is what Lucretius meant it to be.¹¹¹ At the same time, one can also see them sharing the same kind of motivation: to the extent that this is the real end (and we therefore need *to make sense of it* in the form that we have it), all these lines of reading aim in essence to assign the plague with a *deeper* meaning, thus rescuing Lucretius from the charge that he leaves us on a pessimistic note, with no final reminder of his valuable lessons.

One of the wider aims of the present chapter has been to show that the way in which we read the plague is largely dependent on, if not essentially defined by the connections we choose to make between this part of the narrative and other parts of the poem.¹¹² In this respect, it is worth stressing once more that a choice to approach the plague as the climax of the closing sections in Book 3 and 4 yields a closural script which, though remaining sensitive to the psychological dimension of illness, puts the emphasis mainly on the increasing value assigned to the

---

109 Clay 1983, 256; cf. Müller 1978, 217–21; Schiesaro 1994, 102–103; Erler 1997, 82–85. But see Long 1992, 498: "if Lucretius were concerned to disclose and cure anxieties about dying painfully, the plague would be about as effective as a horror movie for inducing pleasant dreams".
110 See Schrijvers 1970, 324; cf. Gale 1994, 228 and Schiesaro 1994. That said, the opening hymn to Venus is not entirely free from associations of violence. According to Porter 2005, 117–18: "There is a slight reductionist tendency to the passage. Mankind is not mentioned but is only implied in its animality ... An undercurrent of violence runs through the whole...: love is compulsive, it "strikes" and "captures" hearts, enslaving them". Although I do no mean to suggest that the Venus-proem resembles even remotely the devastating chaos of the poem's conclusion, we can nonetheless think of how in both cases humans and animals alike are represented as being subjected to nature's superior forces, in a way that renders them effectively helpless.
111 See, however, the scepticism in Volk 2002, 82: "since we cannot be entirely certain that Lucretius intended his poem to end in exactly the way it does, any speculation about the purpose of the finale as it stands is open to doubt".
112 It also depends, of course, on which parts of the plague we choose to put the emphasis on. Commager's conclusion, for instance, that Lucretius' narrative is pervaded by a "movement away from a biological statement towards one with mental or psychic connotations" (1957, 106) focuses entirely on the poet's adaptation of Thucydides' original and ignores completely other crucial parts of the text, such as the clinical list of symptoms in 6.1182–96.

(decay of the) body as we move toward the poem's conclusion.[113] David Sedley aptly notes that the plague brings out a sense of excruciating *physical* suffering; this allows him to read Lucretius' ending as an echo of Epicurus' final moments before his death, allegedly spent in extreme bodily pain caused by sickness.[114] Lying on his deathbed, Epicurus addresses this letter to Idomeneus (Diog. Laert. 10.22 = fr. 52 Arrighetti):

τὴν μακαρίαν ἄγοντες καὶ ἅμα τελευτῶντες ἡμέραν τοῦ βίου ἐγράφομεν ὑμῖν ταυτί· στραγγουρικά τε παρηκολούθει καὶ δυσεντερικὰ πάθη ὑπερβολὴν οὐκ ἀπολείποντα τοῦ ἐν ἑαυτοῖς μεγέθους· ἀντιπαρετάττετο δὲ πᾶσι τούτοις τὸ κατὰ ψυχὴν χαῖρον ἐπὶ τῇ τῶν γεγονότων ἡμῖν διαλογισμῶν μνήμῃ.

I wrote this to you on that blessed day of my life which was also the last. Strangury and dysentery had set in, with all the extreme intensity of which they are capable. But the joy in my soul at the memory of our past discussions was enough to counterbalance all this.[115]

Epicurus is shown here to exhibit a paradigmatic type of calmness in the face of death.[116] Sedley's suggestion that Lucretius meant the plague to create a similar script of narrative exit, one that focuses on terminal suffering and how it should be addressed with the right frame of mind,[117] is plausible, however, it seems to ignore a crucial point of difference: while Epicurus is able to remain mentally composed and to assuage his pain *through memory* of past events,[118] many of the plague's victims are deprived of such comfort: some of them are said in fact to

---

113 The same tendency can be detected in 6.1182–96, discussed above. Lucretius' Hippocratic catalogue of symptoms moves from an account of mental disturbance (e.g. 6.1183–84) to a detailed list of signs indicating a physical breakdown. Several of Lucretius' psychological details in the case of the plague could simply have been meant to illustrate his point that in cases of physical illness the mind is also affected; see e.g. 3.463–64 and 3.471 (where the phrase *contagia morbi* makes its first appearance in the poem), with Penwill 1996, 150.
114 Sedley 1998, 165.
115 Translation in Sedley 1998, 165.
116 For a discussion of Epicurus' death, see Hill 2004, 76–78; Kechagia 2016, 190–98.
117 Sedley 1998, 165: the "triumph of philosophical serenity over the most intense physical pain was surely what Lucretius was preparing to bring into focus at the close of his poem. The panic, terror and misery of the pre-Epicurean Athenians, in the face of bodily suffering hardly worse than Epicurus' own terminal illness, are a brilliantly graphic backdrop to this final lesson in the Epicurean ethical canon".
118 For the prime importance assigned to memory by Lucretius, see the description of Democritus' self-inflicted death in 3.1039–41: *denique Democritum pos quam matura vetustas / admonuit* **memores motus languescere mentis**, */ sponte sua leto caput obvius obtulit ipse*, "Democritus, again, when ripe old age warned him that the recording motions of his mind were beginning to fail, of his own free will himself offered his head to death".

have been affected by "a complete loss of memory" (6.1213–14: *quosdam cepere oblivia rerum / cunctarum*); they could not even tell who they were (6.1214): *neque se possent cognoscere ut ipsi*[119] (both symptoms take on an even more sinister meaning when contrasted with the emphasis placed on *meminisse/memento* in Lucretius' didactic program:[120] the anxiety conferred by the notion of oblivion in the poem's final scene could be said to be only partially related to the plague's victims and to extend also to the readers who — as the narrative is reaching an end — are increasingly exposed to the risk of forgetting what they were being taught in the past six books). Physical pain, as Epicurus claims elsewhere, is either short-lived or mild, and therefore should not be feared (*KD* 4): οὐ χρονίζει τὸ ἀλγοῦν συνεχῶς ἐν τῇ σαρκί, ἀλλὰ τὸ μὲν ἄκρον τὸν ἐλάχιστον χρόνον πάρεστι … αἱ δὲ πολυχρόνιοι τῶν ἀρρωστιῶν πλεονάζον ἔχουσι τὸ ἡδόμενον ἐν τῇ σαρκὶ ἤπερ τὸ ἀλγοῦν, "continuous pain in the flesh does not last long; at its most acute it is present for a very brief time … whereas those sicknesses that are protracted allow pleasure in the flesh even to predominate over pain".[121] Lucretius' plague, by contrast, yields a scene of protracted, unbearable suffering, which is specifically designed to show that bodily pain cannot always be endured.[122] If the poet

---

119 Cf. Thuc. 2.49.8: τοὺς δὲ καὶ λήθη ἐλάμβανε παραυτίκα ἀναστάντας τῶν πάντων ὁμοίως, καὶ ἠγνόησαν σφᾶς τε αὐτοὺς καὶ τοὺς ἐπιτηδείους, "some suffered a total loss of memory straight after their recovery and no longer knew who they themselves or their friends were" (translation in Mynott 2013, 120).
120 See e.g. 2.66: *tu te dictis praebere memento*; 2.891: *illud in his igitur rebus meminisse decebit*; 4.643: *principio meminisse decet quae diximus ante*. For the importance of memory in Lucretius and in Epicurean didaxis more generally, see Epic. *Ep. ad Hdt.* 35–36 and Clay 1983, 176–85; Gale 1994, 116; Schiesaro 2003a; Marcović 2008, 25.
121 Translated and discussed by Gale 2018, 65 and n.8, who is right to observe that Epicurus' solution to the problem of physical pain sounds "rather unsatisfactory". Cf. Warren 2004b, 13–14: "given the amount of time they spend discussing death, the Epicureans have surprisingly little to say about the ethical significance of the process of dying and what they do say is often rather implausible … Notoriously in such discussions, the Epicureans often offer a weak argument in an attempt to show that dying is not to be feared. Any intense pain, they try to reassure us, will be short-lived. Any prolonged pain is not so intense as to be distressing. If this is based merely on empirical argument it is at best questionable"; cf. Warren 2002.
122 Thucydides mentions the loss of bodily parts as a consequence of the disease (2.49.8): κατέσκηπτε γὰρ ἐς αἰδοῖα καὶ ἐς ἄκρας χεῖρας καὶ πόδας, καὶ πολλοὶ στερισκόμενοι τούτων διέφευγον, εἰσὶ δ' οἳ καὶ τῶν ὀφθαλμῶν, "it struck the genitals and the fingers and toes, and many people escaped its clutches only with the loss of these parts — and in some cases their eyes too" (translation in Mynott 2013, 120). In Lucretius this turns to an image of self-inflicted mutilation, e.g. in 6.1208–9: *et graviter partim metuentes limina leti / vivebant ferro privati parte virili*, "and some with the strong fear they had for the threshold of death went on after they had severed the manly part with a knife". Fear of death is mentioned here as causing self-harm but the relief from

meant to recall at this point Epicurus' departure from life, he seems to have done so with the intention of stressing that there are more serious physical illnesses[123] than the ones discussed and conveniently dispensed with by his master.[124]

But the plague emphasizes the suffering of the body also in a way that effectively lays bare the limitations of Lucretius' healing art. In 1.936–50 the poet has presented his philosophy as a "medicine for the soul", suggesting that the body should be left for others to treat. The poem's final scene, as we have seen above, presents us with an illness for which conventional medicine fails to provide a cure (6.1179: *mussabat tacito medicina timore*).[125] Although this type of medicine is different from the one promised by Lucretius in Book 1, its ineffectiveness is brought out in a context which casts a shadow over the poet's own method of healing:[126] *contingunt*, the verb used in 1.938 to describe the smearing of the cup with honey by doctors,[127] is re-employed as a noun in the course of the plague to designate the uncontrollable spread of contamination (6.1235–36): *quippe etenim nullo cessabant tempore apisci / ex aliis alios avidi **contagia morbi**,* "for indeed

---

physical pain is also at play; cf. 3.660–63. Pearcy 2012, 213 argues that Lucretius "says nothing about the possibility that dying, the separation of soul and body, might be painful in itself", and proceeds to draw a connection with Philodemus' (medically influenced) theory according to which death is accompanied at worst by only slight and bearable pain. I find it difficult though to accept that the plague would have been received by the audience with such a theory in mind; the point of the narrative seems to be quite the opposite: that of turning death into a slow and painful process.

123 For the Athenian plague as the representation of sickness in its most acute, devastating form, see Thuc. 2.47.3: οὐ μέντοι τοσοῦτός γε λοιμὸς οὐδὲ φθορὰ οὕτως ἀνθρώπων οὐδαμοῦ ἐμνημονεύετο γενέσθαι.

124 The reference to urine retention (strangury) and dysentery, though presumably aiming to stress the element of bodily pain in Epicurus' death, has also something degrading in it and could have been partly shaped in the environment of a hostile pseudo-biographical tradition. An ironical response can already be traced in Cic. *Fam.* 7.26.1: *ego autem cum omnis morbos reformido tum <eum in> quo Epicurum tuum Stoici male accipiunt quia dicat* στραγγουρικὰ καὶ δυσεντερικὰ πάθη *sibi molesta esse; quorum alterum morbum edacitatis esse putant, alterum etiam turpioris intemperantiae.* Strangury is attributed in this passage to gluttony while dysentery is suspected to result from "shameful intemperance"; rather than evoke pity, the medical details concerning Epicurus' final moments are read as metaphors of hedonism and become, to a certain extent at least, ridiculed. For further discussion, see Shearin 2012, 41–42.

125 For a discussion of this line, see Phillips 1982a.

126 It is tempting to think that already in Lucretius' powerful self-presentation in 1.936–50, there are traces of a certain inhibition as to whether his healing method will work; see e.g. the suggestive use of *conantur* in 1.937 (*cum dare conantur*), showing doctors as *attempting* (without necessarily being successful) to deliver medicine to the children. Cf. 3.652 (a wounded man in the battlefield is struggling to stand on one leg): *inde alius conatur adempto surgere crure.*

127 For the ambivalent meaning of *contingere* in 1.938, see Bartsch 2015, 208.

not for a moment did the contagion of the insatiable disease cease to spread from one to another". The fact that people become contaminated because they are forced to act under the spell, as it were, of the patients' "coaxing" voice only helps to establish further an unsettling sense of affinity with Lucr. 1.936–50. As we read in 6.1243–45: *qui fuerant autem praesto,* **contagibus** *ibant / atque labore, pudor quem tum* **cogebat** *obire /* **blandaque** *lassorum* **vox** *mixta voce querellae*, "but those who remained at hand passed away by contagion, and by the toil which then shame compelled them to face, as those weary with disease uttered appealing cries mingled with lament". The lines present us with a combination of images which are distinctly reminiscent of Lucretius' own seductive and compelling rhetoric as a doctor of the soul: the element of coercion (*cogebat*), combined with the sick people's enticing call for help (*blanda vox*),[128] bring to mind the way in which the poet has presented himself as *forcing* his readers to drink the bitter medicine of philosophy *suaviloquenti carmine* (1.945–46), by means of his "sweet-talking song".[129] The difference is, of course, that whereas in Book 1 persuasion is activated for the patient's own benefit, in Book 6 — where doctors remain silent (6.1179: *mussabat tacito medicina timore*) and the sick people assume a (crumbling) voice of their own — it only helps to spread the infection. More to this point, while 1.936–50 talks about the recuperation of children (1.939–42: *ut puerorum aetas ... recreata valescat*) — the latter serving throughout the narrative as an image for the unenlightened adults who are expected to be cured by Lucretius' intervention[130] — the poem's ending holds in store a gruesome image of their lifeless bodies (6.1256–58): *exanimis pueris super exanimata parentum / corpora nonnumquam posses retroque videre / matribus et patribus natos super edere vitam*, "sometimes you might see the lifeless bodies of parents lying upon their lifeless children, and contrariwise children yielding up their life upon the bodies

---

128 *Blanda vox* in 6.1245 can be understood to belong either to the persons who take care of the sick or to the victims of the plague themselves; see Bailey 1947, 1793 and Dutsch 2008, 56 and n. 22. For the latter interpretation, which I am following here, see e.g. Minyard 1985, 60. In 5.230 the adjective *blandus* is applied to the "gentle" and "broken" speech of the foster nurse, *blanda atque infracta loquella*. Compare how the "broken tongue", *infringi linguam*, in 3.155 foreshadows the inability of the plague's victims to speak properly in 6.1148: *et ulceribus vocis via saepta coibat*. See Segal 1990, 84–85.
129 For the notion of "didactic coercion" in Lucr. 1.936–50, see Mitsis 1993.
130 See e.g. 2.55–58: *nam veluti pueri trepidant atque omnia caecis / in tenebris metuunt, sic nos in luce timemus / interdum nilo quae sunt metuenda magis quam / quae pueri in tenebris pavitant finguntque futura*, "for just as children tremble and fear all things in blind darkness, so we in the light fear, at times, things that are no more to be feared than what children shiver at in the dark and imagine to be at hand".

of mother and father".[131] Powerful and authoritative as it may be, Lucretius' healing method is functional only to the extent that it operates at the level of metaphor, being exclusively tailored for "affections of the soul"; when it comes to the body itself, there is little that the poet's medicine can do to save us from trouble.[132]

2.5 Conclusion

Does this imply a pessimistic reading of the poem's ending? Lucretius' emphasis on the body, as I have been suggesting, brings out a category of illnesses for which the philosopher can claim little intervention. At the same time, however, this emphasis creates also a heightened sense of affinity between the human body and the surrounding world in a way that can ultimately prove relieving. The increasing threat of material dissolution sketched throughout the three endings is combined with a simultaneous move towards more complex forms of being on an atomic level: the patient in Book 3 is like an atom who fails to understand that it is indivisible and fruitlessly attempts to break itself into smaller parts; in Book 4, the lovers fail to merge with each other, just as it is impossible for two atoms to interpenetrate and fuse into a single substance; in Book 6, a society of people — just as any *concilium* of atoms in nature — is destroyed, but only after it has managed to build itself into a concrete and functional unit. This reading would seem to involve a metaphorical interpretation, in the simple sense that it invites us to see the patients in the three book-endings as atoms in disguise. However, unlike the anthropomorphizing metaphors which assign the atoms with human qualities throughout the poem and maintain a figurative representation of the world,[133] the reverse process, that of seeing humans behaving like atoms, has a profoundly

---

131 For the connection between 6.1256–58 and 1.936–42, see Penwill 1996, 148 who observes: "Honey may certainly be a suitable image for the invocation to Venus in Book 1; but the description of the plague is unadulterated wormwood".

132 Cf. Sen. *Ep.* 75.7 (eloquent as a doctor may be, when it comes to a serious bodily disease what really counts is his handling of the matter at hand and not his use of "words"): *Quid aures meas scabis? quid oblectas? aliud agitur: urendus, secandus, abstinendus sum. Ad haec adhibitus es; curare debes morbum veterem, gravem, publicum; tantum negotii habes **quantum in pestilentia medicus**. Circa verba occupatus es? iamdudum gaude si sufficis rebus*, "why do you tickle my ears? Why do you entertain me? There is other business at hand; I am to be cauterized, operated upon, or put on a diet. That is why you were summoned to treat me! You are required to cure a disease that is chronic and serious, — one which affects the general weal. You have as serious a business on hand as a physician has during a plague. Are you concerned about words? Rejoice this instant if you can cope with things" (translation in Gummere 1920, 139–41).

133 See Shearin 2015, 73–82; cf. Kennedy 2007, 385–87.

literalising effect: it essentially reduces us to the matter to which we originally belong. Scholars have noted that Lucretius' narrative develops through an orderly succession of images of creation and destruction, and that the end of it should not worry us because it is easy to imagine that what comes next is yet another scene of (re)creation. Others, in a more factual and pragmatic spirit, have observed that the plague speaks of the ultimate truth; it presents us with "the end towards which our lives proceed as each of us lives through the cycle that all things must follow; and the nature of this end is ... something over which we have no control".[134] Seeing ourselves as part of this bigger picture is precisely what Lucretius wants us to do, however not in psychological but in physical terms; that is, not from a narrowly human but from an inclusively atomic perspective. It is only if we see our bodies as compounds of matter which are destined to dissolve, just as everything else around us is created and then becomes dismantled, that we can overcome our fear of individual extinction; to stop thinking about death and disease requires that we first abandon our self-perception as uniquely privileged individuals and be willing to blend with the rest of the animate and inanimate world as equal partners.

---

134 Penwill 1996, 155. Cf. Müller 2007, 251: the description of the plague serves "as an example for the *motus exitiales* ('destructive movements') of this world ... This description does not leave behind the didactic context of the poem. On the contrary it shows how the *natura rerum* plays its game, this time not promoting, but meaninglessly destroying life".

3 Disease and the Marvellous. Epilepsy in Book 3 and 6

There is a link between imagining disease and imagining foreignness. It lies perhaps in the very concept of wrong, which is archaically identical with the non-us, the alien.

Susan Sontag, *Aids and its Metaphors*

Ποικίλον ἠδὲ ἀλλόκοτον κακὸν ἡ ἐπιληψίη.

Aretaeus of Cappadocia, *On the Causes and Signs of Chronic Diseases* 1.4

Like all natural phenomena, disease is explained in the *DRN* through atoms and the void but the poet — as we had the chance to see in chapter 2 — allows in this context considerable space for Greek medical lore as well. The current view in scholarship is that this combination guarantees a "scientific" treatment of the topic, allowing Lucretius to blend his role as a doctor of the soul with that of a physician who is recording symptoms in an objective and matter-of-fact tone. In one crucial instance, however, the poet hints at the odd nature of the disease: epilepsy in Book 3 is introduced and discussed in what seems to be a clinically detached idiom which, however, fails to suppress entirely the impression that this particular condition is more bizarre than others. This impression is maintained largely through Lucretius' deployment of metaphors, similes and analogies — the "honey" of poetry, in other words, that was presented in 1.936–50 as a necessary ingredient for philosophy's drug — which, on the one hand, toy with the idea that some form of divine agency may be at work while at the same time underlining how deeply transformative and alienating an experience disease can be. Recent work on the phenomenology of illness has stressed the need to stop treating disease as a pathological one-off occurrence, suggesting that we should approach it instead as a process that incurs a radically altered form of being-in-the-world.[1] The most serious of dangers that a patient is faced with during illness (excluding the ultimate hazard of bodily annihilation) is the loss of personal identity, which is felt most intensely at the level of the human's descent into an animal state. As I will argue, while disease is typically described by Lucretius as invading the body as an external force[2] — forming part of what Charles Segal has

---

[1] See Carel 2016.
[2] See e.g. 6.769–80: the earth contains many noxious elements which can cause disease and death; many of them pass through the ears, others through the nostrils; "and not a few exist which the touch must avoid and sight must shun". Disease for Lucretius is something that is

identified as a persistent rhetoric of "violation of corporeal boundaries" in the poem[3] — with epilepsy its cause becomes internalized; the disease blends with our bodies and becomes part of our (naturally frail) constitution. The metaphor of the snake which releases its poison and then retreats back to the deep recesses of our body (3.502–3) is not just a figure of speech employed for the sake of poetic effect; it is essentially designed to show that our bodies retain the capacity to transform, through illness, into something foreign to us. Everything in nature, according to Lucretius, comes down to lifeless atoms and the void — and we humans are no exception to the rule. As epilepsy, however, helps to show, our bodies could be inhabited by more threatening, almost animate forces[4] which standard atomic idiom fails to account for fully, unless it resorts to the use of a bold figurative language whose ultimate effect is one of estranging us from our very own selves. It is at this point, when we begin to realize that even our bodies cannot any more function as a familiar point of reference, that the marvellous (*mirum*), in the sense of the extraordinary and the bizarre, becomes reinstated in the narrative.

According to Robert Wardy,

> From antiquity to the present day atomic theory has demanded that people confront a startling idea: that the world, on scales both very small and very large, is not faithfully represented by the experiences of human subjects ... Theory reveals to the mind's eye a stark, pure vista of colorless, odorless, tasteless, soundless atoms traveling through the never-

---

"produced by the earth and the sky"; when its seeds come in contact with the human body and invade it, they give rise to all sorts of pathological conditions (6.655–64). The plague is a typical example: the seeds of disease traverse a wide expanse of air until they finally reach the Athenians' bodies (6.1138–44). First the head and the mouth become affected; but "when passing through the throat the fell disease had filled the chest ... then indeed the barriers of life did totter" (6.1151–53). In all of these cases, the "morbific particles" (as Wilson 2008, 72–74 calls them) claim an independent existence of their own; in a sense, disease acquires a concrete identity before it reaches and violates the boundaries of the human body. For the idea that there are seeds of disease which come "from outside the world" (*extrinsecus*), see 6.1099–1100 with Nutton 1983, 10–12.

3 Segal 1990, 115–70.
4 According to Varro (*RR* 1.12.2), care must be taken in marshy areas, "because certain small animals breed there" (*quod crescunt animalia quaedam minuta*). One cannot see them with the naked eye (*quae non possunt oculi consequi*) but they can enter the body through the mouth and nostrils and cause severe diseases. As Sallares 2002, 61 points out, Varro must be alluding here to Lucretius' invisible seeds of disease; the fact that Varro speaks of actual little animals (in *RR* 1.12.3 we read of little aggressive creatures, *bestiolae*) could be responding to Lucretius' insinuation that a disease acts as though it had a life of its own; see Phillips 1982b.

ending void. It opens a gap between basic reality and at least the most familiar or basic appearances, threatening to make strangers of us in our own world.[5]

Wardy focuses his attention on the astonishing and profoundly alienating notion that life consists of lifeless atoms. But an equally strong sense of the marvellous can be fueled by the reverse process, through which we are invited — on several occasions throughout the *DRN* — to think of lifeless molecules as animate and deliberating.[6] Epilepsy, attributed to a cause which is acting as though it had a will of its own, falls — as we shall see — to the latter category.

As we move to Book 6, and to a terrain that is inhabited by wondrous, fascinating and yet horrifying forces, epilepsy re-surfaces as a dominant metaphor for the earth's convulsing body. The fact that this body is suggested — through a complex network of analogies between the microcosm and the macrocosm — to belong to a woman, in combination with the poet's reproduction of cultural stereotypes which view the female as an intrinsically strange and unstable creature, only help to put epilepsy into dialogue with another persisting paradox in the poem, thus adding to its mystifying qualities as a disease.

3.1 Epilepsy and the Hippocratic Tradition

Lucretius discusses epilepsy in the course of Book 3, in the context of his argumentation about the mortality of the soul. By providing a vivid description of an epileptic fit, the poet intends to show that the atoms of the soul are subject to extreme pain and suffering even when they are contained and protected by the frame of the human body. This allows him then to reach the conclusion that once dispersed in the air, after the body has died, it is impossible for those atoms to continue to live on their own, without a shelter to hold them together (3.487–509):

> Quin etiam subito vi morbi saepe coactus
> ante oculos aliquis nostros, ut fulminis ictu,
> concidit et spumas agit, ingemit et tremit artus,
> desipit, extentat nervos, torquetur, anhelat
> inconstanter, et in iactando membra fatigat;
> **nimirum** quia vi morbi distracta per artus
> turbat agens anima spumas, ut in aequore salso
> ventorum validis fervescunt viribus undae.

---

5 Wardy 1988, 12.
6 Cf. Kennedy 2007, 384.

exprimitur porro gemitus, quia membra dolore
adficiuntur, et omnino quod semina vocis
eiiciuntur et ore foras glomerata feruntur
qua quasi consuerunt et sunt munita viai.
desipientia fit, quia vis animi atque animai
conturbatur et, ut docui, divisa seorsum
disiectatur eodem illo distracta veneno.
inde ubi iam morbi reflexit causa, reditque
in latebras acer corrupti corporis umor,
tum quasi vaccillans primum consurgit et omnis
paulatim redit in sensus animamque receptat.
haec igitur tantis ubi morbis corpore in ipso
iactentur miserisque modis distracta laborent,
cur eadem credis sine corpore in aere aperto
cum validis ventis aetatem degere posse?

Moreover, we have often seen someone constrained on a sudden by the violence of disease, who, as if struck by a thunderbolt, falls to the ground, foams at the mouth, groans and shudders, raves, grows rigid, twists, pants irregularly, outwearies himself with contortions; assuredly because the spirit, torn asunder by the violence of the disease throughout the frame, is in turmoil and foams, just as in the salt sea the waves boil under the mighty strength of the winds. Further, groans are forced out, because the limbs are afflicted with pain, and in general because seeds of voice are ejected and rush forth from the mouth in a mass, where they have been, as it were, accustomed to pass, where is the established high-road. There is raving, because the strength of mind and spirit is set in a turmoil and, as I have shown, divided apart and separated and drawn asunder by that same poison. Next, when the cause of the disease has already turned back, and the corroding humour of the diseased body has returned to its secret haunts, then first, staggering as it were, the man rises, and by degrees comes back to his full senses and receives back his spirit. Since, therefore, the mind and spirit are tossed about by so great diseases in the very body itself, and are miserably torn asunder and distressed, why do you believe that the same without body, in the open air, amidst mighty winds, are able to live?

This is one of the most extensive descriptions of the disease in Greek and Roman sources since its first appearance in the Hippocratic Corpus. We know of doctors in between who wrote about it and dealt with the problem of its origin and peculiar manifestation, but none of these texts survive except in fragmentary pieces and later testimonies.[7] An obvious model for Lucretius would have been the Hippocratic

---

[7] The list of doctors who discussed epilepsy includes prominent physicians such as Diocles of Carystus (4th cent. BCE), Praxagoras of Cos (4th–3rd cent. BCE), Erasistratus of Chios (3rd cent. BCE) and Asclepiades of Bithynia (2nd–1st cent. BCE). For a detailed account of the disease in antiquity, see Temkin 1971. For Aristotle's views on epilepsy, see Debru 1982 with Lo Presti 2013.

Περὶ ἱερῆς νούσου,[8] a medical treatise of the late part of the 5th century BCE, which is entirely devoted to a pathological condition that has been identified by many as epilepsy.[9] Considering that Lucretius shows himself to be intimately familiar with individual treatises of the Hippocratic Corpus, it is worth dwelling a bit closer on the Greek text in order to see how the poet might have responded to it.

In ch.10 (6.372 L.) the medical author observes that when too much phlegm enters the blood vessels and blocks the circulation of air in the body:

> ἄφωνός γίνεται καὶ πνίγεται, καὶ ἀφρὸς ἐκ τοῦ στόματος ἐκρεῖ, καὶ οἱ ὀδόντες συνηρείκασι, καὶ αἱ χεῖρες συσπῶνται, καὶ τὰ ὄμματα διαστρέφονται, **καὶ οὐδὲν φρονέουσιν.**
>
> The patient becomes speechless and chokes; froth flows from the mouth; he gnashes his teeth and twists his hands; the eyes roll and intelligence fails.[10]

The similarities between this passage and Lucr. 3.487–91 should be obvious. What is particularly interesting is the way in which the Greek text culminates its enumeration of symptoms by mentioning "loss of intelligence" (οὐδὲν φρονέουσιν) — the point here being that the disease, though originating in the body, affects the mind as well. This seems to fit nicely with one of Lucretius' principal argumentative strategies in the course of Book 3: that of speaking about illnesses in which bodily suffering is eventually seen to infect the mind and the soul, by which we are meant to understand that the latter are also subject to death (see e.g. 3.463–73). But there are also additional, more specific points of contact with the Greek text: *subito* in 3.487 could be an allusion to the medical author's observation that the phlegm flows into the veins ἐξαίφνης, causing sudden fits of epilepsy;[11] *ingemit* in 3.489 is likewise reminiscent of the patient's loud cries which are significantly said by the Greek author to resemble the sounds of animals.[12]

---

8 See Kenney 2014, 141.
9 See e.g. Jouanna 1998, 39. For a thorough discussion of the Hippocratic text, see Laskaris 2002.
10 For the text and translation of Περὶ ἱερῆς νούσου, I follow the Loeb edition of Jones 1923.
11 See ch. 10 (6.372 L.): ἄφωνος μέν ἐστιν ὅταν ἐξαίφνης τὸ φλέγμα ἐπικατελθὸν ἐς τὰς φλέβας ἀποκλείσῃ τὸν ἠέρα, the patient becomes "speechless when suddenly the phlegm descends into the veins and intercepts the air". Cf. ch. 13 (6.378–80 L.): τοῖσι δὲ καὶ ἐπειδὰν ἐξαπίνης μετὰ βόρεια πνεύματα νότος μεταλάβῃ, συνεστηκότα τὸν ἐγκέφαλον καὶ εὐσθενέοντα ἔλυσε καὶ ἐχάλασεν, ὥστε πλημμυρεῖν τὸ φλέγμα, καὶ οὕτω τὸν κατάρροον ποιεῖται, "in other cases the cause is that the south wind, suddenly coming on after north winds, loosens and relaxes the brain when it is braced and strong, so that the phlegm overflows, and thus it produces the flux" (translation in Jones 1923, 159 and 167).
12 See ch. 4 (6.360 L.): καὶ ἢν μὲν γὰρ αἶγα μιμῶνται, καὶ ἢν βρύχωνται, ἢ τὰ δεξιὰ σπῶνται, μητέρα θεῶν φασὶν αἰτίην εἶναι. ἢν δὲ ὀξύτερον καὶ εὐτονώτερον φθέγγηται, ἵππῳ εἰκάζουσι, καὶ φασὶ Ποσειδῶνα αἴτιον εἶναι, "if the patient imitates a goat, if he roars or suffers convulsions in

Lucretius' epileptic patient too looks like an animal, as his voice breaks down into fragmented seeds of sound (3.496–97: *semina vocis / eiiciuntur*) and he loses the capacity to produce articulate speech. This is precisely the point that Vergil is making when alluding to the Lucretian text in *G.* 3.515–17: *ecce autem duro fumans sub vomere taurus /* **concidit** *et mixtum* **spumis** *vomit ore cruorem / extremosque ciet* **gemitus**, "But lo, the bull, smoking under the ploughshare's weight, falls: from his mouth he spurts blood, mingled with foam, and heaves his dying groans".[13] The transformation is already at play in Lucretius. The patient's groaning is linked to other passages in the poem which speak of excruciating pain caused by the intimate encounter between human and animal, for example the scene in 5.990–93: *unus enim tum quisque magis deprensus eorum / pabula viva feris praebebat, dentibus haustus, / et nemora ac montis* **gemitu** *silvasque replebat, / viva videns vivo sepeliri viscera busto*, "true, each one was then more likely to be caught and devoured alive by wild beasts, torn by their teeth, and to fill the woods and forests and mountains with groaning as he saw his own flesh buried in a living tomb". There is a peculiar, rhetorically exaggerated, type of merging in these lines:[14] as the human is watching himself while he is being literally eaten alive, his groaning transforms to that of the animal which is devouring him:[15] death takes place in a symbiotic, hybrid space where two lives blend uncomfortably with each other (see especially *viva ... vivo* in 5.993), before one of them predominates in the end. We can compare how the epileptic's loud cries are likewise attributed to a beast, a snake which takes its residence within the patient's body and inflicts suffering at will.

After providing the list of symptoms (3.487–91), Lucretius proceeds to explain them one by one, giving a separate account for the foam at the patient's mouth (492–94), his groans (495–98) and, finally, his loss of intelligence (499–

---

the right side, they say that the Mother of Gods is to blame. If he utters a piercing and loud cry, they liken him to a horse and blame Poseidon" (translation in Jones 1923, 147).

13 Translation in Fairclough/Goold 1999, 213. For the connection between Vergil's bull and Lucretius' epileptic patient, see Farrell 1991, 88–89.

14 Not incidentally, the oxymoron of the "living tomb" applied to predatory animals makes one of its first appearances in Gorgias: γῦπες ἔμψυχοι τάφοι (cited, not without ciriticism, by Long. *Subl.* 3.2 = Gorgias fr. 5a D-K); see Porter 2016, 317. Cf. Enn. *Ann.* 125–26 Skutsch, with Gale 2018, 80 n. 47.

15 The dying man's gemitus (5.992), which fills the woods and forests, recalls the mother cow's moaning in 2.357–59: *omnia convisens oculis loca si queat usquam / conspicere amissum fetum,* **completque querellis** */ frondiferum nemus adsistens*, "as she surveys all the regions if she may espy somewhere her lost offspring, and coming to a stand fills the leafy woods with her moaning". For a discussion of this scene, see Konstan 2013, 198–202.

501). The same structure can be traced back to the Greek medical text. Thus, loss of voice is said to occur when the phlegm suddenly descends into the veins and intercepts respiration; the fact that the veins have been congested by cold phlegm which chills the blood and arrests its motion causes the air to be trapped inside the body and "to rush upwards and downwards", which should explain why the patient is seized by convulsions; finally, the foam which comes from the mouth is produced by the lungs which are squeezed due to the shortage of air, "as if the person was dying" (ch.10, 6.372–74 L.). Each one of these explanations involves the presence of a noxious humour in the body. Although Lucretius subscribes to a different pathological model — what matters principally in his case is the violent rearrangement of the body's atomic fabric caused by the "force of disease" (*vis morbi*) — we should by no means ignore the fact that his account of epilepsy yields one of the most explicit references to humoural pathology in the poem (3.501–3, discussed below; cf. 4.664).[16] The *umor* responsible for the disease remains unspecified, yet its very presence in the text indicates that the poet is willing at points to make use of medical notions and ideas which are not strictly related to Epicurean physics (in fact they may even have been conceptually irreconcilable with it)[17] and whose origin has to be sought elsewhere, in the long-established tradition of Hippocratic writings.[18]

As we move through the Greek text, we realize that while phlegm is considered the principal pathogenic cause, special emphasis is placed also on air in the body and its obstructed circulation. In fact, in the second most detailed account of epilepsy in the Hippocratic Corpus, found in a treatise entitled Περὶ φυσῶν, πνεῦμα/ἀὴρ is revealed to be of fundamental importance for the explanation of the disease (ch.14, 6.112–14 L.):[19]

---

[16] For Lucretius' eclectic combination of atomic materialism with humoural biology, see Tutrone 2012; cf. Pigeaud 1980. Tutrone draws special attention to the distinction made by Grimal 1974 between *primordia/corpora/elementa* and *principia* (a word that is suggesting groups of atoms) in the *DRN*. In a medical context, *principium* — according to Tutrone — could have been used to speak of a compound elementary substance, for example a humour, that is composed of atoms. On the four elementary substances which regulate the psychic life of men and animals (heat, wind, air, and a fourth unnamed element), see Lucr. 3.231–322. The Hippocratic distinction between four different humours in the body could have provided here a model for our poet; see Tutrone 2012, 87–88.
[17] It is worth remembering, for instance, that Asclepiades of Bithynia, a doctor whose medical doctrines have been heavily influenced by Epicurean physics, is strongly criticized by Galen precisely because of his rejection of humoural pathology as a tool for explaining the origin of disease; see Walzer/Frede 1985, xxix; Leigh 2016, 57–58, 78–79.
[18] For the humoural body as the trademark concept of Hippocratic medicine, see King 2013.
[19] For this text which is dated in the last quarter of the 5th cent. BCE, see Craik 2015, 97–102.

Φημὶ δὲ τὴν ἱερὴν νοῦσον ὧδε γίνεσθαι· ὅταν πνεῦμα πολὺ κατὰ πᾶν τὸ σῶμα παντὶ τῷ αἵματι μιχθῇ, πολλὰ ἐμφράγματα γίνεται πολλαχῇ κατὰ τὰς φλέβας· ἐπειδὰν οὖν ἐς τὰς παχείας καὶ πολυαίμους φλέβας πολὺς ἀὴρ βρίσῃ, βρίσας δὲ μείνῃ, κωλύεται τὸ αἷμα διεξιέναι· τῇ μὲν οὖν ἐνέστηκε, τῇ δὲ νωθρῶς διεξέρχεται, τῇ δὲ θᾶσσον· ἀνομοίης δὲ τῆς πορείης τῷ αἵματι διὰ τοῦ σώματος γενομένης, παντοῖαι αἱ ἀνομοιότητες· πᾶν γὰρ τὸ σῶμα πανταχόθεν ἕλκεται καὶ τετίνακται τὰ μέρεα τοῦ σώματος ὑπηρετέοντα τῷ ταράχῳ καὶ θορύβῳ τοῦ αἵματος, διαστροφαί τε παντοῖαι παντοίως γίνονται ... ἀφροὶ δὲ διὰ τοῦ στόματος ἀνατρέχουσιν εἰκότως· διὰ γὰρ τῶν φλεβῶν διαδύνων ὁ ἀὴρ, ἀνέρχεται μὲν αὐτὸς, ἀνάγει δὲ μεθ' ἑωυτοῦ τὸ λεπτότατον τοῦ αἵματος...πότε οὖν παύσονται τῆς νούσου καὶ τοῦ παρεόντος **χειμῶνος** οἱ ὑπὸ τούτου τοῦ νοσήματος ἁλισκόμενοι; ὁπόταν γυμνασθὲν ὑπὸ τῶν πόνων τὸ σῶμα θερμήνῃ τὸ αἷμα· τὸ δὲ διαθερμανθὲν ἐξεθέρμηνε τὰς φύσας, αὗται δὲ διαθερμανθεῖσαι διαφέρονται καὶ διαλύουσι τὴν σύστασιν τοῦ αἵματος, αἱ μὲν συνεξελθοῦσαι μετὰ τοῦ πνεύματος, αἱ δὲ μετὰ τοῦ φλέγματος· ἀποζέσαντος δὲ τοῦ ἀφροῦ καὶ καταστάντος τοῦ αἵματος καὶ γαλήνης ἐν τῷ σώματι γενομένης, πέπαυται τὸ νόσημα.

I hold that the sacred disease is caused in the following way. When much wind has combined throughout the body with all the blood, many barriers arise in many places in the veins. Whenever therefore much air weighs, and continues to weigh, upon the thick, blood-filled veins, the blood is prevented from passing on. So in one place it stops, in another it passes sluggishly, in another more quickly. The progress of the blood through the body proving irregular, all kinds of irregularities occur. The whole body is torn in all directions; the parts of the body are shaken in obedience to the troubling and disturbance of the blood; distortions of every kind occur in every manner [...] Foam naturally rises through the mouth. For the air, passing through the veins, itself rises and brings up with it the thinnest part of the blood. [...] When then will the victims of this disease rid themselves of their disorder and the storm that attends it? When the body exercised by its exertions has warmed the blood, and the blood thoroughly warmed has warmed the breaths, and these thoroughly warmed are dispersed, breaking up the congestion of the blood, some going out along with the respiration, others with the phlegm. The disease finally ends when the foam has frothed itself away, the blood has re-established itself, and calm has arisen in the body.[20]

The idea that the air passes violently through the veins and raises the thinnest part of blood — thereby producing a white substance which comes out as foam from the mouth (διὰ γὰρ τῶν φλεβῶν διαδύνων ὁ ἀὴρ ἀνέρχεται μὲν αὐτὸς, ἀνάγει δὲ μετ' ἑωυτοῦ τὸ λεπτότατον τοῦ αἵματος) — combined with the image of the raging storm which eventually comes to a still (τοῦ παρεόντος χειμῶνος ... γαλήνης ἐν τῷ σώματι γενομένης), provides a solid parallel for Lucretius' simile in 3.493–94: foam is said there to resemble the surging waves of the sea when they

---

20 For the text and translation of the Hippocratic text, I follow the Loeb edition of Jones 1923.

are stirred by the "wind's furious force".²¹ In the opening part of the medical treatise, the author has emphasized that while air is invisible (it can only be grasped by the mind's eye, ἀλλὰ μήν ἐστί γε τῇ μὲν ὄψει ἀφανής, τῷ δὲ λογισμῷ φανερός, ch. 3 = 6.94 L.), its force is nonetheless destructive; this can be inferred from its overwhelming impact on the physical landscape, such as the trees which become uprooted, the sea that swells into waves and the ships which are tossed about.²² A similar line of argument can be found in one of Lucretius' programmatic passages in Book 1, which sets out to explain that though the atoms elude sense-perception, they are undeniably present and they account for everything that takes place in nature (1.271–76). As a proof Lucretius adduces the example of the invisible wind whose devastating force is manifest everywhere around us, first and foremost when it is stirred up and "beats upon the ocean, overwhelming huge ships and scattering the clouds".²³ The hypothesis that 1.271–76 establishes a direct connection with the Hippocratic treatise²⁴ is supported by further parallels between the *DRN* and the medical text. In the section that precedes the account of epilepsy, Lucretius creates the vivid image of a lethargic patient who falls into heavy sleep, as if he were drowning, carried down to the bottom of the sea (3.465–66: *interdumque gravi lethargo **fertur in altum** / aeternumque soporem*). With this we may compare what we find at the beginning of ch.14 of Περὶ φυσῶν (6.110 L.): "when sleep comes upon the body the blood is chilled, as it is of the nature of sleep to cause chill. When the blood is chilled its passages become

---

21 For the connection between the two passages, see Segal 1980, 181–82; cf. Kenney 2014, 140–41. With ἀπο**ζέσαντος** δὲ τοῦ ἀφροῦ in the Greek text, compare the Lucretian *fervescunt ... undae* (3.494).
22 See ch. 3 (6.94 L.): πνεῦμα δὲ τὸ μὲν ἐν τοῖσι σώμασι φῦσα καλεῖται, τὸ δὲ ἔξω τῶν σωμάτων ὁ ἀήρ. οὗτος δὲ μέγιστος ἐν τοῖσι πᾶσι τῶν πάντων δυνάστης ἐστίν· ἄξιον δὲ αὐτοῦ θεήσασθαι τὴν δύναμιν. ἄνεμος γάρ ἐστιν ἠέρος ῥεῦμα καὶ χεῦμα· ὅταν οὖν πολὺς ἀὴρ ἰσχυρὸν ῥεῦμα ποιήσῃ, τά τε δένδρα ἀνασπαστὰ πρόρριζα γίνεται διὰ τὴν βίην τοῦ πνεύματος, τό τε πέλαγος κυμαίνεται, ὁλκάδες τε ἄπειροι τῷ μεγέθει διαρριπτεῦνται, "wind in bodies is called breath, outside bodies it is called air. It is the most powerful of all and in all, and it is worthwhile examining its power. A breeze is a flowing and a current of air. When therefore much air flows violently, trees are torn up by the roots through the force of the wind, the sea swells into waves, and vessels of vast bulk are tossed about" (translation in Jones 1923, 229–31).
23 Compare the passage in the footnote above with Lucr. 1.271–76: *Principio venti vis verberat incita pontum / ingentisque ruit navis et nubila differt; / interdum rapido percurrens turbine campos / arboribus magnis sternit montisque supremos / silvifragis vexat flabris: ita perfurit acri / cum fremitu saevitque minaci murmure ventus*, "first the mighty wind when stirred up beats upon the ocean and overwhelms huge ships and scatters the clouds, and at times sweeping over the plains with rapid hurricane strews them with great trees and flogs the topmost mountains with tree-clashing blasts: so furious and fierce its howling, so savage and threatening the wind's roar".
24 As argued e.g. by Phillips 1984; see also Garani 2007, 117.

more sluggish. This is evident: the body grows heavy and sinks: all heavy things naturally fall downwards"²⁵ (...ῥέπει τὰ σώματα καὶ βαρύνεται· πάντα γὰρ τὰ βαρέα πέφυκεν **ἐς βυσσὸν φέρεσθαι**). The phrase which occurs at the end of the passage, ἐς βυσσὸν φέρεσθαι, corresponds closely to the Lucretian *fertur in altum* in 3.465.

Lucretius, as I have tried to demonstrate briefly, may have combined allusions to more than one medical sources in 3.487–509. Although his explanation of the disease is different from what we find in medical texts — since it is predominantly focused on how the atoms are thrown into disarray — his account remains consistent with Greek scientific thought in that it is designed, among other things, to show that epilepsy is just like any other illness whose origin can be traced in the body. In this context, the use of *nimirum* in 3.492, expressing certainty about a natural occurrence that should give no occasion for wonder,²⁶ is extremely significant.

The idea that people should not feel perplexed and terrified by what they fail to comprehend appears with exceptional frequency throughout the *DRN*. According to Gian Biagio Conte:

> [N]ature freed from the manipulations of a rhetoric of *mirum* becomes a mechanically ordered organism and a field for rational research... One need not be astonished by this phenomenon or that one because it is necessarily connected with this objective rule or that one; it is unworthy of surprise for anyone who has understood the principles of things and their interconnections. The rhetoric of marvel has been replaced by a rhetoric of necessity... which in fact is the contrary of the miraculous.²⁷

Lucretius' attempt to erase wonder becomes particularly evident in the course of Book 6. Phrases which evoke the impressive and frightening nature of thunders, lightnings, violent showers of rain, earthquakes and volcanic eruptions are regularly followed by the formulaic *nec* or *haud mirum*, e.g. in 6.130, 375, 489, 615, 1012. For instance, the fact that a cloud explodes "with a horrifying crash" when it is burst by a thunder should cause "no wonder", considering that "even a small bladder full of air often makes so loud a noise as it is suddenly burst" (6.130–31: ***nec mirum**, cum plena animae vesicula parva / saepe ita dat magnum sonitum displosa repente*). Likewise, the knowledge that there are particles which can

---

25 Translation in Jones 1923, 249.
26 On the etymology of *nimirum*, see Donatus on Ter. *Eun.* 508: *solve nimirum et fac non est mirum ... nam ni ne significat et ne non*, with Schrickx 2011, 186. cf. Fowler 2002, 169.
27 Conte 1994, 21; cf. Gale 2000, 196–201; Fowler 2002, 169 and Kenney 2007, 101.

travel into our sky "from outside the world" (6.483: *extrinsecus*), at a speed "beyond telling", should dispel our astonishment when we see a tempest and darkness cover up in such short time the sea and land with great storm-clouds (6.489–91: **haud igitur mirumst** *si parvo tempore saepe / tam magnis nimbis tempestas atque tenebrae / coperiant maria ac terras inpensa superne*). The same rhetoric is employed also in the case of volcanic eruptions and earthquakes which, as we shall see below, evoke, in a number of significant ways, the epileptic fit described in 3.487–509.

The elimination of wonder and its substitution with a firm knowledge of nature has a long philosophical tradition behind it. One should recall Aristotle's famous statement in *Metaph.* 983a12–21 that philosophy *begins* in wonder (θαυμάζειν): once we start to examine properly the things that look puzzling to us, θαῦμα becomes gradually replaced by knowledge, until in the end it is eradicated.[28] In the case of epilepsy, Lucretius' point that the disease should give no occasion for wonder activates an equally important network of medical intertexts. Not incidentally, the most vivid deconstruction of the idea that a disease could be "marvelous" in the sense of the unaccountable and the truly bizarre — framed by a lively attack against religious forms of healing[29] — is found in the Hippocratic Περὶ ἱερῆς νούσου. In the opening lines of the treatise we read (ch.1, 6.352–54 L.):

> Περὶ τῆς ἱερῆς νούσου καλεομένης ὧδ' ἔχει. οὐδέν τί μοι δοκεῖ τῶν ἄλλων θειοτέρη εἶναι νούσων οὐδὲ ἱερωτέρη, ἀλλὰ φύσιν μὲν ἔχει καὶ πρόφασιν, οἱ δ' ἄνθρωποι ἐνόμισαν θεῖόν τι πρῆγμα εἶναι ὑπὸ ἀπειρίης καὶ **θαυμασιότητος**, ὅτι οὐδὲν ἔοικεν ἑτέροισι ... εἰ δὲ διὰ τὸ **θαυμάσιον** θεῖον νομιεῖται, πολλὰ τὰ ἱερὰ νοσήματα ἔσται καὶ οὐχὶ ἕν, ὡς ἐγὼ ἀποδείξω ἕτερα οὐδὲν ἧσσον ἐόντα **θαυμάσια** οὐδὲ τερατώδεα, ἃ οὐδεὶς νομίζει ἱερὰ εἶναι.

---

28 *Metaph.* 983a12–21: ἄρχονται μὲν γὰρ ... **ἀπὸ τοῦ θαυμάζειν** πάντες εἰ οὕτως ἔχει, καθάπερ <περὶ> τῶν θαυμάτων ταὐτόματα [τοῖς μήπω τεθεωρηκόσι τὴν αἰτίαν] ἢ περὶ τὰς τοῦ ἡλίου τροπὰς ἢ τὴν τῆς διαμέτρου ἀσυμμετρίαν (θαυμαστὸν γὰρ εἶναι δοκεῖ πᾶσι εἴ τι τῷ ἐλαχίστῳ μὴ μετρεῖται)· **δεῖ δὲ εἰς τοὐναντίον** καὶ τὸ ἄμεινον κατὰ τὴν παροιμίαν **ἀποτελευτῆσαι**, καθάπερ καὶ ἐν τούτοις ὅταν μάθωσιν· οὐθὲν γὰρ ἂν οὕτως θαυμάσειεν ἀνὴρ γεωμετρικὸς ὡς εἰ γένοιτο ἡ διάμετρος μετρητή, "For everyone ... starts by wondering at something being the way it is, just as people do at those wondrous automata, when they do not have a theoretical grasp on their cause, or at the turnings of the sun, or at the incommensurability of the diagonal (for it seems a wonder to everyone that a more-than-minimal magnitude is not measurable). It is in the contrary and proverbially the better condition, however, that we must end up, as happens in those other cases when people learn [the cause]. For nothing would make a man who knows geometry wonder more than if the diagonal *were* to turn out to be commensurable" (translation in Reeve 2016, 6). See Nightingale 2004, 254 and 261–65.
29 See King 2006, 247.

I am about to discuss the disease called "sacred". It is not in my opinion any more divine or more sacred than other diseases, but has a nature and a cause, and its supposed divine origin is due to men's inexperience, and to their wonder at its peculiar character, for it looks quite different from other diseases ... But if it is to be considered divine just because it is wonderful, there will be not one sacred disease but many, for I will show that other diseases are no less wonderful and portentous, and yet nobody considers them sacred.[30]

The author goes on to mention "tertian" and "quartan" fevers and "sudden fits of delirium" as equally remarkable with epilepsy — the underlying assumption being that their peculiar manifestation and symptomatology should in principle make these conditions look no less astonishing; yet, as he states, no one "wonders at them" (ὧν οὐ θαυμασίως γ' ἔχουσιν). His aim is not, of course, to propose that one has to, but to suggest instead that people should likewise refrain from attributing to epilepsy any marvellous qualities. The disease, as is implied throughout the text, may be regarded as divine, but only in the sense that "it shares in the divine character of nature in showing a fixed pattern of cause and effect and in being subordinated to what may perhaps be called ... a natural 'law' of regularity".[31] This is the kind of knowledge that requires careful scientific inquiry and is directly opposed to the bewildering effect that epilepsy continues to have on the imagination of lay people.

---

30 Translation in Jones 1923, 139–41 (slightly modified).
31 Van der Eijk 2005, 45. As the medical author claims, it is wrong to believe that "a man's body [can be] defiled by a god, the one being utterly corrupt the other perfectly holy". And he adds: "even should it have been defiled or in any way injured through some different agency, a god is more likely to purify and sanctify it than he is the cause of defilement" (ch.1, 6.362 L.; translation in Jones 1923, 149). This point is not pursued any further; the author's aim is not to actually involve the divine in the therapy of disease but to stress that, by virtue of their holiness, the gods should be left out of discussion; see van der Eijk 2005, 45–73. For a similar line of thought, compare how Epicurus, in his epistle to Menoeceus (§123), supports his argument that the gods have nothing to do with the world of mortals — and should therefore be of no concern to us: πρῶτον μὲν τὸν θεὸν ζῷον ἄφθαρτον καὶ μακάριον νομίζων ... μηθὲν μήτε τῆς ἀφθαρσίας ἀλλότριον μήτε τῆς μακαριότητος ἀνοίκειον αὐτῷ πρόσαπτε ... οἵους δ' αὐτοὺς οἱ πολλοὶ νομίζουσιν, οὐκ εἰσίν· οὐ γὰρ φυλάττουσιν αὐτοὺς οἵους νομίζουσιν. ἀσεβὴς δὲ οὐχ ὁ τοὺς τῶν πολλῶν θεοὺς ἀναιρῶν, ἀλλ' ὁ τὰς τῶν πολλῶν δόξας θεοῖς προσάπτων, "First, believe that god is an indestructible and blessed animal ... and do not ascribe to god anything foreign to his indestructibility or repugnant to his blessedness ... But they are not such as the many believe them to be; for they do not adhere to their own views. The man who denies the gods of the many is not impious, but rather he who ascribes to the gods the opinions of the many" (translation in Inwood/Gerson 1994, 28–29). Cf. Lucr. 6.68–79. Whether Epicurus is expressing here a genuine form of piety or he is just feigning it in order to respond to accusations of impiety was a matter of considerable debate already in antiquity; Cic. *N.D.* 1.123 is clearly in favor of the second interpretation. See also Plut. *Non posse* 1102B–C.

Overall, θαῦμα remains a world of profoundly negative associations in the Hippocratic Corpus. This should explain the frequent use of the formulae θαῦμα δὲ οὐδὲν / οὐδὲν θαυμαστόν /οὐ θαῦμα / οὐ θαυμάσαιμι δ' ἄν,[32] by which doctors wish to stress that, when examined properly, the body, both in illness and in health, holds no secrets.[33] So, for example, in discussing how different people react to pain differently, depending on their individual physical constitutions, a medical author observes that while a wound can cause on certain occasions "so much pain that the person becomes unable to breathe, others, from the pain of that same wound, have no difficulty in breathing, but become delirious and die in fever". As the doctor adds: "one should neither be surprised (ἀλλὰ χρὴ μήτε θαυμάζειν) nor feel dread (μήτε ὀρρωδέειν)" in seeing this, "as he should be aware (εἰδότα) that the minds and the bodies of people differ greatly", and therefore pain is a relative matter ([Hipp.] *Prorrh.* 2.12, 9.34 L.).[34] Knowledge is emphatically said by doctors to lie at the opposite side of wonder (e.g. in [Hipp.] *Vict.* 1.24, 6.496 L.: πολλοὶ θαυμάζουσιν, ὀλίγοι γινώσκουσιν) and, when suitably tested through empirical observation and logical deduction, to effectively eliminate it. Accordingly, medical expertise helps one make sense of complicated medical matters, which common people have the tendency to explain irrationally; this seems to be particularly the case with fevers and symptoms of insanity, hence the emphasis in these contexts on the elimination of the marvellous. As we read in [Hipp.] *Coac.* 80 (5.600 L.): "Fevers that are mild at the beginning and accompanied by throbbing in the head and thin urine have an exacerbation towards their crisis; it would be no wonder in such cases if delirium and sleeplessness also set in", θαῦμα δὲ οὐδέν, εἰ καὶ παρακοπὴ καὶ ἀγρυπνίη γένοιτο.[35] In [Hipp.] *Acut. Sp.* 8 (2.426 L.) the point is made even more forcefully, with the use of a verb in first person: "In fevers accompanied from the beginning by vertigo,

---

32 See e.g. [Hipp.] *Cord.* 3 (9.84 L.); *Genit.* 7 (7.480 L.); *Morb.* 2.47 (7.68 L.); *Morb.* 4.13 (7.566 L.); *Nat. puer.* 26 (7.528 L.).
33 As Holmes 2010b, 38 observes: "However wary scholars have become about using labels like 'secular' and 'rational' to describe Greek medicine in the fifth and fourth centuries, a shift from personal, daemonic explanation to natularizing explanations remains basic to our understanding of learned medicine in this period and the medical tradition that unfolds from it". Lloyd's work remains essential for appreciating the rationalizing agenda of early Greek medicine; see, especially, Lloyd 1979; 1983; 1987.
34 Translation in Potter 1995, 251.
35 Translation in Potter 2010, 123.

throbbing in the head, and thin urine, wait for crises when the fever has its paroxysm; and I would not be at all amazed if patients of that kind were to be affected with delirium" (... οὐ θαυμάσαιμι δ' ἂν οὐδ' εἰ παραφρονήσειαν).[36]

In light of this evidence, Lucretius' suggestion in 3.492 that there is nothing about epilepsy that should cause wonder sounds distinctly medical and should be read in connection with the poet's broader engagement with Hippocratic sources at this point of narrative. The idea that wonder presents an obstacle to knowledge is of equal significance for ancient philosophers and doctors alike. To the extent that Lucretius is combining in 3.487–509 his role as a doctor of the soul with that of a physician who is zooming in on the epileptic patient's symptoms, the use of *nimirum* must be seen as a nod to both traditions.

3.2 Epilepsy Re-considered

And yet, there are several details in Lucretius' account of epilepsy which indicate that, despite his commitment to a lucid and balanced mode of explanation, the poet includes hints at the odd nature of the disease.[37] Starting with 3.488, the observation that the epileptic patient falls to the ground suddenly "as if struck by a thunderbolt", *ut fulminis ictu*, implicates divine interference.[38] When in Book 5 Lucretius tells the myth of Phaethon's punishment by Jupiter, the language that he uses is strikingly similar to that which has been employed throughout 3.487–509:

> at pater omnipotens ira tum percitus **acri** (~ acer, 3.503).
> magnanimum Phaethonta **repenti fulminis ictu** (~ subito, 3.487)
> **deturbavit** equis in terram, Solque cadenti (~ turbat, 3.493 / conturbatur, 3.500)
> obvius aeternam succepit lampada mundi,
> **disiectosque** redegit equos iunxitque **trementis**, (~disiectatur, 3.501/ tremit, 3.489)
> inde suum per iter recreavit[39] cuncta gubernans,
> scilicet ut veteres Graium cecinere poetae. (5.399–405)

---

36 Translation in Potter 1988, 281.
37 Even when it comes to medical sources, epilepsy continues to puzzle authors with its peculiar nature and manifestation. Celsus, for example, includes in his otherwise systematic and clinical discussion of the condition, the striking observation that epileptic patients can sometimes be cured by drinking "the hot blood of a gladiator's cut throat" (*De med.* 3.23.7).
38 See Fratantuono 2015, 187. For thunderbolts as a manifestation of divine retribution in ancient Greek religion and folklore, see Burkert 1985, 252.
39 The restoration of the cosmic order is conveyed here in a language which has been elsewhere applied by Lucretius to the restoration of health in cases of sickness, e.g. in 1.942: *sed potius tali pacto **recreata** valescat.*

But the almighty Father, stirred then with fierce anger, crushed down ambitious Phaethon from his car to the earth with a sudden thunderbolt, and the Sun, meeting his fall, caught up from him the everlasting lamp of the world, and bringing back the scattered horses yoked them in trembling, and then guiding them on their proper path, restored all again — that, you know, is the tale which the old Greek poets have sung.

The story belongs of course to the realm of myth and is straightaway dismissed by Lucretius as pure fiction.⁴⁰ Its close linguistic affinities with 3.487–509, however, reveal in retrospect that the epileptic's sudden fall has been described in terms of an elevated poetic imagery which is subsequently re-employed in a passage that is loaded with supernatural associations and the idea of divine punishment. As in other cases in the *DRN*, Lucretius' dry and clinical tone in the description of a disease does not necessarily entail that the implication of some form divine agency is unequivocally excluded (cf. e.g. 6.1241–42: *poenibat paulo post ... / ... incuria mactans*).⁴¹ One could, of course, object that Book 6 leaves no space for such misunderstandings. In 6.379–422 a series of arguments are adduced to prove that *fulmina* are not god-sent: the fact, for instance, that innocent people are often struck by thunderbolts, instead of guilty ones should be enough to establish that the whole thing is not a matter of divine will and retribution but simply a natural occurrence of pure chance (6.387–95). Even so, *ut fulminis ictu* in 3.488 remains an odd choice of phrase, one which the contemporary audience would have been inclined, in all likelihood, to read as evocative of the divine element.⁴² Lucretius' decision to include it in his account of epilepsy is challenging,

---

40 See 5.406: *quod procul a vera nimis est ratione repulsum*, "but this is all very far indeed removed from true reasoning", with Gale 1994, 33–34. Though discounted as myth, however, Phaethon's story serves as "poetic testimony to a real event: a catastrophic fire that once almost destroyed or did destroy the earth" (Quint 2014, 82).
41 6.1239–42: *nam quicumque suos fugitabant visere ad aegros, / vitai nimium cupidos mortisque timentis / poenibat paulo post turpi morte malaque, / desertos, opis expertis, incuria mactans*, "for if any shirked the visitation of their own sick, avenging Neglectfulness not long after would punish them for their too great greed of life and fear of death, by a death foul and evil deserted and without help". As Hutchinson 2013, 212 observes, "*poenibat paulo post* suggests a divine agency"
42 With the Lucretian sequence *fulminis ictu concidit* (3.488–89) compare, e.g. Cic. *Cons.* fr. 10.36–46 Courtney (~ *Div.* 1.19–20): *nam pater altitonans stellanti nixus Olympo / ipse suos quondam tumulos ac templa petivit / et Capitolinis iniecit sedibus ignis. / tum species ex aere vetus venerataque Nattae / **concidit** ... / hic silvestris erat Romani nominis altrix, / Martia, quae parvos Mavortis semine natos / uberibus gravidas vitali rore rigabat; / quae tum cum pueris flammato **fulminis ictu** / **concidit** atque avolsa pedum vestigia liquit*, "for the Father who thunders on high, resting on starry Olympus, himself struck his own hills and his own temples and hurled his fires at his Capitoline seat. Then fell the ancient and revered bronze image of Natta [...] Here was Mars' wood-haunting nurse of the Roman nation who suckled with life-giving dew from her swollen

to say the least, especially when we take into account that our poet must have been aware of the fact that this of all diseases was misconceived among lay people as being a god-sent affliction. What is at stake here is how far Lucretius is willing to experiment with his use of similes in the course of the poem. As has been amply demonstrated in scholarship, similes in the *DRN* "are carefully tailored to the demands of scientific argumentation";[43] they have a clear illustrative function and, most often, they serve to bridge the gap between what lies manifest before us and the invisible level at which atoms operate.[44] But as 3.488 shows, similes can sometimes also function in ways that prove potentially destabilizing: being introduced, among other reasons, for the sake of poetic effect, they carry a figurative potency which can obscure — whether deliberately or not — their original point of reference, thus meddling with the narrative's principal didactic purpose.[45]

Equally intriguing, in this respect, is the way in which the remission of the disease is described in 3.502–3: *inde ubi iam morbi reflexit causa, reditque / in latebras acer corrupti corporis umor.* The metaphor of the poisonous snake could have been meant as an allusion to the figurative language employed by doctors

---

breasts the young sons of the seed of Mars. At the blow of the flaming lightning bolt she fell with the boys and, once torn from her position, left the marks of her feet" (translation in Wardle 2006, 51–52). Courtney 1993, 166–67 believes that Cicero is reacting here to Lucretius, who believes that the damage inflicted on shrines by thunderbolts is a proof that the gods play no part in the workings of nature (6.417–20). Fellin 1951 and Volk 2013, 99, on the other hand, think that it is Lucretius who is engaging with Cicero's *De consulatu suo*. Be that as it may, Cicero's text is typical in assigning to the thunderbolt a divine origin and purpose. See also Liv. 42.20.1; Ov. *Pont.* 3.1.51; Stat. *Theb.* 10.618.

43 Gale 2007, 62. Cf. Gale 1994, 115 and Kenney 2014, 24: "[I]n Lucretius, both description and imagery, like all his other stylistic characteristics, are *functional*: they assist to carry conviction, and they are employed throughout the poem, in expository and 'pathetic' passages alike, for this purpose".

44 For an extensive discussion of similes in Lucretius, see Garani 2007, 95–150.

45 It might be worth comparing here how metaphors in Lucretius, though indispensable for comprehending reality, often create unresolved tensions in the poem. Take, for instance, Lucretius' presentation of the atoms as miniature individuals acting, suffering and interacting with each other. As Kennedy 2007, 387 points out: "Figuring atoms, which have only size, shape, weight, and movement, in anthropomorphic and biological terms does have the effect of rendering these atoms familiar and their workings more accessible, of naturalizing the discourse in which they are being discussed, but does so precisely by evoking associations which it is the poem's ostensible object to counter"; cf. Bartsch 2015, 208: "metaphors that treat the atomic world as somehow sentient ... gravely distort the philosophical truths of Epicureanism". See also Anderson 1960. For the intrinsic link between metaphor and simile, with reference to Aristotle, see Ricoeur 1996, 337–38.

in medical texts when they speak of the aggressive nature of disease. The use in Hippocratic medicine of adjectives such as θηριώδης and ἄγριος[46] helps to present illness as a wild and devouring force which attacks the individual, penetrates him and, like an animal, feeds on his flesh and mind. Furthermore, considering that Lucretius is thinking here in terms of humoural pathology (3.503: *umor*), it is worth recalling that black bile, believed by some physicians to be the cause of epilepsy,[47] is typically discussed as an "acrid" humour which "bites" the patient. In *De atra bile* 4 (5.115 K.), Galen observes that while there are several black substances regularly evacuated from a patient's body through vomit and faeces, not all of them are black bile, since they lack its distinctive "bite" (δῆξις) and unpleasant smell.[48] In *De locis affectis* 3.11 (8.193–6 K.), the same author notes that epilepsy does not always originate in the brain; often the noxious matter responsible for the disease is located in other parts of the body from where it moves upwards (giving the sensation sometimes of a "cold breeze") till it finally reaches the brain, just as the poison of a scorpion or spider spreads over the body and affects the entire organism.

Lucretius' metaphorical language, however, merits further investigation. The image of the venomous *umor* is highly likely to draw also on poetic texts, some of which bring in the divine element as the ultimate origin of the disease. For a start, one may compare, for instance, Lucr. 3.502–3 with Nic. *Ther.* 282–85 which speaks of a snake that remains hidden in its lurking place, "once it has gorged its fill" (285: ἔνθ' εἰλυθμὸν ἔχεσκεν ἐπεί τ' ἐκορέσσατο φορβῆς).[49] At the same time, there are abundant parallels, especially in Greek tragedy, where intense physical

---

46 See Jouanna 2012, 83–87.
47 See e.g. [Hipp.] *Epid.* 6.8.31 (5.356 L.) which speaks of the tendency of melancholics to become epileptic and that of the epileptics to become melancholic: the material cause, as is suggested, is the same for both conditions: in the case of epilepsy the body is primarily affected, but if the disease turns towards the mind, melancholy ensues. Cf. Philodemus, *De ira* IX 18–X 1 Indelli, who describes the angry person as suffering from "tremblings and shakings of the limbs (τρόμους καὶ κ[ινήσεις] τῶν με[λ]ῶν), just like those which come upon an epileptic (οἷα συμβ[αίνει κ]αὶ τοῖς ἐπιληπτ[ικ]οῖς)". Philodemus continues with the observation that those subject to anger "are always vulnerable to black bile" (καὶ πρὸς μελανχολίας δὲ παρισ[τ]ᾶσιν ἅμ[α] συνεχεῖς), to such an extent that even their hearts "turn black". See Tsouna 2011, 191 and Armstrong 2014, 109.
48 See Stewart 2019, 96. Galen, *De locis affectis* 3.10 (8.189 K.) makes use of the phrase δακνώδη ἀλγήματα in order to describe the pains that attend the excess of black (or yellow) bile in the body.
49 For the affinity between Nicander and Lucretius, see Hollis 1998; cf. Hollis 2007, 101.

and mental pain – sent by the gods – figures as a savage and devouring animal.[50] One particular patient that comes to mind is Philoctetes in Sophocles.[51] His disease, originally caused by the bite of a poisonous snake, continues throughout the play to "feed" on his flesh as an almost animate force with a life of its own (see e.g. 7: νόσῳ διαβόρῳ, 313: τὴν ἀδηφάγον νόσον, 745: βρύκομαι);[52] it moves insidiously like a serpent (787–88: προσέρπει / προσέρχεται τόδ' ἐγγύς) and "goes through him" (743–44: διέρχεται / διέρχεται); it is a beast that dwells inside his body (698: ἐνθήρου ποδὸς).[53] So unbearable is the pain of Philoctetes that the tragic hero actually wants to cut himself into pieces (1207: χρῶτ' ἀπὸ πάντα καὶ ἄρθρα τέμω χερί). It might not be a coincidence that the next time we encounter a snake in *DRN* 3, it is similarly in a context which ties together the themes of mutilation and self-inflicted harm with the illusion that pain can be alleviated through pain.[54] The speculation that a specifically tragic kind of suffering might have informed the poet's account of epilepsy is backed up by another intriguing parallel, Eur. *HF* 861–63: **οὔτε πόντος οὕτω κύμασιν στένων** λάβρος / οὔτε γῆς σεισμὸς **κεραυνοῦ τ' οἶστρος** ὠδῖνας πνέων, / οἳ' ἐγὼ στάδια δραμοῦμαι στέρνον εἰς Ἡρακλέους, "the sea with its roaring waves is not so violent, not so violent the earthquake or the sting of the thunderbolt that fills the air with pain, as will be my dash into the breast of Heracles".[55] The blending between macrocosm and microcosm in Lyssa's words reminds us that Lucretius' patient too is figuratively

---

50 See e.g. Eur. *Med.* 1200–2 (describing the flesh which detaches itself from the bones under the invisible bite of the poison): σάρκες δ' ἀπ' ὀστέων ὥστε πεύκινον δάκρυ / γνάθοις ἀδήλοις φαρμάκων ἀπέρρεον, / δεινὸν θέαμα. Cf. Soph. *Trach.* 1084: ἡ τάλαινα διάβορος νόσος. For the adjective φαγέδαινα applied both by Aeschylus and Euripides to Philoctetes' disease, see Jouanna 2012, 90.
51 For Philoctetes' disease as a divine punishment, see Segal 1995, 111–12.
52 On the devouring force of Philoctetes' disease, see esp. Greengard 1987, 44–45. Cf. Worman 2000 who discusses the relationship between "self" and (monstrous) "otherness" in Sophocles' play.
53 The phrase can be translated as referring to "a foot inhabited by a beast"; see Thumiger 2019, 101. Segal 1990, 55 suggests that the epileptic patient's attempt to stand on his feet (3.504–5) might owe something to the extended scene of Philoctetes' recovery (730–881) in Sophocles. But he does not pursue the connection any further.
54 Lucr. 3.660–63: *omnia iam sorsum cernes ancisa recenti / volnere tortari et terram conspargere tabo, / ipsam seque retro partem petere ore priorem, / volneris ardenti ut morsum premat icta dolore*, [if you cut a snake into pieces] "you will see all the parts cut away writhing separately while the wound is fresh, and bespattering the earth with gore, and the fore turning back and seeking to gnaw itself, that by its bite it may assuage the burning pain of the wound which struck it".
55 Translation in Kovacs 1998, 391.

torn by "winds" and the "surging waves of the sea", and acts "as though he has been struck by a thunderbolt".[56]

Overall, by presenting the patient as being attacked *from within*, Lucretius invites us to view the deep recesses of the human body as an essentially hostile landscape, inhabited by entities which can cause serious harm. One of the standard words in the poem that helps to emphasize the penetrability of our bodies and our exposure to external pain is the verb *insinuare* which combines the meaning of "pushing into something" with that of "moving in as sly, stealthy way".[57] This is how we find it being used, for example, in 6.777–78, in a passage which explains disease by attributing it to harmful substances that reside in the external environment: *multa meant inimica per auris, multa per ipsas / **insinuant** naris infesta atque aspera tactu*, "many pernicious elements pass through the ears, many make their way into the very nostrils noxious and rough to the touch". The verb appears also in 6.955, where Lucretius speaks of the possibility that the seeds of disease have an extra-cosmic origin: they manage to find their way into our world *from without, extrinsecus* (*morbida visque simul, cum extrinsecus insinuatur*).[58] But *insinuare* can also be used to describe the windings and turnings through which a snake moves.[59] Lucretius' picture of epilepsy presents in this respect a kind of inversion: it comes with the unsettling suggestion that apart from the things to which we are exposed and which threaten to "creep into" our bodies at any time, there are also other, more insidious ones, which reside within us. The idea of corporeal boundaries here collapses since the body is revealed to harbour within it the forces from which it is otherwise striving to protect itself.[60]

---

56 For the extended scholarship which discusses Heracles' symptoms of madness in Euripides' play side by side with the description of epilepsy in the Hippocratic *De morbo sacro*, see Papadopoulou 2005, 82, with further bibliography. For the "storm" (that is sent by the gods) as a metaphor for madness in tragedy, see e.g. [Aesch.] *PV* 643: θεόσσυτον χειμῶνα and Soph. *Aj.* 206–7: Αἴας θολερῷ / κεῖται χειμῶνι νοσήσας. For further parallels and discussion, see Padel 1992, 81–88; Hershkowitz 1998, 71.
57 See Segal 1990, 110–11.
58 *Insinuare* is also used by the poet in contexts where he is speaking about the senses, such as touch (2.436), taste (2.684), sound (4.525) and sight (4.331). In commenting on the use of the verb, Graver 1990, 100 observes that the "boundary violations of unpleasant sensation, although we may or may not *feel* them as such, are of a kind with the life-threatening violations of injury and illness".
59 See Paschalis 1997, 103.
60 It is worth noting that in the immediately preceding section (on the effects of wine to the soul), Lucretius concludes with an emphatic use of *insinuare* (3.484–86): *at quaecumque queunt conturbari inque pediri, / significant, paulo si durior **insinuarit** / causa, fore ut pereant aevo privata futuro*, "but if anything can be confused and impeded, this indicates that, if some cause a

Epilepsy in Lucretius brings out the self-harming potential of the human *phusis*. Essentially, it shows how disease can alienate us from our bodies, revealing the latter's capacity to transform into something foreign to us. In Elaine Scarry's words, "the person in great pain experiences his own body as the agent of his agony. The ceaseless, self-announcing signal of the body in pain, at once so empty and undifferentiated and so full of blaring adversity, contains not only the feeling 'my body hurts' but the feeling 'my body hurts me'".[61] In fact, so deep is the sense of self-estrangement and alienation associated with epilepsy, that the living, suffering body of the patient begins to resemble, more and more, a dead man's corpse. Putrefaction and mutilation caused by feral animals typically occur in Lucretius in connection to the decaying body after death or to the process of dying; conceptually they are both linked to the fear that our bodies are constantly exposed to external forces that threaten to dissolve the fabric of our physical being.[62] The venomous *umor* responsible for epilepsy inflicts damage by poisoning and rending the body *from within*,[63] thus turning the agony of sickness

---

little more compelling should penetrate, the thing would perish, and be robbed of its future life". *Insinuare* here might be giving us a foretaste of the serpent metaphor in the lines which follow.
61   Scarry 1985, 47; cf. Napier 1992, 148: "Diseases, like foreigners, are things different from ourselves ... Even our mostly highly trained scientists cannot avoid the vocabulary of the foreign when discussing how diseases take hold of a person. Moreover, the tendency is so deeply rooted that learned discussions of immunology inevitably make use of a vocabulary that can only be described as animistic. Note, for example, how we conceive of allergic reactions, of how "one cell fails to recognize another cell for what it is"".
62   See Segal 1990, 118–36, 144–52.
63   Although putrefaction is not explicitly mentioned by Lucretius, *venenum* in 3.501 points to this direction. In 3.657–63 the writhing body of the dying snake is described as "bespattering the earth with gore", *et terram conspargere* **tabo** (3.661).*Tabescere* is one of the standard verbs used by the poet to describe the rotting of the decaying human body, e.g. in 3.580–81 (the body cannot endure the splitting off of the soul without wasting away in foul stench): *denique cum corpus nequeat perferre animai / discidium, quin in taetro* **tabescat** *odore*. The venomous poison released by the snake in the case of epilepsy is not a random noxious substance but one which is ultimately linked with the dreadful reality of decomposition. With regard to mutilation, often in the poem Lucretius speaks of wild beasts as they are tearing apart human flesh, e.g. in 3.888 (*morsuque ferarum*) and 4.1016 (*pantherae morsu saevive leonis*). *Morsus* is also used to describe the bite of a snake (3.663), whose action in 3.487–509 should thus be imagined as being far more violent than that of producing a simple sting: it effectively threatens to tear the entire mind and spirit apart (409–501): *vis animi atque animai / conturbatur et ... divisa seorsum /* **disiectatur** *eodem illo* **distracta** *veneno*. For Lucretius' frequent use of compounds in *dis-* to convey the dispersive process of mutilation, see Segal 1990, 115–16; and for 3.657–63, see the recent discussion in Possanza 2014.

into a virtual experience of death.⁶⁴ In the ps.-Platonic *Axiochus*, probably inspired by Epicurean sources, the dialogue's eponymous character expresses his fear that when he dies, he will lie there "rotting away, turning into worms and other creeping things" (365c: κείσομαι σηπόμενος, εἰς εὐλὰς καὶ κνώδαλα μεταβάλλων).⁶⁵ Axiochus could be referring here to snakes:⁶⁶ the idea that a human corpse can produce a serpent is abundantly attested in Greek and Roman sources, e.g. in Plut. *Cleom.* 39: ὡς μελίττας μὲν βόες, σφῆκας δὲ ἵπποι κατασαπέντες ἐξανθοῦσι ... τὰ δὲ ἀνθρώπινα σώματα, τῶν περὶ τὸν μυελὸν ἰχώρων συρροήν τινα καὶ σύστασιν ἐν ἑαυτοῖς λαβόντων, ὄφεις ἀναδίδωσι, "as putrefying oxen breed bees, and horses wasps ... so human bodies, when the juices about the marrow collect together and coagulate, produce serpents".⁶⁷ That a snake hides somewhere inside our bodies, exiting on occasions to inflict harm and then returning to its lair — as Lucretius has it — makes us think that decay is constantly at work: a part of our being from the very moment we begin to exist.

The metaphor of the creeping disease (3.502–3), crucially intertwined with notions of strangeness and alienation, appears also in 6.1119–24, which presents the plague as the result of environmental changes which induce a climate that is "foreign" to those who are affected by it: the seeds of pestilence are contained in a dangerous air which "crawls about" and "creeps slowly", like a cloud or mist, causing commotion wherever it goes and compelling change (6.1120–21: *aer inimicus **serpere** coepit, / ut nebula ac nubes paulatim **repit***). When it has reached our sky, "it corrupts it, making it like itself and alien to us" (6.1124: *corrumpat*⁶⁸ *reddatque sui simile atque **alienum***). Prior to this description, epilepsy is echoed also in 6.658–61, in the context of a passing reference to a skin disease known in Greek medical writings as ἐρυσίπελας,⁶⁹ which Lucretius chooses to mention by

---

64 For the idea that disease can turn someone into a "living corpse", see e.g. Soph. *Phil.* 1018: ἐν ζῶσιν νεκρόν, and 1030: ὃς οὐδέν εἰμι καὶ τέθνηχ᾽ ὑμῖν πάλαι.
65 For Lucretius' knowledge of the ps.-Platonic dialogue and his use of it in the course of Book 3, see Nussbaum 1994, 199 and Kenney 2014, 183; 188–89; cf. Warren 2004b, 68–69 and 213–15.
66 Κνώδαλον in ancient Greek is used for "wild creatures" and "beasts" in general. LSJ gives the specific meaning of "serpent" with reference to [Pl.] *Ax.* 365c and Nic. *Th.* 98. See Segal 1990, 145.
67 Translation in Perrin 1921, 141. See also Ov. *Met.* 15.389–90: *sunt qui, cum clauso putrefacta est spina sepulcro, / mutari credant humanas angue medullas*. Cf. Plin. *Nat.* 10.188; Ael. *NA* 1.51; Philostr. *Her.* 8.5–10; Diog. Laert. 5.89–90 = Heraclides of Pontus F16 Wehrli. The following epigram of Archelaus is cited by Antigonus of Carystus (*Mir.* 89): ... ἀνδρὸς γὰρ κοίλης ἐκ μυελοῦ ῥάχεως / δεινὸς γίνετ᾽ ὄφις, νέκυος δειλοῖο σαπέντος (*SH* 129.2–3). See Ogden 2013, 249–50.
68 Compare 3.503: *corrupti corporis*.
69 See [Hipp.] *Progn.* 23 (2.174–78 L.) and *Coac.* 360 (5.660 L.), with Grmek 1991, 203. See also Richter 1912.

its colloquial name, the "sacred fire", without qualifying or dismissing the characterization:

> obturgescit enim subito pes, arripit acer
> saepe dolor dentes, oculos invadit in ipsos,
> existit sacer ignis et urit corpore **serpens**
> quamcumque arripuit partim, **repitque** per artus
>
> For the foot suddenly swells, a sharp aching often seizes the teeth, or invades the eyes themselves, the sacred fire appears creeping over the body and burning each part it takes hold on, and crawls over the limbs.

As with the occurrence of a bold simile in the case of epilepsy (*ut fulminis ictu*), what we witness in this case is the striking use of an adjective which raises the implication of some form of divine interference. *Sacer ignis* occurs once more in the text, in the description of the plague (6.1166–67): *et simul ulceribus quasi inustis omne rubere / corpus, ut est per membra sacer cum diditur ignis*, "the body was red all over with ulcers, as it were, burnt into it, like when the sacred fire spreads all over the limbs". These lines are picked up by Vergil in *G*. 3.561–66: *ne tondere quidem morbo inluvieque peresa / vellera nec telas possunt attingere putris; / verum etiam invisos si quis temptarat amictus, / ardentes papulae atque immundus olentia sudor / membra sequebatur, nec longo deinde moranti / tempore* **contactos artus sacer ignis edebat**, "they could not even shear the fleeces, eaten up with sores and filth, nor touch the rotten web. Nay, if any man donned the loathsome garb, feverish blisters and foul sweat would run along his fetid limbs, and he had not long to wait before the sacred fire was feeding on his stricken limbs".[70] The disease has been said a few lines above (*G*. 3.551–53) to be progressing like the Fury Tisiphone who emerges from the underworld and, driving Sickness and Fear in front of her, becomes greater day by day. The suggestion here

---

70 Translation in Fairclough/Goold 1999, 215–17. For a discussion of these lines, see Fowler 2007, 225.Vergil blends here allusions to Lucretius with references to Greek tragedy, in what appears to be an acknowledgment of the Lucretian text's tendency to invoke tragic scripts of suffering in order to generate scenes of pain and violence in the poem. Compare, especially, *contactos artus sacer ignis edebat* with the poisoned garment in Soph. *Trach*. 1052–54: ὑφαντὸν ἀμφίβληστρον, ᾧ διόλλυμαι. / πλευραῖσι γὰρ προσμαχθὲν ἐκ μὲν ἐσχάτας / **βέβρωκε σάρκας**. The Sophoclean parallel is missed by Thomas 1988 vol.2, 146. See Hardie 1984, 407 n.10, who notes the resemblance between Soph. *Trach*. 770–71: ἴτα φοινίας / ἐχθρᾶς ἐχίδνης ἰὸς ὣς ἐδαίνυτο and Verg. *Aen*. 2.221: *perfusus sanie vittas atroque veneno*.

that the plague could have been a form of divine punishment[71] does not have an explicit parallel in Lucretius. It would, however, be tempting to think that Vergil's choice to place at the very final line of the Noric plague a Lucretian formula (*sacer ignis*) shows how ambiguous Lucretius' language for sickness can be at points and how it effectively lends itself to being interpreted, and reused, as open to supernatural associations.[72]

Lucretius, as I have been arguing in this section, toys with the odd nature of epilepsy primarily through similes and metaphors which, on the one hand, involve the implicit presence of the divine while, on the other hand, they bring out the body's intrinsic capacity to transform into something hostile to us. At the same time this figurative language serves to maintain the text's highly rhetorical nature: Lucretius' aim is not simply to provide an objective recording of symptoms, in a manner that a doctor would have done and would have considered sufficient,[73] but to move beyond that, and create a "spectacle" out of illness (*ante oculos* in 3.488 stands, in this respect, as a marker of rhetorical *enargeia* and betrays the poet's preoccupation with bringing before our eyes what is principally designed to be a vivid and pathetic image of suffering).[74] As I will proceed to illustrate, in Book 6 epilepsy becomes itself a metaphor for a crumbling world that is both intimidating and wondrous. The miraculous properties of the earth will be shown to be intimately linked to its conception as an ailing and convulsing body, just as the one we have encountered in 3.487–509. This in combination with the fact that Book 6 at once diffuses wonder and then reinstates it in the form of an instinctive response to the sublime nature of things will help to show how integral the figurative deployment of disease is for our engagement with the marvellous aspects of this world.

---

71 See Gale 2000, 77: "Given the role played elsewhere by the Furies as instruments of divine vengeance, we might take these lines [Verg. *G*. 3.551–53] as more than a metaphor, and see the plague as a punishment inflicted on the Norici for some unspecified crime". Cf. Harrison 1979.
72 Cf. Sen. *Oed*. 188: *sacer ignis pascitur artus*.
73 This is not to underestimate, of course, the highly rhetorical nature of some of the medical texts among which the Hippocratic Περὶ φυσῶν (full of Gorgianic figures of speech and sound effects; see Jouanna 1988, 10–24, 169–73) stands as a prime example.
74 Cf. [Cic.] *Rhet. Her*. 4.68: *Demonstratio est, cum ita verbis res exprimitur, ut geri negotium et res **ante oculos** esse videatur*, with Fowler 2002, 197. For *ante oculos* in Quintilian, see e.g. *Inst*. 1.12.18, 6.1.11, 8.3.81, 9.2. Cf. Webb 1997, 117–20.

3.3 Epilepsy, Earthquakes and Volcanic Eruptions. Reinstating the Wondrous in a World of Sickness

Book 6 concludes with the plague in Athens. Long before we reach that scene, disease as a notion shapes, both linguistically and conceptually, Lucretius' account of several other natural phenomena, especially the earthquakes (6.535–607) and the eruption of Aetna (6.639–702).

With regard to the earthquakes, the connection with epilepsy[75] is primarily established with reference to the idea of subterranean winds which act as a hidden cause (6.557–600), and that of the "trembling" (cf. 3.489: *tremit artus*) which spreads from the epicenter and "creeps far and wide". Considering that the ground beneath us is hollow and full of caverns (6.535–42), an internal collapse which happens suddenly, *repente*, causes the surface to shake (recall how a sudden epileptic fit is attributed to an invisible substance which traverses the cavities of the human body and unleashes turmoil):

> His igitur rebus subiunctis suppositisque
> terra superne **tremit** magnis concussa ruinis,
> subter ubi ingentis speluncas subruit aetas;
> quippe cadunt toti montes, magnoque **repente**
> concussu late **disserpunt** inde **tremores**. (6.543–47)

> Since therefore she has these things attached and ranged beneath her, the upper earth trembles under the shock of some great collapse when time undermines those huge caverns below; for whole mountains fall, and with the great shock the tremblings in an instant creep abroad from the place far and wide.

---

[75] For the association between bodily convulsions and earthquakes, see Arist. *Mete.* 366b16–30: δεῖ γὰρ νοεῖν ὅτι ὥσπερ ἐν τῷ σώματι ἡμῶν καὶ τρόμων καὶ σφυγμῶν αἴτιόν ἐστιν ἡ τοῦ πνεύματος ἐναπολαμβανομένη δύναμις, οὕτω καὶ ἐν τῇ γῇ τὸ πνεῦμα παραπλήσιον ποιεῖν, **καὶ τὸν μὲν τῶν σεισμῶν οἷον τρόμον εἶναι** τὸν δ' οἷον σφυγμόν ... οἵ τε γὰρ τέτανοι καὶ οἱ σπασμοὶ πνεύματος μέν εἰσιν κινήσεις, τοσαύτην δὲ ἔχουσιν ἰσχὺν ὥστε πολλοὺς ἅμα πειρωμένους ἀποβιάζεσθαι μὴ δύνασθαι κρατεῖν τῆς κινήσεως τῶν ἀρρωστούντων. τοιοῦτον δὴ δεῖ νοεῖν τὸ γιγνόμενον καὶ ἐν τῇ γῇ, **ὡς εἰκάσαι πρὸς μικρὸν μεῖζον**, "for we must suppose that, just as the power of wind trapped within is responsible for both trembling and throbbing in our bodies, likewise, wind in the earth is comparable, as well as the kinds of trembling or throbbing by earthquakes... Tetanuses and spasms are movements of wind, and they have so much force that many people who combine their efforts at restraining those afflicted are unable to hold down their movement. We must suppose that such things happen also in the earth, by way of likening the great to the small" (translation in Wee 2017, 145). Cf. Sen. *QNat.* 3.15.1, 6.24.2–3 with Althoff 1997; Williams 2012, 241–45. Wee 2017 has recently argued that the convulsing body of the epileptic in the Hippocratic *De morbo sacro* may have been meant to recall the image of an earthquake.

At another point, Lucretius speaks of how a huge mass of rocks rolls forwards into some "great and wide pool of water". The earth is then shaken by the commotion of the subterranean lake, "just as a vessel sometimes cannot remain still, unless the water within it ceases to be moved about in waves to and fro", *ut vas interdum non quit constare, nisi* **umor** */ destitit in dubio fluctu iactarier intus* (6.555–56).[76] The use of *umor* and *vacillans* (6.554: *terra vacillans*) in the same context are reminiscent of the staggering patient in 3.504 (*tum quasi vaccillans primum consurgit*) who is gradually recovering his senses once the noxious humour (3.503: *acer umor*) comes to a still.

In the case of the Aetna, Lucretius introduces his account with the claim that just as the world contains many seeds which cause diseases among men, in the same way the universe contains many elements which cause natural upheavals in the world. One of the diseases spotlighted by the poet is the "sacred fire" whose connection with epilepsy has been discussed above (6.655–69):

> Numquis enim nostrum **miratur**, siquis in artus
> accepit calido febrim fervore coortam
> aut alium quemvis morbi per membra dolorem?
> obturgescit enim subito pes, arripit acer
> saepe dolor dentes, oculos invadit in ipsos,
> existit sacer ignis et urit corpore serpens
> quamcumque arripuit partim, repitque per artus,
> **nimirum** quia sunt multarum semina rerum,
> et satis haec tellus morbi caelumque mali fert,
> unde queat vis immensi procrescere morbi.
> sic igitur toti caelo terraeque putandumst
> ex infinito satis omnia suppeditare,
> unde repente queat tellus concussa moveri
> perque mare ac terras rapidus percurrere turbo,
> ignis abundare Aetnaeus, flammescere caelum.

> For is there any of us who feels wonder, if someone has got into his limbs a fever that gathers with burning heat, or any other pain from disease throughout his body? For the foot suddenly swells, a sharp aching often seizes the teeth, or invades the eyes themselves, the sacred fire appears creeping over the body and burning each part it takes hold on, and crawls over the limbs. There is nothing to wonder about it, because there are seeds of many things, and this earth and sky produce enough noxious disease that from it may grow forth an immeasurable quantity of disease. In this way therefore we must believe that a supply of all things is brought up from the infinite to the whole heaven and earth, enough to enable the

---

76 For this passage, see Garani 2007, 145–46.

earth on a sudden to quake and move, the swift whirlwind to scour over land and sea, Aetna's fires to overflow, the heaven to burst in a blaze.

The text opens with a rhetorical question (6.655: *numquis enim nostrum miratur?*), asking whether any of us would really feel astonished if s/he happened to fall ill. Lucretius appeals here to common human experience, implying that disease is as much part of life as health is and therefore subject to its norms and regularities. This allows him accordingly to make the observation that earthquakes and volcanic eruptions are premised on the same natural principles, the only difference being that disease in that case occurs on a grander scale (6.664: *unde queat vis immensi procrescere morbi*).

Epilepsy is echoed in both passages (6.543–47, 6.655–59) and becomes embedded in narratives which maintain that we should *not* wonder at things since virtually everything in the world, however odd or terrifying it might look, can be explained by atoms and the void. As Lucretius adds in 6.647–54, it also helps to keep in mind how immense the universe is so that we cease to be astonished by phenomena which are ultimately revealed to convey a *false* sense of greatness: the eruption of Aetna may inspire wonder and awe, but when we think of it as only an infinitesimal fraction of the universe, we then stop finding it frightening (6.653–54: *quod bene propositum si plane contueare / ac videas plane*, **mirari multa relinquas**).

Book 6, however, operates simultaneously on many different levels between which several tensions exist. According to James Porter, although Lucretius is indeed committed to the principle of substituting *mirum* with *ratio*, nature continues nonetheless to retain its marvellous qualities:

> The attraction to natural prodigies is irresistible, even erotic; wonder comes naturally, as does the desire to transgress the limits of phenomena ... Lucretius' surface lesson, 'And if you kept my proposition clearly in mind, you would cease to wonder at many things' (6.653–4), is too easily understood as an injunction not to wonder at anything (*nil admirari*) in nature. But that is surely the wrong conclusion to draw. After all, even the reflection of the sky in a puddle [4.414–19] is a 'marvellous' thing (*mirande*), both as an appearance of nature and as an index to the wondrous truths of physics.[77]

Thus, in the case of the Aetna, the wind which has grown hot in the caverns beneath the mountain bursts out and "carries its fire afar, scatters ashes far abroad, rolls the smoke all thick and black and thrusts out rocks of *wonderful* weight", *extruditque simul* **mirando** *pondere saxa* (6.690–92). The passage reminds us of

---

[77] Porter 2007, 173. Cf. Shrijvers 1970, 264–65; Hardie 1986, 171; Ferri 1993, 117–22.

the earlier discussion of the thunderbolt: "the speed, moreover, and heavy blow (*fulminis ... gravis ictus*) of the thunderbolt comes about, and the bolts usually run with so quick a fall, because first of all within the clouds a force is always aroused and collects itself and takes on a mighty energy of movement, and then, when the cloud can no longer contain the increasing rush, the force is pressed out and therefore flies with a *wonderful* rush", ... *exprimitur vis atque ideo volat impete **miro*** (6.323–28). Lucretius' use of *mirandum/mirum* in these passages[78] should not go unnoticed: it is essentially designed to underscore that while we should not feel perplexed by all those terrifying phenomena which prevent us from attaining *ataraxia*, it would still be a mistake to turn a blind eye on their extraordinary qualities, as this would entail our no longer being able to appreciate the beauty inherent in the world. Wonder persists–only this time, instead of being associated with ignorance, it becomes transformed to a deep admiration of nature. In Stephen Greenblatt's words: "it might seem at first sight that" the comprehension of the world which Lucretius promises "would inevitably bring with it a sense of cold emptiness. But being liberated from harmful illusions is not the same with disillusionment". Rather than assume that knowledge lays wonder to rest, "in Lucretius' account the process is something like the reverse: it is knowing the way things are that awakes the deepest wonder".[79] This must also be what Seneca has in mind when, in a discussion of earthquakes that owes a lot to Lucretius Book 6, he notes (*QNat.* 6.4.2): "compared to the knowledge of nature, there is nothing greater (*quo nullum maius est, nosse naturam*). For the handling of this material does not contain anything more beautiful ... than that it engages a person with its own magnificence and is cultivated not because of financial payment but out of wonder" (*quam quod hominem magnificentia sui detinet nec mercede **sed miraculo colitur***).[80] Philosophical inquiry, as Seneca's passage amply illustrates, does not render the world mundane but has instead an intensifying

---

78 See also 6.186 (on clouds piled high one above another in a wonderful mass), *extructis aliis alias super impete miro*) and 6.436–37 (on whirlwinds): *quam cum discidit, hinc prorumpitur in mare venti / vis et fervorem mirum concinnat in undis*, "and when the force of the wind has torn it asunder, it bursts forth from the cloud upon the sea and causes a wonderful boiling in the waves". The fact that the *Aetna* poet (ca. 1st cent. CE), who is heavily indebted to Lucretius, endorses the "miraculous" as a positive and undisputed quality of the natural world is suggestive in itself. See e.g. *Aetna* 155–56: *quod si spissa foret, solido si staret in omni, / nulla daret miranda sui spectacula tellus*; 180: *plurima namque patent illi miracula monti*; cf. 252–53. See Porter 2016, 508–16.
79 Greenblatt 2011, 169.
80 Cf. Sen. *QNat* 6.4.1 (on earthquakes): ***mille miracula*** *movet faciemque mutat locis et defert montes*, with Williams 2012, 43–44 and 250–51; 2016.

effect on the sense of wonder and thrill that we experience when interacting with nature.[81]

But the wonder resulting from *ratio* remains a profoundly unsettling feeling. The moment when Lucretius declares his ultimate knowledge of the universe is notoriously one that combines delight with a penetrating sense of "shuddering" (3.28–30): *his ibi me rebus quaedam divina voluptas / percipit atque* **horror**, *quod sic natura tua vi / tam manifesta patens ex omni parte retecta est*, "thereupon from all these things a sort of divine delight gets hold upon me and a shuddering, because nature thus by your power has been so manifestly laid open and uncovered in every part".[82] *Horror* — a word that is intimately linked in Latin with *mirum* —[83] could be translated here as referring to the excitement and thrill of knowledge but we should not lose sight of the fact that it is also the standard term employed

---

81 In a similar way, while Aristotle (*Metaph.* 983a12–21), as we have seen, considers *thauma* a cognitive and affective state which betrays one's ignorance, on other occasions he endorses it as a positive concept: the word can also designate the kind of admiration that only those who have contemplated, and have come to understand, the true nature of things are able to enjoy. This is precisely what lies behind Aristotle's statement in *Part. an.* 645a17, that "in all natural things, there is something wonderful" (θαυμαστόν). In the following lines, the philosopher speaks of the mental effort which is required before we manage to comprehend how every tiny part in the body is there for a reason; to understand a bodily part's function and ascribe it with a purpose immediately qualifies it as beautiful (*Part. an.* 645a25–27): τὸ γὰρ μὴ τυχόντως ἀλλ' ἕνεκά τινος ἐν τοῖς τῆς φύσεως ἔργοις ἐστὶ καὶ μάλιστα· οὗ δ' ἕνεκα συνέστηκεν ἢ γέγονε τέλους, τὴν τοῦ καλοῦ χώραν εἴληφεν, "in the works of nature purpose and not accident is predominant; and the purpose or end for the sake of which those works have been constructed or formed has its place among the beautiful" (translation in Peck/Forster 1937, 101). See Tipton 2014, 68–69.

82 Gale 1994, 29 n.106 observes that "there is a world of difference between the awe, *divina voluptas atque horror* (3.28f.), which Epicurus' teachings inspire in the poet, and the *metus*, the crippling fear, experienced by the worshippers of Cybele [e.g. in 2.609, 619, 623, 632] or by kings and commoners alike in the face of storms and lightning (5.1218–40)"; cf. Kenney 2014, 79. But see also Bullard 2011, 103 who, I think, is right in pointing out that Lucr. 3.28–30 "works as a powerful poetic irony ... the materialist natural philosophy offered by the 'master' Epicurus as a cure to the anxieties of ignorance and superstition is itself a source of spiritual experience — divine ecstasies, tremblings and so on". For a similar reading of these lines, see Kennedy 2007, 380: the "expropriation of the language and images associated with religion is a game played for high stakes. Whatever Lucretius might have wanted for his own text, he could not wholly determine its reception. Expressing his vision in the language of religion may serve to naturalize and domesticate it, but it also leaves open the possibility of a recuperation, the reappropriation of the text of the *DRN* for the very position it ostensibly claims to be opposing".

83 For the association between *horror* and *mirari/mirabile/mirum* in Latin, see e.g. Pl. *Am.* 1117–18 (cited in the note below); Verg. *G.* 4.441–42; *Aen.* 3.26, 7.78; Stat. *Theb.* 8.4; *Ach.* 1.375: *mirantur et horrent*.

elsewhere the poem in order to designate an unwelcome feeling of dread.⁸⁴ In 4.31–37, for instance, the adverb *horrifice* describes a mixed reaction of wonder and panic when people see images of the dead in their sleep; in 5.1220 reference is made to the "horrible impact" (*fulminis horribili ... plaga*) which is produced when a thunderbolt hits the ground and makes the earth tremble, leaving people astonished and terrified by what they misconceive to be an act of god. At the same time, by making use of a word which — just like *phrikē* in Greek⁸⁵ — conveys what is principally a physical and instinctive reaction,⁸⁶ Lucretius diverts our attention from his mental and affective state to a convulsing (and sick) body.⁸⁷ In 6.592–95

---

84 *Percipit horror*, the formula used by Lucretius in 3.29, is attested for the first time in Latin in Pacuv. 224 R (*ROL* II 265): *diversi circumspicimus, horror percipit*, "we looked around us from all sides; horror seized us". The exact context in which the line occurred in Pacuvius' play is difficult to reconstruct. Fantham 2003, 109 cautiously places it in a scene which "sounds as though it was partly modelled on the opening of Euripides' *Iphigenia in Tauris*"; for further discussion, see Schierl 2006, 365. Plautus' reworking of Pacuvius' line also points to a reaction of pure dread (*Am.* 1117–18): *Mira memoras, nimis formidolosum facinus praedicas;* / *nam mihi* **horror** *membra misero* **percipit** *dictis tuis*, "...utter dread at your words grips the limbs of my poor self". These are the only two occurrences of *percipit horror* in Latin before it appears again in Lucretius. Given the poet's in depth engagement with Roman drama (see the recent discussion of Taylor 2016), I would venture the hypothesis that Lucr. 3.29 has a poignant, tragic quality in it.

85 Compare the *visual* language which frames the emergence of Lucretian *horror* in 3.28–30 (*tam manifesta patens*) with Philodemus' suggested line of treatment in *De ira*, according to which negative images (of anger's harmful effects) should be set before the pupil's eyes (τιθέναι πρὸ ὀμμάτων), so that the latter *sees* the error of his ways. Philodemus' point is that these vivid images can produce "a great shudder" (μεγάλην ἐνποιεῖ **φρίκην**, *De ira* col. III 14–15 Indelli) which functions as a kind of shock tactics; see Tsouna 2003 and Gale 2018, 65–67. The idea that Lucretius could be alluding to Philodemus' notion of shudder intensifies the sinister overtones of *horror*. The hypothesis seems to be further supported by the fact that φρίκη for Philodemus is not simply a negative emotion but has a transcendental air to it; see e.g. *De oec.* col. XXIV.3–4: ἐκστατικὴ φρίκη θεῶν καὶ θανάτου. Cf. Lovatt 2013, 100 on the "ecstatic proem" of Lucretius Book 3.

86 See Cairns 2015, 76: The sensory and cognitive aspects of *phrikē* in tragedy, "essential though they may be for the specification of the emotion ... do not suffice to make *phrikē* what it is — for *phrikē* is fundamentally a physical experience, the experience of a body that shivers and shudders"; cf. Cairns 2013. For the association between *horror* and *phrikē*, see Burkert 2010, 52. In medical Latin, *horror* translates φρίκη. See e.g. Cels. 3.3.3: *Frigus uoco, ubi extremae partes membrorum inalgescunt,* **horrorem,** *ubi corpus totum intremit* and compare it with [Hipp.] *De morbis* 4.15 (7.574 L.): **τετάρακται** μὲν δὴ ὁ ἄνθρωπος, ὁκόταν πυρεταίνῃ· σημήϊον δὲ τοῦτο, ὅτι **φρίκη διαΐσσει διὰ τοῦ σώματος** ἄλλοτε καὶ ἄλλοτε, "when a person is having a fever, he is stirred up, as is shown by the fact that shivering spreads through his body from time to time" (transl. in Potter 2012, 137–39).

87 For the bodily qualities of *horror* (deriving from *horreo* = "stand erect, bristle"; the noun points to the idea of hair standing on end), see e.g. Pl. *Am.* 1118 (cited above); Verg. *Aen.* 3.29–

the winds move through the interstices underground and cause the earth to tremble just as when a patient is seized by a shivering fit: ... *fera vis venti per crebra foramina terrae / dispertitur **ut horror**, et incutit inde tremorem, / frigus uti nostros penitus cum venit in artus, / concutit invitos cogens tremere atque movere*, "the furious force of wind is distributed abroad through the many interstices of the earth like an ague, and thus transmits the trembling; just as when cold penetrates deep into our limbs, it shakes them, making them tremble and quake against our will". The lines bear a striking resemblance to the description of the epileptic fit, especially by means of focusing our attention on the earth's "forced" trembling (compare **vis** ... *incutit tremorem* and **cogens** *tremere* with *vi morbi saepe* **coactus** in 3.487). The passage, with its emphasis on *horror*, is also reminiscent of 3.28–30. What presents itself as the defining, climactic moment for Lucretius' intellectual pursuits in the poem thus transpires to be combined with a heightened awareness of the body's fragile state, foreshadowing in this way the violent images of sickness and material dissolution, which will occupy most of Book 3.[88]

What I am suggesting is that wonder in Lucretius is always linked — in some way or another — to an obtrusive feeling of mental and physical uneasiness.[89] While a distinction between the "negative" and "positive" sublime,[90] between dumbstruck astonishment and informed admiration, is undeniably present in the poem, the line between the two is not always easy to draw: terrifying phenomena continue to carry an aesthetic value even for those who fail to comprehend them

---

30: *mihi frigidus horror / membra quatit*; Sen. *Tro.* 457: *mihi gelidus horror ac tremor somnum excutit*. Lucr. 3.290-91 is rather illuminating: *est et frigida multa comes formidinis aura, / quae ciet horrorem membris et concitat artus*, "[the mind] has also abundance of that cold air, fear's comrade, which makes the limbs shiver and stirs the frame".

88 Book 3, along with Book 5, contains the highest number of *horror* terms in the poem, all of them appearing in negative contexts associated with fear of/and death: see e.g. 3.170 (*vis horrida teli*); 3.905 (*horrifico busto*); 3.1012 (*Tartarus horriferos eructans faucibus aestus*). Among these occurrences, 3.170-73 is perhaps the most intriguing: *si minus offendit vitam* **vis horrida** *teli / ossibus ac nervis disclusis intus adacta, / at tamen insequitur languor terraeque petitus /* **suavis**, "if the grim force of a weapon driven deep to the dividing of bones and sinews fails to hit the life, yet a languor follows and a blissful fall to the ground". The pairing of *horrida vis* with *suavis* recalls the paradoxically symbiotic relationship between *horror* and *voluptas* in 3.28–29.

89 For the proem to Book 3 and the portrayal of Epicurus as a mystagogue leading the poet from darkness to light, see Gale 1994, 194 who notes that *horror* in this context "is particularly reminiscent of the θάμβος ('awe') or κατάπληξις ('amazement') which the initiand is sometimes said to experience" (p.194), citing as primary evidence Plutarch fr.178 Sandbach: the passing from darkness to light is marked by "shivering, trembling, sweating and astonishment" (... φρίκη καὶ τρόμος καὶ ἱδρὼς καὶ θάμβος).

90 For Lucretius' "contrasting sublimities", see Hardie 2009, 76.

while, inversely, the beauty of knowledge — grounded as it may be on a firm grasp of atomic principles — is never free from a subverting feeling of shudder and dread. The intrinsic link between knowledge, admiration and the eventual realization of our mortality is of the essence here. Lucretius' marveling over nature is often generated by instances in which the earth unveils its majestic qualities under conditions which bring out, vividly and compellingly, its state as porous and dissoluble matter. The enlightened admiration promised by the poet for those who will be able to follow his teaching goes hand in hand with an increased awareness that our world is destined to die. Convulsion, functioning as an index to disease and death but also to knowledge, emerges in this case as a crucial notion: it provides the substrate both for the epileptic's excruciating spasms and for the less intense, though equally insidious, trembling which casts a shade over the poet's delight when the absolute truth is being revealed to him. In its turn, the world to which this truth allows us to have a privileged access is often presented as trembling and shaking.

The description of the earthquake — yet another marvel to behold — ends with the remark that our world will not last forever (6.607: *et fiat mundi confusa ruina*) and mentions the fear that the ground beneath us may collapse in an instant (6.605–6: *ne pedibus raptim tellus subtracta feratur / in barathrum*) — just as epilepsy strikes suddenly, shaking the human frame and causing the patient to fall without a warning. The fact that epilepsy is caused by an unseen substance which inflicts harm and then retreats back to its secret haunts provides a fitting parallel for the unseen winds which rage underground and then abate, allowing the earth to hold still again (6.570–74): "As it is, because in turns the winds abate and gather force, and rally as it were and come back and then are driven back in retreat, for this reason the earth more often threatens to fall than it does fall; for it inclines forward and then again springs back, and after tumbling forward recovers its proper place in equilibrium", ... *inclinatur enim retroque recellit / et recipit prolapsa suas in pondere sedes* (cf. 3.504–5: *tum quasi* **vaccillans** *primum consurgit et omnis / paulatim redit in sensus animamque receptat*). In the case of the earthquake, the fact that the trembling eventually stops is not enough to alleviate our anxiety that the world will come to an end. As Lucretius asks: since we see that the earth is shaken so violently, how can we possibly believe that the world is everlasting (6.601–7)? Likewise, the epileptic patient's recovery (3.504–5) creates only a momentary sense of comfort and relief; the fact remains that the soul, along with the body, is destined to die: for if the atoms of our mind and soul are subject to agonizing suffering even when they are protected by the human body, what reasons do we have to believe that they will continue to exist once they leave it (3.506–9)?

In discussing the analogy between microcosm and macrocosm in Lucretius, Pieter Shrijvers points out that:

> The comparisons established between grandiose cosmic phenomena and the minute scale of the human body have the psychological consequence that, thanks to these parallels, the miraculous and terrifying quality of the *paradoxa* is diminished. Lucretius' cosmology has the effect of belittling the importance of things usually experienced as awe-inspiring.[91]

But while analogy, as Schrijvers points out, can in fact be designed to make things that look strange and terrifying become familiar, the constant association between the diseased human body and the terrestrial wonders in Book 6 can also have the opposite effect, that of enhancing our sense of exposure to an incredible amount of pain and suffering as individuals. One of the reasons, for example, why Lucretius' account of the plague at the end of the poem looks so unsettling has precisely to do with the fact that the patients' bodies have become larger, as it were, and blend in with images that extend beyond the microcosm of the human body. Consider, for instance, the burning feeling in 6.1168–69 (*intima pars hominum vero flagrabat ad ossa, / flagrabat stomacho flamma* **ut fornacibus** *intus*) in connection with the flames which Aetna breathes out of its "vast furnaces" in 6.680–81: *inritata repente / flamma foras* **vastis** *Aetnae* **fornacibus** *efflet*.

Epilepsy plays a pivotal role in establishing this uncomfortable sense of affiliation between the human body and the external world. As has been observed, the figurative deployment of the sea and the winds in 3.487–509 provides the only instance in the poem in which we can speak of "the representation of the human being as a microcosm, in the strict sense".[92] This is subsequently complemented by epilepsy's dominant presence as a metaphor for the earth's convulsing body in Book 6. But as I have tried to argue, this metaphor is ultimately disconcerting: while it forms part of a strategy that aims to present phenomena such as earthquakes and volcanic eruptions in terms that look familiar to us, it also alienates us from our bodies by exposing them to an ongoing association with a crumbling world. The wonder that we feel about this world continues in essence to be a profoundly unsettling feeling: realizing that the earth shakes and trembles like an epileptic body may help us abandon our initial response of blind terror and fear — it can even allow us to enter a state of informed admiration about how things work in nature; but the more we think of the connection, the more estranged we become from our bodies, seeing how they can relate to the rest of the world

---

91 Schrijvers 2007, 276.
92 Schrijvers 2007, 271.

through — what Lucretius himself calls — an "immeasurable" amount of disease and suffering (6.664: *vis immensi morbi*).

3.4 Epilepsy and the Female in the Paradoxographical Tradition

The epileptic patient makes a final appearance in the poem in 6.791–93. Lucretius argues at this point that the earth contains many noxious substances which can harm us through smell, taste, touch, sight or hearing (6.769–80). To support this observation, the poet provides an unusually extensive list of random, unfortunate interactions between the human body and the external environment (6.781–817). The text runs as follows (6.769–805):

> Principio hoc dico, quod dixi saepe quoque ante,
> in terra cuiusque modi rerum esse figuras:
> multa, cibo quae sunt, vitalia, multaque, **morbos incutere et mortem** quae possint adcelerare.
> [...]
> arboribus primum certis gravis umbra tributa
> usque adeo, capitis faciant ut saepe dolores,
> siquis eas subter iacuit prostratus in herbis.
> est etiam magnis Heliconis montibus arbos
> floris odore hominem taetro consueta necare.
> scilicet haec ideo terris ex omnia surgunt,
> multa modis multis multarum semina rerum
> quod permixta gerit tellus discretaque tradit.
> nocturnumque recens extinctum lumen ubi acri
> nidore offendit nares, consopit ibidem,
> concidere et spumas qui **morbo mittere suevit**.
> castoreoque gravi mulier sopita recumbit,
> et manibus nitidum teneris opus effluit ei,
> tempore eo si odoratast quo menstrua solvit.
> multaque praeterea languentia membra per artus
> solvunt atque animam labefactant sedibus intus.
> denique si calidis etiam cunctere lavabris
> plenior et fueris, solio ferventis aquai
> quam facile in medio fit uti des saepe ruinas!
> carbonumque gravis vis atque odor insinuatur
> quam facile in cerebrum, nisi aquam praecepimus ante!
> at cum membra hominis percepit fervida febris,
> tum fit odor vini plagae mactabilis instar.

> In the first place, I say this, as I have said often before, that in the earth are elements of every kind of thing: many (which belong to food) being useful to life, and many such as can strike us with disease and make death come quickly … Firstly, certain trees have a shade so dangerous that they often cause headache, if one has lain beneath stretched out on the herbage. There is also in the great mountains of Helicon a tree which is accustomed to kill men by the vile stench of its flower. You may be sure that the reason why all these things rise from the soil is that the earth has many seeds of many things which she holds mixed up in many ways and separates apart before passing them on. And when a night-light newly extinguished meets the nostrils with a sharp smell, it stupefies on the spot one who is accustomed to fall and foam at the mouth through disease. The heavy scent of castor makes a woman fall back asleep, dropping the dainty work from her tender hands, if she has smelt it at the time of her monthly courses. And many other things besides loosen the languid limbs all through the frame and shake the spirit in its habitations within. Again, if you should ever tarry along in the hot baths after a full meal, how easily you often collapse in the middle of the bath of hot water! And how easily the strong heavy fumes of charcoal creep into the brain, unless we have taken water before! But when a burning fever is in possession of a man's limbs, then the odour of wine has the effect of a deadly blow.

Compared to the context in which we have first encountered it in Book 3, epilepsy is surrounded here by phenomena which look far more astonishing and harder to explain. Lucretius' answer is that the earth contains multiple elements, both beneficial and harmful, which can help maintain life or, inversely, cause sickness and death (6.769–72); yet one gets the impression that the point is subsequently overshadowed by what evolves into a quick and dense narrative pace which highlights how wondrous and at the same time inhospitable the world can be. The passage looks back at 2.398–477 where it has been stated that some things are agreeable to our senses while others are not. As Lucretius explains there, the sensible qualities of an object — its sweetness or bitterness, its pleasantness or foulness, and so on — are grounded on its physical structure and the shape of its constituting atoms: some are smooth to the touch, while others are rough and harsh (2.422–25).[93] However, while Lucr. 2.398–477 provides a balanced view of a world which contains both pleasant and unpleasant sensations (honey and wormwood, sweet melodies and the harsh grating of a strident saw, enjoyable scents and smelly corpses, nice colours and nasty sights), the list that we find in 6.781–817 is predominantly focused on the ugly side of things. The intrinsic link between wonder and dread — a dread which is ultimately arising from the awareness that as beings we are constantly exposed to sickness and death; 6.771–72: *morbos / incutere et mortem* — comes, once more, to the fore.

---

93 See Graver 1990, 103.

Lucretius draws his material in 6.781–817 mainly from Greek paradoxographical sources, collections of wondrous occurrences (θαύματα) which resist a rational explanation.[94] Wonder in paradoxography is often generated in contexts which present nature as an insidious force. Disease, accordingly, is given in these texts a prominent position: poisonous plants which make the body wither and bring death in an instant, spring water which leaps into people's eyes and causes them to suffer from dropsy and consumption, rivers which turn everything that falls in them into dead matter,[95] all these occurrences shape a vision of a world which can harm us in an astonishing variety of ways. At the same time, these marvels help to convey the feeling that behind shining appearances there always lurk unimaginable dangers. In fact, one way of understanding this peculiar world is by reading it as an inversion of an idealized pastoral setting.[96] Lucretius responds appropriately: on the one hand, the marvels listed in 6.781–817 bring out disease as a dominant theme: headache (6.784), fever (6.804–5), epilepsy (6.791–93), even menstruation (6.794–96) give to the text a distinctly medical tone. On the other hand, the reference to trees which cause headache to those who lie under their shadow and, more significantly, the tree in Helicon which kills people with its vile stench, reveal a concrete awareness on the poet's part that the world of paradox is construed as a *locus amoenus* that has been turned upside down and has lost its usual appeal.[97]

Epilepsy presents a particularly favorite theme for paradoxographers. In [Arist.] *Mir. Ausc.* 66 we read that "when the spotted lizard has sloughed its skin like a snake, it turns round and devours it". This is observed "by physicians because of the skin's value for epileptics". In [Arist.] *Mir. Ausc.* 77 we learn that when the seal is caught, it vomits a liquid substance which is "good for epileptics". An equally intriguing paradox is reported in [Arist.] *Mir. Ausc.* 18: "At Trapezus in Pontus honey from boxwood has a heavy scent; and they say that healthy

---

94 For ancient paradoxography, see Jacob 1983; Sassi 1993; Schepens and Delcroix 1996; Petsalis-Diomidis 2010, 151–67; Pajón-Leyra 2011; Geus/King 2018.
95 See [Arist.] *Mir. ausc.* 78, 95, 152.
96 For a similar inversion in Nicander's poetry, which propagates a deliberately "anti-bucolic" agenda, see Overduin 2014; for Nicander and paradoxography, see Overduin 2019.
97 The headache caused by the tree's shade in Lucr. 6.783–85 has distinctively anti-pastoral implications; cf. Theocr. 3.52: ἀλγέω τὰν κεφαλάν, τὶν δ' οὐ μέλει. **οὐκέτ' ἀείδω**, "my head aches, but you don't care. I'll sing no more". Lucretius' shade is echoed in Verg. *Ecl.* 10.75–76: *surgamus: **solet esse gravis cantantibus umbra**, / iuniperi gravis umbra; nocent et frugibus umbrae*; for these lines, see Hardie 2006, 277–78.

men go mad but that epileptics are cured by it immediately".⁹⁸ It is worth noting that in all of these stories nature is revealed to hold in store marvels which have curative properties. Indeed, although paradoxography, as I noted above, displays a deep fascination with sickness and decay,⁹⁹ what is principally at stake is how different elements in nature are webbed into a virtually endless network of sympathies and antipathies¹⁰⁰ which work in unpredictable and inexplicable ways: the same substance that proves vital for some can be fatal for others. Conceptually, this is not very different from Lucretius' antiprovidentialist worldview.¹⁰¹

Paradoxography is primarily concerned with laying before us a natural world full of θαύματα, without providing an answer as to how these phenomena occur: "the key to the genre", in Nita Krevans' words, "is the objective and rational presentation of an item which appears to break the laws of nature"; its "aim is not the satisfied 'aha!' of understanding but the round-eyed 'oh!' of wonder".¹⁰² Paradoxography operates at the opposite side of what Aristotle sees as true knowledge. The philosopher, according to *Metaph.* 983a12–21,¹⁰³ begins by wondering why certain perplexing things are as they are; when their causes have

---

98 For the translations of the ps.-Aristotelian Περὶ θαυμασίων ἀκουσμάτων I follow the Loeb edition of Hett 1936.
99 See e.g. [Arist.] *Mir. ausc.* 78: Λέγεται δὲ περὶ τὴν Ἰταλίαν ἐν τῷ Κιρκαίῳ ὄρει φάρμακόν τι φύεσθαι θανάσιμον, ὃ τοιαύτην ἔχει τὴν δύναμιν ὥστε, ἂν προσρανθῇ τινί, παραχρῆμα πίπτειν ποιεῖ, καὶ τὰς τρίχας τὰς ἐν τῷ σώματι ἀπομαδᾶν, καὶ τὸ σύνολον τοῦ σώματος διαρρεῖν τὰ μέλη, ὥστε τὴν ἐπιφάνειαν τοῦ σώματος εἶναι τῶν ἀπολλυμένων ἐλεεινήν, "it is said that in Italy near the mountain Circe a fatal drug grows, which has this property, that when it is sprinkled on anyone, it makes him fall immediately and causes his hair to fall out; all the limbs of his body grow weak, so that the appearance of the body of those who are dying is pitiful".
100 A now lost treatise, entitled 'On Sympathies and Antipathies', is attributed to Bolus of Mendes (late 3rd / first half of the 2nd cent. BCE), a shadowy figure working at the crossroads of natural philosophy, paradoxography and learned magic; see Gaillard-Seux 2009, with Holmes 2017, 248. Some of Lucretius' passages bear traces of this tradition, for instance, 4.710–21 which tells of how the cock makes the lion flee in panic while it leaves humans unaffected. Schrijvers 1999, 129 argues that this example of sympathy and antipathy was first anthologized by Bolus.
101 See Schiesaro 2006, 432 with reference to Lucr. 6.788–90 (on the multiple elements which earth holds in store): "The concept fits neatly within Lucretius' antiprovidentialist outlook… Some trees are good, some can be dangerous; the same element can produce positive or negative effects on human beings, since no element of the natural world was created for us (or, for that matter, against us)".
102 Krevans 2005, 91.
103 As Aristotle has explained a few lines above, we begin to wonder about "unusual" (*atopa*) things which lie close at hand, before we gradually move to matters of greater significance (*Metaph.* 982b13–15): ἐξ ἀρχῆς μὲν τὰ πρόχειρα τῶν ἀτόπων θαυμάσαντες, εἶτα κατὰ μικρὸν οὕτω προϊόντες καὶ περὶ τῶν μειζόνων διαπορήσαντες, see Warren 2014, 71. It could be said that what

been properly investigated and theoretical knowledge has been attained, wonder becomes effectively erased. By way of a reversal, paradoxography presents us, in a matter-of-fact tone, with sensational material whose main aim is to astonish and leave us bewildered and confused; even if we assume that θαῦμα in that case functions implicitly as an impulse to further mental inquiry, the latter remains a process which the text declines to actualize, creating instead a sense of suspense that has no obvious closure.[104]

Lucretius has been shown to engage critically with the paradoxographical tradition,[105] especially in the latter part of Book 6, where the narrative focuses on exotic marvels of foreign lands: the Nile, the magnet and the peculiarities of springs and wells.[106] As Monica Gale observes, the poet "takes up this tradition in order to emphasize the all-embracing power of *ratio*: however extreme, however peculiar such phenomena may seem, they can all be accounted for by the movements of atoms and atomic compounds in space".[107] The same could be said to apply to the list of wondrous phenomena in 6.769–817: strange as they might seem, they can all be explained as the result of exhalations of noxious atoms released from the earth.[108]

---

is dismissed by Aristotle in this passage as a trivial kind of oddity (useful only to the extent that it subsequently makes us wonder about more important things), constitutes the prime material of paradoxography–a genre which lingers on wondrous trivialities without aiming at any kind of resolution. This is the kind of wonder that constitutes an impediment to knowledge. See Rubenstein 2008, 202: properly experienced, "wonder is self-destructive" and should act only as a provocation for the knowledge of increasingly complex ideas".
104 Munson 2001, 134.
105 This critical engagement is hinted already in 1.726–30 (the lines praising Empedocles): *quae cum magna modis multis **miranda** videtur / gentibus humanis regio visendaque fertur, / rebus opima bonis, multa munita virum vi, / nil tamen hoc habuisse viro praeclarius in se / nec sanctum magis et **mirum** carumque videtur*, "which mighty region [i.e. Sicily], while it seems wonderful in many ways to the nations of mankind and is famed as a place to see, fat with good things, fortified with mighty store of men, yet it seems to have contained in it nothing more illustrious than this man, nor more sacred and wonderful and dear". Sicily was traditionally treated by paradoxographers as the land of wonders par excellence. Lucretius is certainly hinting at the tradition, proposing instead Empedocles — an advocate of philosophy and reason — as the island's real wonder.
106 For correspondences between Lucretius' narrative and specific paradoxographical *topoi*, see Gale 2000, 200–201 and Bakker 2016, ch.3.
107 Gale 2000, 200.
108 We should note, however, that in contrast with other wondrous phenomena in Book 6, which are exhaustively accounted for by the poet, sometimes through the use of multiple explanations (Hardie 2009, 231–63; Hankinson 2013), the list of marvellous occurrences in 6.769–817 is accompanied only by a brief explanatory comment (all of them result from noxious substances

And yet, I would like to conclude with the suggestion that the image of the epileptic who is stupefied by the sharp smell of the extinguished lamp (6.791–93) is something more than simply yet another wonder in a long list of strange occurrences which can be explained rationally. By virtue of its significant association with the menstruating woman who falls asleep with the scent of castor oil, epilepsy emerges from this passage as a strange condition that activates the same sense of persisting paradox with that generated by the unsettling presence of the female body throughout the poem.

A link between menstruation and epilepsy can already be traced back to Hippocratic gynecology, and has a long history thereafter.[109] What underlies many of the relevant sources is the emphasis placed on the bizarre nature of a woman's body and the capacity of menstrual blood to act in wondrous ways when found in close proximity with an epileptic patient. Pliny the Elder, for instance, notes that the epileptic can recover his senses when you get someone (preferably a woman) to rub his feet with menstrual blood.[110] This is in line with the long list of the marvellous properties of menstrual fluid provided by the author in *Nat.* 7.63–65 and 28.77–84: harmful as it may turn out to be in some cases (turning fresh wine sour, causing plants to wither, corroding bronze and iron with rust), in others it can prove extremely useful (when, for example, applied as a successful remedy for malaria and rabies). All this sounds way too fanciful by medical standards, but as I have argued elsewhere, the line between paradoxography and medicine in antiquity becomes extremely thin when it comes to the female body.[111] Fundamental medical concepts, such as the notion of the "wandering womb"[112] and the idea that female patients can be cured by drugs consisting of

---

contained in the earth, 6.771–72). This is not to say that Lucretius does not provide in this case a sufficient explanation, but that the discourse of wonder persists at this point somewhat more vividly and intensely compared to other occasions.

109 See e.g. the Hippocratic *De virginum morbis* (8.466–70 L.) which draws a link between the retention of menses and the occurrence of epileptic fits; for a discussion, see Flemming/Hanson 1998. Cf. Cels. 3.23.1.

110 See especially, Plin. *Nat.*28.83: "Sotira the midwife claims that to anoint the soles of the patient's feet with menstrual fluid is a most efficacious cure for tertian and quartan malaria; it is much more effective if it is done by the woman herself without the patient's knowledge. The same remedy also awakens an epileptic"; translation and discussion in Plant 2004, 122.

111 Kazantzidis 2018. See also the collections of essays edited in Kazantzidis 2019.

112 According to which the womb acts almost as if it were an entity of its own and travels throughout the body seeking for moisture, sometimes causing delirium and suffocation. For some illuminating discussions, see Manuli 1983, 147–92; Hanson 1990, esp. 319–21 and Dean-Jones 1994, 69–77.

animal excrement[113] betray an intimate association with non-scientific, folklore beliefs which tend to treat the female body as unstable, threatening and filthy. According to Brooke Holmes, "medical writers, while lively polemicists, in many cases provided new justification for conventional wisdom. The constructed and "fantastic" nature of what the medical writers believe about the body is particularly evident in their ideas about the female body, which dovetail neatly with long-held cultural stereotypes about female inferiority".[114] Menstruation is a case in point.[115] Aristotle, to cite a famous example, observes in a matter-of-fact tone in *Insomn*. 459b–460a that when a menstruating woman looks into a mirror, the surface of the mirror becomes stained with a bloody cloud (ἐν γὰρ τοῖς ἐνόπτροις τοῖς σφόδρα καθαροῖς, ὅταν τῶν καταμηνίων ταῖς γυναιξὶ γινομένων ἐμβλέψωσιν εἰς τὸ κάτοπτρον, γίνεται τὸ ἐπιπολῆς τοῦ ἐνόπτρου οἷον νεφέλη αἱματώδης).[116] Although he proceeds to explain the phenomenon scientifically, by relying on a conventional, extramission theory of vision,[117] this does not suffice to eliminate the underlying assumption that female dirt is uncontainable and infects the external environment.[118]

Lucretius, I submit, not only is extremely alert to this blurring of boundaries between medical science and paradox when it comes to female anatomy and pathology but, significantly, he allows considerable space for it in the poem. As a result, we could speak of a reproduction of cultural stereotypes which show that the poet, though sensitive to the dominant role of female figures in the narrative

---

113 According to von Staden 1992, the underlying notion of combating female filth with animal filth resonates with the widespread belief across Greek ritual, magic and religion that women, unlike men, are excessively susceptible to impurity and pollution. See also von Staden 2008.
114 Holmes 2010b, 10.
115 On Greek attitudes towards menstruation, see Dean-Jones 1994, 223–53.
116 For this passage (whose authenticity is disputed by some scholars), see Cole 2004, 108–11 and Bartsch 2006, 64. For the impurity of menstrual blood, cf. Arist. *HA* 581b1–2: a young girl's menstrual blood is οἷον νεόσφακτον, "like that of a freshly-slaughtered beast". For the female in Aristotle, see Connell 2016.
117 See Rakoczy 1996, 28–31.
118 Not incidentally, the menstruant's bloody gaze is reported only once again in ancient literature, in a passage by Pliny the Elder which speaks of the menstrual blood's polluting properties in a context that is clearly influenced by the principles of sympathetic magic (*Nat.* 7.64): "But it would be difficult to find anything more bizarre than a woman's menstrual flow. Proximity to it turns new wine sour; crops tainted with it are barren, grafts die, garden seedlings shrivel, fruit falls from the tree on which it is growing, mirrors are clouded by its very reflection' (translation in Beagon 2005, 72); cf. *Nat.* 28.82. For this passage, see Richlin 1997, 203–204; Bettini 1999, 113–15; Lowe 2015, 133–35.

(what Don Fowler calls the "feminine principal" in Lucretius),[119] is still not willing to distance himself completely from a long established tradition that sees the female as an odd and unstable creature.[120] This becomes especially evident in the course of Book 5, with the poet's theory of the early earth's multiple wombs from which humans and other creatures spring spontaneously (5.805–20)–an image that stands in clear contrast with Lucretius' down-to-earth and informed account of the mechanics of reproduction in Book 4. The idea — whose precedent has been traced by some back to Empedocles, while being attributed by others to Epicurus — is mocked for its absurdity in ancient sources, some of which are chronologically prior to Lucretius: Critolaus, a distinguished member of the Peripatetic school and a thinker of no little influence in Rome, calls it "dreadfully stupid", εὐήθεια δεινή (ap. Philo De Aet. Mund. 66–67).[121] As Gordon Campbell notes, the theory "is certainly the closest Lucretius comes to Empedocles' hallucinatory early world, where separated limbs and organs wander the earth".[122] What is more, the underlying assumption that a womb exists independently, feeding its offspring and taking care of it, recalls the peculiar concept of the wandering womb which Plato conceives as an organ with its own intelligence and appetites, an animal within an animal (Ti. 91 b–d). The female reproductive organ continues subsequently to dominate the horrifying landscape of Book 6. The sudden production of celestial wonders is consistently embedded in a language which evokes what is described by Hippocratic physicians as a rupturing of the womb during birth. Consider, for instance, how in the case of thunder the wind is trapped within the cloud and whirls round and round trying to find its way out; "when the wind's power and fierce impulse have weakened it, then the cloud is torn and explodes with a most horrifying crush" (6.128–29). The violence of the scene reminds us of a fetus described by doctors to "push with his hand and feet" until the membranes which contain it become ruptured, allowing it consequently to "advance rapidly", "forcing and widening the womb as it passes through".[123]

---

119 Fowler 1996.
120 See, especially, Nugent 1994. For a recent reading of Lucretius as an "anti-modern" poet, adhering to beliefs which contravene scientific progress in a variety of epistemic fields, see Farrell 2016.
121 For Critolaus, see Hahm 2007.
122 Campbell 2003, 75.
123 [Hipp.] De nat. pueri 30 (7.530–38 L.) with Hanson 1991, 88–89 and Bettini 2013, 66–67. As Demand 1994, 19 observes: "the Hippocratic physician, in keeping with the Greek view of women as passive, saw the pains and contractions of the woman as responses to the violent efforts of the infant".

As we move from the sky down to the earth, terrestrial wonders continue to have a distinctly female air. In fact, what makes them look so astonishing and terrifying results from a combined configuration of the earth *as a female and diseased entity at the same time*. Lucretius' reference to the epileptic in 6.791–93 comes at a point in the narrative where the poet has turned his attention to Avernian places,[124] regions in the earth which drive animal life away with their mephitic vapors and poisonous exhalations (a concrete parallel could be drawn here with the way in which a woman's menstrual fluids – a harmful substance that is impossible to contain within the limits of the human body – infects the animal and plant life that lies close to it). The earth's presentation in this section of the poem in terms of a moist and porous mass,[125] as Georgia Nugent has brilliantly illustrated, constitutes a clear reference to all those qualities which characterize physiologically the female body.[126] In Book 5 Lucretius explained that the earth is the "lowest" and "less pure" part of the world: once it started to form itself into a concrete mass, it began to squeeze out the finer and smaller particles out of which the sea, the stars, the sun and the moon were made; the soil on which we stand is "the mud of creation, so to speak, which flowed together by its weight and settled to the bottom like dregs" (5.495–97: *sic igitur terrae concreto corpore pondus / constitit, atque omnis mundi **quasi limus** in imum / confluxit gravis et subsedit funditus **ut faex**). This is not a very attractive image for our place of birth and habitation as humans; it effectively allows Lucretius to establish that disease is not only something that "invades our world from without" (6.955: *extrinsecus*) but, crucially, also a quality inhering in the earth itself. To quote Nugent: "The very terms of this opposition posit a sense in which evil occurrences, whether earthquakes or pestilence, are 'intrinsic' to earth; they are implicitly seen as 'natural' to her, rising up from the porous, moist, putrid mass which *is* her nature".

---

124 6.738ff.
125 Women's flesh, according to medical writers, has a distinctly loose and porous texture; this makes them liable to absorbing excessive quantities of moisture (subsequently evacuated through menstruation) and renders them less stable in comparison to the solid male bodies. See Holmes 2018, 75.
126 Nugent 1994. See especially p. 196: "Thus with disease ... distinction is drawn between dangers arising from what is 'extrinsic' (*extrinsecus*) and those inhering in the earth itself. The very terms of this opposition posit a sense in which evil occurrences, whether earthquakes or pestilence, are 'intrinsic' to earth; they are implicitly seen as 'natural' to her, rising up from the porous, moist, putrid mass which *is* her nature"; cf. Keith 2000, 39–40. Compare how in Hippocratic medicine most of the female patients' symptoms are ultimately linked to uterine problems; what allows women to procreate is also what makes them vulnerable to a number of violent pathologies from which men stay safe. See Holmes 2018, 76.

The analogy with menstruation could, once more, prove useful. The convulsive state of the ailing earth — be it in the case of Aetna or the earthquakes — is intrinsically linked to the image of a massive body which excretes on a regular basis a surplus of substances (mostly the winds) that have been collected inside it in excessive quantities. We could think of how menstruation is also about evacuation — a releasing of fluids, which comes about naturally but turns out to be extremely harmful when those fluids are trapped inside the body for longer than nature allows — and of how, once the process has been completed, the body regains its physical balance (till the same thing happens again).

Lucretius' feminization of the earth is not an innocent process. To the extent that this metaphor is operative, especially in Book 6, it reproduces the assumption that the female body is unstable and filthy.[127] This is precisely the point where we can see the dividing line between medical science and paradox collapsing. Let us take, for instance, the element of dirt: the notion that the earth is female emerges in paradoxographical sources primarily through its capacity to give birth to all sorts of wonders, but this is also fleshed out by means of the earth's presentation as an inhospitable habitat: foul and stinking places in the world — just like those appearing in the course of Lucretius' Book 6 — become assimilated to the bodies of women discussed, in their turn, as repulsive and threatening.[128] Farfetched as it may sound, the same emphasis on the inferiority of the female body is attested also in medical texts, sometimes in even more straightforward terms: when a physician, for example, advises that a sick woman should drink a potion made of an animal's faeces and urine, he is obviously relying on the homeopathic principle that a woman's body is impure and should thus be treated with the use of unclean substances. The female is in fact so elusive that when a medical scientist and a paradoxographer deal with it they end up speaking the same language.

---

127 For the filth of the female body in Roman authors, see von Staden 1991, who observes that the analogies employed in Celsus' *De medicina* to describe a woman's anatomy suggest "impurity and ... the aesthetically disagreeable" (p. 279): thus, the vagina is like the male anus; a woman's breasts or nipples resemble a nasal polyps; and the labia looks like an ulcer.

128 Compare, for instance, the following two accounts: the first comes from [Arist.] *Mir. Ausc.* 81: ... ἔστι δὲ καὶ λίμνη, ὡς ἔοικε, πλησίον τοῦ ποταμοῦ, ὕδωρ ἔχουσα θερμόν· **ὀσμὴ δ' ἀπ' αὐτῆς βαρεῖα καὶ χαλεπὴ ἀποπνεῖ**, καὶ οὔτε ζῷον οὐδὲν πίνει ἐξ αὐτῆς οὔτε ὄρνεον ὑπερίπταται, ἀλλὰ πίπτει καὶ ἀποθνῄσκει, "[In the Electrides islands] there is a lake apparently near the river, containing hot water. A heavy and unpleasant smell comes from it, and no animal ever drinks from it nor does bird fly over it without falling and dying". The second comes from Antigonus of Carystus, *Mir.* 118: τὰς δὲ Λημνίας **δυσόσμους γενέσθαι** Μηδείας ἀφικομένης μετ' Ἰάσονος καὶ φάρμακα ἐμβαλούσης εἰς τὴν νῆσον· κατὰ δή τινα χρόνον καὶ μάλιστα ἐν ταύταις ταῖς ἡμέραις, ἐν αἷς ἱστοροῦσιν τὴν Μήδειαν παραγενέσθαι, **δυσώδεις αὐτὰς οὕτως γίνεσθαι, ὥστε μηδένα προσιέναι**. For Antigonus' implicit reference to menstruation here, see Jackson 1990, 81.

This fusion between "scientific" and "non-scientific" modes of understanding the female body is also attested in Lucretius, and generates an intriguing contrast throughout Book 6: on the one hand, paradoxography — as has been amply demonstrated in scholarship — is throughout attacked: specific themes, such as the magnet and the Nile, which had long held readers in suspense and fascination, are systematically explained in atomic terms and are revealed to be nothing more than natural occurrences.[129] At the same time, the poet can be seen to operate on an overarching metaphor, that of the unstable and inferior female body,[130] whose origins can be commonly traced back to medical science and paradoxography — or, rather, back to a fluid cultural tradition where the blending between folklore and science runs so deep that it renders the distinction between the two meaningless. It is to this strange, imperfect and almost constitutionally ill world that epilepsy — providing yet another dominant metaphor throughout the poem's concluding book — comes to add its own share of oddity.

The poet's excursus in 6.738–839 on the earth's noxious exhalations — in the context of which the epileptic and the menstruant appear side by side — brings to mind an enigmatic scene earlier in the poem. As the lover enters his mistress' house, he is hit with an unbearable stench and flees in panic (4.1174–81):

> nempe eadem facit — et scimus facere — omnia turpi,
> et miseram taetris se suffit odoribus ipsa,
> quam famulae longe fugitant furtimque cachinnant.
> at lacrimans exclusus amator limina saepe
> floribus et sertis operit postisque superbos
> unguit amaracino et foribus miser oscula figit;
> quem si, iam ammissum, venientem **offenderit** aura
> una modo, causas abeundi quaerat honestas.

> The truth is she [i.e. the woman one is in love with] does all the same things as the ugly woman does, and we know it, fumigating herself, poor wretch, with rank odors while her maidservants give her a wide berth and giggle behind her back. But the lover shut out, weeping, often covers the threshold with flowers and wreaths, anoints the proud doorposts with oil of marjoram, presses his love-sick kisses upon the door; but if he is let in, once he gets but one whiff as he comes, he would seek some decent excuse for taking his leave.

---

129 See Gale 2000, 200.
130 In Nugent's words (1994, 194), "[w]hile it is fair to say that Lucretius and indeed atomism tends to reduce phenomena to primary physical components, yet only with the female is the result fetid air!"

Several scholars have traced here an allusion to menstruation,[131] observing that the same sense of anxiety and repulsion is conferred by the earth's female, oozing body in Book 6. The tension between male and female in this curious scene blends elements of attraction and desire with an unfailing awareness that the female poses a serious danger: this should explain the reference to the oil of the marjoram with which the woman's doorposts are anointed. Plutarch mentions how tortoises eat marjoram after swallowing snakes to protect themselves from the poison; the same herb, according to Pliny the Elder, is consumed by storks as a medicine which cures them from disease.[132] The implication should be obvious: just as animals in the wild pursue self-preservation by acting on an intuitive knowledge of the antidotes which nature holds in store, the afflicted lover in Lucretius — who already experiences desire as a disease — takes his own prophylactic measures in the knowledge that his appetite is putting his health at risk. But when the door eventually opens, the patient is suddenly overwhelmed by a disgusting odour: *venientem **offenderit** aura* (4.1180). The phrasing is similar to 6.791–92, which describes the way in which the sharp smell of the lamp hits the nostrils of the epileptic: *acri / nidore **offendit** nares*. The linguistic echo is not accidental: it derives in part from Lucretius' tendency to associate menstruation and epilepsy in contexts in which the human body is seen to behave in odd ways. Ultimately, this oddity is disclosed as being part of (our) nature but the way it is expounded creates also a profound sense of self-estrangement. In 6.821–23 Lucretius tells us of a bird which is trapped in a poisoned mass of air exhaled from the earth's porous body: *quo simul ac primum pennis delata sit ales, / impediatur ibi **caeco** correpta **veneno**, / ut **cadat** e regione loci, qua derigit aestus*, "so that, as soon as the bird has winged its way thither, it may be caught by the unseen poison and checked there, and so may fall straight down to the place where the exhalation directs it". The idea of an "unseen poison" (for some, a figure for menstrual blood here) which brings about a creature's fall (*cadat*) has already occurred in the case of epilepsy in 3.501 (*veneno*), where the patient hits the ground (*concidit*) without apprehending the cause. In both instances the threat of disease and death is intrinsic to a body which, familiar as it may seem, preserves the capacity to inflict harm at its own will.

---

131 See Nussbaum 1994, 178–81; Nugent 1994, 193–94 (who refers generally to "feminine bodily fluids"); Dawson 2008, 191–96. Brown 2017 believes that the reference is scatological. For menstrual blood and dirt in Roman culture, see Lennon 2010.
132 Plut. *Mor.* 918 B–E; Plin. *Nat.* 8.98.

3.5 Conclusion

In a programmatic passage in Book 7 of *Natural History*, Pliny the Elder makes the following statement about the human oddities found in nature (7.32):

> Haec atque talia ex hominum genere ludibria sibi, **nobis miracula ingeniosa fecit natura**. ex singulis quidem quae facit in dies ac prope horas, quis enumerare valeat? ad detegendam eius potentiam satis sit **inter prodigia** posuisse gentes.
>
> Nature has cleverly contrived these and similar species of the human race to amuse herself and to amaze us. As for the individual creations she produces every day, and almost every hour, who could possibly reckon them? Let it be a sufficient revelation of her power to have placed entire races among her miracles.[133]

Nature's wondrous aspects, according to Pliny, are often impenetrable.[134] The idea that bizarre things have been created by it as some kind of "private joke" establishes a clear hierarchy between a superior, knowing force and the humans' limited capacity to grasp the world for what it really is.[135] As humans we are meant to be observing and sensitive to marvels, but this by no means entails that we are also expected to understand the reasoning behind them. In fact, as Pliny himself tells us, his purpose is not to probe too deeply into causes and that explanations do not exist for everything.[136] Sometimes it is up to the reader to take the text as a starting point and seek for the causes himself: "all matters contain some deeply hidden mysteries which each person must use his own intelligence to penetrate".[137] The idea that there are mysteries in the world which defy a solid scientific explanation could be appropriately placed in a Stoic context: the marvellous,

---

[133] Translation in Beagon 2005, 65–66. Cf. Plin. *Nat.* 11.6: *nam mihi contuenti semper suasit rerum natura nihil incredibile existimare de ea*, "the more I observe Nature, the less prone I am to consider any statement about her to be impossible" (translation in Healy 1999, 64).

[134] See Murphy 2004, 90 on Plin. *Nat.* 7.32: "This is a conclusion that concludes nothing: it makes no inferences, and forms no general principles. By cataloguing only the most bizarre shapes in which the human race appears, and then invoking the marvellous (*miracula*) and the monstrous (*prodigia*) to explain these strange and divergent instances, the *Natural History* in fact makes analysis impossible. The emphasis on the bizarre seems to defy attempts at further explanation".

[135] Compare Pliny's use of *ludibrium* with Pl. *Leg.* 644d8–9: for all we know, we humans could have been created as the gods' παίγνιον. See Annas 2017, 130.

[136] See Conte 1994, 102: Pliny's primary aim is to astonish the reader. For *mirabilia* in Pliny's work, see Healy 1999, 63–70; Carey 2003, 84–101; Beagon 2011; Naas 2011.

[137] Plin. *Nat.* 17.29; translation and discussion in Beagon 2011, 85. See also Plin. *Nat.*2.101: some causes are too deeply hidden in nature.

even when it remains inexplicable, can always be transferred to a superior power whose designing of things is not necessarily comprehensible in its entirety.[138]

Nothing could be further from Lucretius' worldview. Unlike Pliny, our poet is strongly dedicated to the principle that there is nothing that philosophy cannot explain, however strange and perplexing it might look at first sight. And yet, as I have tried to show in this chapter, there are cases in the poem where the marvellous persists, in a symbiotic relationship with Lucretius' reductive rhetoric according to which everything comes down to atoms and the void. Recent scholarship has stressed that the best way to understand the persisting marvellous in the *DRN* is by interpreting it as an informed admiration and appreciation of the beauty inhering in the world, a beauty which is grounded on (and can only be revealed to those with) a firm understanding of atomic principles. But Lucretius is not altogether blind to the puzzles posed by nature, some of which continue to fascinate and confuse us even when a rational account has been provided. Epilepsy presents such a contested site of interpretation. While being originally introduced in 3.487–509 as yet another natural occurrence to be explained by means of atomic principles, the disease gives the opportunity to the poet to delve a bit further into its extraordinary qualities, primarily through a figurative language that adds extra layers of meaning to the text: the simile of the striking thunderbolt and the metaphor of the snake in 3.488 and 3.501–2, fit somewhat uneasily with the poet's attempt to defuse the mystifying qualities of the disease. Accordingly, in Book 6 the dominant analogy between an epileptic fit and the earth's convulsing body produces horrifying and wondrous spectacles at the same time. That the shaking earth is specifically conceptualized as a woman's body only helps to blend epilepsy with another paradox, that of the female's innately bizarre nature, which Lucretius not only refrains from dismissing explicitly but reproduces eagerly at various points in the poem.

---

138 For the Stoic connotations of Plin. *Nat.* 7.32, see Parker 2008, 96.

4 From Callimachean Aesthetics to the Sublime. The Plague in Book 6

> Perhaps in the world's destruction it would be possible at last to see how it was made. Oceans, mountains. The ponderous counterspectacle of things ceasing to be. The sweeping waste, hydroptic and coldly secular. The silence.
>
> Cormac McCarthy, *The Road*

As we have seen in the previous chapter, the dialogue that is developed between disease and the discourse of wonder in the *DRN* is an intricate one. My emphasis has been on the ways in which *morbus* continues on occasions to puzzle and astonish the readers either by means of being presented in a metaphorical language which has an alienating effect or by serving itself as a metaphor for a crumbling world that inspires awe and admiration but is also profoundly unsettling at the same time. In the fourth and final chapter, I expand on the connection between *morbus* and *mirum* by focusing my attention on the sublime potential of disease and its use as a theme which is employed by the poet in order to produce magnificent spectacles of destruction that equal in beauty and intensity images of birth and creation in the poem. Considerable attention has been drawn in recent years to the topic of the sublime in Lucretius, especially with regard to the celestial and earthly marvels in Book 6, but no due emphasis has been placed on the plague in this context. In this chapter I argue that instead of simply trying to decipher the exact meaning and function of the poem's final scene in philosophical terms, we should also take a moment to look at it as a piece of poetry and appreciate its powerful literary qualities. The plague, as I will attempt to illustrate, revolves principally around images of filth, excess and impurity, which bring out Lucretius' uncomfortable relationship with Callimachus throughout the *DRN*. At the same time, it is precisely out of the messy and disordered world of disease that the poet aspires to create a spectacle that is appalling and exciting at the same time, horrifying and yet deeply fascinating. The feeling of dread that emerges as a response to the plague, I suggest, does not present itself as an exclusively negative emotion but forms part of a complicated aesthetic script which is ultimately designed to stir the poem's readers, for one last time, with the thrill of the sublime.

4.1 Lucretius and Callimachean Aesthetics

Lucretius' relationship to Callimachus has never been an easy subject to tackle. In the most recent systematic survey of Callimachean reception in Rome, Lucretius remains conspicuously absent.[1] Edward Kenney's 1970 article, entitled 'Doctus Lucretius', continues to be cited in scholarship as a turning-point, a discussion which helped classicists abandon the "excessively isolationist"[2] view of Lucretius' poetry and paved the way for more integrated readings of his work, which link it to the neoteric agenda that influenced his contemporaries. It would therefore be useful to make a start by revisiting some of Kenney's main points and consider what they have to tell us about Lucretius.

Kenney's argument is not without its problems. On the one hand, the author focuses, somewhat exclusively and abstractly, on the concept of *doctrina*, stating clearly that he is not interested in assigning Lucretius to a school or sect of poets. The reason for doing so is that we lack concrete evidence as to whether such a school existed in the first place, and if so in what form. To quote Kenney:

> So much has been written on the *novi poetae* and the 'neoterics' that we are in some danger of forgetting how slender is the actual evidence on these matters. Even supposing that such terms as οἱ νεώτεροι, 'the newer poets', and *cantores Euphorionis*, 'those who sing (or sing the praises of) Euphorion' conveyed some defined and special meaning to Cicero's contemporaries, are we really in a position to distinguish it with anything like precision? It is indeed not unlikely, if one's experience of modern polemic and modern party spirit is any guide, that those contemporaries would themselves have been hard put to it to define exactly what they meant by such terms except insofar as they expressed coterie animus and purely personal likes and dislikes.[3]

This is a remarkably strong point; it inevitably leaves us, however, with a rather vague understanding of the intellectual environment in which Lucretius should be placed. Kenney's attempt to establish that *doctrina* is an essential quality of Lucretius' poetry does not seem to implicate the existence of a larger underlying agenda; his discussion of individual passages from the *DRN* is meant to reveal the "refined" qualities of the poet's work but without always making it clear whether such refinement serves to maintain a sustained dialogue with Hellenistic

---

1 Hunter 2006 (apart from scattered references, e.g. in p. 8, 84, 113, 118 and 134–35).
2 Kenney 1970, 368.
3 Kenney 1970, 368. Cf. Crowther 1970 and Bramble 1974, 180–81. Contra: Lyne 1978. At any rate, the idea that the neoteric poets in Rome conceived of "modernity" in a spirit of total negation of archaic and old-fashioned models (e.g. Ennius) should not be exaggerated; see the discussion in Zetzel 1983.

aesthetics — a concept that remains ultimately as elusive as Lucretius' presumed engagement with it. On the other hand, Kenney's practice throughout is to point out parallels and sources that show Lucretius to have been thoroughly familiar with Hellenistic poetry, especially with Hellenistic epigram at the end of Book 4, the diatribe against love and sex.[4] Again, it is not made entirely clear whether these allusions should qualify as points of contact with the neoteric environment or whether they are used to signpost a break from it. Lucretius is said at first to be enforcing his message, namely that all love is meaningless and painful, by borrowing motifs from a class of erotic poetry which he deemed to be light and frivolous, "worthless" even, and to make fun of an audience which was "excessively familiar" with low-standard art of this type. At the same time, Kenney also claims that it is precisely the poet's self-implicating irony, his expressed distaste for a mode of writing which is heavily imitated and reproduced in the course of his argument that allows him to partake in the Hellenistic spirit. To quote him again: in his preference for the oblique and ironical allusion, "Lucretius may perhaps be seen as more Alexandrian than Catullus or, in the next generation, Horace".[5] Leaving aside the question why "irony" should be considered a specifically Hellenistic quality (and not a quality intrinsic to every literary text), it should be stressed that Kenney's discussion of Lucretius' allusions to erotic epigram is highly selective; it is narrowly focused on specific authors (e.g. Meleager, Asclepiades), and fails to take into account some memorable — and, for what matters here, trickier — passages, most notably Callimachus, *Ep.* 28. The image of the περίφοιτος ἐρώμενος (28.3) occurs in that case in a polemical context; it is something that Callimachus finds aesthetically inappropriate, since being shared by many comes in stark contrast with his idea of exclusivity — his belief that a work of real craftsmanship and art should be enjoyed by a select few and should remain, more or less, inaccessible to the rest.[6] What we witness at the end of Lucretius Book 4 is a striking reversal of that image: the only remedy to the mental and physical pain inflicted by love is — according to the poet — promiscuity, a "random roaming Venus" (4.1071: *volgivaga Venere*)[7] as he calls it: to avoid obsession

---

4 See, especially, Kenney 1970, 380–85. Cf. Brown 1987, 132–35, with Edmunds 2002.
5 Kenney 1970, 391.
6 As the first four lines of the epigram read: ἐχθαίρω τὸ ποίημα τὸ κυκλικόν, οὐδὲ κελεύθῳ / χαίρω, τίς πολλοὺς ὧδε καὶ ὧδε φέρει· / μισέω καὶ περίφοιτον ἐρώμενον, οὐδ' ἀπὸ κρήνης / πίνω· σικχαίνω πάντα τὰ δημόσια. For a recent discussion, see Acosta-Hughes/Stephens 2012, 96–97.
7 Lucretius could be responding here, in a critical way, to Pl. *Symp.* 181a–b: οὕτω δὴ καὶ τὸ ἐρᾶν καὶ ὁ Ἔρως οὐ πᾶς ἐστι καλὸς οὐδὲ ἄξιος ἐγκωμιάζεσθαι, ἀλλὰ ὁ καλῶς προτρέπων ἐρᾶν. ὁ μὲν οὖν τῆς **Πανδήμου** Ἀφροδίτης ὡς ἀληθῶς **πάνδημός** ἐστι καὶ ἐξεργάζεται ὅτι ἂν τύχῃ· καὶ οὗτός ἐστιν ὃν οἱ φαῦλοι τῶν ἀνθρώπων ἐρῶσιν· ἐρῶσι δὲ οἱ τοιοῦτοι πρῶτον μὲν οὐχ ἧττον γυναικῶν

with a single object of desire, one should strive to have sex with as many partners as possible. This is precisely what Callimachus claims to despise.

Whether Lucretius in Book 4 is deliberately opposed to Callimachus remains open to speculation.[8] The tension, as it stands, should however make us consider the possibility that the poet's philosophical agenda (in this particular instance, his hostility towards erotic infatuation and compulsive desire) may sometimes turn out to be an inhospitable environment to — what we have come to know and refer to as — Callimachean aesthetics.

A brief example will help to illustrate this point. In 3.11 Lucretius compares himself to honeybees feeding on Epicurus' "golden words" (3.9–13):

tu pater es, rerum inventor, tu patria nobis
suppeditas praecepta, tuisque ex, inclute, chartis,
floriferis ut apes in saltibus omnia libant,
omnia nos itidem **depascimur** aurea dicta,
aurea, perpetua semper dignissima vita.

You are our father, the discoverer of truths, you supply us with a father's precepts, from your pages, illustrious man, as bees in the flowery glades sip all the sweets, so we likewise feed on all your golden words, your words of gold, ever most worthy of life eternal.

ἢ παίδων, ἔπειτα ὧν καὶ ἐρῶσι τῶν σωμάτων μᾶλλον ἢ τῶν ψυχῶν, ἔπειτα ὡς ἂν δύνωνται ἀνοητοτάτων, πρὸς τὸ διαπράξασθαι μόνον βλέποντες, "love is not in himself noble and worthy of praise; that depends on whether the sentiments he produces in us are themselves noble. Now the Common Aphrodite's Love is himself truly common. As such, he strikes wherever he gets a chance. This, of course, is the love felt by the vulgar, who are attached to women no less than to boys, to the body more than to the soul, and to the least intelligent partners, since all they care about is completing the sexual act" (translation by Nehamas/Woodruff in Cooper 1997). In Plato's vein, Callimachus expresses his distaste for "public" love (see σικχαίνω πάντα τὰ δημόσια in the note above); unlike both of them, Lucretius sees in it an easy and practical way of achieving peace of mind.

8 Interestingly enough, in *Sat.* 1.2 Horace endorses the Lucretian model of care-free sex while dismissing at the same time the discriminating elitism of Callimachus. In lines 105–8 Horace paraphrases Call. *Ep.* 31 in which the Hellenistic poet praises the thrill of chasing the object of desire: *leporem venator ut alta / in nive sectetur, positum sic tangere nolit, / cantat et adponit 'meus est amor huic similis; nam / transvolat in medio posita et fugientia captat'*, "the huntsman pursues the hare mid the deep snow, but declines to touch it when it is available; so he sings and adds: 'my love is like this, for it passes over what is served to all and chases flying game'" (translation in Fairclough 1942, 27; modified). Horace then goes on to criticize Callimachus' "silly lines" (1.2.109: *versiculis*), stating that they are not enough to ease one's pain when afflicted by the sorrows of love (1.2.109–10). What we should do instead is enjoy the advantages of the Lucretian *parabilis Venus* (1.2.119). See Gowers 2012, 112–13, with Harrison 2007, 94–95. It might be argued that Horace's combined allusion to Lucretius and Callimachus at this point brings out precisely the kind of tension between the two that is already present in *DRN* 4.

The image is reminiscent of the frequent occurrence of honey and bees in Hellenistic poetry.[9] In Call. *Aetia* fr.1.9–12 Harder Mimnermus is called "sweet", γλυκύς, in a context which clearly associates poetic elegance with composition executed on a small-scale (1.9: ὀλιγόστιχος); similarly, in Call. *Ep.* 27, Aratus' "slender lines" (27.3–4: λεπταί ῥήσιες), are praised as the "sweetest of verses", τὸ μελιχρότατον τῶν ἐπέων (27.2–3) — the allusion here seems to go back to Hesiod, mentioned in the epigram's opening line, for whom it is said that when he was an infant, a swarm of bees came to settle in his mouth, either because his breath was already too sweet or because his singing would one day be so.[10] Sweetness, in all these cases, is conceived as the prime objective; it is the ultimate goal of a poetry that has been painstakingly distilled and is now presented to the readers in its purest form. When it comes to Lucretius, however, honey is not the final product, but simply the means of achieving something else. It is virtually impossible to read 3.11 without recalling the famous passage in 1.936–50,[11] where Lucretius states explicitly that his purpose is "to spread with the honey of the Muses" (1.947: *quasi musaeo dulci contingere melle*) a bitter doctrine, just as a doctor spreads the lips of a cup with honey to trick children into drinking wormwood. Sweetness in Lucretius transpires to be a disguise, and what essentially lies behind it is an "unpleasant medicine" (1.936: *absinthia taetra*); even if the metaphor of honeybees brings to mind earlier poetic uses, the text's philosophical agenda ultimately imposes its own priorities and radically transforms the meaning of the motif. Robert Brown is right, in this respect, to observe that "ideas which Callimachus used to clarify his aesthetic standards are appropriated by Lucretius for the different role of alluring his audience".[12] In this context, it should be added that while bees stand as a symbol of selectiveness and variety in poetry (e.g. in Call. *In Apollinem* 110),[13] Lucretius' use of the image is linked to an extreme and exclusive diet: the poet in 3.12 "devours", *depascimur*, and becomes stuffed with "everything", *omnia*, that is found in Epicurus' writings, in a spirit that someone like Callimachus would have undoubtedly denounced as undiscerning and, in effect, tasteless. Lucretius makes use of *depascor* only once in the poem, but the verb's occurrence elsewhere in Latin poetry suffices to establish that it is consistently applied to big animals (bulls in Verg. *G.* 4.539; the giant serpents which devour

---

9 E.g. in Call. *In Apollinem* 110–12 and Theoc. *Id.* 1.146–51. Cf. *SH* 1001, with Nünlist 1998, 62, 208 and 302.
10 See T26 in Most 2006, 177. Cf. Worman 2015, 83–85.
11 For the intratextual link between the two passages, see Volk 2002, 112.
12 Brown 2007, 339.
13 See Huxley 1971, with Morgan 1998, 262–64.

Laocoon and his children in *Aen.* 2.215) and carries with it associations of avid, insatiable feasting.¹⁴ The contrast with *libant* ("sip", "nibble", "sample") in 3.11 is thus inevitable. Kenney acknowledges that there might be a certain "incongruity" between the two words,¹⁵ while David Sedley observes that *depascimur* (unlike the sampling process indicated by *libant*) is meant to underline Lucretius' "singular devotion" and his "exclusive dependence" on Epicurus.¹⁶ Lucretius' aim — one would have thought — was to create an intensifying effect, but this seems to be done in a way which disrupts the analogy between the two lines, transforming a refined type of diet (*libant*) into what is essentially a poetics of avid consumption (*depascimur*).

Lucretius' commitment to Epicurus, as Sedley observes, "is so all-consuming as to obviate any interest in later philosophical or scientific developments":¹⁷

> Even if it were in the future to turn out, in one or two isolated cases, that Lucretius was aware of some philosophical or scientific development which demonstrably postdated Epicurus that would not alter the general picture. Some such snippet of information could have reached him through his non-philosophical reading, through a chance encounter, or even through marginal scholia in the copy of Epicurus which he consulted. It would still be his lack of such contact, and his preference for the unmediated arguments of Epicurus, that predominantly characterized the content of his poem.¹⁸

Sedley's (overdrawn) picture of Lucretius' philosophical conservatism is subsequently balanced by the author's following remark: "in every other respect [Lucretius] shows himself an acute observer of his own society, sensitive and subtle in argument and thoroughly versed in the literary traditions of both Italy and Greece, including Hellenistic as well as Greek poetry ... It is only in his hard-core scientific and philosophical beliefs that his fundamentalism shows itself".¹⁹ Indeed, Lucretius' multifaceted engagement with earlier and contemporary literary traditions²⁰ makes it quite implausible that he would have been in principle opposed to a "neoteric agenda", in its Callimachean or, more broadly, Hellenistic

---

14 Vergil uses it also in *G.* 3.458 (*quin etiam, ima dolor balantum lapsus ad ossa / cum furit atque artus depascitur arida febris*, 3.457–58) in his account of the diseases which affect the flock, a few lines before he begins the description of the Noric plague.
15 Kenney 2014, 76.
16 Sedley 1998, 68.
17 Sedley 1998, xvi.
18 Sedley 1998, 91.
19 Sedley 1998, 72.
20 For some illuminating discussions, see Fowler 2000, 138–55 and Sharrock 2013.

form. The question remains, however, whether there are certain, intrinsic qualities in the Roman poet's work that make him diverge from Callimachean aesthetics in a way which, though not necessarily intentional, ends up creating a rift between the two that is both meaningful and hard to ignore. Recent discussions of Lucretius and the sublime have revealed one such angle.[21]

In an article published in 2011, entitled "Against ΛΕΠΤΟΤΗΣ: Rethinking Hellenistic Aesthetics", James Porter has advanced a provocative reappraisal of the critical vocabulary used to discuss Hellenistic poetry. He claims that the presumed centrality of λεπτότης in the Hellenistic period — a notion according to which we tend to think of "refinement" as a quality that can only be conceived and executed on a small-scale — has to be contested, since attention to detail does not necessarily maintain "an aesthetic of the detail".[22] Starting with the observation that the Hellenistic poets reveal "an intense capacity to think through things", in the sense that they are particularly sensitive to the material dimensions of art, Porter illustrates how the "object-obsessed" quality of this period's poetry breeds a model of "aesthetic materialism"[23] in which "purity of form" is gradually substituted by what he calls a "sensuous engagement with art", a kind of aesthetic experience that is grounded in an object's material coordinates.[24] It is in the context of attending to "sensuous detail" where the interplay between magnitude and smallness becomes most evident: marveling at a picture engraved on a minute stone (e.g. Posidippus AB15 = 20 G-P) implies a logic of "contrastive scales";[25] details are not designed to be meaningful by themselves but only as long as they interact, conceptually as well as aesthetically, with larger magnitudes of perception. To quote Porter: "the grandeur is an effect of magnification.

---

21 A contrast between Callimachus and Lucretius on the grounds of what may be understood as an antithesis between a pedantic and a sublime mode of writing respectively can already be traced in the following remark by Clausen 1964, 183–84: "The poetry of Callimachus and others like him could be appreciated by only a very few readers as learned or nearly as learned as themselves. Theirs was a bibliothecal poetry, poetry about poetry, self-conscious and hermetic. It is easy enough to understand why these umbratile poets were drawn to the composition of didactic poetry. For in such poetry they had everywhere the chance to show off their erudition and to demonstrate by how much their manner excelled their matter. Hence their choice of inert or apparently intractable subjects to versify. Their aim was to shine, not to persuade; *and in their poetry breathed no Lucretian fire* (emphasis added)".
22 Porter 2011, 295.
23 The notion is exhaustively discussed in Porter 2010.
24 See, especially, pp. 271–74.
25 Pp. 293–94.

It occurs whenever one inspects the material of poetry from up close and that material suddenly fills, and overfills, one's field of vision".[26]

Porter's main example is Posidippus; he is particularly interested in showing how small material objects in his poetry are designed to evoke an expanding empire that contains in it all kinds of marvels.[27] Callimachus, on the other hand, is more or less absent. In fact, in his recent book on the concept of the sublime in antiquity, Porter mentions Callimachus a handful of times, calling him "squeamish", a poet unable to appreciate the sublimity potentially contained in aesthetic details.[28] Such criticism gives us a good reason to start thinking whether a great deal of the critical vocabulary we use to praise Callimachus is opposed to the very meaning and essence of the sublime. Consider, for instance, the notion of "excess" and the idea that the sublime generates by its nature *oversized* conceptual products.[29] As Marco Fantuzzi and Richard Hunter point out, Callimachus' poetry

---

26 Porter 2011, 291.
27 Cf. Bing 2005 and Thompson 2005.
28 Porter 2016, 146 n. 212. Callimachus' antipathy to tragedy in general and to Aeschylus in particular is read accordingly as yet another sign of the poet's anti-sublime feelings (Porter 2016, 333–34; cf. Sistakou 2016, 49–50). We should recall at this point that while Long. *Subl.* 33.4–5 mentions Apollonius of Rhodes and Theocritus, there is no reference to Callimachus. But even Apollonius and Theocritus in this passage do not escape criticism for being too perfectionist in their exercise of the craft: "I have myself cited a good many faults in Homer and the other greatest authors, and though these slips certainly offend my taste, yet I prefer to call them not wilful mistakes but careless oversights, let in casually almost and at random by the heedlessness of genius (ὅμως δὲ οὐχ ἁμαρτήματα μᾶλλον αὐτὰ ἑκούσια καλῶν ἢ παροράματα δι' ἀμέλειαν εἰκῆ που καὶ ὡς ἔτυχεν ὑπὸ μεγαλοφυΐας ἀνεπιστάτως παρενηνεγμένα). In spite, then, of these faults I still think that the greatest excellences, even if they are not sustained throughout at the same level, should always be voted the first place, if for nothing else, for the greatness of mind they reveal. Apollonius, for instance, is an impeccable (ἄπτωτος) poet in the *Argonautica*, and Theocritus — except in a few extraneous matters — is supremely successful (ἐπιτυχέστατος) in his pastorals. Yet would you not rather be Homer than Apollonius?" (translation in Fyfe / Russell 1995, 269). Russell 1989, 308 describes Longinus ch.33 as "a manifesto directed against what we may call the Callimachean ideal"; cf. Fuhrmann 1992, 199–202. Contra: Hunter 2011, 234: "Callimachus was... just too big a fish, in both the Greek and Roman critical traditions, for 'Longinus' to take on: his silent absence from the firing-line in *On the Sublime* 33 is in fact a most eloquent tribute to his reputation".
29 For a list of μεγ- words in Longinus' text, see Porter 2016, 180–81, mentioning, among others: μέγεθος ("magnitude / grandeur"), μέγας ("grand"), τὰ μεγάλα ("great things"), μεγαλοφυές ("great in nature"), μεγαλοφυΐα ("greatness of nature"), μεγαλοψυχία ("greatness or haughtiness of mind"), μεγαλοφροσύνη ("greatness / elevation in thought"), μεγαλοπρεπές ("magnificent"), μεγαληγορία ("loftiness of diction"), μεγαλορρήμων ("magniloquent"), μεγεθύνω ("making grand / sublime"). Nothing could be further from the famous saying attributed to Callimachus: μέγα βιβλίον μέγα κακόν (fr. 465 Pf.). An anonymous scholion on Call. *In Apollinem* 106 tells us that the

is characterized by a "remarkable lack of obvious verbal adornment"; it displays "a sense of control, of an elimination of excess" which is replaced "by a severe poetic discretion".³⁰ By contrast, the sublime is grounded on the "sense that control has been lost and that limits have been breached through an excess".³¹

What makes a writer sublime, according to Longinus, is his capacity to induce feelings of "ecstasy" to the audience, similar to the ones experienced by himself (*Subl.* 1.4: οὐ γὰρ εἰς πειθὼ τοὺς ἀκροωμένους ἀλλ' **εἰς ἔκστασιν** ἄγει τὰ ὑπερφυᾶ).³² So, for example, Demosthenes is said to utter words of incredible force "in a sudden moment of inspiration, as if possessed by the divine" (*Subl.* 16.2: ἀλλ' ἐπειδὴ καθάπερ ἐμπνευσθεὶς ἐξαίφνης ὑπὸ θεοῦ καὶ οἱονεὶ φοιβόληπτος γενόμενος); it is as though he had access to "heaven-sent gifts which it would be impious to call human" (*Subl.* 34.4: θεόπεμπτά τινα δωρήματα, οὐ γὰρ εἰπεῖν θεμιτὸν ἀνθρώπινα). Archilochus is like a rapid stream which sweeps away everything in its way, acting under the influence of outbursts of divine inspiration (*Subl.* 33.5: Ἀρχιλόχου πολλὰ καὶ ἀνοικονόμητα παρασύροντος, κἀκείνης τῆς ἐκβολῆς τοῦ δαιμονίου πνεύματος ἦν ὑπὸ νόμον τάξαι δύσκολον). Surely, this kind of language has very little to do with Callimachus' view that poetry achieves its purest and most elevated form through a somber-minded exercise of the craft; the idea of inspiration, though not entirely absent from his writings, is considerably toned down and gives place to the primacy of technical skill.³³

Recent scholarship on the sublime has drawn attention to Lucretius' central place in the history of the concept.³⁴ Though little credence can be given to it,

---

poet was actually forced to produce the *Hecale* as a response to those criticizing him that he was unable to write "a big poem": ἐγκαλεῖ διὰ τούτων τοὺς σκώπτοντας αὐτὸν μὴ δύνασθαι ποιῆσαι μέγα ποίημα, ὅθεν ἠναγκάσθη ποιῆσαι τὴν Ἑκάλην. The phrase μέγα ποίημα can carry multiple meanings: on the one hand, it could be referring to criteria of length; but it can also mean that Callimachus was accused — already by his contemporaries — of failing to reach grandeur in subject matter or style; see Gutzwiller 2012, 221–30.
30 Fantuzzi/Hunter 2004, 44.
31 Porter 2016, 173.
32 Cf. Halliwell 2011, 367: "The human soul itself — its capacity to reach beyond the material, beyond the present, and beyond its mundane ego — is the true locus of Longinian sublimity. The sublime is the greatness of the cosmos, and even of an infinity 'beyond the cosmos', internalized in the spaces of the mind. And that is the place where ecstasy and truth can meet".
33 According to Fantuzzi/Hunter 2004, 449, the style of poetry which Callimachus rejected "could certainly be associated with Dionysiac frenzy". Cf. Knox 1985, with Sens 2016, 232.
34 See, especially, Porter 2007; 2016, 38–41 and 445–57; Hardie 2009, 65–228; Most 2012. Cf. Segal 1990, 74–80; Ferri 1993, 122–25; Conte 1994, 1–34.

Jerome's testimony, according to which the *DRN* was composed "during the intervals of Lucretius' insanity",[35] is worthy of attention to the extent at least that it interacts with other sources in antiquity that tend to treat the poet as an exalted, ecstatic genius.[36] As Gerard Passannante has recently argued, the phrase *per intervalla insaniae* is deliberately ambiguous: it can either mean that the poem was written "in rare moments of lucidity between fits of madness" or, alternatively, that it was produced "during the fits of the poet's madness".[37] The task upon which Lucretius sets himself is inspired by the firm laws of physics: everything in nature can be explained through atoms and the void. This does not mean, however, that the reaction to the scientific insights offered by philosophy cannot have a destabilizing effect, giving rise to an intensely felt emotional and cognitive experience that does not always sit easily with the calm rationality preached elsewhere by the poet. The language of ecstasy makes its presence felt at various points in Lucretius' poem,[38] most significantly in the proem to Book 3. The poet's sublime flight of mind and the epiphany of atoms falling endlessly into the void create there a setting of mystic revelation. Lucretius' "divine delight and shuddering" (3.28–30) has been read by some as simply a rhetorical way of emphasizing the thrill of knowledge. But the appropriation of this kind of imagery, according to Duncan Kennedy, "is a game played for high stakes … Expressing his vision in the language of religion may serve to naturalize and domesticate it, but it also leaves open the possibility of a recuperation, the reappropriation of the text of the *DRN* for the very position it ostensibly claims to be opposing".[39]

Lucretius' universe is violent and unsettling: earthquakes, erupting volcanoes, thunderbolts and lighting, the endless void — all these elements create a vision of the world that approximates what has been called "a cosmic sublime".[40] As humans, Longinus notes, we are naturally drawn to magnitude; but a crucial aspect of the sublime pertains to the realization that magnitude is not always immediately evident: every single thing, despite its apparently finite nature, contains in it a "superfluity" (*Subl.* 35.3: τὸ περιττὸν ἐν πᾶσι) — it retains, in other

---

35 The full text, cited and discussed in detail by Holford–Strevens 2002, reads as follows: *Titus Lucretius poeta nascitur: qui postea amatorio poculo in furorem versus, cum aliquot libros per intervalla insaniae conscripsisset, quos postea Cicero emendavit, propria se manu interfecit anno aetatis XLIIII.* See also Hadzits 1935, 4–7; Butler 2011, 37–39; Butterfield 2018.
36 See e.g. Stat. *Silv.* 7.76: *docti furor arduus Lucreti.* Cf. Pers. *Sat.* 3.83–84, with Luck 1988.
37 Passannante 2012, 104–105.
38 See, especially, 1.922–25.
39 Kennedy 2007, 380.
40 See Porter 2007.

words, the capacity to become enlarged by means of the perceiving subject's sensitive imagination.[41] Lucretius is typically drawn to excess as this is reflected in seemingly small details. A tiny pool of water trapped between the stones on a paved street in 4.414–19 is a "marvel" to look at (419: *mirande*) not in and of itself but because, by virtue of the perceptual illusion it creates, it reflects the high gaping mouth of the heaven above (417: *caeli patet altus hiatus*) and makes us think of the celestial bodies in the sky as if they were lying deep beneath the earth. What is proposed by Callimachus as an "aesthetics of purity", contained in distilled dew drops[42] and small fountains, turns in Lucretius to an "aesthetics of vastness": the reason why we are drawn to tiny puddles of water is ultimately their function as reflections of the boundless universe.

Lucretius' vision of the world is grounded on a constant interplay between the miscroscopic level of atoms and their function as the material substrate for impressively large constructions. Size is forever relative; even that which looks vast offers only a glimpse of an even greater vastness that lies beyond the grasp of ordinary human experience. As we are told in 6.608–15, we should not wonder that the sea stays the same and never increases its measure, for all that is poured into it, through great rivers, the wandering showers and the flying tempests, is no more than a single drop when we compare it to the vast ocean (6.613–14: *tamen ad maris omnia summam / guttai vix instar erunt unius adaugmen*) — in the same way that the ocean and the world we inhabit are almost nothing compared to the universal sum of things (6.678–79: *cum tamen omnia cum caelo terraque marique / nil sint ad summam summai totius omnem*).

This is hardly a world with which Callimachus would have fit easily. To him, anything that exceeds a small scale runs the risk of rendering itself impure, just like Euphrates, at the end of the *Hymn to Apollo*, which carries with it all kind of filth (108–9: Ἀσσυρίου ποταμοῖο μέγας ῥόος, ἀλλὰ τὰ πολλὰ / **λύματα** γῆς καὶ πολλὸν ἐφ' ὕδατι **συρφετὸν** ἕλκει). The Nile, by contrast, presents for Lucretius a source of deep fascination precisely because of its unique capacity to regularly transgress its limits and inundate the plains around it — to mingle water with earth (6.712–13: *Nilus in aestatem crescit campisque redundat / unicus in terris, Aegypti totius amnis*). Although in 6.712–37 the poet sets out to explain rationally how this happens by adducing a series of alternative explanations, the language that is used throughout the section ultimately intensifies the sublime effect of this wonder of nature. The inundation happens "at the height of the hot season" (6.714: *medium per saepe calorem*); the winds that blow against the current "are

---

41 See Porter 2016, 176.
42 See, Call. *Aetia* 1.33–34 Harder.

driven from the cold stars of the pole" (6.720: *gelidis ab stellis axis aguntur*), causing the river "to rise deep" (6.717–18: *et, undas / cogentes sursus, replent*). A few lines below, and in the context of a different explanation, we read of how "a vast mass of sand" (6.724: *magnus congestus harenae*) swept inshore by the sea accumulates at the river's mouths and obstructs its waves. Another possibility is that the river "swells deep among the lofty Ethiopian mountains" (6.735–36: *forsitan Aethiopum penitus de montibus altis / crescat*) when the sun's rays dissolve the snow and make it depart to the plains. Nothing could lie closer to a muddying of waters with earth than the image represented by the Nile. And yet, as Longinus — another author with a soft spot for cataclysmic outpourings and big rivers[43] — observes, this is precisely the point where the sublime effect is generated: the greatest intellects, just like massive currents of water, are also the "most impure" (αἱ ὑπερμεγέθεις φύσεις ἥκιστα καθαραί); to reach for the sublime requires that one has left behind any obsession with details and, in a spirit of all-encompassing grandeur, allows for minor imperfections in his work.[44]

The tension between Lucretius and Callimachus, as I have been suggesting so far, does not always have to be intentional; rather, the spectacle of the world revealed through Epicurean philosophy often turns out to be aesthetically incongruous, by its very nature, with Callimachean minimalism. That said, there are instances in which Lucretius appears to be targeting the Hellenistic poet in a more focused and intricate way. These instances usually involve allusions to specific Callimachean passages and ideas, which on a closer reading reveal an attitude of subversion rather than imitation. In 4.909–11 Lucretius promises to explain sleep *suavidicis potius quam multis versibus*, "in sweet-speaking rather than many verses" and compares the "small song", *parvus canor*, of swans to the dis-

---

43 *Subl.* 35.4: ἔνθεν φυσικῶς πως ἀγόμενοι μὰ Δί' **οὐ τὰ μικρὰ ῥεῖθρα θαυμάζομεν, εἰ καὶ διαυγῆ** καὶ χρήσιμα, ἀλλὰ **τὸν Νεῖλον** καὶ Ἴστρον ἢ Ῥῆνον, πολὺ δ' ἔτι μᾶλλον τὸν Ὠκεανόν.
44 The passage, which is then followed by Longinus' criticism of Apollonius Rhodius and Theocritus — two poets who pay too much attention to detail — reads as follows (*Subl.* 33.2): ἐγὼ δ' οἶδα μέν ὡς αἱ ὑπερμεγέθεις φύσεις ἥκιστα καθαραί· τὸ γὰρ ἐν παντὶ ἀκριβὲς κίνδυνος μικρότητος, ἐν δὲ τοῖς μεγέθεσιν, ὥσπερ ἐν τοῖς ἄγαν πλούτοις, εἶναί τι χρὴ καὶ παρολιγωρούμενον· μήποτε δὲ τοῦτο καὶ ἀναγκαῖον ᾖ, τὸ τὰς μὲν ταπεινὰς καὶ μέσας φύσεις διὰ τὸ μηδαμῇ παρακινδυνεύειν μηδὲ ἐφίεσθαι τῶν ἄκρων ἀναμαρτήτους ὡς ἐπὶ τὸ πολὺ καὶ ἀσφαλεστέρας διαμένειν, τὰ δὲ μεγάλα ἐπισφαλῆ δι' αὐτὸ γίνεσθαι τὸ μέγεθος, "now I am well aware that the greatest natures are least immaculate. Perfect precision runs the risk of triviality in great writing as in great wealth there must be something overlooked. Perhaps it is inevitable that humble, mediocre natures, because they never run risks and never aim at the heights, should remain to a large extent safe from error, while in great natures their very greatness spells danger" (translation in Fyfe/Russell 1995, 267–69).

tasteful *clamor* of cranes. The image, as has been aptly pointed out in scholarship,[45] ultimately derives from Callimachus' rejection of the "one continuous song in many thousand verses" (ἓν ἄεισμα διηνεκές ... ἐν πολλαῖς ... χιλιάσιν) in *Aetia* fr. 1.3–4 Harder. What seems to have been ignored, though, in discussions of this passage is the critical, even suspicious, eye with which we readers are expected to understand Lucretius' promise. For in another programmatic statement in Book 1, this one also involving the element of sweetness, the poet has said something significantly different (1.410–17): "if you shrink even a little from the daunting task that lies ahead of you", he says to Memmius, "I give a solemn pledge: to use my mellow tongue and, from my mind's rich store, pour forth copious drafts of wisdom, welling from deep springs" (1.412–13: *usque adeo largos haustus e frontibus magnis / lingua meo suavis diti de pectore fundet*). There is admittedly little relevance here between the trickling Callimachean spring (see e.g. *In Apollinem* 111–12) and the robust-sounding *fontes* of Lucretius.[46] That the contrast is not incidental is further supported by what we read in the immediately following lines. So many things has Lucretius in mind to tell Memmius that he fears old age and death might overcome them both before he has the time to finish all he has to say (1.414–17: *ut verear ne tarda prius per membra senectus / serpat et in nobis vitai claustra resolvat, / quam tibi de quavis una re **versibus** omnis / argumentorum sit **copia** missa per auris*). Lucretius' capacity to speak in "sweet verses" is revealed to be combined with a poem that has potentially no ending — if needed, it can carry on *ad infinitum*, just like the universe it sets out to describe.[47]

The tension with Callimachus is primarily played out at the level of size. Another good example of this tendency is provided by Lucretius' praise of Empedocles in 1.714–41. The passage pays homage to the philosopher's intellectual achievements through a description of his native island's natural wonders, linking the beauty and sublimity of Sicily with Empedocles' "divine mind". In 1.718–19, we read of Sicily's seaboard:

---

[45] See e.g. Newman 1967, 96; Minyard 1978, 79.
[46] See Ferrero 1949, 22.
[47] As Smith 2001, 14 n. 30 observes: "Engagingly, Lucretius makes gentle fun of his missionary zeal, though one should not doubt that he is completely serious in his declared readiness to do whatever is necessary in his attempt to convert Memmius to Epicureanism ... Although this passage is Lucretius' own, he may have taken his cue from Epicurus, who at the end of *On Nature* 28 makes fun of his garrulity; and so may Diogenes of Oinoanda, author of the massive Epicurean inscription ... who humorously mentions the vast number of letters he has converted into stone for the information and salvation of his readers (fr. 116)".

quam fluitans circum **magnis anfractibus** aequor
Ionium glaucis aspargit virus ab undis.

Around which the Ionian deep, flowing with its vast windings, sprinkles the salt brine from its green waves.

With these lines compare Callimachus' praise of Apollo's birthplace in *Hymn* 4.13–14:

ὁ δ' ἀμφί ἑ πουλύς ἑλίσσων
Ἰκαρίου πολλὴν ἀπομάσσεται ὕδατος ἄχνην.

The sea, strongly surging around her [i.e. Delos], wipes off much foam from the Icarian water.[48]

Despite the obvious similarities between the two passages (*quam fluitans circum* – ἀμφί ἑ πουλύς ἑλίσσων, *aequor Ionium* – Ἰκαρίου ὕδατος, *aspargit virus* – ἀπομάσσεται ἄχνην), Lucretius has revised the original both in detail and, more importantly, in tone.[49] Robert Brown is right to observe that the image of Sicily "is rather more elevated than in Callimachus, thanks largely to the resounding periphrasis"[50] in 1.718. It should be added that (*magnis*) *anfractibus*, a hapax in Lucretius, deliberately evokes a topography of enlarged dimensions: Manilius also uses the noun once, in *Astr.* 2.363 (*sexque per anfractus curvatur virgula in orbem*), to describe the "curving" of the line round a circle of stars that make up a constellation. Before him, Cicero has employed the same word in his account of the sphere as the perfect shape on which the universe's body has been modelled, so that it has "no curvatures or angles" (*Tim.* 17: *nihil incisum angulis, nihil anfractibus*).[51] Lucretius' revisionist attitude towards Callimachus[52] materializes as a conscious attempt to invoke a sense of sublime, cosmic vastness that is missing from the Greek model.

---

48 Translation in Stephens 2015, 173.
49 For a detailed discussion, see Brown 2007, 340–41.
50 Brown 2007, 341.
51 See also Roche 2009, 350 on Lucan 1.605: *longis anfractibus*. Cf. Kidd 1997, 191 and 195.
52 This is not the only subversive allusion to the Callimachean text. In 1.738–39 Empedocles' revelations are compared to those of the Delphic oracle, and they are found to be superior: *sanctius et multo certa ratione magis quam / Pythia quae tripodi a Phoebi lauroque profatur*, "with more sanctity and far more certainty than the Pythia who speaks forth from Apollo's tripod and laurel". The idea of speaking more accurately than the Delphic oracle echoes the words of the unborn Apollo in Callimachus, *Hymn* 4.94: ἀλλ' ἔμπης ἐρέω τι τομώτερον ἢ ἀπὸ δάφνης. Lucre-

In what follows, I will attempt to read the plague along the same lines. On the one hand, I will discuss the poem's final scene as a section that affords numerous allusions to Callimachus' work, made in a spirit of subversion rather than imitation. On the other hand, I will discuss how the plague is designed to generate what is essentially conceived as a magnificent spectacle of destruction. Lucretius' appeal to the imagery and language of the sublime will effectively be shown to be combined with a simultaneous distancing from Callimachus, in a way which suggests that the two aesthetic agendas can hardly be reconciled — to Lucretius' mind at least — with each other.

4.2 Lucretius' Plague and Callimachus

Attempts to unlock the plague's elusive meaning have turned over the years to be impeded by two kinds of interpretative obstacles. On the one hand, the shadow cast by Thucydides over Lucretius' text has inevitably led to the impression that there is only limited space left in this part of the narrative for other sustained allusions to previous Greek literature. On the other hand, it has become an established belief that, whatever sense we make of it, the plague has to be deciphered primarily in philosophical terms. Some, as we have seen, see the plague as a symbol of an unenlightened life spent in fear and agony; others view it as a test for the audience's capacity to stay calm in the face of death. A philosophical perspective, as I have been arguing in the first two chapters, is indeed crucial for understanding the plague: death, as the poet stresses time and again, is only a catalyst that allows for the never-ending recycling of matter into newly fixed atomic compounds; our fear of individual extinction — brought out by the plague in the most powerful and violent way — could thus be counterbalanced by the soothing thought that some kind of immortality is preserved on the microscopic level of atoms. That said, we should not lose sight of the fact that the plague also serves as a kind of poetic signature which can be meaningful in ways that need not be directly related to the poem's core philosophy. My intention in this section is to shift the focus from a narrowly philosophical reading of the text to examine more closely what the narrative's final scene has to tell us about Lucretius' poetics more generally by paying special attention to the dialogue that is developed with

---

tius' allusion to Callimachus effectively undermines Apollo's status as a god of prophecy. In harmony with Epicurean doctrine, the poet maintains that *ratio*, represented in this case by Empedocles, should be preferred to any misguided notion of divine foreknowledge. The tension with Callimachus is once more evident. See Brown 2007, 341–42.

Callimachus. I wish to read the plague, in other words, as a scene whose significance extends beyond the poem's didactic/philosophical scope and touches upon wider aesthetic concerns that might have occupied Lucretius' mind as a poet.

The plague creates a sense of disorder that is profoundly disconcerting also in a (meta)poetic sense. The scene that emerges throughout could be read as forming the exact opposite of what we normally identify as the typical topography and ecology of poetic initiation in Greek and Latin literature:[53] filth, contaminated fountains, crowded public spaces and an overbearing sense of pollution that spreads across people indiscriminately, all these details produce what is primarily an aesthetically unsettling effect. In the course of Book 6, we have witnessed how an idyllic and inspiring countryside has been gradually transforming into a haunting landscape inhabited by death. In 1.117–18 Lucretius has mentioned Ennius "who first brought down from pleasant Helicon a chaplet of evergreen leafage", *Ennius ut noster cecinit, qui primus **amoeno** / detulit ex **Helicone** perenni fronde coronam*. In 6.786–87 the information is added that "in the great mountains of Helicon there exists a tree which is accustomed to kill men by the vile stench of its flower", *est etiam magnis Heliconis montibus arbos / floris odore hominem taetro*[54] *consueta necare*.[55] When we eventually reach the plague, the contrast with the pastoral world — as this has been unveiled for the first time in the opening hymn to Venus (1.1.–49) — becomes even more pointed.[56] The image of the patients lying on the ground half-dead while they are seeking to extinguish their insatiable thirst in 6.1262–71 (discussed below) is meaningfully juxtaposed to the leisurely contentment of primitive men in 5.1392–96: *saepe itaque inter se*

---

53 For an exhaustive discussion of scenes of poetic initiation in Greek and Latin literature, see Kambylis 1965.

54 With *odore...taetro* in 6.787 compare *ulceribus taetris* in 6.1271.

55 The laurel of Phoebus, another symbol representing the production of poetry and art (see 2.505; cf. 1.739), is also involved in a scene of destruction in 6.150–55: *aridior porro si nubes accipit ignem, / uritur ingenti sonitu succensa repente, / lauricomos ut si per montis flamma vagetur / turbine ventorum comburens impete magno; / **nec res ulla magis quam Phoebi Delphica laurus** / **terribili sonitu flamma crepitante crematur***, "if, further, the cloud be drier when it receives the lightning, it is suddenly kindled and burns up with a loud din, as if the mountains were covered with laurel, and a flame were driven over by a tempest of winds, consuming them with mighty rush; and there is no other thing that burns with more terrible sound in the crackling flames than the Delphic laurel of Phoebus".

56 For the designed contrast between the plague and the opening hymn to Venus in 1.1–49, see Liebeschuetz 1967/8; Minadeo 1965; Schiesaro 1994. Compare e.g. "the fertile zephyr's breath which blows free and strong", *et reserata viget genitabilis aura favoni* (1.11) with the sick people's "heavy and uneven breathing" moments before they die in 6.1186: *creber spiritus aut ingens raroque coortus*.

***prostrati** in gramine molli / **propter aquae rivom** sub ramis arboris altae / non magnis opibus iucunde corpora habebant, / praesertim cum tempestas ridebat et anni / tempora pingebant viridantis floribus herbas*, "often therefore stretched in groups on the soft grass hard by a stream of water under the branches of a tall tree they gave pleasure to their bodies at cheap cost, above all when the weather smiled and the season of the year painted the green herbage with flowers". The picture drawn in these lines is not simply about care-free jest; it also provides the appropriate setting for the production of arts, music and dance.[57] To this thriving world of creativity the plague stands as a pathological foil, substituting the sound of song with laments and turning people's laughter to inarticulate cries.

It is in this context that I would like to read the plague as recalling and recasting in a pathological light certain passages in the poem that have been thought to bear Callimachean overtones. Let us take, for instance, the lines which introduce Lucretius' powerful poetic manifesto towards the end of Book 1, subsequently repeated in the proem to Book 4 (1.926–30 = 4.1–5):

> avia Pieridum peragro loca nullius ante
> trita solo. iuvat integros accedere fontis
> atque haurire, iuvatque novos decerpere flores
> insignemque meo capiti petere inde coronam
> unde prius nulli velarint tempora Musae.

> I traverse pathless tracts of the Pierides never yet trodden by any foot. I love to approach virgin springs and there to drink; I love to pluck new flowers, and to seek an illustrious chaplet for my head from fields whence before this the Muses have crowned the brows of none.

Scholars have observed that among Lucretius' multiple models in this passage we should definitely include Callimachus' ideas about poetic purity and innovation.[58] Indeed, one can detect combined allusions to Apollo's advice in the *Aetia* prologue that the poet should avoid the wide road and stay on the narrow path (fr. 1.25–28 Harder); to *Epigram* 28, where Callimachus expresses his disgust for public streets and fountains; and to the *Hymn to Apollo* which emphasizes the

---

[57] See, especially, 5.1398: *agrestis enim tum musa vigebat*, "for then the rustic muse was in its prime". For discussion, see Hardie 2006, 289.
[58] See Kenney 1970, 369–70 and Brown 1982, 80–82; cf. Gale 1994, 58; Volk 2002, 87–88. For a different interpretation, see Knox 1999. The prominence of the water symbol in the tradition of poetic initiation must be ascribed to Callimachus and his followers; see Kambylis 1965, 73–74, 98–102, 110–12.

ideal of a small and pure spring (110–12) by contrasting it to the filth that a big river carries with it.

Consider, now, how the idyllic scenery outlined in 1.926–30 is fundamentally revised in 6.1262–71, the moment when Lucretius describes the victims of the plague crowding Athens and creating an asphyxiating atmosphere:

> omnia conplebant loca tectaque; quo magis aestu
> confertos ita acervatim mors accumulabat.
> multa siti prostrata viam per proque voluta
> corpora silanos ad aquarum strata iacebant
> interclusa anima nimia ab dulcedine aquarum,
> multaque per populi passim loca prompta viasque
> languida semanimo cum corpore membra videres
> horrida paedore et pannis cooperta perire
> corporis inluvie, pelli super ossibus una,
> ulceribus taetris prope iam sordeque sepulta.

They filled all places and buildings; so by the stifling heat death all the more piled them in heaps, being thus packed. Many bodies, thrown down by thirst and rolling over the road, lay stretched by the water-spouts, cut off from the breath of life by the too great sweetness of water; many in public places and roads you might see all about, bodies half-dead with fainting limbs caked with squalor and covered with rags, perishing in filth of body, nothing but skin on their bones, and that almost buried in foul ulcers and dirt.

Leaving aside its undeniable links to Thucydides,[59] one way of making sense of this passage is by reading it as an inversion of Lucr. 1.926–30. Note, for instance, the contrast that is built between the two texts in spatial terms: the "pathless tracks", *loca nullius ante trita solo* — an indication of freedom of movement and

---

59 Lucr. 6.1262–71 is modelled on Thuc. 2.52.1–2: Ἐπίεσε δ' αὐτοὺς μᾶλλον πρὸς τῷ ὑπάρχοντι πόνῳ καὶ ἡ ξυγκομιδὴ ἐκ τῶν ἀγρῶν ἐς τὸ ἄστυ, καὶ οὐχ ἧσσον τοὺς ἐπελθόντας. οἰκιῶν γὰρ οὐχ ὑπαρχουσῶν, ἀλλ' ἐν καλύβαις πνιγηραῖς ὥρᾳ ἔτους διαιτωμένων ὁ φθόρος ἐγίγνετο οὐδενὶ κόσμῳ, ἀλλὰ καὶ νεκροὶ ἐπ' ἀλλήλοις ἀποθνῄσκοντες ἔκειντο καὶ ἐν ταῖς ὁδοῖς ἐκαλινδοῦντο καὶ περὶ τὰς κρήνας ἁπάσας ἡμιθνῆτες τοῦ ὕδατος ἐπιθυμίᾳ, "their general misery was aggravated by people crowding into the city from the fields, and the worst affected were the new arrivals. There were no houses for them but they lived in huts that were stifling in the heat of summer and they were visited by death in conditions of total disorder. The bodies of those dying were heaped on each other, and in the streets and around the springs half-dead people reeled about in a desperate desire for water" (translation in Mynott 2013, 121–22). A quick look at the two passages shows that, in comparison to Thucydides, Lucretius pays more emphasis on the element of *dirt*. See Foster 2009, 394 n. 64: "in Thucydides' description the corpses die upon one another in the road, or gather at the springs, or die in temples. Lucretius abandons most of the urban landscape (he mentions roads) and focuses almost exclusively on the filth of the half living".

inspiring wilderness[60] — give place to a suffocating lack of space due to the crowd's containment within the city walls: *omnia conplebant loca ... acervatim ... accumulabat* (6.1262–63). The untouched springs, *integri fontes*, become substituted by public fountains in the middle of the agora, *silanos ad aquarum* (6.1265), which carry water that has been contaminated by the seeds of disease. The sipping of water, which marks a crucial moment of poetic initiation, *iuvat integros fontes haurire*,[61] transforms into a horrendous, insatiable thirst: the more "sweet liquid" the patients consume, the more their condition deteriorates: *interclusa anima nimia ab dulcedine aquarum* (6.1266).[62]

As we take a closer look at the plague, one particular Callimachean patient comes to mind: Erysichthon in the *Hymn to Demeter* suffers from a terrible λιμός that is sent by the goddess as a punishment for the violation of her sacred grove (65–67): ἃ μὲν τόσσ' εἰποῖσ' Ἐρυσίχθονι τεῦχε πονηρά. / αὐτίκα οἱ χαλεπόν τε καὶ ἄγριον ἔμβαλε λιμόν / αἴθωνα κρατερόν, μεγάλᾳ δ' ἐστρεύγετο νούσῳ, "with these words she brought misery to Erysichthon. At once she cast on him a wild and dreadful hunger, burning and powerful, and he was tortured by the great disease".[63] Before I turn to a close reading of the hymn, it is worth stressing in advance that a reason why Erysichthon would have caught Lucretius' attention[64]

---

60 For the association between remoteness and poetic inspiration, see Rimmel 2015, 100; cf. Schiesaro 2009.
61 Both *iuvat* and *integros* in Latin have medical connotations, indicating health. For *(ad)iuvare*, see e.g. Cels. 1.9.5; 3.2.71; 3.2.10; and for *integer*, see Cels. 2.10.5; 2.17.5; 3.3.3.
62 With *haurire* in 1.928 contrast the image of the plague "drenching" the city of its people: *exhausit civibus urbem* (6.1140). Compare also how *splendidus umor,* a phrase that could have been used to describe the shining water of a spring, is used by Lucretius in 6.1187 to describe the sweat of the patients, and is subsequently combined with the disgusting image of spittle (6.1187–89): *sudorisque madens per collum splendidus umor, / tenvia sputa minuta, croci contacta colore / salsaque,* "dank sweat streaming and shining over the neck, fine thin spittle, salt and yellow in color".
63 Translation in Hopkinson 1984, 67.
64 For Lucretius' good knowledge of the Callimachean hymns, see Brown 2007. Farrell 2008 argues that one of the structural models for the six books of the *DRN* — more specifically, for the poem's composition in three groups of two books each — might have been Callimachus' collection of six hymns. This proposition, of course, would seem to place Lucretius under Callimachus' shadow; it would make him a follower rather than a dissenting figure. But Farrell is careful to note that his argument does not entail a full and blind endorsement: "By structuring the six books of *DRN* as three pairs of books, Lucretius may have been inspired by Callimachus' arrangement ... But by incorporating a different structure not found in Callimachus, one based on two groups of three books, Lucretius may have been overlaying his Callimachean structure with that of an Ennian hexad as well ... Interestingly, this involves a combination of Callimachean and Ennian structures in ways that are not just formally opportune, but thematically interesting as

is that the Callimachean text is already engaged in dialogue with Thucydides' plague. A significant allusion to the Greek historian's account can be traced in line 59, where Callimachus uses the adjective ἡμιθνῆτες to describe the reaction of Erysichthon's companions as Demeter appears suddenly in front of them (59–60):

οἱ μὲν ἄρ' ἡμιθνῆτες, ἐπεὶ τὰν πότνιαν εἶδον,
ἐξαπίνας ἀπόρουσαν ἐνὶ δρυσὶ χαλκὸν ἀφέντες.

When they saw the goddess they started away, half-dead with fear, leaving their bronze implements in the trees.[65]

ἡμιθνῆτες, "half-dead", is an extremely rare adjective in Greek literature before Callimachus.[66] It is by no means a coincidence that one of its rare appearances is attested in Thucydides' account of the plague in 2.52.2: ἀλλὰ καὶ νεκροὶ ἐπ' ἀλλήλοις ἀποθνῄσκοντες ἔκειντο καὶ ἐν ταῖς ὁδοῖς ἐκαλινδοῦντο καὶ περὶ τὰς κρήνας ἁπάσας **ἡμιθνῆτες** τοῦ ὕδατος ἐπιθυμίᾳ, "the bodies of those dying were heaped on each other, and in the streets and around the springs half-dead people reeled about in a desperate desire for water".[67] The word's occurrence in Callimachus would appear to have a proleptic use: although it is not applied to Erysichthon as a patient, it nonetheless anticipates the disease by which he is going to be afflicted a few lines below. The conceptual link between Erysichthon's λιμός and the plague (λοιμός) is supported by a number of parallels in Greek literature: evidence of a close association between the two nouns can be found in Hesiod (*Op.* 243), Herodotus (7.171) and, most memorably, Thucydides (2.54.2–3).[68] The historian concludes his account of the disease by mentioning an old, disputed

---

well. In terms of scale, Lucretius' poem, both in whole and in part, represents a middle way between Callimachean minimalism and Ennian grandiosity. Thematically, Lucretius borrows from a collection of religious hymns and from a historical epic. Again, his own poem rejects the hypostasization either of conventional religiosity or of history as determiners of meaning or as means to salvation. As in other respects, Lucretius' command of the poetic tradition and his admiration for the literary masters of the past does not prevent him from going his own way philosophically. Indeed, his adaptation of these formal elements may serve to underline the distinctive message of his own poem" (2008, 15). One important consequence of accepting Farrell's hypothesis is the fact that the end of Lucretius' Book 6 should be in dialogue with the sixth, and final, hymn of Callimachus, the story of Erysichthon.
65 Translation in Hopkinson 1984, 67.
66 Before the 3rd cent. BCE it occurs only in Thuc. 2.52.2; Ar. *Nub.* 504 and Aeschin. 3.159.
67 Translation in Mynott 2013, 121–22.
68 See Mitchell-Boyask 2008, 25 and Bremmer 2008, 177 and 306. For a detailed discussion of the connections between famine and pestilence in antiquity, see Gourevitch 2013.

oracle that gave rise to different interpretations among the people: some believed that it had been predicting war combined with "famine" (λιμός) while others thought that what it meant was "plague" (λοιμός). Thucydides notes that, in view of the disease that eventually afflicted Athens, people opted for the version of the oracle predicting a λοιμός, thus matching their memories to their sufferings at present.[69]

Erysichthon's sickness in Callimachus is throughout invested with carefully crafted medical details.[70] At the same time, it bears a striking resemblance to the general pathology outlined by Thucydides, especially with regard to the feeling of inextinguishable hunger and thirst, which afflicts the patient (compare e.g. Call. *In Cererem* 87–90[71] with Thuc. 2.49.5). As a result, any attempt to determine whether Lucretius is alluding to the Greek historian or to the Hellenistic poet — or simultaneously to both — involves a number of difficulties. That said, there are significant pathological details in the Latin text which are missing from Thucydides but, suggestively enough, are present in Callimachus. One of them relates to Lucretius' emphasis on the people's extreme state of emaciation moments before they die in 6.1267–71:

> multaque per populi passim loca prompta viasque
> languida semanimo cum corpore membra videres
> horrida paedore et pannis cooperta perire
> corporis inluvie, pelli super ossibus una,
> ulceribus taetris prope iam sordeque sepulta.

The phrase *pelli super ossibus una* in 6.1270 does not have a parallel in Thucydides; in fact, there is no point in the historian's description, at which emaciation is explicitly mentioned as a consequence of the disease. On the contrary, Thucydides comments on the bodies' astonishing endurance during the plague (2.49.6): καὶ τὸ σῶμα, ὅσονπερ χρόνον καὶ ἡ νόσος ἀκμάζοι, οὐκ ἐμαραίνετο, ἀλλ' ἀντεῖχε παρὰ δόξαν τῇ ταλαιπωρίᾳ, "the body did not waste away while their illness was

---

69 See Demont 1990.
70 See Cairns 2016, 219–20. Cf. Acosta-Hughes 2002, 253 n. 96, with Langholf 1986.
71 In lines 87–90 the imagery of hunger blends with that of thirst: ἐνδόμυχος δῆπειτα πανάμερος εἰλαπιναστὰς / ἤσθιε μυρία πάντα· κακὰ δ' ἐξάλλετο γαστὴρ / αἰεὶ μᾶλλον ἔδοντι, **τὰ δ' ἐς βυθὸν οἷα θαλάσσας** / ἀλεμάτως ἀχάριστα κατέρρεεν εἴδατα πάντα, "meanwhile, closeted in the house, he banqueted all day long and consumed countless things. His wretched belly leapt as he ate more and more and all his food flowed down into him as if into the depths of the sea" (translation in Hopkinson 1984, 69).

at its height but was surprisingly resistant to the ordeal".[72] Erysichthon's ravenous hunger, on the other hand, has a terrible wasting effect on his body (88–93):

> κακὰ δ' ἐξάλλετο γαστὴρ
> αἰεὶ μᾶλλον ἔδοντι, τὰ δ' ἐς βυθὸν οἷα θαλάσσας
> ἀλεμάτως ἀχάριστα κατέρρεεν εἴδατα πάντα.
> ὡς δὲ Μίμαντι χιών, ὡς ἀελίῳ ἔνι πλαγγών,
> καὶ τούτων ἔτι μέζον ἐτάκετο μέστ' ἐπὶ νευράς·
> δειλαίῳ **ῥινός τε καὶ ὀστέα** μῶνον ἔλειφθεν.

His wretched belly leapt as he ate more and more, and all his food flowed down into him as if into the depths of the sea. Like snow on Mimas or a wax doll in the sun – even more quickly than these he wasted away to the very sinews: only skin and bone were left to the wretch.[73]

Lucretius' *pelli super ossibus una* corresponds closely with Callimachus' ῥινός τε καὶ ὀστέα μῶνον.[74] The use of *inluvie* in the same line – a word whose original meaning is that of a wash of water that gathers impurities[75] – could be a further nod to Erysichthon's miserable state towards the end of the hymn, as we see him sitting in the middle of the street, begging for scraps of food, which have been thrown away from a feast (114–15): ἐνὶ τριόδοισι καθῆστο / αἰτίζων ἀκόλως τε καὶ ἔκβολα **λύματα** δαιτός. Erysichthon here consumes the very matter which Callimachus sees as making poetry impure. The word λύματα brings to mind Call. *In Apollinem* 105–12:

> ὁ Φθόνος Ἀπόλλωνος ἐπ' οὔατα λάθριος εἶπεν·
> 'οὐκ ἄγαμαι τὸν ἀοιδὸν ὃς οὐδ' ὅσα πόντος ἀείδει.'
> τὸν Φθόνον ὡπόλλων ποδί τ' ἤλασεν ὧδέ τ' ἔειπεν·
> 'Ἀσσυρίου ποταμοῖο μέγας ῥόος, ἀλλὰ τὰ πολλὰ
> **λύματα γῆς** καὶ πολλὸν ἐφ' ὕδατι συρφετὸν ἕλκει.
> Δηοῖ δ' οὐκ ἀπὸ παντὸς ὕδωρ φορέουσι μέλισσαι,
> ἀλλ' ἥτις καθαρή τε καὶ ἀχράαντος ἀνέρπει
> πίδακος ἐξ ἱερῆς ὀλίγη λιβὰς ἄκρον ἄωτον.'

---

72 Translation in Mynott 2013, 120.
73 Translation in Hopkinson 1984, 69.
74 Before Lucretius, the phrase is found in Latin only in Pl. *Aul.* 564 (*quia ossa ac pellis totust, ita cura macet*) and *Capt.* 135: *ossa atque pellis sum miser a macritudine*. Cf. Theoc. *Id.* 2.90 (ὀστί' ἔτ' ἧς καὶ δέρμα) and Ap. Rhod. *Argon.* 2.200–1 (describing Phineus' appalling state when Jason and his companions meet him): πίνῳ δέ οἱ αὐσταλέος χρὼς / ἐσκλήκει, ῥινοὶ δὲ σὺν ὀστέα μοῦνον ἔεργον. Scholars argue that Apollonius derived his inspiration from Callimachus' Erysichthon; see De Forest 1994, 75; cf. Murray 2004, 208–12.
75 See Lowe 2015, 127; cf. Felton 2013, 414.

Envy spoke secretly into Phoebus' ear: "I do not admire the singer who does not sing even as much as the sea". Phoebus pushed Envy off with his foot and spoke the following: "The flow of the Assyrian river is vast, but it draws along much refuse from the land and much garbage on its waters. Not from any sources do bees carry water to Demeter, but from what comes up pure and undefiled from a holy fountain, a small drop, the choicest of waters".[76]

In a similar way, the excessive drinking of the plague's victims in Lucretius generates a tension with what is presented elsewhere in the narrative as an ideal philosophical diet. It could be argued that the image of the Athenians jumping into the wells with their mouths wide open, *ore patente*, stands in contrast to the "copious drafts from large springs", *largos haustus e fontibus magnis*, promised to Memmius by the poet in 1.412–13. Both passages involve the image of avid drinking; however, while in 1.412–13 a point is made about the nourishing sweetness of Lucretius' redeeming text, in the case of the plague the water that is consumed in large quantities is nothing but pure poison. The sick in Lucretius are deceived into believing that the water is sweet (6.1266: *dulcedine aquarum*); they are unable to tell that it has been contaminated by the seeds of disease or — according to one of the rumors reported by Thucydides[77] — that it has been poisoned by their enemies. The sweetness of Lucretius' text also involves a considerable degree of deception, but what is covered underneath is ultimately a life-sustaining drug (1.936: *absinthia taetra*) designed to purge people from the sickness of fear and anxiety. In a way, the victims of the plague represent an audience that is no more fit to keep up with Lucretius' refined diet. Similar to Erysichthon in Callimachus, they end up devouring filth and dirt, being oblivious to the fact that this only helps to make their condition worse.

Vergil and Ovid appear both to have been alert to the connection between Lucretius' plague and Callimachus' Erysichthon. Vergil's Noric plague in *Georgics* 3[78] radically transforms an idyllic landscape into a neutral space that is void of aesthetic meaning; the pastoral world, as we are told in *G.* 3.520–24, has lost all its appeal since its infected population can no more appreciate its soothing beauty: *non umbrae altorum nemorum, non mollia possunt / prata mouere animum, non qui per saxa uolutus / **purior electro** campum petit amnis; at ima /*

---

76 Translation in Stephens 2015, 81.
77 Thuc. 2.48.2: ἐς δὲ τὴν Ἀθηναίων πόλιν ἐξαπιναίως ἐσέπεσε, καὶ τὸ πρῶτον ἐν τῷ Πειραιεῖ ἥψατο τῶν ἀνθρώπων, ὥστε καὶ ἐλέχθη ὑπ' αὐτῶν ὡς οἱ Πελοποννήσιοι **φάρμακα** ἐσβεβλήκοιεν ἐς τὰ φρέατα.
78 Whose main model is that of Lucretius; see the discussions in Harrison 1979; West 1979; cf. Gale 2000, 45–48.

soluuntur latera, atque oculos stupor urget inertis / ad terramque fluit deuexo pondere ceruix, "no shades of deep woods, no soft meadows can touch his heart, no stream purer than amber, rolling over the rocks in its course towards the plain; but his flanks are unstrung throughout, numbness weighs upon his languid eyes, and his neck sinks with drooping weight to earth".[79] The phrase *purior electro*, "purer than amber", in 3.522 is a clear allusion to Callimachus' description of the goddess' sacred grove in the *Hymn to Demeter* (27–29): ἐν πίτυς, ἐν μεγάλαι πτελέαι ἔσαν, ἐν δὲ καὶ ὄχναι, / ἐν δὲ καλὰ γλυκύμαλα· τὸ δ' **ὥστ' ἀλέκτρινον ὕδωρ** / ἐξ ἀμαρᾶν ἀνέθυε, "within were pines, large elms, and pear-trees, and fair sweet apples; and the amber coloured water boiled up from ditches".[80] It is this *locus amoenus* that Erysichthon subsequently violates, by trespassing on Demeter's holy grove. Vergil's plague, I suggest, echoes Erysichthon's devastating impact on nature. It is tempting to argue that this is done in close imitation of Lucretius where the same Callimachean figure blends in with the violent disruption caused by the plague on the natural order of things.

With regard to Ovid, Erysichthon in *Metamorphoses* 8 first experiences hunger in a dream, only to find out that even when he is awake, food remains equally insubstantial (8.823–27): *lenis adhuc Somnus placidis Erysicthona pennis / mulcebat: petit ille dapes sub imagine somni, / oraque vana movet dentemque in dente fatigat, / exercetque cibo delusum guttur inani / proque epulis tenues nequiquam devorat auras*, "still gentle Sleep on wings of quietness soothed Erysichthon. In his sleep he dreamed of food and feasting, chewed and champed on nothing, wore tooth on tooth, stuffed down his cheated gullet imaginary food, and course on course devoured the empty air".[81] As Philip Hardie aptly observes, the image conveyed in these lines evokes "the insatiability of the Lucretian lover in 4.1097–1104":[82] *ut bibere in somnis sitiens quom quaerit, et umor / non datur, ardorem qui membris stinguere possit, / sed laticum simulacra petit frustraque laborat / in medioque sitit torrenti flumine potans, / sic in amore Venus simulacris ludit amantis*, "as when in dreams a thirsty man seeks to drink, and no water is forthcoming to quench the burning in his frame, but he seeks the image of water, striving in vain, and in the midst of a rushing river thirsts while he drinks: so in love Venus mocks lovers with images" (4.1097–1101). Crucially, the lover's delusion, as I have discussed in detail in chapter 2, resurfaces at the end of the poem, this time affecting

---

79 Translation in Fairclough/Goold 1999, 213.
80 Translation in Hopkinson 1984, 63. Vergil's allusion to Callimachus is spotted by Thomas 1988, 139.
81 Translation in Melville 1986, 196.
82 Hardie 2012, 173.

the sick men who are unable to extinguish their thirst (cf. 6.1176–77). The intratextual link could hardly have escaped Ovid's attention.[83] Indeed, a closer look at his personified Hunger in *Met.* 8.796–808 yields a number of intriguing points of contact with the symptoms of the plague in Lucretius, such as the hollow eyes, the rough skin, the infected throat and the emaciated body.[84] Ovid is blending here λιμός with λοιμός, in the same way that the two have already become conflated in Lucretius through the allusive presence of Callimachus' Erysichthon.

Lucretius' response to Callimachus at the end of his poem has not gone unnoticed by Vergil and Ovid. But what precisely does this response indicate? Are we meant to understand it simply as a case of imitation or is there a more subversive attitude built into it? Erysichthon embodies, in many ways, the exact opposite of λεπτότης.[85] On the one hand, his impious actions against Demeter are portrayed in a language which evokes martial epic,[86] of the kind that Callimachus has dismissed in the *Aetia* prologue. According to Jackie Murray, the violation of the goddess' sacred grove and his attempt to use the material, ὕλη, of the trees to build a banquet hall — the place where epic story-telling normally takes place — constitutes a direct affront to Callimachean poetics.[87] On the other hand, Erysichthon's ravenous hunger and the vast quantities of food and filth he consumes turn him, as we have seen above, into the exact opposite of poetic refinement as the latter has been presented at the end of the *Hymn to Apollo*. Even his emaciated body, materializing through the shocking image of "skin and bones", may have

---

[83] For some allusions to Lucretius' plague in Ovid's story of Erysichthon, see also Piazzi 2019, 18.

[84] I provide here an indicative list of similar symptoms between Ovid's *Fames* (*Met.* 8.796–808) and the victims of the plague in Lucretius: **Hollow eyes:** *cava lumina* (8.801) — *cavati oculi, cava tempora* (6.1194). **Rough skin:** *dura cutis* (8.803) — *frigida pellis / duraque, in ore iacens rictum, frons tenta manebat* (6.1194–95). **Infected throat:** *scabrae rubigine fauces* (8.802) — *sudabant etiam fauces intrinsecus atrae / sanguine, et ulceribus* (6.1147–48). **Emaciation:** *ossa sub incurvis exstabant arida lumbis* (8.804) — *pelli super ossibus una* (6.1270). **Burning disease transforms into madness:** *ut vero est expulsa quies, furit ardor edendi / perque avidas fauces incensaque viscera regnat* (8.828–29) — *furiosus voltus et acer* (6.1184). Ovid's familiarity with the symptomatology outlined in Lucr. 6.1138–1286 becomes evident in his account of the plague in Aegina in *Met.* 7.523–613, which draws heavily on Lucretius' text; for a recent discussion, see Hutchinson 2013, 210–19. Cf. Garani 2013, 255–57.

[85] For a metapoetic reading of Callimachus' Erysichthon, see Müller 1987. Cf. Bulloch 1977; Murray 2004; Morrison 2007, 170–78; Harder 2018.

[86] See Hopkinson 1984, 6–7.

[87] Murray 2004, 214.

an ironic touch in it: this is a kind of "slenderness", λεπτότης, that has gone a bit too far.[88]

It is precisely this un-Callimachean imagery that Lucretius chooses to reproduce in the course of the plague. What we are dealing with here appears to be a complex kind of "antiphrastic allusion"[89] through which the source text becomes effectively undermined. By turning his attention to Erysichthon and by replicating the details of a pathology which has already been conceived by the Hellenistic poet as a violation of his own aesthetic principles, Lucretius essentially marks his distance from Callimachus, allowing the messy and disordered world of disease to take over and occupy through images of filth, excess and pollution the poem's final lines.

4.3 Lucretius' Plague and the Sublime

Lucretius' uncomfortable relationship with Callimachus in the course of the plague is combined with a simultaneous attempt on the poet's part to bring out the sublime qualities of the disease. The plague inevitably elicits a response of deep fear and anxiety, revolving as it does around images of mass death and annihilation. At the same time, it is precisely its presentation as a horrifying spectacle, one from which we can keep a relative distance as readers,[90] that allows it to lay claim to a potentially sublime effect. As Carolyn Korsmeyer observes:

---

[88] In an anecdote reported by Athenaeus about Philetas of Cos — the great scholar and poet of the early Hellenistic period, and a leading figure of the neoteric movement in Alexandria — we read: "the poet Philetas was rather thin (λεπτότερος), and on account of his slender build (διὰ τὴν τοῦ σώματος ἰσχνότητα) he used to have leaden balls attached to his feet so that he would not be overturned by the wind" (*Deipn.* 12.552 B). The story is also found in Aelian, *VH* 10.6: "they say that Philetas was very slightly built (λεπτότατον γενέσθαι τὸ σῶμα). Since the slightest cause would throw him off his feet, it is reported that he wore shoes with lead soles, to prevent his being overturned by the wind whenever it blew hard" (translation of the passages in Lightfoot 2009, 27–29). Both anecdotes have as their obvious target Philitas' excessive elegance, by turning λεπτότης from a stylistic and aesthetic concern to a medical condition that affects the body. Erysichthon's wasting disease likewise turns him into a poor reflection of what an ideally slender body should have looked like.
[89] For a discussion of "antiphrastic allusion" in Latin poetry, see Narducci 1979, 31–79.
[90] The plague brings us face to face with our fear of personal death. Still, as a narrative, it describes events that happened a long time ago and, in this respect, one could say that it is not of our immediate concern. Cf. 3.830–37: the Punic war had a devastating effect of cosmic proportions, yet we were not there to experience it and be affected by it; horrifying as it might have been, to us it is only a story that belongs to the distant past. As Porter 2016, 451 aptly notes, "all of book 6 has this feel of detached spectacle about it".

A person in the grip of actual terror enjoys nothing; the emotion overwhelms and produces intolerable distress. However, if it is possible to regard a mighty and fearsome object from a position of relative safety, or to achieve psychological distance that lessens the grip of fear, then one may observe terrifying things and be stirred with the thrill of the sublime ... The sublime is not itself an experience of terror–at least not only terror. But without the underlying terror that its objects inspire, there would be no experience of the sublime. Here a supremely uncomfortable and aversive emotion is transmogrified into powerful and transportive aesthetic insight. Just how this occurs is hard to fathom, but that it occurs is indisputable.[91]

The plague functions as a kind of climax to the spectacular phenomena discussed in Book 6: thunders and lightings, earthquakes and volcanic eruptions, storms and whirlwinds, they have all served to present us with a view of the world that is profoundly unsettling but also immensely thrilling at the same time. It is important, therefore, to start by observing that disease is not presented as an exclusively negative force but is expected instead to be understood in close association with other earthly and celestial marvels.[92] The theme of *morbus* is formally introduced in 6.1090–1137. Lucretius makes an important distinction at this point between diseases that arise from the damp, putrefied earth (6.1100–102) and those whose seeds "fly about in the air" (6.1096: *volare*) and "descend upon us through the sky" (6.1099–100: *superne / per caelum veniunt*). The plague belongs to the latter category. As we read in 6.1141–43: *nam penitus veniens Aegypti finibus ortus, / **aera permensus multum camposque natantis**, / **incubuit** tandem populo Pandionis omni*, "for beginning from the innermost parts of Egypt, and traversing a wide expanse of air and the swimming plains, it fell at length upon all the people of Pandion". The introduction of the mythical element through the reference to "the people of Pandion",[93] in combination with the vast expanses of air and the swimming plains mentioned in 6.1142, confer an epic tone to the passage.[94] The

---

91 Korsmeyer 2011, 133.
92 For the plague as "a spectacular ... conclusion to the *De rerum natura*", see West 1979, 75.
93 See also 6.1138–39: *haec ratio quondam morborum et mortifer aestus / **finibus in Cecropis** funestos reddidit aegros*, "such a cause of disease and death-bringing current once in the realms of Cecrops poisoned the countryside".
94 For Lucretius' allusions to the plague in Book 1 of the *Iliad*, see Gale 1994, 113–14. For the use of *permetior* in the context of an epic journey, see Verg. *Aen.* 3.156–59 (the images of the Trojan household gods speak to Aeneas in his sleep during the plague in Crete): *nos te Dardania incensa tuaque arma secuti, / nos tumidum sub te **permensi** classibus **aequor**, / idem venturos tollemus in astra nepotes / imperiumque urbi dabimus*, "we followed you and your arms when Dardania was burned; under you we traversed on ships the swelling sea; we, too, shall exalt to heaven your sons that are to be, and give empire to their city" (translation in Fairclough/Goold 1999, 382). Cf. Enn. *Ann.* 67: *campum ... permensa*.

image brings to mind the flights of Homeric gods when they are said to be covering distances which are hard to fathom and then to rush downwards to the world of mortals, e.g. in *Od.* 5.44–50: αὐτίκ' ἔπειθ' ὑπὸ ποσσὶν ἐδήσατο καλὰ πέδιλα, / ἀμβρόσια χρύσεια, τά μιν φέρον **ἠμὲν ἐφ' ὑγρὴν / ἠδ' ἐπ' ἀπείρονα γαῖαν** ἅμα πνοιῇς ἀνέμοιο ... / Πιερίην δ' ἐπιβὰς **ἐξ αἰθέρος ἔμπεσε** πόντῳ, "immediately he [i.e. Hermes] bound upon his feet the fair sandals, golden and immortal, that carried him over the water as over the dry boundless earth abreast of the wind's blast ... He stood on Pieria and launched himself from the bright air across the sea".[95] Although its damage is mainly felt on the land's people and animals, the plague remains principally linked to the sky; its origin transports us to the high altitudes that lie above our heads (*permensus* has been used one more time in the poem, in 4.394, to describe the travelling stars)[96] and implies that cosmic forces might be at work, which can result in destruction of immense, legendary proportions.[97]

The skies present for Lucretius an endless source of fascination. Everything that takes place there is "elevated" by its nature. This is how the poet introduces his discussion of thunder in 6.96–98: *principio tonitru quatiuntur caerula caeli / propterea quia concurrunt* **sublime** *volantes / aetheriae nubes contra pugnantibus ventis*, "in the first place, the blue sky is shaken with thunder, because flying clouds rush together high in the ether, when winds fight against each other". The adjective *sublimis* has already been used in Book 1, 2 and 4, always with reference

---

95 Translation in Lattimore 1965, 89. Although the immediate context of these lines does not involve death (Hermes is about to convey to Calypso that Odysseus has to return to Ithaca), the reference to the god's wand in *Od.* 5.47–48 (εἵλετο δὲ ῥάβδον, τῇ τ' ἀνδρῶν ὄμματα θέλγει, / ὧν ἐθέλει, τοὺς δ' αὖτε καὶ ὑπνώοντας ἐγείρει) serves as a reminder of his role as crosser of the infernal frontier and "as guide of the shades in their transition from the upper world to Hades" (Sourvinou-Inwood 1995, 105).
96 4.391–94: *Sidera cessare aetheriis adfixa cavernis / cuncta videntur, et adsiduo sunt omnia motu, / quandoquidem longos obitus exorta revisunt, / cum* **permensa** *suo sunt* **caelum** *corpore claro*, "the stars all seem to be fixed and stationary in the vaults of ether, yet all are in constant motion since they rise and return to their far distant settings when they have traversed the sky with bright body".
97 With *incubuit ... populo* in 6.1143 compare 5.345–47 (on legends of flood and fire which, if believed, prove that the earth is mortal): *nam cum res tantis morbis tantisque periclis / temptarentur, ibi si tristior* **incubuisset** */ causa, darent late cladem magnasque ruinas*, "for when things were assailed by so great afflictions and so great dangers, if then a more serious cause had come upon them, there would have been widespread destruction and a mighty fall".

to the heights of heaven.[98] But the word is not simply meant by the poet to indicate distance and remote objects; it is also pregnant with an aesthetic meaning, to the extent at least that altitude is seen to provide the conceptual space for "marvellous" things to keep happening:[99] in 6.185–86 we read of thick clouds "piled high one above another in a wonderful mass" (*hoc densis fit nubibus et simul alte / extructis aliis alias super impete miro*); in 6.328 the thunderbolt flies with "a wonderful rush" (*volat impete miro*); in 6.431–37 a cloud depressed by the wind descends as a column to the sea and stirs it up causing "a wonderful boiling in the waves" (6.436–37: ... *hinc prorumpitur in mare venti / vis et fervorem mirum concinnat in undis*).

The sublimity inherent in these passages persists throughout the plague. The disease is said to hang "suspended in the air above" (6.1128: *suspensa manet vis aere in ipso*), threatening to fall upon humans at any instant; when it eventually does so, it resembles a whirlwind which strikes the sea and causes commotion (see 6.1099–100: **superne** / *per caelum* **veniunt** and compare it with 6.424–25: *presteras Graii quos ab re nominitarunt, / in mare qua missi* **veniant** *ratione* **superne**). The plague creeps through the air, slowly and insidiously like a serpent (6.1120–21: *aer inimicus serpere coepit, / ut nebula ac nubes paulatim repit*), but when the time has come to unleash its power, this occurs suddenly (6.1125: *subito*; cf. 6.1090: *repente*). Its manifestation evokes the sudden explosion of thunders (6.131: *saepe ita dat magnum sonitum displosa repente*) and lightning bolts (6.181–82: *dissipat ardoris quasi per vim expressa repente / semina quae faciunt nictantia fulgura flammae*); it reminds us of the way in which rough flying bodies rapidly come together to form clouds (6.451–53: *nubila concrescunt, ubi corpora multa volando / hoc super in caeli spatio coiere repente / asperiora*). Lucretius repeatedly makes use of *nubes / nebula* to refer to the cloud of atoms, which carries the disease (6.1099; 6.1121). Not only does this help to maintain a general link with the elevated cloudy landscape that dominates the first part of Book 6,[100] it also provides the ground for specific connections. The disease, as we have seen,

---

98 1.340 (on things that move through the sea, the earth and the sky): *per maria ac terras sublimaque caeli*; 2.206 (on shooting stars): *nocturnasque faces caeli sublime volantis*; 4.132–33 (on the formation of *simulacra* in the air): *constituuntur in hoc caelo qui dicitur aer, / quae multis formata modis sublime feruntur*.

99 Not incidentally, Ovid (*Am.* 1.15.23) uses the adjective *sublimis* to praise Lucretius' outstanding poem (see the discussion below).

100 In 6.96–534, Lucretius discusses (a) thunders (b) lightnings (c) thunderbolts (d) waterspouts (e) clouds and (f) rain. By far the commonest term in this section of the poem is the noun *nubes*, occurring over fifty times.

is transmitted through contact (6.1236: *ex aliis alios avidi contagia morbi*) in a congested urban landscape where the victims of the plague are literally piled one upon the other. The same sense of enforced containment is brought out by the discussion of the elements which are trapped within the clouds. So, for instance, in the case of the thunderbolt the wind that is confined in a hollow cloud is said to be ignited by its own incessant movement or through *contact* with fire (6.280: *e contagibus ignis*) which occupies the same space and does not allow it to move freely.[101]

Clouds serve throughout to enhance our sense of altitude: while obstructing our access to the sky, they help nonetheless to stir our imagination into picturing thick masses of matter extending far beyond the reach of vision. It would be impossible, Lucretius tells us, to have thunderbolts and heavy rains were it not for the thick clouds which are "piled up high" upon each other (see, respectively, 6.246–47: *fulmina gignier e crassis* **alte**que *putandumst / nubibus* **extructis** and 6.266–68: *nec tanti possent venientes opprimere imbres, / flumina abundare ut facerent camposque natare, / si non* **extructis** *fore* **alte** *nubibus aether*). Such is the "wonderful" height which a mass of clouds can reach that we can only capture it through our imagination (6.185–88): *scilicet hoc densis fit nubibus et simul* **alte** */* **extructis** *aliis alias super impete* **miro***; / ne tibi sit frudi quod nos inferne videmus / quam sint lata magis quam sursum extructa quid extent*, "you may be sure that this [i.e. the lightning] is what happens, when clouds are thick and at the same time piled high one above another in a wonderful mass, that you may not be deceived because from below we see more readily how wide they are than how far they extend piled upwards". The end of the poem affords a clear view to a different pile of bodies, that of the dead people who have lost their lives in the plague (6.1262–63): *omnia conplebant loca tectaque; quo magis aestu / confertos ita acervatim mors accumulabat*, "they kept on filling up all the places and buildings, so that death kept on heaping them up all the more in piles, packed together in that heat".[102] In the poem's final lines, the image returns with added force (6.1283–86): *namque suos consanguineos aliena rogorum /* **insuper extructa** *ingenti clamore locabant / subdebantque* **faces***, multo cum sanguine saepe / rixantes potius quam corpora desererentur*, "for they would lay their own kindred amidst loud lamentation upon piles of woods not their own, and would set light to the fire, often

---

101 For the emphasis on the narrow space, see 6.277: *insinuatus ibi vertex versatur in arto*.

102 With *confertos* in 6.1263 compare 6.507–9 (on the production of rain): *quo cum bene semina aquarum / multa modis multis convenere undique adaucta, /* **confertae nubes** *umorem mittere certant*, "and when into these clouds very many seeds of waters in many ways have gathered together, being increased from all sides, the clouds stuffed full strive to discharge the moisture".

brawling with much shedding of blood rather than abandon the bodies". The plural *faces* has been used twice so far in the narrative, both times with reference to the captivating brightness of shooting stars (2.206: *nocturnasque faces caeli sublime volantis*; 5.1191: *noctivagaeque faces caeli flammaeque volantes*). The description of the deceased as they are being placed on pyres could thus be said to produce yet another point of contact between the plague's grim reality and the heavenly realm, implying an ascending movement from the blazing corpses to the blazing stars as well as a collapse of established boundaries and hierarchies — between "low" and "high", "earthly" and "celestial" — that takes place precisely at the moment of death.[103] Just as the clouds have been said in 6.250–55 to block all light and leave one suddenly feeling as though "all the darkness of Acheron has escaped and filled the sky with the countenance of black terror", so does the plague's infernal setting — by way of creating an inverse mirror effect — provide a reflection of the sublime world which lies above our heads. An additional link is established through the notion of burial: suspension of customary funerary rites during the plague gives rise to great masses of unburied bodies piled up high on the earth's surface; in their turn, the majestic clouds, which collect above the lofty mountains, stay still with great masses of wind "buried on every side".[104] Death and the accumulation of inert matter, whether understood

---

103 This is a point missed by those who choose to focus exclusively on the dark aspects of the poem's ending, e.g. Kenney 2007, 109 (on 6.1282–86): "Lucretius has not merely embellished Thucydides' picture; he contradicts it, replacing the silent departure of the mourners by a noisily and shockingly undignified brawl". And yet, these lines transpire to be particularly dignifying in tone, especially if we consider the possibility that Lucretius invites us here to see the fires of the dead transforming, as it were, into bright stars in the night sky. For the transition from funeral pyres to glittering stars, cf. Verg. *Aen.* 11.185–202: *huc corpora quisque suorum / more tulere patrum*, **subiectisque ignibus** *atris / conditur in tenebras altum caligine caelum / ... tum litore toto / ardentis spectant socios semustaque servant / busta, neque avelli possunt, nox umida donec / invertit caelum* **stellis ardentibus** *aptum*, "here, after the fashion of their fathers, they each brought the bodies of their kin, and as the murky fires are lit beneath, high heaven is veiled in the gloom of darkness ... Then, all along the shore, they watch their comrades burning, and keep guard above the charred pyres, and they cannot tear themselves away till dewy night rolls round the heaven, inset with gleaming stars" (translation in Fairclough/Goold 2000, 249–51). As Gransden 1991, 90 observes, "here we move from the blazing corpses to the blazing stars, from man-made fires to the fires of heaven; the camera tracks away to form a magnificent close". I would suggest that the idea is already implicitly present in Lucretius.
104 See 6.189–93: *contemplator enim, cum mentibus adsimulata / nubila portabunt venti transversa per auras, / aut ubi per magnos montis cumulata videbis / insuper esse aliis alia atque urgere superne / in statione locata* **sepultis undique ventis**, "for do but apply your scrutiny when the winds carry clouds like mountains across through the air, or when you see them piled about the

literally or metaphorically, are essential in both cases for creating a daunting spectacle.

As James Porter has illustrated, Lucretius' appeal to the sublime throughout the *DRN* is mainly played out on two levels: on the one hand, it takes the form of a deep and unsettling thrill generated at the point when we come to realize how the invisible world of microscopic atoms interacts, materially as well as conceptually, with larger dimensions which overfill our imagination in the form of vast objects, grand natural phenomena and, ultimately, the boundless universe. An analogy between a rain of atoms and a heavy storm that sweeps everything in its way, a puddle of water that reflects and captures in it the celestial bodies in the sky above, the suffering body of a patient which resembles that of the earth when we see the latter trembling and shaking during an earthquake or a volcanic eruption, all these images inspire a sublime feeling that is grounded on "the collision and confusion of two incommensurable scales ... of micro- and macro-levels, whereby the infinitesimally small can appear infinitely and forbiddingly large".[105] On the other hand, sublime sensations are generated through glimpses of the void, "whereby void is to be understood not simply as an agent or precondition of motion but also as an agent of commotion, terror, and destabilization".[106] In its most extreme form, the sublime void can be seen to encompass death itself which represents an absolute vacuity and gives rise to spectacles which stimulate mixed responses of horror and fascination. The plague, as I will proceed to illustrate, participates in both those scripts of the sublime.

In 2.49.5 Thucydides observes crisply that the diseased were burning on the inside: καὶ τὸ μὲν ἔξωθεν ἁπτομένῳ σῶμα οὔτ' ἄγαν θερμὸν ἦν οὔτε χλωρόν, ἀλλ' ὑπέρυθρον, πελιτνόν, φλυκταίναις μικραῖς καὶ ἕλκεσιν ἐξηνθηκός· τὰ δὲ ἐντὸς οὕτως ἐκάετο ὥστε μήτε τῶν πάνυ λεπτῶν ἱματίων καὶ σινδόνων τὰς ἐπιβολὰς μηδ' ἄλλο τι ἢ γυμνοὶ ἀνέχεσθαι, "externally, the body was not particularly hot to the touch nor pale but was reddish and livid, breaking out in small blisters and sores; internally, however, sufferers were on fire and could not bear contact with the lightest of clothing and linens or anything other than going naked".[107] In Lucretius the image has been adapted so as to accommodate the implication of an oversized body. In 6.1168–69 we read that "a flame burnt in the stomach as in a furnace": *intima pars hominum vero flagrabat ad ossa, / flagrabat stomacho*

---

great mountains one above another, pressing down from above, and lying still with the winds deep buried on every side". See Pope 2020, 214.
105 Porter 2016, 446.
106 Porter 2016, 449.
107 Translation in Mynott 2013, 119–20.

*flamma **ut fornacibus intus**. Fornacibus intus* serves to maintain a link between the microcosm of the human body and the figurative language that has been applied in the course of Book 6 to large scale natural phenomena taking place on sky and the earth. In 6.202 we are told of how lightings originate from winds which are trapped within the "hollow furnaces" of clouds, *cavis ... fornacibus intus*. The same applies to thunderbolts in 6.277–78: *insinuatus ibi vertex versatur in arto / et calidis acuit fulmen fornacibus intus*, "the whirlwind, finding its way in [the hollow cloud], turns about there in the narrow space, and sharpens the thunderbolt in the hot furnace within". In 6.680–81 the image is employed to describe this time the flame which "suddenly breathes out of the vast furnaces of Aetna", *repente / flamma foras vastis Aetnae fornacibus efflet*.[108] A closer look at Lucretius' adaptation of Thucydides' passage reveals that the historian's reference to "small blisters and sores" (φλυκταίναις μικραῖς καὶ ἕλκεσιν) has been elided and has become substituted instead by ulcers that looked as if they were "burnt in" the patients' skin (6.1166–67): *et simul ulceribus quasi **inustis** omne rubere / corpus*. Once again, Lucretius directs our attention to thunderbolts and the way in which they have been introduced in 6.219–21: *quod superest, quali natura praedita constent / fulmina, declarant ictus et **inusta** vaporis / signa notaeque gravis halantes sulpuris auras*, "furthermore, what kind of a nature thunderbolts have, is made clear by the strokes and the marks of heat burnt in, and the dints breathing offensive gusts of sulphur". Overall, and compared to Thucydides, the victims of the plague in Lucretius have been made larger: their disease is not presented simply as an obliterating force but allows them to function as images of phenomena — such as lightnings, thunderbolts and volcanic eruptions — which transcend the narrow limits of the human body and, crucially, inspire throughout the poem feelings of awe and admiration. The aesthetic effect here is produced by the way in which *morbus* is seamlessly employed to conjure up analogies between the microcosm and the macrocosm:[109] the suffering body,

---

108 See also the interplay between the "throat" of Aetna (6.639–40: *per fauces ut Aetnae / expirent ignes*; 6.689: *tollit se ac rectis ita faucibus eicit alte*; 6.701–2: *in summo sunt vertice enim crateres, ut ipsi / nominitant, nos quod fauces perhibemus et ora*, "for on the topmost summit are craters, as they themselves call them, what we speak of as the throat or the mouth") and that of the diseased in 6.1147–48: *sudabant etiam fauces intrinsecus atrae*, "the throat also, black within, sweated blood"; cf. 6.1151: *per fauces pectus complerat* and 6.1189: *per fauces rauca vix edita tussi*.
109 This is a common practice throughout the poem. The most vivid analogies between our individual bodies and the macrocosm involve illness as a common point of reference. An ailing — and not a healthy — body, Lucretius seems to suggest, is more fit to provide us with a better

through its experience of pain and sickness, becomes extended as it were into something bigger and more imposing than it is normally thought to be and, thus, increasingly assimilated to the grand natural forces that seem otherwise to dominate our lives.

Equally important for the plague's sublime effect is the emphasis placed on void in the poem's final section. Thucydides describes the sick people's attempt to satisfy their thirst as follows (2.49.5): ἥδιστά τε ἂν ἐς ὕδωρ ψυχρὸν σφᾶς αὐτοὺς ῥίπτειν. καὶ πολλοὶ τοῦτο τῶν ἠμελημένων ἀνθρώπων καὶ ἔδρασαν ἐς φρέατα, τῇ δίψῃ ἀπαύστῳ ξυνεχόμενοι, "and what they most felt like was throwing themselves into cold water. Indeed many who were not being looked after actually did so, jumping into rain-tanks, possessed by a thirst that could not be quenched".[110] The Greek text is closely imitated by Lucretius but, once again, the people's agony becomes intensified as they are said to throw themselves into the wells "from high above" and with "their mouths wide open" (6.1172–75): *in fluvios partim gelidos ardentia morbo / membra dabant nudum iacientes corpus in undas. / multi praecipites lymphis putealibus* **alte** */ inciderunt, ipso venientes* **ore patente**, "some cast their frame burning with the plague into cool streams, throwing the body naked into the waters. Many fell headlong from a height into wells of water, which they struck first with gaping mouth as they came". *Patente* in 6.1175 is a word which has been consistently used in the narrative to describe vast apertures and long distances beyond calculation. In 4.398 it describes a massive channel of water that keeps two mountains apart from each other (*liber patet exitus ingens*); in 4.417 Lucretius uses it to speak of the lofty gaping of the sky that is stretching above us (*caeli patet altus hiatus*). But the verb's most distinctive meaning is the one which points to the void — to the immeasurable breadth and depth at which emptiness can spread.[111] At the end of the poem, such emptiness is intrinsically linked to the vanishing of life.[112] *Ore patente* seems specifically designed to recall the huge gaping mouth of death which awaits to devour the world

---

understanding of the *mortal* world we inhabit. See, especially, 5.338–50, 6.591–607, 6.655–69, with Segal 1990, 94–114.

110 Translation in Mynott 2013, 120.

111 See 1.954–57: *item quod inane repertumst / seu locus ac spatium, res in quo quaeque gerantur, / pervideamus utrum finitum funditus omne / constet an* **immensum pateat vasteque profundum**, "likewise as regards the void which has been found to exist, or place and space for all things to be done, let us see clearly whether it be limited in its essence or spread to breadth immeasurable and vasty depth". Lucretius' answer to this question is that the universe knows no ends or limits (1.958ff.); see also 2.92–93: *spatium sine fine modoquest, / immensumque* **patere** *in cunctas undique partis*.

112 For death as a state of "absolute vacuity", see Porter 2016, 448.

in its final moments before destruction (5.373–75): *haud igitur leti praeclusa est ianua caelo / nec soli terraeque neque altis aequoris undis, / sed* **patet** *immani et vasto respectat* **hiatu**, "the door of death therefore is not closed for the heavens, nor for sun and earth and the deep waters of the sea, but stands open and awaits them with vast and hideous maw".[113] As Charles Segal points out, "the gate of death becomes virtually a living mouth, a huge gaping maw … The vastness of the aperture is vividly portrayed by the expressive hyperbaton and elision (*immani et vasto respectat hiatu*). Cosmic destruction here, personal destruction in the remote past (5.990–98): both take the same form, actual or anticipated, of engulfement by fierce jaws".[114] But while in the passages mentioned by Segal the human body is treated as a passive object, waiting to be consumed by death and wild beasts, in the course of the plague it has been transformed into something different: the detail of the patients' open mouths looks at once discouraging – a symptom of utter despair and helplessness – but also invigorating in a sense, and sublimely so, since it elevates them into active participants of their own demise. While throughout the poem vacuity represents a notion that is alien and hostile to the human body – which, as every other compound object, requires that matter is present and that it has been fixed in an appropriately condensed form – the book's final scene holds in store a surprising twist by turning that same body into a devouring force which resembles the consuming void. Lucretius' analogy between microcosm and macrocosm thus comes full circle: not only can our bodies serve as reflections of the vast and solid compounds of matter which surrounds us; they can also stand as analogues for the absence of that matter,[115] by gesturing towards what remains by its nature invisible and intangible: the gaping void itself.

---

113 For the link between 5.373–75 and the plague, see Segal 1990, 98–99: "The power of the disintegrative process … to engulf the entire universe has its human counterpart in the engulfement of the entire city of Athens by the plague at the end of the poem. This is the human, social equivalent to the chaos at the end of the world".
114 Segal 1990, 136.
115 According to Porter 2016, 449, the central theme of Book 6 "is the porosity and voiding of sensible matter, and ultimately void as the absence (or unintelligibility) of matter itself. Hence the extraordinary frequency of terms for emptiness in this book: *cava, cavernae, vacuum, inanis, fauces, foramina, hiatus, barathrum*, and so on. Hence, too, the focus of the book, namely bodies lapsing into emptiness, collapsing, and caving in. Earthquakes, volcanic eruptions, vast cloud formations riddled with thunderbolts, empty spaces underground and overhead, and the boundless universe itself, are all analogues for this emptying out of sensation's contents within the objects of sensation". For a similar image of emptiness increasingly gaining ground over matter, see the description of the faces of the diseased in 6.1194: **cavati** *oculi,* **cava** *tempora*.

The plague is not the only destructive event with sublime aspirations in the poem. Already in the proem to Book 2, Lucretius has given us a taste of what it feels like to watch a scene of death and suffering from an elevated standpoint (2.1–6):[116] **Suave**, *mari magno turbantibus aequora ventis, / e terra magnum alterius **spectare** laborem; / non quia vexari quemquamst **iucunda voluptas**, / sed quibus ipse malis careas quia **cernere suave** est. / **suave** etiam belli certamina magna **tueri** / per campos instructa tua sine parte pericli,* "pleasant it is, when on the great sea the winds trouble the waters, to gaze from shore upon another's great tribulation: not because any man's troubles are a delectable joy, but because to perceive what ills you are free from yourself is pleasant. Pleasant is it also to behold great encounters of warfare arrayed over the plains, with no part of yours in the peril". The combined emphasis on pleasure and spectacle inevitably lends an aesthetic value to what Lucretius claims to be actually enjoying in these lines; although his *voluptas* is said to derive from the knowledge that he is safe (and not from the pain of others as such),[117] it is also emerging as a response to the intrinsic sublimity contained in majestic catastrophes. Ovid picks up the hint in *Amores* 1.15.23–24, when he speaks of "the songs of sublime Lucretius [that] will perish only on the day that sees the destruction of the earth",[118] *carmina* **sublimis** *tunc sunt peritura Lucreti, /* **exitio** *terras cum* **dabit una dies**. Reference here is made to Lucr. 5.93–96: *quorum naturam triplicem, tria corpora, Memmi, / tris species tam dissimilis, tria talia texta, /* **una dies dabit exitio**, *multosque per annos / sustentata ruet moles et machina mundi,* "this threefold nature [i.e. the earth, the sea and the sky], these three masses, Memmius, these three forms so different, these three textures so interwoven, one day shall consign to destruction; the mighty and complex system of the world, upheld through many years, shall crash into ruins". While Lucretius' poem evolves as a narrative of endless birth, death and

---

116 For the sublime in Lucr. 2.1–19, see Most 2012, 247–48; cf. Day 2013, 144. It has long been observed that the plague at the end of the poem provides a spectacle that is supposed to remind us of the scenes of suffering encountered in the proem to Book 2; see, more recently, Morrison 2013, 223–24.
117 See the discussions in Holtsmark 1967; De Lacy 2007; Winter 2019, 397–405, 411ff.
118 Translation in Hardie 2009, 197, with further discussion; see also Hardie 2007, 116–17. Cf. Ov. *Tr.* 2.423–26: *utque suo Martem cecinit gravis Ennius ore / Ennius ingenio maximus arte rudis: / explicat ut causas rapidi Lucretius ignis, / casurumque triplex vaticinator opus,* "Ennius, solemnly, with appropriate voice, was the singer of Mars; Ennius sublime for energy, artistically a primitive; Lucretius unfolds the causes of the devastating fire, and prophetizes a catastrophe for the threefold structure of the universe"; translation in Barchiesi 1997b, 24–25, with further discussion. See also Ov. *Fast.* 1.301 (*sublimia pectora*), with Schiesaro 2014, 91–92.

recreation, the sublime feeling, so Ovid suggests, is mainly inspired by the dismantling of things; the coming together of matter can be captivating and thrilling but it is only with its counterpart, the dissolution of compound bodies, that horror creeps in and, along with fascination, produces sublime sensations. The plague provides us with a glimpse into what this final day of sublime destruction, foreseen in 5.93–96, might look like. The overarching combat between fire and water that shapes the entire scene brings to mind Lucretius' earlier description in Book 5 of the ongoing struggle between elemental forces in the universe — a struggle that will be resolved only when one of those elements will prevail, and the world as we know it will come to an end (5.380–84): *denique tantopere inter se cum maxima mundi / pugnent membra, pio nequaquam concita bello, / nonne vides aliquam longi certaminis ollis / posse dari finem? vel cum sol et vapor omnis /* **omnibus epotis umoribus** *exsuperarint*, "again, since the greatest members of the world fight so hard together, stirred by most unrighteous war, do you not see that some end may be given to their long strife? Either when sun and all heat shall prevail, having drunk up all the waters...". *Omnibus epotis umoribus* in 5.384 foreshadows the drinking of vast quantities of water during the plague as the patients strive to extinguish the unbearable burning feeling that is torturing them. As we eventually see those patients throwing themselves into rivers and wells, water appears to take the upper hand (6.1172–75) — reminding us of an alternative scenario for the world's destruction (5.394–95): *cum semel interea fuerit superantior ignis / et semel, ut fama est,* **umor regnarit** *in arvis*, "although in the meanwhile fire won the mastery once, and once, as the story goes, water was king over the fields". This is an "impious" war (5.380: *pio nequaquam concita bello*; 5.382: *certaminis*), a civil strife of sorts.[119] Likewise, the plague in Athens shifts the focus from the external enemy lurking outside the city's walls into the dismantling of the civic body from the inside: *rixantes*, the participle which dominates the poem's final line (6.1286), shows the citizens fighting among each other over their dead, like warriors in a battlefield.[120]

The plague brings out the struggle between elemental forces in the universe and creates the environment for a sublime ending, and an equally stupendous restart, of the world.[121] In 6.1125 the disease is introduced as *clades* **nova** *pestilitasque*. The adjective *novum* here is meant to stress that the sickness invades a

---

119 See Gee 2013, 54–55.
120 See also 6.1247–48: *inque aliis alium, populum sepelire suorum / certantes* and compare it with *certaminis* in 5.382.
121 In this respect, it creates a sort of contrast with the slow decay of the earth, as the latter has been described at the end of Book 2; see especially 2.1173–74: *nec tenet omnia paulatim tabescere*

part of the world to which it does not naturally belong; *novitas caeli* has been mentioned a few lines above (6.1103) in association with the odd looking effects which different environmental conditions have on the inhabitants of remote places around the globe (6.1103–15). What is exceptional in the case of the plague is that this "novelty of climate" is not confined within its place of origin (Egypt) but travels through the air and enters the land of Attica as a complete stranger; not only does the plague threaten human and animal life, it also brings large scale confusion into the orderly distribution of diverse climates across different parts of the world.[122] On a broader cosmological level, *nova pestilitas* brings to mind the "strange storm", *nova tempestas*, out of which our world was created– a point in time when no rules applied and order was missing since everything existed as a confused mass of atoms (5.436–42). The world which we currently inhabit, Lucretius suggests, has no space left for such "novelty": a long time has passed since the infancy of the earth (5.780: *novitas mundi*), when things still retained the ability to inspire wonder because they looked new and unusual; the universe has now come to be governed by deeply fixed laws, which leaves only little space to the possibility of experiencing feelings of pure astonishment.[123] And yet, with cosmic destruction looming as an inevitable reality, a return to a strange primordial state of things is also unavoidable. In a universe where no divine providence exists to guarantee the orderly formation of a new world, the dissolution of things will bring with it, once more, a confusion that is bound to last before the

---

et ire / ad scopulum, spatio aetatis defessa vetusto, "nor does the farmer comprehend that all things gradually decay, and go to the reef of destruction, outworn by the ancient lapse of years". With *paulatim tabescere* compare the quick-killing disease in 6.1201: *posterius tamen hunc **tabes** letumque manebat*.

122 See, especially, 6.1106–13: *nam quid Brittannis caelum **differre** putamus, / et quod in Aegypto est qua mundi claudicat axis, / quidve quod in Ponto est **differre**, et Gadibus atque / usque ad nigra virum percocto saecla colore? / quae cum quattuor inter se **diversa** videmus / quattuor a ventis et caeli partibus esse, / tum color et facies hominum **distare** videntur / largiter et morbi generatim saecla tenere*, "for what difference must we suppose to be between the climate of Britain and that of Egypt where the world's pole leans aslant? What between that which is in Pontus, and at Gades right onwards to the tribes of black men with their roasted skin? And as we see these four climates to be diverse under the four winds and quarters of heaven, so the colour and aspect of men are seen to be widely different and diseases to posses the nations after their kind". The emphasis placed on difference in these lines implies a state of order that is maintained through fixed boundaries and divisions; cf. *tris species **tam dissimilis*** (5.94), used for the three different forms of the earth, the sky and the sea, which have to remain apart from each other so that the complex system of the world continues to be operative. The plague is no ordinary disease precisely because it brings with it a collapse of those boundaries, as different parts of the world (in this case, Egypt and Greece) are seen to come perilously close to each other.
123 See Hardie 2009, 38–39.

atoms find their ways again into operative compounds of matter. The plague at the end of the poem activates two different perspectives of time, and derives sublime meaning from both: to the extent that it is presented as an event which already occurred in the past, it assumes the form of a stunningly horrifying spectacle; at the same time, and insofar as it can be seen to function as a metaphor for the approaching cosmic destruction, it signals the arrival of yet another *nova tempestas* — a point in the future when a magnificent *discordia rerum* will be restored in full force, until something new will emerge out of it.[124]

4.4 Conclusion

As I have tried to argue in the last section, Lucretius spends considerable effort creating a spectacle out of the plague, either by linking it to celestial phenomena that inspire awe and admiration or by implying its intrinsic connection to images of cosmic chaos and destruction that exist far beyond the realm of ordinary human experience. In this section, and by way of conclusion, I would like to consider the possibility that Thucydides may have served as a source of inspiration for Lucretius, since the Greek historian's text appears also to be engaged at points with what may be termed the plague's sublime potential.

Thucydides' description of the plague makes it abundantly clear from the very beginning that this was no ordinary disease.[125] In 2.49.2 he introduces it by saying that those people who were healthy fell ill "all of a sudden", without there being an obvious πρόφασις (τοὺς δὲ ἄλλους ἀπ' οὐδεμιᾶς προφάσεως, ἀλλ' ἐξαίφνης ὑγιεῖς ὄντας); this is precisely the kind of language that a doctor would have used to speak of an illness that is lacking an evident cause and which makes prognosis difficult.[126] In 2.51.1 Thucydides mentions ἀτοπία: the account he is about to

---

124 See 5.436–39: *sed nova tempestas quaedam molesque coorta / omnigenis e principiis, discordia quorum / intervalla vias conexus pondera plagas / concursus motus turbabat proelia miscens*, "a sort of strange storm [was to be seen], all kinds of beginnings gathered together into a mass, while their discord, exciting war amongst them, made a confusion of intervals, courses, connections, weights, blows, meetings, motions". For universal discord and the sublime, see Porter 2016, 500–501; cf. Hardie 2009, 99–107 and 119–22.
125 The historian even implies at points that the disease might have been sent by the gods; see Kallet 2013 and Michelakis 2019, 386–87. For a review of the scholarship on Thucydides' treatment of religion in relation to the plague, see Rubel 2000, 123–34. Cf. Polybius 36.17: certain events are simply beyond human understanding, such as natural disasters like storms, droughts and plagues.
126 See Hankinson 1988, 57–58. For *prophasis* in Thucydides, see Rood 1998, 208–10. Weidauer 1954, 8–20 examines the term in Thucydides and the Hippocratic texts. Ludwig 2002, 157 n. 109

give, he tells us, will reproduce the general picture of the disease (ἰδέα) but it will leave out details that may look too "extraordinary" or even "absurd" to be included (τὸ μὲν οὖν νόσημα, **πολλὰ καὶ ἄλλα παραλιπόντι ἀτοπίας**, ὡς ἑκάστῳ ἐτύγχανέ τι διαφερόντως ἑτέρῳ πρὸς ἕτερον γιγνόμενον, τοιοῦτον ἦν ἐπὶ πᾶν τὴν ἰδέαν, "this, then, was the general character of the disease, leaving aside its many peculiarities in the different ways it affected different people").[127] There is a clear indication here that the disease was too odd to lend itself to a thorough and exhaustive account. In fact, as is explicitly stated in 2.50.1–2, the plague "defied all reason":

γενόμενον γὰρ **κρεῖσσον λόγου** τὸ εἶδος τῆς νόσου τά τε ἄλλα χαλεπωτέρως ἢ κατὰ τὴν ἀνθρωπείαν φύσιν προσέπιπτεν ἑκάστῳ καὶ ἐν τῷδε ἐδήλωσε μάλιστα ἄλλο τι ὂν ἢ τῶν ξυντρόφων τι· τὰ γὰρ ὄρνεα καὶ τετράποδα ὅσα ἀνθρώπων ἅπτεται, πολλῶν ἀτάφων γιγνομένων ἢ οὐ προσῄει ἢ γευσάμενα διεφθείρετο. τεκμήριον δέ· τῶν μὲν τοιούτων ὀρνίθων ἐπίλειψις σαφὴς ἐγένετο, καὶ οὐχ ἑωρῶντο οὔτε ἄλλως οὔτε περὶ τοιοῦτον οὐδέν.

Indeed the form the plague took defied all reason. When it attacked anyone it was beyond all human endurance and in one respect in particular it showed itself quite different from any of the more familiar diseases. Despite there being many unburied bodies the birds and animals which feed on human flesh either kept away from the corpses or if they started eating them died themselves. The evidence for this is that there was a marked absence of such birds, which were not to be seen at the bodies or anywhere else at all.[128]

The phrase κρεῖσσον λόγου is a hapax in Thucydides.[129] The historian could be suggesting that the disease, due to its uncommon nature and the way in which it infected humans and animals alike, was beyond human understanding. Pericles

---

is right to observe that ἀπ' οὐδεμιᾶς προφάσεως should be associated with the historian's subsequent admission in 2.50.1 that his description "fails to capture the *eidos* of the disease".

127 Translation in Mynott 2013, 121. For the association between *atopon* and *thaumasion* and their opposition to the notions of nature (*phusis*) and cause (*aitia*), see Schiefsky 2007, 80–81. For *atopon* in Thucydides, see Sears 2013, 255.
128 Translation in Mynott 2013, 120.
129 According to Demont 2013, 75, Thucydides' claim that the disease was κρεῖσσον λόγου must have sounded rather unusual by contemporary Hippocratic standards. A doctor around that time would not have easily admitted to the fact that there are things in the human body — whether in health or sickness — that could escape his power of understanding. Cf. Michelakis 2019, 392–93: "In Thucydides, the plague is an all-encompassing disease that pushes and redefines the boundaries of what disease is. It is different from any of the familiar diseases … It stands over and above one's ability to describe, explain, and predict … It is also disproportionately powerful for human nature … The unusual superiority of the plague over domains such as reason, language, predictability, and human nature, and its alien character compared to ordinary diseases, bring about what Thucydides sums up as "such a great upheaval" (τοσαύτης μεταβολῆς, 2.48.3)".

insists on this point when he calls it in 2.61.3 a "sudden, unexpected and completely unaccountable" event (τὸ αἰφνίδιον καὶ ἀπροσδόκητον καὶ **τὸ πλείστῳ παραλόγῳ** ξυμβαῖνον). At the same time, Thucydides' phrasing could be alluding to the actual difficulty of "putting into words" the disastrous effects of the disease (cf. 2.51.1: πολλὰ καὶ ἄλλα παραλιπόντι).[130] To be in "loss of words"[131] is a typical reaction to something that looks "wonderful", θαυμάσιον, whether in a positive or a negative sense;[132] as a response, it is suitably applied to emotional states which emerge from an encounter with a dauntingly sublime spectacle or sensation.[133] Not incidentally, one of the few occurrences of the phrase κρεῖσσον λόγου in Greek literature, with the meaning of something that is "beyond description", is attested in Josephus' account of Herod's splendid palace in *BJ* 5.177–80:

---

130 So Demont 2013, 75, who adopts Charles Forster Smith's Loeb translation of γενόμενον γὰρ κρεῖσσον λόγου τὸ εἶδος τῆς νόσου as: "the character of the disease proved such that it baffles description".

131 Loss of words is also present in Lucretius, though in a slightly different form (6.1178–79): *nec requies erat ulla mali: defessa iacebant / corpora.* **mussabat** *tacito medicina timore*, "nor was there any rest from pain. Medicine muttered below her breath, scared into silence". This striking image of impotence and fear in the face of the plague could be an allusion to Thucydides: the disease is once again seen to compromise speech, first by rendering the patients voiceless as they literally choke in their own blood (6.1147–50) and then by virtue of its presentation as a force of nature which cannot be handled by medical science and imposes silence on those who attempt to speak about it and explain it. The uncommon verb *mussare* ("to mutter", "stand quiet") in 6.1179 is not a random choice of word in this context: its first occurrence in Latin is attested in Ennius (*Ann.* 6.168, 10.327, 17.435. See Elliott 2013, 435); significantly, Vergil then uses it to convey the people's emotional reaction elicited by the thrilling and captivating sight of an epic battle, the bull-like clash between Aeneas and Turnus (*Aen.* 12.718).

132 See e.g. Eur. *IT* 839–40 (Iphigenia discovers her brother among the Taurians): **θαυμάτων / πέρα καὶ λόγου πρόσω** τάδ' ἀπέβα. But see also Eur. *Bacch.* 666–67 (the Messenger is about to disclose to Pentheus the abominable acts of the frenzied women): ἥκω φράσαι σοι καὶ πόλει χρῄζων, ἄναξ, / ὡς δεινὰ δρῶσι **θαυμάτων τε κρείσσονα**. To be "beyond wonder/ speech" is especially favourite as a notion among the Greek tragedians. Even when it is emerging as a response to a painful event, it still contains in it an element of thrill and excitement: the Messenger in Euripides' *Bacchae* is enthralled by the sight of the maenads as much as he is appalled by it. A similar mix of feelings could be detected throughout Thucydides' account of the plague. For the link between loss of speech and wonder, see Neer 2010, 60–62.

133 See e.g. Xen. *Mem.* 3.11: Γυναικὸς δέ ποτε οὔσης ἐν τῇ πόλει καλῆς ... μνησθέντος αὐτῆς τῶν παρόντων τινὸς καὶ εἰπόντος ὅτι κρεῖττον εἴη λόγου τὸ κάλλος τῆς γυναικός, καὶ ζωγράφους φήσαντος εἰσιέναι πρὸς αὐτὴν ἀπεικασομένους, and Diod. Sic. 3.46.4: θεία γάρ τις φαίνεται καὶ λόγου κρείττων ἡ προσπίπτουσα καὶ κινοῦσα τὰς ἑκάστων αἰσθήσεις εὐωδία. For ineffability and the sublime, see Porter 2016, 48, 52, 22–27.

Adjoining and on the inner side of these towers, which lay to the north of it, was the king's palace, baffling all description (παντὸς λόγου κρείσσων) ... It was completely enclosed within a wall thirty cubits high, broken at equal distances by ornamental towers, and contained immense banqueting-halls and bedchambers for a hundred guests. The interior fittings are indescribable — the variety of the stones (for species rare in every other country were here collected in abundance), ceilings wonderful both for the length of the beams and the splendor of their surface decoration (ἐν οἷς **ἀδιήγητος** μὲν ἡ ποικιλία τῶν λίθων ἦν, συνῆκτο γὰρ πολὺς ὁ πανταχοῦ σπάνιος, **θαυμασταὶ** δὲ ὀροφαὶ μήκει τε δοκῶν καὶ λαμπρότητι προκοσμημάτων), the host of apartments with their infinite varieties of design, all amply furnished, while most of the objects in each of them were of silver or gold.[134]

The hypothesis that the notion of the sublime is built into Thucydides' account of the plague would not have sounded strange to someone like Longinus. In *Subl.* 38.3 Longinus discusses the figure of "hyperbole", saying that it should not be exaggerated and that the best kind of it is that which conceals itself "when it is uttered under stress of emotion to suit the circumstances of a great crisis".[135] The passage that is cited to illustrate this thesis bears close resemblance to the plague: "This is what Thucydides does in speaking of those who were killed in Sicily. 'For the Syracusans went down and began to slaughter chiefly those in the river. The water was immediately tainted but nonetheless they kept on drinking it, foul though it was with mud and gore, and most of them were still ready to fight for it' [Thuc. 7.84]. That a drink of mud and gore should yet still be worth fighting for is made credible only by the height of the emotion which the circumstances arouse (...'οἵ τε γὰρ Συρακούσιοι' φησὶν 'ἐπικαταβάντες τοὺς ἐν τῷ ποταμῷ μάλιστα ἔσφαζον, **καὶ τὸ ὕδωρ εὐθὺς διέφθαρτο· ἀλλ' οὐδὲν ἧσσον ἐπίνετο ὁμοῦ τῷ πηλῷ ἡματωμένον καὶ τοῖς πολλοῖς ἔτι ἦν περιμάχητον**'. αἷμα καὶ πηλὸν πινόμενα ὅμως εἶναι περιμάχητα ἔτι ποιεῖ πιστὸν ἡ τοῦ πάθους ὑπεροχὴ καὶ περίστασις)".[136] The Athenians' disaster in Sicily is narrated by Thucydides in a way that seems specifically designed to recall the great plague in Book 2.[137] The reference to the polluted water in the passage cited by Longinus is crucial for establishing a link with 2.48.2, at which point Thucydides introduces us to the disease by mentioning the suspicion that the water of the city was poisoned by the Peloponnesians (ὥστε καὶ ἐλέχθη ὑπ' αὐτῶν ὡς οἱ Πελοποννήσιοι φάρμακα ἐσβεβλήκοιεν ἐς τὰ φρέατα). Further comparison between the two texts yields a

---

134 Translation in Thackeray 1928, 55.
135 *Subl.* 38.3: μήποτ' οὖν ἄρισται τῶν ὑπερβολῶν, ὡς καὶ ἐπὶ τῶν σχημάτων προείπομεν, αἱ αὐτὸ τοῦτο διαλανθάνουσαι ὅτι εἰσὶν ὑπερβολαί. γίνεται δὲ τὸ τοιόνδε, ἐπειδὰν ὑπὸ ἐκπαθείας μεγέθει τινὶ συνεκφωνῶνται περιστάσεως.
136 Translation in Fyfe/Russell 1995, 283.
137 See Rood 2012, 159.

number of significant affinities in terms of content and language. The miserable state of the imprisoned Athenians in 7.87.1–2 (ἐν γὰρ κοίλῳ χωρίῳ ὄντας καὶ ὀλίγῳ πολλοὺς οἵ τε ἥλιοι τὸ πρῶτον καὶ τὸ πνῖγος ἔτι ἐλύπει διὰ τὸ ἀστέγαστον καὶ αἱ νύκτες ἐπιγιγνόμεναι τοὐναντίον μετοπωριναὶ καὶ ψυχραὶ τῇ μεταβολῇ ἐς ἀσθένειαν ἐνεωτέριζον, πάντα τε ποιούντων αὐτῶν διὰ στενοχωρίαν ἐν τῷ αὐτῷ καὶ προσέτι τῶν νεκρῶν ὁμοῦ ἐπ᾽ ἀλλήλοις ξυννενημένων, οἵ ἔκ τε τῶν τραυμάτων καὶ διὰ τὴν μεταβολὴν καὶ τὸ τοιοῦτον ἀπέθνῃσκον, καὶ ὀσμαὶ ἦσαν οὐκ ἀνεκτοί, καὶ **λιμῷ** ἅμα καὶ δίψῃ ἐπιέζοντο)[138] could in fact be read as a replay of the plague in condensed form, evoking, among others, details such as the "foul breath" of the patients (2.49.2: καὶ πνεῦμα ἄτοπον καὶ δυσῶδες ἠφίει), the terrible need for water (2.49.5: τῇ δίψῃ ἀπαύστῳ ξυνεχόμενοι) and the suffocating lack of space (2.52.2: οἰκιῶν γὰρ οὐχ ὑπαρχουσῶν, ἀλλ᾽ ἐν καλύβαις πνιγηραῖς ὥρᾳ ἔτους διαιτωμένων ὁ φθόρος ἐγίγνετο οὐδενὶ κόσμῳ ἀλλὰ καὶ νεκροὶ ἐπ᾽ ἀλλήλοις ἀποθνῄσκοντες ἔκειντο).

In Longinus' understanding, what matters principally is the intensity of emotion generated by a certain text. Disease, as theme, seems to fit well in this picture. It is worth stressing that the famous quotation of Sappho fr.31 Voigt in *Subl.* 10.2 is followed by an observation that shows Longinus dealing with the Greek text almost as though it were a medical list of symptoms: οὐ θαυμάζεις, ὡς, ὑ<πὸ τὸ> αὐτὸ τὴν ψυχὴν τὸ σῶμα τὰς ἀκοὰς τὴν γλῶσσαν τὰς ὄψεις τὴν χρόαν, πάνθ᾽ ὡς ἀλλότρια διοιχόμενα ἐπιζητεῖ καὶ καθ᾽ ὑπεναντιώσεις ἅμα ψύχεται κάεται, ἀλογιστεῖ φρονεῖ [ἢ γὰρ φοβεῖται ἢ παρ᾽ ὀλίγον τέθνηκεν] ἵνα μὴ ἕν τι περὶ αὐτὴν πάθος φαίνηται, **παθῶν δὲ σύνοδος,** "is it not wonderful how she summons at the same time, soul, body, hearing, tongue, sight, skin, all as though they had wandered off apart from herself? She feels contradictory sensations, freezes, burns, raves, reasons [she is either afraid or at the point of death] so that she displays not a single emotion, but a whole congeries of emotions" (*Subl.* 10.3).[139] The phrase used by Longinus for the combined presence of conflicting emotions, παθῶν σύνοδος, has medical overtones.[140] In the Galenic corpus, for example, σύνοδος συμπτωμάτων designates as

---

138 "There were large numbers of them in a small space in the pits, and as there was no roof they were first oppressed by the heat of the sun by day and by the stifling air; the nights that followed were in contrast autumnal and chilly and the men's condition was further weakened by the change in temperature. Besides, because of the confined space they had to do everything in the same spot and to make matters worse the bodies of the dead were heaped one on top of another (whether dying from wounds, from the change in temperature or from other such causes) and the stench was intolerable" (translation in Mynott 2013, 509).
139 Translation in Fyfe/Russell 1995, 201.
140 See Fowler 2000, 153. For the medical imagery in Sappho's fragment, see Ferrari 2001, with Thumiger 2017, 129–30.

a technical term a concurrence of symptoms, which point as a group to a specific medical condition.[141] The clinical profiling applied to the Sapphic text implies that Longinus sees disease as a theme that can be appropriately used to elicit a strong emotional response from the audience and, along with it, to produce sublime feelings.

Whether apart from responding to Thucydides' account of the plague as something "ineffable" and "extraordinary" Lucretius is also engaging with a wider tradition that tends to treat sickness as a potentially sublime theme is hard to tell. However this might have been, the end of *DRN* 6 displays a clear tendency to establish disease as an aesthetically meaningful subject, by inviting the readers to respond to it with a mix of horror and fascination and to view death not only as an intimidating reality but also as a grand exit from life. Lucretius is by no means blind to the fact that disease entails disorder, a lack of κόσμος on the human level, as Thucydides puts it (2.52.2: ὁ φθόρος ἐγίγνετο οὐδενὶ κόσμῳ). But in the same way that the Greek historian invites us to marvel at the λοιμός as a superior disease which transcends the boundaries of ordinary human experience, so does Lucretius' plague emerge throughout as an elevated force of nature which, despite the pain and gruesome death it brings to the people of Athens, can still claim its own peculiar place in the domain of the sublime and the beautiful.

4.5 Appendix

Recent discussions of the reception of the Lucretian sublime in Latin literature have revealed an ambivalent response by later authors, such as Horace and Ovid.[142] With regard to Horace, Philip Hardie identifies "a combination of attraction to and distancing from Lucretius" and an "alternation between an investment in a Lucretian earnestness and a belittling of that earnestness".[143] One of the central passages for Hardie's discussion is *Odes* 1.1.35–36, addressed to Maecenas: *quodsi me lyricis vatibus inseres, / **sublimi** feriam sidera vertice*, "but if you enroll me among the lyric bards, I shall knock against the stars with my head held high". The lines are echoed at the end of the *Ars Poetica*, at the point where Horace ridicules the caricature of the mad poet whose sublime aspirations make him

---

141 See e.g. ps.-Galen, *Definitiones medicae* 169 (19.395 K.): Συνδρομή ἐστι σύνοδος τῶν συμπτωμάτων. ἢ τὸ τῶν συμπτωμάτων ἄθροισμα. ἢ τὸ τῶν συμπτωμάτων ἄθροισμα φαινομένων ἐναργῶς ἅπασιν. For the intersection of medicine and literary criticism in Longinus' text, see Arthur-Montagne 2017.
142 See Hardie 2009, 180–228 and Schiesaro 2014, on Horace and Ovid respectively.
143 Hardie 2009, 180 and 181.

fall into a pit (455–60): *vesanum tetigisse timent fugiuntque poetam / qui sapiunt, agitant pueri incautique sequuntur. / hic, dum **sublimis** versus ructatur et errat, / si veluti merulis intentus decidit auceps / in puteum foveamve, licet 'succurrite' longum / clamet, 'io cives', non sit qui tollere curet*, "men of sense are afraid to touch a mad poet and flee him; reckless children follow after and harass him. Suppose, as he weaves along with his head in the clouds,[144] belching his poems, he falls down into a pit or a well, like a birdcatcher intent on blackbirds; though he yell loud and long "Ho, fellow-citizens, help, help!" no one will bother to pull him out".[145] Considering that the mad poet's (premeditated) fall is subsequently associated with Empedocles' suicide (463–66), it is possible, according to Hardie, that Horace is poking fun here at Lucretius, who is hiding behind the figure of the Greek philosopher:[146] the higher one aspires to reach, the more dangerous it becomes for him to fall; sublime yearnings are noble but they also make you lose sight of what lies just under your feet.

More recently, Alessandro Schiesaro has read Phaethon's story in Ovid *Met.* 1.747–2.400 along the same lines, as an episode which reflects on the virtues and limits of Lucretius' sublime aspirations and ends up in an active confrontation and pointed contrast with the Epicurean poet.[147] While Ovid, according to Schiesaro, gives credit to Lucretius for his literary qualities and his striving for the sublime, he is at the same time criticizing him because the gods have been deprived of any meaningful presence in his universe. Epicurus' flight of mind in search of the ultimate truth, which is praised by Lucretius in *DRN* 1.72–77, turns in Ovid's hands into an ill-fated ride that brings disaster all over the world. Among the immediate victims, Ovid mentions the swans crowding the bank of the river Cayster in Maeonia (2.252–53). "Ovid's combusted swans", as Schiesaro observes, "may suggest that what is ending up in flames here is also Epicurus-the-swan as mentioned…in the proem to Book 3 of *DRN* and his dream of a poetry which can be both precious and all-revealing".[148]

---

144 Compare Vergil's description of Tisiphone (a personification of the plague) in *G.* 3.551–53: *saevit et in lucem Stygiis emissa tenebris / pallida Tisiphone Morbos agit ante Metumque, / inque dies avidum surgens **caput altius effert***, "ghastly Tisiphone rages, and, let forth in light from Stygian gloom, drives before her Disease and Dread, while day by day, uprising, she rears still higher her greedy head" (translation in Fairclough/Goold 1999, 215).
145 Translation in Oliensis 1998, 216, who offers a sensitive reading of these lines, focusing especially on Horace's self-implicating ironies, in pp. 215–23.
146 For the Empedocles/Lucretius association, see Canfora 1993, 99–105.
147 Schiesaro 2014.
148 Schiesaro 2014, 95.

In what follows, I want to expand briefly on this critical attitude towards the Lucretian sublime by considering the possibility that, on occasions, such critique involves specific allusions to the plague. My aim is to corroborate further that a sublime discourse underlies the end of Lucretius' poem and that later authors read it (and criticized it) as such.

Starting with Horace, it has so far escaped attention that the end of the *Ars Poetica* recalls the plague in more than one way.[149] The element of madness side by side with the image of someone falling into a pit/well (*Ars* 455–60, cited above) are also prominent in Lucretius' account: the victims of the plague — a contagious disease (cf. Hor. *Ars* 453–55: *ut mala quem scabies*[150] *aut morbus regius urget* ... / *vesanum tetigisse timent fugiuntque poetam / qui sapiunt*, "as with a man afflicted by a repulsive rash or jaundice ... men of sense are afraid to touch a mad poet and flee him") — throw their bodies naked into cool streams, and "many fall headlong from *high* above into wells of water, which they strike with gaping mouth" (6.1174–75: *multi praecipites*[151] *lymphis putealibus alte / inciderunt ipso venientes ore patente*).[152] That they do so in a state of extreme mental discomfort is sufficiently established by such passages as Lucr. 6.1180–81 (*totiens ardentia morbis / **lumina versarent oculorum** experta somno*, "they so often rolled their staring

---

149 For one thing, the fact that Horace decides to end his entire work with the description of a disease in the final lines of the *Ars Poetica* is enough to alert us to the closural function of the plague in Lucretius' poem as a possible model.

150 *Scabies* has been mentioned by Horace earlier in the poem: high-aspiring Roman poets are just like children who boast of their "marvellous" poems (*Ars* 416: *ego mira poemata pango*) before going back to their silly games (417): *occupet extremum scabies*, "the last one's got the scabies!". As Rimell 2019, 121 n. 48 observes, it is possible that Horace is poking fun here at Lucr. 1.933–934: *deinde quod obscura de re tam lucida pango / carmina, musaeo contingens cuncta lepore*, "next because the subject is so dark and the lines I write so clear, as I touch all with Muses' grace".

151 The Lucretian *praecipites ... alte inciderunt* could have caught Horace's attention as an image pregnant with aesthetic / sublime associations. See Hardie 2009, 215–16: "Horace already uses *praeceps* as a stylistic term of the headlong dithyrambic rush of a dithyramb at *Ars Poet.* 217 *facundia praeceps*. Later *praeceps* is used specifically of the vice that corresponds to the virtue of sublimity, by Quintilian at *Inst.* 12.10.73 *corruptum dicendi genus, quod ... praecipitia pro sublimibus habet aut specie libertatis insanit* ... and by Pliny in a letter that closely parallels material in ps.-Longinus, *Ep.* 9.26.2 *debet orator erigi attolli ... ecferri, ac saepe accedere ad praeceps*".

152 *Lymphis putealibus* in 6.1174 is highly poetic. One is tempted to think that even at the moment of excruciating suffering, the plague's victims continue to occupy an aesthetically charged landscape. With *lymphis putealibus* (6.1174) and *fluvios gelidos* (6.1172), compare, for instance, Hor. *Od.* 1.1.30–32 (on the poet's Bacchic inspiration): *me gelidum nemus / nympharumque leves cum Satyri chori / secernunt populo* (Horace's lines recall Lucr. 4.580–94; see Hardie 2009, 218–19).

eyes, fiery with the plague and knowing no sleep") and 6.1183–84: *perturbata animi mens in maerore metuque, / triste supercilium, **furiosus voltus** et acer*, "a mind disordered in all this sorrow and fear, a gloomy brow, a mad and fierce look". A close reading of Lucr. 6.1172–5 reveals further affinities with Horace: *ore patente* in 6.1175 lends itself to comparison with *ructatur* in Hor. *Ars* 457: *dum sublimis versus **ructatur** et errat*. As we picture the mad poet "belching his poems" with his mouth wide open, we may be further reminded that the victims of the plague display a similar symptom (6.1160–62): ***singultusque** frequens noctem per saepe diemque / corripere adsidue nervos et membra coactans / dissoluebat eos, defessos ante, fatigans*, "retching persisted often through night and day, constantly causing cramps in the muscles and limbs, which quite broke them up, wearying those who were already wearied out". Belching in Horace implies an involuntary biological process, a point of collapse at which the body takes over the mind and wind comes out of the mouth inadvertently;[153] *ructatur* (= ἐρεύγεσθαι) in this context lies rather close to *evomere*[154] and as such it reminds us even more of the medical picture drawn by Lucretius, which is especially focused on fluids bursting out of the upper orifices of the body (see e.g. 6.1147–48, 1188–89, 1203). When we move to Empedocles' suicide (463–66) — mentioned by Horace as an example of the *vesanus poeta* — the allusions to Lucretius continue. "Longing to be thought an immortal god" (464–65: *deus immortalis haberi / dum cupit*) and reach the ultimate stage of sublimity, Empedocles jumps into the flames of Aetna at a moment when his body is seized by "excessive coldness" (465–66: ***ardentem frigidus** Aetnam / insiluit*).[155] The contrast between heat and cold recalls,

---

153 Brink 1971, 424 allows the possibility that by the time of Horace *ructatur* "had lost its coarseness... as ἐρεύγομαι had in Hellenistic Greek ... Hence *versus ructatur* may be 'to mouth, come out with, verses'". But see Bartsch 2015, 59 and n. 119, who believes that the verb hints at a digestive problem and helps to bring out a fragile bodily constitution. For the reception of Horace's "mad poet" in Persius *Sat.* 1 and 3 (the latter of the two poems ends with a scene of actual vomit which causes death), see Hooley 1997, 26–63, with Bartsch 2017, 297–99.
154 See Bramble 1974, 65.
155 Hor. *Ars* 465–66 echoes Verg. *G.* 2.483–86; see Brink 1969, 139. In the immediately preceding lines, Vergil has expressed his wish to compose a poem on natural philosophy (2.475–82) but he suddenly feels that he will not be able to carry out his plan; in this case, so he maintains, he would still be content with enjoying, without though fully comprehending, the beauties of the natural world around him (2.483–86): *sin has ne possim naturae accedere partis / frigidus obstiterit circum praecordia sanguis, / rura mihi et rigui placeant in vallibus amnes, / flumina amem silvasque inglorius*, "but if the chill blood about my heart bar me from reaching those realms of nature, let my delight be the country, and the running streams amid the dells–may I love the waters and the woods, though I be unknown to fame" (translation in Fairclough/Goold 1999, 171). Vergil's lines recall Empedocles' doctrine according to which intelligence is situated in the

in reverse, Lucr. 6. 1172–73: *in fluvios partim **gelidos ardentia** morbo / membra dabant nudum iacientes corpus in undas.*

Echoes of Lucretius' plague can also be traced in Seneca's description of the deluge which will drown the earth, in *Naturales Quaestiones* 3.27–30.[156] Seneca conceives of it as a "grand" topic, stressing clearly from the outset that compared to birth, destruction can generate more magnificent and sublime spectacles (*QNat.* 3.27.2):

> Nihil difficile naturae est, utique ubi in finem sui properat. Ad originem rerum parce utitur viribus dispensatque se incrementis fallentibus; subito ad ruinam toto impetu venit… Urbes constituit aetas, hora dissolvit; momento fit cinis, diu silva; magna tutela stant ac vigent omnia, cito ac repente dissiliunt.
>
> Nothing is difficult for nature, especially when she is hurrying toward her own finale. For the creation of everything, she uses her powers sparingly and rations herself out in barely perceptible increments; but she arrives at destruction suddenly … Cities take an age to establish, an hour to demolish; ashes are produced in a moment, a forest takes a long time. Everything needs plenty of protection to survive, but it disintegrates swiftly.[157]

Seneca's *Natural Questions* are full of allusions to the themes and topics discussed in Lucretius' Book 6.[158] Lucretius places the plague in a timeless, mythological setting (6.1138–40), which allows him subsequently to present it as a catastrophe of cataclysmic proportions — as an image of the dismantling of the world's fabric, which has been mentioned in 5.93–96. In the same way, though in a different philosophical context, Seneca speaks of the deluge as the moment which will signal the world's destruction — it is an event that is conceived as "parallel and analogous" to a Stoic *ekpurōsis* which has been decreed by the god

---

blood around the heart (see Hardie 1986, 42–43); but they are also pregnant with allusions to Lucretius: for instance, the poet's inhibitions as to whether he will be able "to approach" the ultimate truths of nature (*G.* 2.483: *sin has ne possim naturae **accedere** partis*), brings to mind the description of Lucretius' poetic initiation in *DRN* 1.927: *iuvat integros **accedere** fontis*; see Hardie 2008, 167. A few lines below (*G.* 2.490ff.: *felix quit potuit rerum cognoscere causas…*), Vergil's engagement with Lucretius becomes obvious. As Schiesaro 2014, 93 observes: "'felix qui potuit' refers … to an impossible aspiration, one immediately abandoned for the safer option of devoting oneself to the care of rural gods". All in all, Empedocles' "icy state" in Hor. *Ars* 465–66 activates an intertextual network of references which, through Vergil, points ultimately to a critical and at points ironic engagement with Lucretius' sublime aspirations.

156 For Sen. *QNat.* 3.27–30, see Hutchinson 1993, 128–31; Berno 2003, 93–102; Gauly 2004, 235–67; Mazzoli 2005; Williams 2012, 110–16.
157 Translation in Hine 2010, 44–45.
158 See, more recently, Schiesaro 2015, 246–51, with further bibliography.

(*QNat.* 3.28.7).¹⁵⁹ Both Lucretius' plague and Seneca's flood are intensely preoccupied with cosmic disasters which, in the context of the respective works, surpass by far all others. What is more, Lucretius presents the plague as a deluge of sorts. Legends of flood have been mentioned in 5.341–44 (*aut ex **imbribus** adsiduis exisse rapaces / per terras amnes atque oppida coperuisse, / tanto quique magis victus fateare necessest / exitium quoque terrarum caelique futurum*, "[if you believe that] after incessant rains rivers have issued out to sweep over the earth and overwhelm their towns, so much the more you must own yourself worsted, and agree that destruction will come to earth and sky"), without being explicitly dismissed. The end of Book 6 draws our attention to the overpowering force of water as the patients are seen almost to drown themselves by throwing their bodies into rivers and wells (6.1172–77). Just as the deluge has been assimilated to a disease by Lucretius (see 5.411–12: *umor item quondam coepit **superare coortus**, / ut fama est* and compare it with e.g. 4.664: *febris bili **superante coorta** est*), so does the plague bring out the implication of a flood which sweeps everything in its way.

Overall, there is a good chance that the end of *DRN* 6 lies at the background of Seneca *QNat.* 3.27–30. This would seem to suggest that, in conceiving of the flood as a magnificent spectacle, Seneca is responding positively to the sublime qualities of Lucretius' plague. On closer inspection, however, the flood appears to give Seneca an opportunity to take his distance from Lucretius, rather than establish a sense of affiliation.¹⁶⁰ This is how he describes the people who climb on the mountains' peaks to save themselves from the waters in *QNat.* 3.27.11–12:

> Iam omnia, qua prospici potest, aquis obsidentur; omnis tumulus in profundo latet et **immensa** ubique **altitudo** est. Tantum **in summis** montium iugis vada sunt; in ea **excelsissima** cum liberis coniugibusque fugerunt actis ante se gregibus. Diremptum inter miseros commercium ac transitus, quoniam, quicquid submissius erat, id unda complevit. **Editissimis** quibusque adhaerebant reliquiae generis humani, quibus **in extrema** perductis hoc unum solacio fuit quod transierat **in stuporem** metus. **Non vacabat timere mirantibus**, nec dolor quidem habebat locum; quippe vim suam perdit in eo qui ultra sensum mali miser est.

> Now everything, as far as the eye can see, is covered in water. Every hill is hidden beneath the sea, and everywhere the depth is enormous. Only on the highest mountain ridges are there shallows. People have fled to the tallest peaks with their children and wives, driving

---

159 See Mader 1983, 64.
160 On divergent forms of sublimity in Lucretius and Seneca, see the recent discussion in Shearin 2019.

their flocks before them. Communication and travel is cut off between these wretched people, for all the lower-lying land is filled with water. The remnants of the human race were clinging to all the highest points. In their extremity their only source of comfort was that fear had turn to bewilderment. In their dumbstruck state they had no time to be afraid; there was not even an opportunity for grief, since it loses its hold over someone who is too wretched to be aware of suffering.[161]

The Senecan sublime in this passage, expressed in terms which denote immense depths and extreme heights, is articulated in a way that establishes a clear contrast with Lucretian poetics and philosophy. Relief from fear and suffering does not come as a result of reasoning (*ratio*) but because everyone is so bewildered by the spectacle that s/he has virtually no space left to accommodate any other feelings: *non vacabat timere mirantibus*.[162] The sort of dumbstruck astonishment which in this case proves soothing is precisely what Lucretius promises, time and again, to dispel in the course of Book 6. For Lucretius, the true sublime is experienced as commensurate to a state of revelation and heightened awareness; it is the shuddering which seizes us the moment when we have come to *understand* how things around us work. In *QNat*. 3.27.11–12 Seneca suggests an alternative view: when nature's destructive forces are unleashed on such a grand scale, the sublime occupies our entire mental and emotional vision: even fear — which is so intensely felt throughout Lucretius' plague — becomes in the end eliminated. This state of pure bewilderment would seem to be in line with the philosophical context in which Seneca operates: it is ultimately linked to the belief that divine forces are constantly at work (even at the moment of the world's destruction),[163] which we as mortals will never be able to comprehend fully. This is something

---

161 Translation in Hine 2010, 46–47.
162 Cf. Sen. *Tranq*. 1.14: *Rursus ubi se animus cogitationum magnitudine levavit, ambitiosus in verba est altiusque ut spirare ita eloqui gestit et ad dignitatem rerum exit oratio; oblitus tum legis pressiorisque iudicii* **sublimius feror** *et ore iam non meo*, "again, when my mind has been uplifted by great thoughts, it is seized by ambition for words and a desire to make loftier expression match loftier aspirations, so that language emerges in keeping with the dignity of the topic; then I forget my rule and more restrictive judgement and soar to loftier heights, uttering words no longer my own" (translation in Davie 2007, 114). As Schiesaro 2003b, 53 observes: "Poetry, as an irrational force, smashes the barriers of both rationality and decorum, and overrides any hesitation enforced by timor". Cf. Staley 2010, 42–47.
163 See *QNat*. 3.28.7: both the deluge and the conflagration occur when the god has decided to inaugurate a new world and end the old one. According to Schiesaro 2015, 246, despite the broad structural and thematic affinities, the "ultimate goals" of *DRN* and *Naturales Quaestiones* "remain irreconcilable, since the understanding of nature's workings is, for Lucretius, a means to "exclude the gods from earth" (*Ep*. 90.35), while, in Seneca's eyes, the wonders of nature are a powerful reminder of divine providence"; cf. Berno 2015, 85–86.

that Lucretius would not have tolerated as a thought, neither when it comes to our perception of reality nor in our experience of its terrifying beauty.

5 Afterword

> Titus Lucretius poeta nascitur: qui postea amatorio poculo in furorem versus, cum aliquot libros per intervalla insaniae conscripsisset, quos postea Cicero emendavit, propria se manu interfecit anno aetatis XLIIII.[1]

> Titus Lucretius is born. Later, having been driven mad by a love-philtre, after writing during the intervals of his insanity several books, which Cicero subsequently edited, he died by his own hand in the forty-fourth year of his life.

Little credence can be given to the biographical information conveyed in these lines which have been rightly read and interpreted as a hostile comment, made by a Christian author, against the ramblings of an atheist writer. The mention of *furor* in connection to the theme of love constitutes a clear allusion to what Jerome must have taken to be a deeply unsettling and disturbing description of sexual intercourse in *DRN* 4. At the same time, the appearance of a love-philtre in the story could be alluding to Lucretius' own preparation of the drug of philosophical therapy in 1.936–50: ironically, the philosopher who proclaims his expertise in fixing the right therapeutic cocktail for his patients/readers, ends up drinking the wrong stuff. The result of this is not an immediate death, but a poem first. The phrase *per intervalla insaniae*, as was mentioned above, has an ambiguous meaning: it can either mean that the *DRN* was composed in moments of lucidity — that is, between bouts of insanity — or that it was produced during the poet's madness. Jerome's famous story puts disease at the centre of Lucretius' biography and makes it an essential part of the poem's disturbed state and composition: *morbus* lies at the beginning of the text's generation but it also presents an obstacle — an impediment that accounts for the narrative's curious contents and its incomplete state. Suicide, mentioned in the final line of Jerome's testimony, suggests an abrupt and premature end, for the poet's life as well as for his text.

The present book has been an attempt to show that, unlike what Jerome might have been inclined to believe, disease emerges as a profoundly important concept for the poetics and design of the *DRN*, adding unity and meaning to the poem's form and content. The notion of design underlies the understanding of disease as an "architect of death" — as a crucial catalyst, in other words, for the coming-to-be and consequent dissolution of things in a world of ever-flowing atoms. Equally important, in this respect, is its employment as a structural device

---

[1] Jerome, *Interpretatio chronicae Eusebii Pamphili*, in Migne, *PL* 27: 523.

that brings coherence to the narrative and guarantees its escalating progression towards closure. At the same time, disease is by no means exclusively conceived as a horrifying evil: to the extent that it occupies our lives and imagination as a natural force of grand proportions — one which can occasionally elude our full perception and transcend the limits of our knowledge — disease can instill feelings of wonder, similar to those which we experience when interacting with the world's (terrifying) beauty. This is perhaps another way by which Lucretius is attempting to erase our anxiety for death: for once disease becomes endorsed as a meaningful part of our lives and once we manage to take a certain distance from it and even contemplate it as an aesthetic object, we can then override our fear of it and see it as part and parcel of our mortal existence.

Bibliography

Acosta-Hughes, B. (2002), *Polyeideia: The Iambi of Callimachus and the Archaic Iambic Tradition*, Berkeley.
Acosta-Hughes, B. (2010), *Arion's Lyre: Archaic Lyric into Hellenistic Poetry*, Princeton.
Acosta-Hughes, B./Stephens, S.A. (2012), *Callimachus in Context: From Plato to the Augustan Poets*, Cambridge.
Adams, J.N. (1995), *Pelagonius and Latin Veterinary Terminology in the Roman Empire*, Leiden.
Adams, J.N. (2003), *Bilingualism and the Latin Language*, Cambridge.
Algra, K. (2003), "Stoic Theology", in: B. Inwood (ed.), *The Cambridge Companion to the Stoics*, Cambridge, 153–78.
Allen, J. (2015), "Aristotle on Chance as an Accidental Cause", in: M. Leunissen (ed.), *Aristotle's Physics: A Critical Guide*, Cambridge, 66–87.
Althoff, J. (1997), "Vom Schicksal einer Metapher: Die Erde als Organismus in Senecas *Naturales Quaestiones*", in: K. Döring/B. Herzhoff/G. Wöhrle (eds.), *Antike Naturwissenschaft und ihre Rezeption 7*, Trier, 95–110.
Anderson, W.S. (1960), "Discontinuity in Lucretian Symbolism", *TAPA* 91, 1–29.
Annas, J. (2017), *Virtue and Law in Plato and Beyond*, Oxford.
Annas, J./Barnes, J. (2000), (ed.) *Sextus Empiricus: Outlines of Scepticism*, Cambridge.
Annas, J./Woolf, R. (2001), *Cicero: On Moral Ends*, Cambridge.
Armisen-Marchetti, M. (1989), *Sapientiae Facies: Étude sur les images de Sénèque*, Paris.
Armstrong, D. (2004), "Horace's *Epistles* 1 and Philodemus", in: D. Armstrong et al. (eds.), *Vergil, Philodemus, and the Augustans*, Austin, 267–98.
Armstrong, D. (2014), "Horace's Epicurean Voice in the *Satires*", in: M. Garani/D. Konstan (eds.), *The Philosophizing Muse: The Influence of Greek Philosophy on Roman Poetry*, Newcastle upon Tyne, 91–127.
Arnott, W.G. (1998), "Notes on Menander's *Phasma*", *ZPE* 123, 35–48.
Arnott, W.G. (2000), (ed.) *Menander. Vol. III*, Cambridge, Mass./London (Loeb Classical Library).
Arthur-Montagne, J. (2017), "Symptoms of the Sublime: Longinus and the Hippocratic Method of Criticism", *GRBS* 57, 325–55.
Bailey, C. (1928), *The Greek Atomists and Epicurus: A Study*, Oxford.
Bailey, C. (1947), *Lucretius. De Rerum Natura: Edited, with Prolegomena, Critical Apparatus, Translation and Commentary* (3 vols.), Oxford.
Bakker, F.A. (2016), *Epicurean Meteorology: Sources, Method, Scope and Organization*, Leiden.
Balme, M. (2001), *Menander: The Plays and Fragments*, Oxford.
Barchiesi, A. (1997a), "Endgames: Ovid's *Metamorphoses* 15 and *Fasti* 6", in: D.H. Roberts/F.M. Dunn/D. Fowler (eds.), *Classical Closure: Reading the End in Greek and Latin Literature*, Princeton, 181–208.
Barchiesi, A. (1997b), *The Poet and the Prince: Ovid and Augustan Discourse*, Berkeley.
Bartsch, S. (2006), *The Mirror of the Self: Sexuality, Self-Knowledge, and the Gaze in the Early Roman Empire*, Chicago/London.
Bartsch, S. (2014), "Persius' Fourth *Satire*: Socrates and the Failure of Pedagogy", in: M. Garani/D. Konstan (eds.), *The Philosophizing Muse: The Influence of Greek Philosophy on Roman Poetry*, Newcastle upon Tyne, 245–68.
Bartsch, S. (2015), *Persius: A Study in Food, Philosophy and the Figural*, Chicago/London.

Bartsch, S. (2017), "Philosophy, Physicians, and Persianic Satire", in: R. Seaford/J. Wilkins/ M. Wright (eds.), *Selfhood and the Soul: Essays on Ancient Thought and Literature in Honour of Christopher Gill*, Oxford, 273–302.
Beagon, M. (2005), *The Elder Pliny on the Human Animal: Natural History, Book 7*, Oxford.
Beagon, M. (2011), "The Curious Eye of the Elder Pliny", in: R. Gibson/R. Morello (eds.), *Pliny the Elder: Themes and Contexts*, Leiden, 71–88.
Berno, F.R. (2003), *Lo specchio, il vizio e la virtù: Studio sulle Naturales Quaestiones di Seneca*, Bologna.
Berno, F.R. (2015), "Exploring Appearances: Seneca's Scientific Works", in: S. Bartsch/ A. Schiesaro (eds.), *The Cambridge Companion to Seneca*, Cambridge, 82–92.
Berressem, H. (2005), "*Incerto Tempore Incertisque Locis*: The Logic of the *Clinamen* and the Birth of Physics", in: N. Abbas (ed.), *Mapping Michel Serres*, Ann Arbor, 51–71.
Berryman, S. (2009), *The Mechanical Hypothesis in Ancient Greek Natural Philosophy*, Cambridge.
Betensky, A. (1980), "Lucretius and Love", *CW* 73, 291–99.
Bett, R. (1997), *Sextus Empiricus: Against the Ethicists (Adversus Mathematicos XI)*, Oxford.
Bett, R. (2005), *Sextus Empiricus: Against the Logicians*, Cambridge.
Bettini, M. (1999), *The Portrait of the Lover*, Berkeley.
Bettini, M. (2013), *Women and Weasels: Mythologies of Birth in Ancient Greece and Rome*, Chicago/London.
Bignone, E. (1945), *Storia della letteratura latina*, Florence.
Biles, Z.B./Olson, S.D. (2015), *Aristophanes Wasps: Edited with Translation and Commentary*, Oxford.
Bing, P. (2005), "The Politics and Poetics of Geography in the Milan Posidippus, Section One: On Stones (AB 1–20)", in: K. Gutzwiller (ed.), *The New Posidippus: A Hellenistic Poetry Book*, Oxford, 119–40.
Bobzien, S. (2000), "Did Epicurus Discover the Free Will Problem?", *OSAP* 19, 287–337.
Bolton, R. (2015), "The Origins of Aristotle's Natural Teleology in *Physics* II", in: M. Leunissen (ed.), *Aristotle's Physics: A Critical Guide*, Cambridge, 121–43.
Bonanno, M.G. (1990), *L'allusione necessaria: Ricerche intertestuali sulla poesia greca e latina*, Rome.
Bonelli, G. (1984), *I motivi profondi della poesia lucreziana*, Brussels.
Booth, J. (1997), "All in the Mind: Sickness in Catullus 76", in: S.M. Braund/C. Gill (eds.), *The Passions in Roman Thought and Literature*, Cambridge, 150–68.
Borgo, A. (1998), *Lessico morale di Seneca*, Naples.
Boyancé, P. (1963), *Lucrèce et l'épicurisme*, Paris.
Bramble, J.C. (1974), *Persius and the Programmatic Satire: A Study in Form and Imagery*, Cambridge.
Bremmer, J. (2008), *Greek Religion and Culture, the Bible and the Ancient Near East*, Leiden.
Bright, D.F. (1971), "The Plague and the Structure of the *De rerum natura*", *Latomus* 30, 607–32.
Brink, C.O. (1969), "Horace and Empedocles' Temperature: A Rejected Fragment of Empedocles", *Phoenix* 23, 138–42.
Brink, C.O. (1971), *Horace on Poetry, vol. 1: The 'Ars Poetica'*, Cambridge.
Brittain, C. (2006), *Cicero: On Academic Scepticism*, Indianapolis/Cambridge.
Broadie, S. (2012), *Nature and Divinity in Plato's Timaeus*, Cambridge.
Bronowski, A. (2019), *The Stoics on Lekta: All There is to Say*, Oxford.

Brooks, P. (1984), *Reading for the Plot: Design and Intention in Narrative*, Oxford.
Brown, D. (2013), *The Poetry of Victorian Scientists: Style, Science and Nonsense*, Cambridge.
Brown, P.M. (1997), *Lucretius De rerum natura III: Translated with Introduction and Notes*, Warminster.
Brown, R.D. (1987), *Lucretius on Love and Sex: A Commentary on De rerum natura IV, 1030–1287, with Prolegomena, Text, and Translation*, Leiden.
Brown, R.D. (1994), "The Bed-Wetters in Lucretius 4.1026", *HSCPh* 96, 191–96.
Brown, R.D. (2007), "Lucretius and Callimachus", in: M.R. Gale (ed.), *Oxford Readings in Lucretius*, Oxford, 328–50 [originally published in *ICS* 7 (1982), 77–97].
Brown, R.D. (2017), "Lucretius' Malodorous Mistress (*De Rerum Natura* 4.1175)", *CJ* 113, 26–43.
Buchheit, V. (2007), "Epicurus' Triumph of the Mind", in: M.R. Gale (ed.), *Oxford Readings in Lucretius*, Oxford, 104–131 [originally published in German in *Hermes* 99 (1971), 303–23].
Bullard, P. (2011), *Edmund Burke and the Art of Rhetoric*, Cambridge.
Bulloch, A.W. (1977), "Callimachus' Erysichthon, Homer and Apollonius Rhodius", *AJPh* 98, 97–123.
Burkert, W. (1985), *Greek Religion* (transl. J. Raffan), Cambridge; Mass.
Burnyeat, M.F. (2012), *Explorations in Ancient and Modern Philosophy. Vol. I*, Cambridge.
Butler, S. (2011), *The Matter of the Page: Essays in Search of Ancient and Medieval Authors*, Wisconsin.
Butterfield, D. (2018), "Lucretius the Madman on the Gods", in: J. Bryan/R. Wardy/J. Warren (eds.), *Authors and Authorities in Ancient Philosophy*, Cambridge, 222–43.
Cabisius, G. (1985), "Social Metaphor and the Atomic Cycle in Lucretius", *CJ* 80, 109–20.
Cairns, D. (2013), "A Short History of Shudders", in: A. Chaniotis/P. Ducrey (eds.), *Unveiling Emotions II: Emotions in Greece and Rome: Texts, Images, and Material Culture*, Stuttgart, 85–107.
Cairns, D. (2015), "The Horror and the Pity: *Phrikē* as a Tragic Emotion", *Psychoanalytic Inquiry* 35, 75–94.
Cairns, F. (2016), *Hellenistic Epigrams: Contexts of Exploration*, Cambridge.
Campbell, G.L. (2000), "Zoogony and Evolution in Plato's *Timaeus*: The Presocratics, Lucretius, and Darwin", in: M.R. Wright (ed.), *Reason and Necessity: Essays on Plato's Timaeus*, Swansea, 145–80.
Campbell, G.L. (2003), *Lucretius on Creation and Evolution: A Commentary on De rerum natura Book Five, Lines 772–1104*, Oxford.
Campbell, G.L. (2007), "Bicycles, Centaurs and Man-faced Ox-creatures: Ontological Instability in Lucretius", in: S.J. Heyworth (ed.), *Classical Constructions: Papers in Memory of Don Fowler, Classicist and Epicurean*, Oxford, 39–62.
Canfora, L. (1993), *Vita di Lucrezio*, Palermo.
Carel, H. (2016), *Phenomenology of Illness*, Oxford.
Carey, S. (2003), *Pliny's Catalogue of Nature: Art and Empire in the Natural History*, Oxford.
Castagnoli, L. (2013), "Democritus and Epicurus on Sensible Qualities in Plutarch's *Against Colotes* 3–9", *Aitia. Regards sur la culture hellénistique au XXIe siècle*, III [Open access at http:aitia.revues.org/622].
Caston, R.R. (2006), "Love as Illness: Poets and Philosophers on Romantic Love", *CJ* 101, 271–98.
Classen, C.J. (1968), "Poetry and Rhetoric in Lucretius", *TAPA* 99, 77–118.
Clausen, W. (1964), "Callimachus and Latin Poetry", *GRBS* 5, 181–96.
Clay, D. (1983), *Lucretius and Epicurus*, Ithaca/London.

Clay, D. (2003), "Lucretius' Honeyed Muse: The History and Meaning of a Simile", in: A. Monet (ed.), *Le jardin romain: épicurisme et poésie à Rome*, Villeneuve-d'Ascq, 183–96.
Clay, D. (2007), "The Sources of Lucretius' Inspiration", in: M.R. Gale (ed.), *Oxford Readings in Lucretius*, Oxford, 18–47 [originally published in: J. Bollack/A. Laks (eds.), *Études sur l'épicurisme antique* (*Cahiers de Philologie* 1. Lille) 205–27].
Cole, S.G. (2004), *Landscapes, Gender, and Ritual Space: The Ancient Greek Experience*, Berkeley.
Commager, H.S. (1957), "Lucretius' Interpretation of the Plague", *HSCPh* 62, 105–18 [reprinted in M.R. Gale (ed.) *Oxford Readings in Lucretius*, Oxford (2007), 182–98].
Connell, S. (2016), *Aristotle on Female Animals: A Study of the Generation of Animals*, Cambridge.
Conte, G.B. (1994), *Genres and Readers: Lucretius, Love Elegy, Pliny's Encyclopedia* (transl. G.W. Most), Baltimore.
Cooper, J.M. (1997), *Plato: Complete Works*, Indianapolis/Cambridge.
Courtney, E. (1993), *The Fragmentary Latin Poets*, Oxford.
Craik, E.M. (2001), "Thucydides on the Plague: Physiology of Flux and Fixation", *CQ* 51, 102–108.
Craik, E.M. (2015), *The 'Hippocratic' Corpus: Content and Context*, London/New York.
Crowther, N.B. (1970), "ΟΙ ΝΕΩΤΕΡΟΙ, Poetae Novi, and Cantores Euphorionis", *CQ* 20, 322–27.
D'Angour, A. (2013), "Love's Battlefield: Rethinking Sappho Fragment 31", in: E. Sanders et al. (eds.), *Erōs in Ancient Greece*, Oxford, 59–71.
Davie, J.N. (2007), *Seneca: Dialogues and Essays*, Oxford.
Dawson, L. (2008), *Lovesickness and Gender in Early Modern English Literature*, Oxford.
Day, H. (2013), *Lucan and the Sublime: Power, Representation and Aesthetic Experience*, Cambridge.
Dean-Jones, L.A. (1992), "The Politics of Pleasure: Female Sexual Appetite in the Hippocratic Tradition", *Helios* 19, 72–91.
Dean-Jones, L.A. (1994), *Women's Bodies in Classical Greek Science*, Oxford.
Debru, A. (1982), "L'épilepsie dans le *De somno* d'Aristote", in: G. Sabbah (ed.), *Médecins et médecine dans l'antiquité*, Saint-Étienne, 25–41.
De Forest, M.M. (1994), *Apollonius' Argonautica: A Callimachean Epic*, Leiden.
De Lacy, P. (1969), "Limit and Variation in the Epicurean Philosophy", *Phoenix* 23, 104–13.
De Lacy, P. (1983), "Lucretius and Plato", in: G.P. Carratelli (ed.), *ΣΥΖΗΤΗΣΙΣ: Studi sull'epicureismo greco e romano offerti a Marcello Gigante*, vol. i, Naples, 291–307.
De Lacy, P. (2007), "Distant Views: The Imagery of Lucretius 2", in: M.R. Gale, (ed.), *Oxford Readings in Lucretius*, Oxford, 146–57 [originally published in *CJ* 60 (1964), 49–55].
Demand, N. (1994), *Birth, Death, and Motherhood in Classical Greece*, Baltimore.
Demastes, W.W. (1998), *Theatre of Chaos: Beyond Absurdism, Into Orderly Disorder*, Cambridge.
De Melo, W. (2011), *Plautus: Vol. II*, Cambridge, Mass./London (Loeb Classical Library).
Demont, P. (1990), "Les oracles delphiques relatifs aux pestilences et Thucydide", *Kernos* 3, 147–56.
Demont, P. (2013), "The Causes of the Athenian Plague and Thucydides", in: A. Tsakmakis/ M. Tamiolaki (eds.), *Thucydides Between History and Literature*, Berlin/Boston, 73–87.
Devinant, J. (2018), "Mental Disorders and Psychological Suffering in Galen's Cases", in: P.N. Singer/C. Thumiger (eds.), *Mental Illness in Ancient Medicine: From Celsus to Paul of Aegina*, Leiden/Boston, 198–221.

Di Benedetto, V. (1985), "Intorno al linguaggio erotico di Saffo", *Hermes* 113, 145–56.
Domenicucci, P. (1981), "Lucrezio IV, 1160 sgg. e Alessi, fr. 98 Edmonds", *Atene e Roma* 26, 175–82.
Drabkin, I.E. (1955), "Remarks on Ancient Psychopathology", *Isis* 46, 223–34.
Dudley, J. (2012), *Aristotle's Concept of Chance: Accidents, Cause, Necessity, and Determinism*, Albany.
Dutsch, D. (2008), *Feminine Discourse in Roman Comedy: On Echoes and Voices*, Oxford.
Edmunds, L. (2002), "Mars as Hellenistic Lover: Lucretius, *De rerum natura* 1.29–40 and its Subtexts", *International Journal of the Classical Tradition* 8, 343–58.
Elliott, J. (2013), *Ennius and the Architecture of the Annales*, Cambridge.
Erbse, H. (1981), "Thukydides über die Ärzte Athens", *RhM* 124, 29–41.
Erler, M. (1997), "Physics and Therapy: Meditative Elements in Lucretius' *De rerum natura*', in: K. Algra/M.H. Koenen/P.H. Schrijvers (eds.), *Lucretius and his Intellectual Background*, Amsterdam, 79–92.
Everson, S. (1999), 'Epicurean Psychology', in: K. Algra et al. (eds.), *The Cambridge History of Hellenistic Philosophy*, Cambridge, 542–59.
Fairclough, H.R. (1942), *Horace: Satires, Epistles, Ars Poetica*, Cambridge, Mass./London (Loeb Classical Library).
Fairclough, H.R./Goold, G.P. (1999), *Virgil: Eclogues, Georgics, Aeneid 1–6*, Cambridge, Mass./ London (Loeb Classical Library).
Fairclough, H.R./Goold, G.P. (2000), *Virgil: Aeneid 7–12, Appendix Vergiliana*, Cambridge, Mass./ London (Loeb Classical Library).
Fantham, E. (2011), *Roman Readings: Roman Responses to Greek Literature from Plautus to Statius and Quintilian*, Berlin/New York.
Fantuzzi, M./Hunter, R. (2004), *Tradition and Innovation in Hellenistic Poetry*, Cambridge.
Farrell, J. (1991), *Vergil's Georgics and the Traditions of Ancient Epic: The Art of Allusion in Literary History*, Oxford/New York.
Farrell, J. (2007), "Lucretian Architecture: The Structure and the Argument of *De Rerum Natura*", in: S. Gillespie/P. Hardie (eds.), *The Cambridge Companion to Lucretius*, Cambridge, 76–91.
Farrell, J. (2008), "The Six Books of Lucretius' *De rerum natura*: Antecedents and Influence", *Dictynna* 5: http://dictynna.revues.org/385
Farrell, J. (2016), "Lucretius and the Symptomatology of Modernism", in: J. Lezra/L. Blake (eds.), *Lucretius and Modernity: Epicurean Encounters Across Time and Disciplines*, New York, 39–55.
Fellin, A. (1951), "Risonanze del *De consulatu* ciceroniano nel poema di Lucrezio", *RFIC* 79, 307–16.
Felton, D. (2013), "Were Vergil's Harpies Menstruating?", *CJ* 108, 405–18.
Ferrari, F. (2001), "Saffo: nevrosi e poesia", *SIFC* 19, 3–31.
Ferrero, L. (1949), *Poetica nuova in Lucrezio*, Florence.
Ferri, R. (1993), *I dispiaceri di un epicureo: uno studio sulla poetica oraziana delle Epistole (con un capitolo su Persio)*, Pisa.
Filippetti, A. (2007), "Ippocrate e Lucrezio: i colori della *facies*", *Aion* 29, 127–34.
Fitzgerald, W. (1984), "Lucretius' Cure for Love in the *De Rerum Natura*", *CW* 78, 73–86.
Flemming, R. (2000), *Medicine and the Making of Roman Women: Gender, Nature, and Authority from Celsus to Galen*, Cambridge.

Flemming, R./Hanson, A.E. (1998), "Hippocrates' 'Peri Partheniôn' (Diseases of Young Girls): Text and Translation", *Early Science and Medicine* 3, 241–52.
Foster, E. (2009), "The Rhetoric of Materials: Thucydides and Lucretius", *AJPh* 130, 367–99.
Fowler, D. (1989), "First Thoughts on Closure: Problems and Prospects", *Materiali e Discussioni* 22, 75–122.
Fowler, D. (1991), Review of C. Segal, *Lucretius on Death and Anxiety* (1990) and A. Schiesaro, *Simulacrum et imago: gli argomenti analogici nel De Rerum Natura* (Pisa 1990), *G&R* 39, 237–39.
Fowler, D. (1995), "From Epos to Cosmos: Lucretius, Ovid, and the Poetics of Segmentation", in: D. Innes/H. Hine/C. Pelling (eds.), *Ethics and Rhetoric: Classical Essays for Donald Russell on his Seventy-Fifth Birthday*, Oxford, 3–18.
Fowler, D. (1996), "The Feminine Principal: Gender in the *De Rerum Natura*", in: G. Giannantoni/ M. Gigante (eds.), *Epicureismo greco e romano*, Naples, 813–22.
Fowler, D. (1997), "Second Thoughts on Closure", in: D.H. Roberts/F.M. Dunn/D. Fowler (eds.), *Classical Closure: Reading the End in Greek and Latin Literature*, Princeton, 3–22.
Fowler, D. (2000), *Roman Constructions: Readings in Postmodern Latin*, Oxford.
Fowler, D. (2002), *Lucretius on Atomic Motion: A Commentary on De rerum natura: Book 2, Lines 1–332*, Oxford.
Fowler, D. (2007), "Lucretius and Politics", in: M.R. Gale (ed.), *Oxford Readings in Lucretius*, Oxford, 397–431 [originally published in: M. Griffin/J. Barnes (eds.), *Philosophia Togata I*, Oxford 1989, 120–50].
Fowler, P.G. (1983), 'A Commentary on Part of Lucretius *De rerum natura* Book Six', Oxford (D. Phil thesis).
Fowler, P.G. (2007), "Lucretian Conclusions", in: M.R. Gale (ed.), *Oxford Readings in Lucretius*, Oxford, 199–233. [originally published in: D.H. Roberts/F.M. Dunn/D. Fowler (eds.), *Classical Closure: Reading the End in Greek and Latin Literature*, Princeton, 112–38].
Fratantuono, L. (2015), *A Reading of Lucretius' De rerum natura*, Lanham/Boulder/New York/London.
Frede, M. (1983), "The Method of the So-called Methodical School of Medicine", in: J. Barnes et al. (eds.), *Science and Speculation: Studies in Hellenistic Theory and Practice*, Cambridge, 1–23.
Frede, M. (1986), "The Stoic Doctrine of the Affections of the Soul", in: M. Schofield/G. Striker (eds.), *The Norms of Nature: Studies in Hellenistic Ethics*, Cambridge, 93–110.
Freudenburg, K. (1993), *The Walking Muse: Horace on the Theory of Satire*, Princeton.
Freudenburg, K. (2001), *Satires of Rome: Threatening Poses from Lucilius to Juvenal*, Cambridge.
Fuhrmann. M. (1992), *Die Dichtungstheorie der Antike*, Darmstadt.
Furley, D. (1967), *Two Studies in the Greek Atomists*, Princeton.
Furley, D. (1993) "Democritus and Epicurus on Sensible Qualities", in: J. Brunschwig/M. Nussbaum (eds.), *Passions and Perceptions: Studies in Hellenistic Philosophy of Mind*, Cambridge, 72–94.
Fyfe, W.H./Russell, D. (1995), *Longinus: On the Sublime*, in: S. Halliwell *et al. Aristotle Poetics, Longinus On the Sublime, Demetrius On Style*, Cambridge, Mass./London (Loeb Classical Library).
Gaillard-Seux, P. (2009), "Un pseudo-Démocrite énigmatique: Bolos de Mendès", in: F. Le Blay (ed.), *Transmettre les savoirs dans les mondes hellénistique et romain*, Rennes, 223–43.
Gale, M.R. (1994), *Myth and Poetry in Lucretius*, Cambridge.

Gale, M.R. (2000), *Virgil on the Nature of Things: The Georgics, Lucretius and the Didactic Tradition*, Cambridge.
Gale, M.R. (2007), "Lucretius and Previous Poetic Traditions", in: S. Gillespie/P. Hardie (eds.), *The Cambridge Companion to Lucretius*, Cambridge, 59–75.
Gale, M.R. (2009), *Lucretius: De Rerum Natura V,* Warminster.
Gale, M.R. (2018), "Contemplating Violence: Lucretius' *De rerum natura*", in: M.R. Gale/J.H.D. Scourfield (eds.), *Texts and Violence in the Roman World*, Cambridge, 63–86.
Galloway, A. (1986), "Lucretius' Materialist Poetics: Epicurus and the "Flawed" *Consolatio* of Book 3", *Ramus* 15, 52–73.
Garani, M. (2007), *Empedocles Redivivus: Poetry and Analogy in Lucretius*, London/New York.
Garani, M. (2013), "Lucretius and Ovid on Empedoclean Cows and Sheep", in: D. Lehoux/A.D. Morrison/A. Sharrock (eds.), *Lucretius: Poetry, Philosophy, Science,* Oxford, 233–59.
Gardner, H.H. (2019), *Pestilence and the Body Politic in Latin Literature*, Oxford.
Gauly, B.M. (2004), *Senecas Naturales Quaestiones: Naturphilosophie für die römische Kaiserzeit*, Munich.
Gee, E. (2013), *Aratus and the Astronomical Tradition*, Oxford.
Gellar-Goad, T.H.M. (2020), *Laughing Atoms, Laughing Matter: Lucretius' De Rerum Natura and Satire*, Ann Arbor.
Geus, K./King, C.G. (2018), "Paradoxography", in: P.T. Keyser/J. Scarborough (eds.), *Oxford Handbook of Science and Medicine in the Classical World*, Oxford, 431–44.
Gibbs, R.W. (1994), *The Poetics of Mind: Figurative Thought, Language, and Understanding*, Cambridge.
Gigante, M. (1975), "Philosophia Medicans in Filodemo", *Cronache Ercolanesi* 5, 53–61.
Gillespie, S./Hardie, P. (2007), "Introduction", in: S. Gillespie/P. Hardie (eds.), *The Cambridge Companion to Lucretius*, Cambridge, 1–15.
Giussani, C. (1897), *T. Lucreti Cari De rerum Natura Libri Sex. Vol. 2*, Torino.
Görler, W. (1997), "Storing up Past Pleasures: The Soul-Vessel Metaphor in Lucretius and in his Greek Models", in: K.A. Algra/M.H. Koenen/P.H. Shrijvers (eds.), *Lucretius and his Intellectual Background*, Amsterdam, 193–207.
Gourevitch, D. (1983), "La psychiatrie de l'antiquité gréco-romaine", in: J. Postel/C. Quétel (eds.), *Nouvelle histoire de la psychiatrie*, Toulouse, 13–31.
Gourevitch, D. (2013), *LIMOS KAI LOIMOS: A Study of the Galenic Plague*, Paris.
Gowers, E. (1993), *The Loaded Table: Representations of Food in Roman Literature*, Oxford.
Gowers, E. (2012), *Horace: Satires, Book 1*, Cambridge.
Grams, L. (2009), "Medical Theory in Plato's *Timaeus*", *Rhizai* 6, 161–92.
Gransden, K.W. (1991), *Virgil: Aeneid XI*, Cambridge.
Graver, M.R. (1990), "The Eye of the Beholder: Perceptual Relativity in Lucretius", *Apeiron* 23, 91–116.
Graver, M.R. (2002), *Cicero on the Emotions: Tusculan Disputations 3 and 4*, Chicago/London.
Graver, M.R. (2003), "Mania and Melancholy: Some Stoic Texts on Insanity", in: J. Sickinger/G. Bakewell (eds.), *Gestures: Essays on Ancient History, Literature, and Philosophy in Honor of Alan Boegehold*, Oxford, 40–54.
Graver, M.R. (2008), *Stoicism and Emotion*, Chicago/London.
Greenblatt, S. (2011), *The Swerve: How the World Became Modern*, New York/London.
Greengard, C. (1987), *Theatre in Crisis: Sophocles' Reconstruction of Genre and Politics in Philoctetes*, Amsterdam.
Griffith, M./Most, G.W. (2013), *Sophocles II*, Chicago/London [3rd edition].

Grimal, P. (1974), "Elementa, primordia, principia dans le poème de Lucrèce", in: *Mélanges de philosophie, de littérature et d'histoire ancienne offerts à P. Boyancé*, Rome, 357–66.

Grmek, M.D. (1991), "La dénomination latine des maladies considérées comme nouvelles par les auteurs antiques", in: G. Sabbah (ed.), *Le latin médical. La constitution d'un langage scientifique: réalités et langage de la médecine dans le monde romain*, Saint-Étienne, 195–214.

Gummere, R.M. (1920), *Seneca: Epistles 66–92*, Cambridge, Mass./London (Loeb Classical Library).

Gutzwiller, K. (2012), "The Hecale and Hellenistic Conceptions of Short Hexameter Narratives", in: S. Bär/M. Baumbach (eds.), *Brill's Companion to Greek and Latin Epyllion and its Reception*, Leiden/Boston, 221–44.

Guyau, J.-M. (1878), *La morale d'Épicure*, Paris.

Hadzits, G.D. (1935), *Lucretius and his Influence*, London.

Hahm, D.E. (2007), "Critolaus and Late Hellenistic Peripatetic Philosophy", in: A.M. Ioppolo/D.N. Sedley (eds.), *Pyrrhonists, Patricians, Platonizers: Hellenistic Philosophy in the Period 155–86 B.C.*, Naples, 47–101.

Halliwell, S. (2011), *Between Ecstasy and Truth: Interpretations of Greek Poetics from Homer to Longinus*, Oxford.

Hampe, B. (2017), "Embodiment and Discourse: Dimensions and Dynamics of Contemporary Metaphor Theory", in: B. Hampe (ed.), *Metaphor: Embodied Cognition and Discourse*, Cambridge, 3–23.

Hankinson, J.R. (1998), *Cause and Explanation in Ancient Greek Thought*, Oxford.

Hankinson, J.R. (2013), "Lucretius, Epicurus and the Logic of Multiple Explanations", in: D. Lehoux/A.D. Morrison/A. Sharrock (eds.), *Lucretius: Poetry, Philosophy, Science*, Oxford, 69–98.

Hanses, M. (2015), 'The Life of Comedy after the Death of Plautus: The *Palliata* in Roman Life and Letters' (PhD thesis, Columbia).

Hanson, A.E. (1990), "The Medical Writer's Woman", in: D.M. Halperin/J.J. Winkler/F.I. Zeitlin (eds.), *Before Sexuality: The Construction of Erotic Experience in the Ancient Greek World*, Princeton, 309–38.

Hanson, A.E. (1991), "Continuity and Change: Three Case Studies in Hippocratic Gynecological Therapy and Theory", in: S.B. Pomeroy (ed.), *Women's History and Ancient History*, Chapel Hill/London, 73–110.

Hanson, A.E./Green, M. (1994), "Soranus of Ephesus: *Methodicorum Princeps*", *ANRW* II 37.2, 984–1075.

Harder, A. (2018), "Callimachus", in: K. De Temmerman/E. van Emde Boas (eds.), *Characterization in Ancient Greek Literature*, Leiden, 100–15.

Hardie, P. (1984) "The Sacrifice of Iphigeneia: An Example of 'Distribution' of a Lucretian Theme in Virgil", *CQ* 34, 406–12.

Hardie, P. (1986), *Virgil's Aeneid: Cosmos and Imperium*, Oxford.

Hardie, P. (1997), "Closure in Latin Epic", in: D.H. Roberts/F.M. Dunn/D. Fowler (eds.), *Classical Closure: Reading the End in Greek and Latin Literature*, Princeton, 139–62.

Hardie, P. (2002), *Ovid's Poetics of Illusion*, Cambridge.

Hardie, P. (2006), "Cultural and Historical Narratives in Virgil's *Eclogues* and Lucretius", in: M. Fantuzzi/T. Papanghelis (eds.), *Brill's Companion to Greek and Latin Pastoral*, Leiden, 275–300.

Hardie, P. (2007), "Lucretius and Later Latin Literature", in: S. Gillespie/P. Hardie (eds.), *The Cambridge Companion to Lucretius*, Cambridge, 111–30.
Hardie, P. (2008), "Cosmology and National Epic in the *Georgics* (*Georgics* 2.458–3.48)", in: K. Volk (ed.), *Oxford Readings in Vergil's Georgics*, Oxford, 161–81.
Hardie, P. (2009), *Lucretian Receptions: History, The Sublime, Knowledge*, Cambridge.
Hardie, P. (2012), *Rumour and Renown: Representations of Fama in Western Literature*, Cambridge.
Harris, C.R.S. (1973), *The Heart and the Vascular System in Ancient Greek Medicine: From Alcmaeon to Galen*, Oxford.
Harris, W.V. (2009), *Dreams and Experience in Classical Antiquity*, Cambridge, Mass.
Harrison, E.L. (1979), "The Noric Plague and Virgil's Third *Georgic*", *PLLS* 2, 1–65.
Harrison, S. (2007), *Generic Enrichment in Vergil and Horace*, Oxford.
Healy, J.F. (1999), *Pliny the Elder on Science and Technology*, Oxford.
Henry, D. (2013), "Optimality Reasoning in Aristotle's Natural Teleology", *OSAP* 45, 225–63.
Hershkowitz, D. (1998), *The Madness of Epic: Reading Insanity from Homer to Statius*, Oxford.
Hett, W.S. (1936), *Aristotle: Minor Works*, Cambridge; Mass./London (Loeb Classical Library).
Hill, T. (2004), *Ambitiosa Mors: Suicide and the Self in Roman Thought and Literature*, New York/London.
Hine, H.M. (2010), *Seneca: Natural Questions*, Chicago.
Hoenig, C. (2018), *Plato's Timaeus and the Latin Tradition*, Cambridge.
Holford-Strevens, L. (2002), "*Horror vacui* in Lucretian Biography", *Leeds International Classical Studies* 1, 1–23.
Hollis, A.S. (1998), "Nicander and Lucretius", *PLLS* 10, 169–84.
Hollis, A.S. (2007), *Fragments of Roman Poetry, c. 60 BC – AD 20*, Oxford.
Holmes, B. (2010a), "Body, Soul, and Medical Analogy in Plato", in: K. Bassi/J. Euben (eds.), *When Worlds Elide: Classics, Politics, Culture*, Lanham, 345–85.
Holmes, B. (2010b), *The Symptom and the Subject: The Emergence of the Physical Body in Ancient Greece*, Princeton.
Holmes, B. (2013), "Causality, Agency, and the Limits of Medicine", *Apeiron* 46, 302–26.
Holmes, B. (2016), "Michel Serres's Non-Modern Lucretius: Manifold Reason and the Temporality of Reception", in: J. Lezra/L. Blake (eds.), *Lucretius and Modernity: Epicurean Encounters Across Time and Disciplines*, New York, 21–38.
Holmes, B. (2017), "The Generous text: Animal Intuition, Human Knowledge and Written Transmission in Pliny's Books on Medicine", in: M. Formisano/P.J. van der Eijk (eds.), *Knowledge, Text and Practice in Ancient Technical Writing*, Cambridge, 217–30.
Holmes, B. (2018), "Body", in: P.E. Pormann (ed.), *The Cambridge Companion to Hippocrates*, Cambridge, 63–88.
Holtsmark, E.B. (1967), "On Lucretius 2.1–19", *TAPA* 98, 193–204.
Hooley, D.M. (1997), *The Knotted Thong: Structures of Mimesis in Persius*, Ann Arbor.
Hopkinson, N. (1984), *Callimachus: Hymn to Demeter*, Cambridge.
Hübner, W. (2010), *Manilius, Astronomica. Buch V. Band 1: Einführung, Text und Übersetzung*, Berlin/New York.
Hunter, R.L. (2004), *Plato's Symposium*, Oxford.
Hunter, R.L. (2006), *The Shadow of Callimachus: Studies in the Reception of Hellenistic Poetry at Rome*, Cambridge.
Hunter, R.L. (2011), "The Reputation of Callimachus", in: D. Obbink/R. Rutherford (eds.), *Culture in Pieces: Essays on Ancient Texts in Honour of Peter Parsons*, Oxford, 220 –38.

Hunter, R./Russell, D. (2011), *Plutarch: How to Study Poetry (De audiendis poetis)*, Cambridge.
Husner, F. (1924), *Leib und Seele in der Sprache Senecas*, Leipzig.
Hutchinson, G.O. (1993), *Latin Literature from Seneca to Juvenal: A Critical Study*, Oxford.
Hutchinson, G.O. (2013), *From Greek to Latin: Frameworks and Contexts for Intertextuality*, Oxford.
Huxley, G. (1971), "Callimachus, the Assyrian River and the Bees of Demeter", *GRBS* 12, 211–15.
Inwood, B. (1985), *Ethics and Human Action in Early Stoicism*, Oxford.
Inwood, B./Gerson, L.P. (1994), *The Epicurus Reader: Selected Writings and Testimonia*, Indianapolis/Cambridge.
Jackson, S. (1990), "Myrsilus of Methymna and the Dreadful Smell of the Lemnian Women", *ICS* 15, 77–83.
Jacob, C. (1983), "De l'art de compiler à la fabrication du merveilleux: Sur la paradoxographie grecque", *Lalies* 2, 121–40.
Johnson, W.R. (1993), *Horace and the Dialectic of Freedom: Readings in Epistles 1*, Ithaca/London.
Johnson, M.R. (2013), "Nature, Spontaneity, and Voluntary Action in Lucretius", in: D. Lehoux/A.D. Morrison/A. Sharrock (eds.), *Lucretius: Poetry, Philosophy, Science*, Oxford, 99–130.
Jones, W.H.S. (1923), *Hippocrates: Vol. II*, Cambridge, Mass./London (Loeb Classical Library).
Jouanna, J. (1988), *Hippocrate: Des vents. De l'art*, Paris.
Jouanna, J. (1998), "The Birth of Western Medical Art", in: M.D. Grmek (ed.), *Western Medical Thought from Antiquity to the Middle Ages*, Cambridge, Mass./London, 22–71.
Jouanna, J. (2012), *Greek Medicine from Hippocrates to Galen: Selected Papers* (transl. N. Allies), Leiden/Boston.
Kallet, L. (2013), "Thucydides, Apollo, the Plague, and the War", *AJPh* 2013, 355–82.
Kambylis, A. (1965), *Die Dichterweihe und ihre Symbolik: Untersuchungen zu Hesiodos, Kallimachos, Properz und Ennius*, Heidelberg.
Kaster, R.A. (2005), *Emotion, Restraint, and Community in Ancient Rome*, Oxford/New York.
Kaster, R.A. (2011), *Macrobius: Saturnalia, Books 1–2*, Cambridge, Mass./London (Loeb Classical Library).
Kazantzidis, G. (2013), "*Quem nos furorem, μελαγχολίαν illi vocant*: Cicero on Melancholy", in: W.V. Harris (ed.), *Mental Disorders in the Classical World*, Leiden/Boston, 245–64.
Kazantzidis, G. (2018), "Medicine and the Paradox in the Hippocratic Corpus and Beyond", in: M. Gerolemou (ed.), *Recognizing Miracles in Antiquity and Beyond*, Berlin/Boston, 31–61.
Kazantzidis, G. (2019), (ed.), *Medicine and Paradoxography in the Ancient World*, Berlin/Boston.
Keane, C. (2006), *Figuring Genre in Roman Satire*, Oxford/New York.
Kechagia, E. (2016), "Dying Philosophers in Ancient Biography: Zeno the Stoic and Epicurus", in: K. De Temmerman/K. Demoen (eds.), *Writing Biography in Greece and Rome*, Cambridge, 181–99.
Keith, A. (2000), *Engendering Rome: Women in Latin Epic*, Cambridge.
Kennedy, D. (2002), *Rethinking Reality: Lucretius and the Textualization of Nature*, Ann Arbor.
Kennedy, D. (2007), "Making a Text of the Universe: Perspectives on Discursive Order in the *De Rerum Natura* of Lucretius", in: M.R. Gale (ed.), *Oxford Readings in Classical Studies: Lucretius*, Oxford, 376–96.
Kenney, E.J. (1970), "Doctus Lucretius", *Mnemosyne* 23, 366–92 [reprinted in: M.R. Gale (ed.), *Oxford Readings in Lucretius*, Oxford, 300–27].
Kenney, E.J. (1977), *Lucretius*, Oxford.

Kenney, E.J. (2007), "Lucretian Texture: Style, Metre and Rhetoric in the *De rerum natura*", in: S. Gillespie/P. Hardie (eds.), *The Cambridge Companion to Lucretius*, Cambridge, 92–110.
Kenney, E.J. (2014), *Lucretius: De rerum natura, Book III* (2nd edition), Cambridge.
Kidd, D. (1997), *Aratus' Phaenomena*, Cambridge.
King, H (2006), "The Origins of Medicine in the Second Century A.D.", in: S. Goldhill/R. Osborne (eds.), *Rethinking Revolutions through Ancient Greece*, Cambridge, 246–63.
King, H. (2013), "Female Fluids in the Hippocratic Corpus: How Solid was the Humoral Body?", in: P. Horden/E. Hsu (eds.), *The Body in Balance: Humoral Medicines in Practice*, New York, 25–52.
Klingner, F. (1956), *Romische Geisteswelt*, Munich.
Knox, P. E. (1985), "Wine, Water, and Callimachean Poetics", *HSCPh* 89, 107–19.
Knox, P. E. (1999), "Lucretius on the Narrow Road", *HSCPh* 99, 275–87.
Konstan, D. (2013), "Lucretius and the Epicurean Attitude Towards Grief", in: D. Lehoux/A.D. Morrison/A. Sharrock (eds.), *Lucretius: Poetry, Philosophy, Science*, Oxford, 193–210.
Korsmeyer, C. (2011), *Savoring Disgust: The Foul and the Fair in Aesthetics*, Oxford/New York.
Kovacs, D. (1998), *Euripides: Suppliant Women, Electra, Heracles*, Cambridge, Mass./London (Loeb Classical Library).
Krevans, N. (2005), "The Editor's Toolbox: Strategies for Selection and Presentation in the Milan Epigram Papyrus", in: K. Gutzwiller (ed.), *The New Posidippus: A Hellenistic Poetry Book*, Cambridge, 81–96.
Kyriakidis, S. (2004), "Middles in Lucretius' *DRN*: The Poet and his Work", in: S. Kyriakidis/F. de Martino (eds.), *Middles in Latin Poetry*, Levante, 27–49.
Landolfi, L. (2006), "Patologia dell'eros e metaforesi in Lucrezio *De rerum natura* 4.1058–1090", *La parola del passato* 61, 87–109.
Langholf, V. (1986), "Kallimachos, Komödie und hippokratische Frage", *Medizinhistorisches Journal* 21, 3–30.
Langholf, V. (1990), *Medical Theories in Hippocrates: Early Texts and the 'Epidemics'*, Berlin.
Langslow, D.R. (1991), "The Development of Latin Medical Terminology: Some Working Hypotheses", *PCPS* 37, 106–30.
Langslow, D.R. (1999), "The Language of Poetry and the Language of Science: The Latin Poets and 'Medical Latin'", in: J.N. Adams/R.G. Mayer (eds.), *Aspects of the Language of Latin Poetry: Proceedings of the British Academy* 93, Oxford, 183–225.
Langslow, D.R. (2000), *Medical Latin in the Roman Empire*, Oxford.
Laskaris, J. (2002), *The Art is Long: On the Sacred Disease and the Scientific Tradition*, Leiden.
Lattimore, R. (1965), *The Odyssey of Homer*, New York.
Lee, M.-K. (2005), *Epistemology after Protagoras: Responses to Relativism in Plato Aristotle, and Democritus*, Oxford.
Leigh, R. (2016), *On Theriac to Piso, Attributed to Galen: A Critical Edition with Translation and Commentary*, Leiden/Boston.
Leith, D. (2009), "The Qualitative Status of the *Onkoi* in Asclepiades' Theory of Matter", *OSAP* 36, 283–320.
Leith, D. (2012), "Pores and Void in Asclepiades' Physical Theory", *Phronesis* 57, 164–91.
Lennon, J. (2010), "Menstrual Blood in Ancient Rome: An Unspeakable Impurity?", *C&M* 61, 71–87.
Lévy, C. (2003), "Cicero and the *Timaeus*", in: G. Reydams-Schils (ed.), *Plato's Timaeus as Cultural Icon*, Notre Dame, 95–110.

Liapis, V. (2009), "Polyphemus' Throbbing Πόδες: Theocritus Idyll 11.70–71", *Phoenix* 63, 156–61.
Liebeschuetz, J.H.W.G. (1967/8), "The Cycle of Growth and Decay in Lucretius and Virgil", *PVS* 7, 30–40.
Lightfoot, J. (2009), *Hellenistic Collection: Philitas, Alexander of Aetolia, Hermesianax, Euphorion, Parthenius*, Cambridge, Mass./London (Loeb Classical Library).
Lloyd, G.E.R. (1979), *Magic, Reason and Experience: Studies in the Origin and Development of Greek Science*, Cambridge.
Lloyd, G.E.R. (1983), *Science, Folklore and Ideology: Studies in the Life Sciences in Ancient Greece*, Cambridge.
Lloyd, G.E.R. (1987), *The Revolutions of Wisdom: Studies in the Claims and Practice of Ancient Greek Science*, Berkeley.
Long, A.A. (1977), "Chance and Natural Law in Epicureanism", *Phronesis* 22, 63–88.
Long, A.A. (1985), "The Stoics on World-Conflagration", *The Southern Journal of Philosophy* 23, 13–37.
Long, A.A. (1992), Review of C. Segal, *Lucretius on Death and Anxiety* 1990, *Ancient Philosophy* 12, 493–99.
Long, A.A./Sedley, D.N. (1987), *The Hellenistic Philosophers: Vol. 1: Translations of the Principal Sources with Philosophical Commentary*, Cambridge.
Long, A.G. (2019), *Death and Immortality in Ancient Philosophy*, Cambridge.
Lonie, I.M. (1981), *The Hippocratic Treatises 'On Generation', 'On the Nature of the Child', 'Diseases IV': A Commentary*, Berlin.
Lo Presti, R. (2013), "Mental Disorders and the Perils of Definition: Characterising Epilepsy in Greek Scientific Discourse (5th–4th Centuries BC)", in: W.V. Harris (ed.), *Mental Disorders in the Classical World*, Leiden/Boston, 195–222.
Lovatt, H. (2013), *The Epic Gaze: Vision, Gender and Narrative in Ancient Epic*, Cambridge.
Lowe, D. (2015), *Monsters and Monstrosity in Augustan Poetry*, Ann Arbor.
Luck, G. (1988), "Was Lucretius Really Mad?", *Euphrosyne* 16, 289–94.
Ludwig, P.W. (2002), *Eros and Polis: Desire and Community in Greek Political Theory*, Cambridge.
Lyne, R.O.A.M. (1978), "The Neoteric Poets", *CQ* 28, 167–87.
MacGregor, A. (2005), "Was Manilius Really a Stoic?", *ICS* 30, 41–65.
Mader, G. (1983), "Some Observations on the Senecan Götterdämmerung", *Acta classica* 26, 61–71.
Manuli, P. (1983), "Donne mascoline, femmine sterile, vergini perpetue: la ginecologia greca tra Ippocrate e Sorano", in: S. Campese/P. Manuli/G. Sissa (eds.), *Madre Materia: Sociologia e biologia della donna greca*, Turin, 147–92.
Marcović, D. (2008), *The Rhetoric of Explanation in Lucretius' De rerum natura*, Leiden/Boston.
Maso, S. (2005), "Clinamen ciceroniano", in: C. Natali/S. Maso (eds.), *La catena delle cause: Determinismo e antideterminismo nel pensiero antico e in quello contemporaneo*, Amsterdam, 255–68.
Mazzoli, G. (2005), "La retorica del destino: la *demonstratio diluvii* in Seneca, *Nat. Quaest.* III 27–30", *Pallas* 69, 167–78.
Melville, A.D. (1986), *Ovid: Metamorphoses*, Oxford.
Michelakis, P. (2019), "Naming the Plague in Homer, Sophocles and Thucydides", *AJPh* 140, 381–414.
Michels, A.K. (1955), "Death and Two Poets", *TAPA* 86, 160–79.

Minadeo, R. (1965), "The Formal Design of the *De rerum natura*", *Arion* 4, 444–61.
Minyard, J.D. (1978), *Mode and Value in the De rerum natura: A Study in Lucretius' Metrical Language*, Wiesbaden.
Minyard, J.D. (1985), *Lucretius and the Late Republic: An Essay in Roman Intellectual History*, Leiden.
Mitchell-Boyask, R. (2008), *Plague and the Athenian Imagination: Drama, History, and the Cult of Asclepius*, Cambridge.
Mitsis, P. (1988), *Epicurus' Ethical Theory*, Ithaca.
Mitsis, P. (1993), "Committing Philosophy on the Reader: Didactic Coercion and Reader Autonomy in *De rerum natura*", in: A. Schiesaro/P. Mitsis/J.S. Clay (eds.), *Mega Nepios. Il destinatario nell'epos didascalico/The Addressee in Didactic Epic (MD 31)*, Pisa, 111–28.
Montiglio, S. (2006), "Should the Aspiring Wise Man Travel? A Conflict in Seneca's Thought", *AJPh* 127, 553–86.
Morgan, T. (1998), *Literate Education in the Hellenistic and Roman Worlds*, Cambridge.
Morrison, A.D. (2007), *The Narrator in Archaic Greek and Hellenistic Poetry*, Cambridge.
Morrison, A.D. (2013), "*Nil igitur mors est ad nos*? Iphianassa, the Athenian Plague, and Epicurean Views of Death", in: D. Lehoux/A.D. Morrison/A. Sharrock (eds.), *Lucretius: Poetry, Philosophy, Science*, Oxford, 211–32.
Most, G.W. (2006), *Hesiod: Theogony, Works and Days, Testimonia*, Cambridge, Mass./London (Loeb Classical Library).
Most, G.W. (2012), "The Sublime, Today?", in: B. Holmes/W.H. Shearin (eds.), *Dynamic Reading: Studies in the Reception of Epicureanism*, Oxford, 239–66.
Muecke, F. (2005), "Rome's First 'Satirists': Themes and Genre in Ennius and Lucilius", in: K. Freudenburg (ed.), *The Cambridge Companion to Roman Satire*, Cambridge, 33–47.
Müller, C.W. (1987), *Erysichthon: Der Mythos als narrative Metapher im Demeterhymnos des Kallimachos*, Mainz/Stuttgart.
Müller, G. (2007), "The Conclusions of the Six Books of Lucretius", in: M.R. Gale (ed.), *Oxford Readings in Lucretius*, Oxford, 234–54 [originally published in German in O. Gigon (ed.), *Lucrèce*, Geneva (1978), 197–221.
Munson, V. (2001), *Telling Wonders: Ethnography and Political Discourse in the Work of Herodotus*, Ann Arbor.
Murphy, T. (2004), *Pliny the Elder's Natural History: The Empire in the Encyclopedia*, Oxford.
Murray, J. (2004), "The Metamorphoses of Erysichthon: Callimachus, Apollonius and Ovid", in: M.A. Harder et al. (eds.), *Callimachus II*, Leuven, 207–42.
Mussehl, J. (1912), *De Lucretiani libri primi condicione ac retractatione*, Tempelhof.
Mynott, J. (2013), *Thucydides: The War of the Peloponnesians and the Athenians*, Cambridge.
Naas, V. (2011), "Imperialism, *Mirabilia*, and Knowledge: Some Paradoxes in the *Naturalis Historia*", in: R. Gibson/R. Morello (eds.), *Pliny the Elder: Themes and Contexts*, Leiden, 57–70.
Napier, D.A. (1992), *Foreign Bodies: Performance, Art, and Symbolic Anthropology*, Berkeley.
Narducci, E. (1979), *La provvidenza crudele: Lucano e la distruzione dei miti augustei*, Pisa.
Neer, R. (2010), *The Emergence of the Classical Style in Greek Sculpture*, Chicago/London.
Nehamas, A. (1998), *The Art of Living: Socratic Reflections from Plato to Foucault*, Berkeley.
Nethercut, J. (2019), "Provisional Argumentation and Lucretius' Honeyed Cup", *CQ* 68, 523–33.
Newman, J.K. (1967), *Augusts and the New Poetry*, Brussels.
Nightingale, A.W. (2004), *Spectacles of Truth in Classical Greek Philosophy: Theoria in its Cultural Context*, Cambridge.

Notaro, E. (2002), "Lucrezio e le fonti mediche", *Vichiana* 4, 163–94.
Nugent, S.G. (1994), "*Mater* Matters: The Female in Lucretius", *Colby Quarterly* 30, 179–205.
Nünlist, R. (1998), *Poetologische Bildersprache in der frühgriechischen Dicthung*, Stuttgart.
Nussbaum, M.C. (1986), "Therapeutic Arguments: Epicurus and Aristotle", in: M. Schofield/ G. Striker (eds.), *The Norms of Nature*, Cambridge, 31–74.
Nussbaum, M.C. (1994), *The Therapy of Desire: Theory and Practice in Hellenistic Ethics*, Princeton.
Nutton, V. (1983), "The Seeds of Disease: An Explanation of Contagion and Infection from the Greeks to the Renaissance", *Medical History* 27, 1–34.
Nutton, V. (2004), *Ancient Medicine*, London.
Ogden, D. (2013), *Drakōn: Dragon Myth and Serpent Cult in the Greek and Roman Worlds*, Oxford.
O'Hara, J.J. (2007) *Inconsistency in Roman Epic: Studies in Catullus, Lucretius, Vergil, Ovid and Lucan*, Cambridge.
O'Keefe, T. (1997), "The Ontological Status of Sensible Qualities for Democritus and Epicurus", *Ancient Philosophy* 17, 119–34.
O'Keefe, T. (2005), *Epicurus on Freedom*, Cambridge.
Oliensis, E. (1998), *Horace and the Rhetoric of Authority*, Cambridge.
Overduin, F. (2014), "The Anti-bucolic World of Nicander's *Theriaca*", *CQ* 64, 623–41.
Overduin, F. (2019), "In the Realm of the Two-Headed Snake: Pragmatics and Aesthetics of *Mirabilia* in Nicander's *Theriaca* and *Alexipharmaca*", in: G. Kazantzidis (ed.), *Medicine and Paradoxography in the Ancient World*, Berlin/Boston, 73–93.
Owen, W.H. (1968), "The Lacuna in Lucretius' II, 164", *AJPh* 89, 406–18.
Padel, R. (1992), *In and Out of the Mind: Greek Images of the Tragic Self*, Princeton.
Page, D.L. (1953), "Thucydides' Description of the Great Plague at Athens", *CQ* 3, 97–119.
Pajón-Leyra, I. (2011), *Entre ciencia y maravilla: el género literario de la paradoxografía griega*, Zaragoza.
Papadopoulou, T. (2005), *Heracles and Euripidean Tragedy*, Cambridge.
Papanghelis, T.D. (1987) *Propertius: A Hellenistic Poet on Love and Death*, Cambridge.
Park, E.C. (2012), 'Plato and Lucretius as Philosophical Literature: A Comparative Study', Oxford DPhil thesis.
Parker, G. (2008), *The Making of Roman India*, Cambridge.
Parry, A. (1969), "The Language of Thucydides' Description of the Plague", *BICS* 16, 106–18.
Paschalis, M. (1997), *Virgil's Aeneid: Semantic Relations and Proper Names*, Oxford.
Passannante, G. (2012), "Reading for Pleasure: Disaster and Digression in the First Renaissance Commentary on Lucretius", in: B. Holmes/W.H. Shearin (eds.), *Dynamic Reading: Studies in the Reception of Epicureanism*, Oxford, 89–112.
Pearcy, L.T. (2012), "Does Dying Hurt? Philodemus of Gadara, *De Morte* and Asclepiades of Bithynia", *CQ* 62, 211–22.
Peck, A.L./Forster, E.S. (1937), *Aristotle: Parts of Animals, Movement of Animals, Progression of Animals*, Cambridge, Mass./London (Loeb Classical Library).
Penwill, J.L. (1996), "The Ending of Sense: Death as Closure in Lucretius Book 6", *Ramus* 25, 146–69.
Perelli, L. (1969), *Lucrezio: Poeta dell'angoscia*, Florence.
Perrin, B. (1921) *Plutarch's Lives: Vol. X*, Cambridge, Mass./London (Loeb Classical Library).
Petsalis-Diomidis, A. (2010), *Truly Beyond Wonders: Aelius Aristides and the Cult of Asklepios*, Oxford.

Pezzini, G. (2018), "The Early Lucilius and the Language of the Roman *palliata*", in: B.W. Breed/ E. Keitel/R. Wallace (eds.), *Lucilius and Satire in Second-Century BC Rome*, Cambridge, 162–83.
Phillips, J.H. (1982a), "Lucretius on the Inefficacy of the Medical Art: 6.1179 and 6.1226–38", *Classical Philology* 77, 233–35.
Philips, J.H. (1982b), "On Varro's *animalia quaedam minuta* and Etiology of Disease", *Transactions and Studies of the College of Physicians of Philadelphia* 4, 12–25.
Phillips, J.H. (1984), "Lucretius and the (Hippocratic) *On Breaths*: Addenda", in: G. Sabbah (ed.), *Textes Médicaux Latins Antiques*, Saint-Étienne, 83–85.
Piazzi, L. (2019), "Il modello di Lucrezio nell'episodio ovidiano di Erisittone", *MD* 82, 9–21.
Pigeaud, J. (1980), "La physiologie de Lucrèce", *REL* 58, 176–200.
Pigeaud, J. (1981), *La maladie de l'âme: Étude sur la relation de l'âme et du corps dans la tradition médico-philosophique antique*, Paris.
Pinault, J.R. (1992), "The Medical Case for Virginity in Early Second Century C.E.: Soranus of Ephesus, *Gynecology* 1.32", *Helios* 19, 123–39.
Plant, I.M. (2004), *Women Writers of Ancient Greece and Rome: An Anthology*, London.
Polito, R. (2005), "Matter, Medicine and the Mind: Asclepiades vs. Epicurus", *OSAP* 29, 285–335.
Polito, R. (2013), "Asclepiades of Bithynia and Heraclides Ponticus: Medical Platonism?", in: M. Schofield (ed.), *Aristotle, Plato and Pythagoreanism in the First Century BC: New Directions for Philosophy*, Cambridge, 118–38.
Pope, M. (2019), "Embryology, Female *Semina* and Male Vincibility in Lucretius, *De Rerum Natura*", *CQ* 69, 229–45.
Pope, M. (2020), "Bodies Piled High: Lucretius, Lucan, and the Un/Natural Costs of Civil War", *CPh* 115, 209–26.
Porter, J.I. (2005), "Love of Life: Lucretius to Freud", in: S. Bartsch/T. Bartscherer (eds.), *Erotikon: Essays on Eros, Ancient and Modern*, Chicago/London, 113–41.
Porter, J.I. (2007), "Lucretius and the Sublime", in: S. Gillespie/P. Hardie (eds.), *The Cambridge Companion to Lucretius*, Cambridge, 167–85.
Porter, J.I. (2010), *The Origins of Aesthetic Thought in Ancient Greece: Matter, Sensation, and Experience*, Cambridge.
Porter, J.I. (2011), "Against ΛΕΠΤΟΤΗΣ: Rethinking Hellenistic Aesthetics", in: A. Erskine/L. Llewellyn Jones (eds.), *Creating a Hellenistic World*, Swansea, 271–312.
Porter, J.I. (2016), *The Sublime in Antiquity*, Cambridge.
Possanza, M.D. (2014), "Serpentine Constructions: Lucretius, *De Rerum Natura* 3.657–63", *CQ* 64, 197–206.
Potter, P. (1988), *Hippocrates: Vol. VI*, Cambridge; Mass./London (Loeb Classical Library).
Potter, P. (1995), *Hippocrates: Vol. VIII*, Cambridge, Mass./London (Loeb Classical Library).
Potter, P. (2010), *Hippocrates: Vol. IX*, Cambridge; Mass./London (Loeb Classical Library).
Potter, P. (2012), *Hippocrates: Vol. X*, Cambridge, Mass./London (Loeb Classical Library).
Quint, D. (2014), *Inside Paradise Lost: Reading the Designs of Milton's Epic*, Princeton.
Rackham, H. (1931), *Cicero: On Ends*, Cambridge; Mass./London (Loeb Classical Library, 2nd ed.).
Rackham, H. (1933), *Cicero: On the Nature of Gods; Academica*, Cambridge, Mass./London (Loeb Classical Library).
Rakoczy, T. (1996), *Böser Blick, Macht des Auges und Neid der Götter: Eine Untersuchung zur Kraft des Blickes in der griechischen Literatur*, Tübingen.
Rawson, E. (1982), "The Life and Death of Asclepiades of Bithynia", *CQ* 32, 358–70.

Reeve, C.D.C. (2016), *Aristotle: Metaphysics. Translation with Introduction and Notes*, Indianapolis/Cambridge.
Reinhardt, T. (2004), "Readers in the Underworld: Lucretius, *De rerum natura* 3.912–1075", *JRS* 94, 27–46.
Reydams-Schils, G. (2013), "The Academy, the Stoics and Cicero on Plato's *Timaeus*", in: A.G. Long (ed.), *Plato and the Stoics*, Cambridge, 29–58.
Richlin, A. (1997), "Pliny's Brassiere: Roman Medicine and the Female Body", in: J.P. Hallett/ M.B. Skinner (eds.), *Roman Sexualities*, Princeton, 197–220.
Richter, P. (1912), "Die Bedeutung des Milzbrandes für die Geschichte der Epidemien", *Archiv für Geschichte der Medizin* 6, 281–97.
Ricoeur, P. (1996), "Between Rhetoric and Poetics", in: A. Rorty (ed.), *Essays on Aristotle's Rhetoric*, Berkeley, 324–84.
Riedweg, C. (1990), "The "Atheistic" Fragment from Euripides' "Bellerephontes" (286N²)", *ICS* 15, 39–53.
Rimell, V. (2015), *The Closure of Space in Roman Poetics: Empire's Inward Turn*, Cambridge.
Rimell, V. (2019), "The Creative Superiority of Self-Reproach: Horace's *Ars Poetica*", in: S. Matzner/S. Harrison (eds.), *Complex Inferiorities: The Poetics of the Weaker Voice in Latin Literature*, Oxford, 107–28.
Rist, J.M. (1972), *Epicurus: An Introduction*, Cambridge.
Roche, P. (2009), *Lucan: De bello civili, Book I*, Oxford.
Rood, T. (1998), *Thucydides: Narrative and Explanation*, Oxford.
Ross, D.O. (1987), *Virgil's Elements: Physics and Poetry in the Georgics*, Princeton.
Rouse, W.H.D./Smith, M.F. (1992), *Lucretius: De Rerum Natura*, Cambridge, Mass./London (Loeb Classical Library).
Rozelaar, M. (1943), *Lukrez: Versuch einer Deutung*, Amsterdam.
Rubel, A. (2000), *Die Stadt in Angst: Religion und Politik in Athen während des Peloponnesischen Krieges*, Darmstadt.
Rubenstein, M.-J. (2008), *Strange Wonder: The Closure of Metaphysics and the Opening of Awe*, New York.
Rubenstein, M.-J. (2014), *Worlds Without End: The Many Lives of the Multiverse*, New York.
Rudolph, K.C. (2018), "Tastes of Reality: Epistemology and the Senses in Ancient Philosophy", in: K.C. Rudolph (ed.), *Taste and the Ancient Senses*, New York/London, 45–59.
Russell, D. (1989), "Greek Criticism of the Empire", in: G.A. Kennedy (ed.), *The Cambridge History of Literary Criticism*, Cambridge, 297–329.
Rzepka, A. (2012), "Discourse *Ex Nihilo*: Epicurus and Lucretius in Sixteenth Century England", in: B. Holmes/W.H. Shearin (eds.), *Dynamic Reading: Studies in the Reception of Epicureanism*, Oxford, 113–32.
Sallares, R. (2002), *Malaria and Rome: A History of Malaria in Ancient Italy*, Oxford.
Sandbach, F.H. (ed.) (1990), *Menandri Reliquiae Selectae*, Oxford.
Sassi, M.M. (1993), "Mirabilia", in: G. Cambiano/L. Canfora/D. Lanza (eds.), *Lo spazio letterario della Grecia antica* (vol. 1), Rome, 449–68.
Scarry, E. (1985), *The Body in Pain: The Making and Unmaking of the World*, New York/Oxford.
Schepens, G./Delcroix, K. (1996), "Ancient Paradoxography: Origin, Evolution, Production and Reception", in: O. Pecere/A. Stramaglia (eds.), *La letteratura di consumo nel mondo greco-latino*, Cassino, 373–460.

Schiefsky, M. (2007), "Art and Nature in Ancient Mechanics", in: B. Bensaude-Vincent/W.R. Newman (eds.), *The Artificial and the Natural: An Evolving Polarity*, Cambridge, Mass., 67–108.
Schierl, P. (2006), *Die Tragödien des Pacuvius*, Berlin.
Schiesaro, A. (1994), "The Palingenesis of *De rerum natura*", *PCPhS* 40, 81–107.
Schiesaro, A. (2003a), "Rhétorique, Politique et *Didaxis* chez Lucrèce", in: A. Monet (ed.), *Le jardin romain: Epicurisme et poésie à Rome*, Villaneuve d'Ascq., 57–75
Schiesaro, A. (2003b), *The Passions in Play: Thyestes and the Dynamics of Senecan Drama*, Cambridge.
Schiesaro, A. (2006), "A Dream Shattered? Pastoral Anxieties in Senecan Drama", in: M. Fantuzzi/T. Papanghelis (eds.), *Brill's Companion to Greek and Latin Pastoral*, Leiden/Boston, 427–49.
Schiesaro, A. (2009), "Horace's Bacchic Poetics", in: L. Houghton/M. Wyke (eds.), *Perceptions of Horace*, Cambridge, 61–79.
Schiesaro, A. (2014), "*Materiam superabat opus*: Lucretius Metamorphosed", *JRS* 104, 73–104.
Schiesaro, A. (2015), "Seneca and Epicurus: The Allure of the Other", in: S. Bartsch/A. Schiesaro (eds.), *The Cambridge Companion to Seneca*, Cambridge, 239–51.
Schrickx, J. (2011), *Lateinische Modalpartikeln: Nempe, quippe, scilicet, videlicet und nimirum*, Leiden.
Schrijvers, P.H. (1970), *Horror ac Divina voluptas: Études sur la poétique et la poésie de Lucrèce*, Amsterdam.
Schrijvers, P.H. (1999) (ed.), *Lucrèce et les Sciences de la Vie*, Leiden.
Schrijvers, P.H. (2007), "Seeing the Invisible: A Study of Lucretius' Use of Analogy in the *De rerum natura*", in: M.R. Gale (ed.), *Oxford Readings in Lucretius*, Oxford, 255–88 [originally published in French in: O. Gigon (ed.), *Lucrèce*, Geneva (1978), 77–114].
Sears, M.A. (2013), *Athens, Thrace and the Shaping of Athenian Leadership*, Cambridge.
Sedley, D.N. (1988), "Epicurean Anti-Reductionism", in: J. Barnes/M. Mignucci (eds.), *Matter and Metaphysics*, Naples, 295–327.
Sedley, D.N. (1998), *Lucretius and the Transformation of Greek Wisdom*, Cambridge.
Sedley, D.N. (2007), *Creationism and its Critics in Antiquity*, Berkeley.
Sedley, D.N. (2013), "Cicero and the *Timaeus*", in: M. Schofield (ed.), *Aristotle, Plato and Pythagoreanism in the First Century BC: New Directions for Philosophy*, Cambridge, 187–205.
Sedley, D.N./Long, A.A. (1987),*The Hellenistic Philosophers. Volume I*, Cambridge.
Segal, C. (1970), "Lucretius, Epilepsy and the Hippocratic *On Breaths*", *CPh* 65, 180–182
Segal, C. (1990), *Lucretius on Death and Anxiety: Poetry and Philosophy in De Rerum Natura*, Princeton.
Segal, C. (1995), *Sophocles' Tragic World: Divinity, Nature, Society*, Cambridge, Mass./London.
Sens, A. (2016), "Death, Wine and Closure in Hellenistic Sympotic Epigram", in: V. Cazzato/ D. Obbink /E.E. Prodi (eds.), *The Cup of Song: Studies on Poetry and the Symposion*, Oxford, 230–46.
Serres, M. (2000), *The Birth of Physics* (transl. J. Hawkes), Manchester.
Setaioli, A. (2014), "Ethics I: Philosophy as Therapy, Self-transformation, and 'Lebensform'", in: A. Heil/G. Damschen (eds.), *Brill's Companion to Seneca: Philosopher and Dramatist*, Leiden/Boston, 239–56.
Sharples, R.W. (1991–3), "Epicurus, Carneades, and the Atomic Swerve", *BICS* 38,174–90.
Sharrock, A. (2013), "Introduction", in: D. Lehoux/A.D. Morrison/A. Sharrock (eds.), *Lucretius: Poetry, Philosophy, Science,* Oxford, 1–24.

Shearin, W.H. (2012), "Haunting Nepos: *Atticus* and the Performance of Roman Epicurean Death", in: B. Holmes/W.H. Shearin (eds.), *Dynamic Reading: Studies in the Reception of Epicureanism*, Oxford, 30–51.

Shearin, W.H. (2015), *The Language of Atoms: Performativity and Politics in Lucretius' De rerum natura*, Oxford/New York.

Shearin, W.H. (2019), ""The Deep-Sticking Boundary Stone": Cosmology, Sublimity, and Knowledge in Lucretius' *De Rerum Natura* and Seneca's *Naturales Quaestiones*", in: P.S. Horky (ed.), *Cosmos in the Ancient World*, Cambridge, 247–69.

Sinclair, B.W. (1981), "Thucydides, the *Prognostika*, and Lucretius: A Note on *De Rerum Natura* 6.1195", in: G.S. Shrimpton/D.J. McCargar (eds.), *Classical Contributions: Studies in Honour of Malcolm Francis McGregor*, New York, 145–52.

Singer, I. (2009), *The Nature of Love, 1: Plato to Luther* (2nd edition), Cambridge, Mass./London.

Singer, P.N. (forthcoming), "What is a *Pathos*? Where Medicine Meets Philosophy", in: G. Kazantzidis/D. Spatharas (eds.), *Medical Understandings of Emotions in Antiquity*, Berlin/Boston.

Sistakou, E. (2016), *Tragic Failures: Alexandrian Responses to Tragedy and the Tragic*, Berlin/Boston.

Skutsch, O. (1968), *Studia Enniana*, London.

Smith, M.F. (2001), *Lucretius: On the Nature of Things. Translated with Introduction and Notes*, Indianapolis/Cambridge.

Smith, J.H./Kerrigan, W. (1984), *Taking Chances: Derrida, Psychoanalysis, and Literature*, Baltimore/London.

Snyder, J.M. (1980), *Puns and Poetry in Lucretius' De Rerum Natura*, Amsterdam.

Solmsen, F. (1951), "Epicurus and Cosmological Heresies", *AJPh* 72, 1–23.

Solmsen, F. (1961), "Greek Philosophy and the Discovery of the Nerves", *Museum Helveticum* 18, 150–97.

Sourvinou-Inwood, C. (1995), *'Reading" Greek Death: To the End of the Classical Period*, Oxford.

Spencer, W.G. (1935), *Celsus: On Medicine, Vol. I*, Cambridge, Mass./London.

Staley, G.A. (2010), *Seneca and the Idea of Tragedy*, Oxford.

Stephens, S. (2015), *Callimachus: The Hymns*, Oxford.

Stewart, K.A. (2019), *Galen's Theory of Black Bile: Hippocratic Tradition, Manipulation, Innovation*, Leiden.

Stoddard, K. (1996), "Thucydides, Lucretius and the End of *De rerum natura*", *Maia* 48, 107–28.

Stok, F. (1996), "Follia e malattie mentali nella medicina dell'età romana", in: *ANRW* II 37.2, 2282–409.

Stover, T. (1999), "*Placata posse omnia mente tueri:* 'Demythologizing' the Plague in Lucretius", *Latomus* 58, 69–76.

Taylor, B. (2016), "Rationalism and the Theatre in Lucretius", *CQ* 66, 140–54.

Taylor, C.C.W. (2007), "Democritus and Lucretius on Death and Dying", in: A. Brancacci/P.-M. Morel (eds.), *Democritus: Science, The Arts, and the Care of the Soul*, Leiden, 77–86.

Temkin, O. (1956), *Soranus' Gynaecology*, Baltimore.

Temkin, O. (1971), *The Falling Sickness: A History of Epilepsy from the Greeks to the Beginnings of Modern Neurology* (2nd edition, revised), Baltimore.

Thackeray, H.St.J. (1928), *Josephus: The Jewish War, Books 5–7*, Cambridge, Mass./London (Loeb Classical Library).

Thomas, R.F. (1979), "New Comedy, Callimachus, and Roman Poetry", *HSCPh* 83, 179–206.

Thomas, R.F. (1988), *Virgil: Georgics. Volumes I and II*, Cambridge.
Thomas, R.F. (2008), "Prose into Poetry: Tradition and Meaning in Virgil's *Georgics*", in: K. Volk (ed.), *Oxford Readings in Classical Studies: Vergil's Georgics*, Oxford, 43–80.
Thomas, Rosalind (2006), "Thucydides' Intellectual Milieu and the Plague", in: A. Rengakos/ A. Tsakmakis (eds.), *Brill's Companion to Thucydides*, Leiden, 87–108.
Thomas, R. (2017), "Thucydides and his Intellectual Milieu", in: R. Balot/S. Forsdyke/E. Foster (eds.), *The Oxford Handbook of Thucydides*, Oxford, 567–86.
Thompson, D.J. (2005), "Posidippus, Poet of the Ptolemies", in: K. Gutzwiller (ed.), *The New Posidippus: A Hellenistic Poetry Book*, Oxford, 269–86.
Thumiger, C. (2013), "Mad *Erōs* and Eroticized Madness in Tragedy", in: E. Sanders et al. (eds.), *Erōs in Ancient Greece*, Oxford, 27–40.
Thumiger, C. (2016), "Patient Function and Physician Function in the Hippocratic Cases", in: G. Petridou/C. Thumiger (eds.), *Homo Patiens: Approaches to the Patient in the Ancient World*, Leiden/Boston, 107–37.
Thumiger, C. (2017), *A History of the Mind and Mental Health in Classical Greek Medical Thought*, Cambridge.
Thumiger, C. (2018), "Doctors and Patients", in: P. Pormann (ed.), *The Cambridge Companion to Hippocrates*, Cambridge, 263–91.
Thumiger, C. (2019), "Animality, Illness and Dehumanization: The Phenomenology of Illness in Sophocles' *Philoctetes*", in: G.M. Chesi/F. Spiegel (eds.), *Classical Literature and Posthumanism*, London, 95–102.
Tipton, J.A. (2014), *Philosophical Biology in Aristotle's Parts of Animals*, Heidelberg.
Toohey, P. (2004), *Melancholy, Love, and Time. Boundaries of the Self in Ancient Literature*, Ann Arbor.
Totelin, L. (2018), "Bitter Herbs and Sweet Honey: Taste in Botany, Medicine and Science in Antiquity", in: K. Rudolph (ed.), *Tastes and the Ancient Senses*, London/New York, 60–71.
Townend, G.B. (1978), "The Fading of Memmius", *CQ* 28, 267–83.
Traill, A. (2008), *Women and the Comic Plot in Menander*, Cambridge.
Traina, A. (1981), "*Dira libido* (sul linguaggio lucreziano dell'eros)", in: A. Traina, *Poeti latini (e neolatini)* II, Bologna, 11–34.
Tsouna, V. (2003) ""Portare davanti agli occhi": una tecnica retorica nelle opere morali di Filodemo", *Cronache Ercolanensi* 33, 243–47.
Tsouna, V. (2009), "Epicurean Therapeutic Strategies", in: J. Warren (ed.), *The Cambridge Companion to Epicureanism*, Cambridge, 249–65.
Tsouna, V. (2011), "Philodemus, Seneca and Plutarch on Anger", in: J. Fish/K.R. Sanders (eds.), *Epicurus and the Epicurean Tradition*, Cambridge, 183–210.
Turner, E.G. (1969), "The *Phasma* of Menander", *GRBS* 10, 307–24.
Tutrone, F. (2012), "Between Atoms and Humours: Lucretius' Didactic Poetry as a Model of Integrated and Bifocal Physiology", in: M. Horstmanshoff/H. King/C. Zittel (eds.), *Blood, Sweat and Tears: The Changing Concepts of Physiology from Antiquity into Early Modern Europe*, Leiden, 83–102.
Vallance, J.T. (1990), *The Lost Theory of Asclepiades of Bithynia*, Oxford.
van der Eijk, P.J. (2005), *Medicine and Philosophy in Classical Antiquity: Doctors and Philosophers on Nature, Soul, Health and Disease*, Cambridge.
van der Eijk, P.J. (2017), "The Place of Disease in a Teleological World-view: Plato, Aristotle, Galen", in: J. Rocca (ed.), *Teleology in the Ancient World: Philosophical and Medical Approaches*, Cambridge, 217–41.

van Sickle, J. (1980), "The Book-Roll and Some Conventions of the Poetic Book", *Arethusa* 13, 5–42.
Volk, K. (2002), *The Poetics of Latin Didactic. Lucretius, Vergil, Ovid, Manilius*, Oxford.
Volk, K. (2013), "The Genre of Cicero's *De consulatu suo*", in: T. D. Papanghelis/S.J. Harrison/ S. Frangoulidis (eds.), *Generic Interfaces in Latin Literature: Encounters, Interactions and Transformations*, Berlin/Boston, 93–112.
von Staden, H. (1991), "*Apud nos foediora verba*: Celsus' Reluctant Construction of the Female Body", in: G. Sabbah (ed.), *Le latin médical: La constitution d'un langage scientifique*, Saint-Étienne, 271–96.
von Staden, H. (1992), "Women and Dirt", *Helios* 19, 7–30.
von Staden, H. (2000), "Body, Soul, and Nerves: Epicurus, Herophilus, Erasistratus, the Stoics and Galen", in: J.P. Wright/P. Potter (eds.), *Psyche and Soma: Physicians and Metaphysicians on the Mind-body Problem from Antiquity to Enlightenment*, Oxford, 79–116.
von Staden, H. (2008), "Animals, Women, and *Pharmaka* in the Hippocratic Corpus", in: V. Boudon-Millot/V. Dasen/B. Maire (eds.), *Femmes en médecine*, Paris, 171–204.
Wallach, B. (1976), *Lucretius and the Diatribe against the Fear of Death: De Rerum Natura III.830–1094*, Leiden.
Walzer, R./Frede, M. (1985), *Galen: Three Treatises on the Nature of Science*, Indianapolis/ Cambridge.
Wardle, D. (2006), *Cicero: On Divination, Book 1*, Oxford.
Wardy, R. (1988), "Lucretius on what Atoms are Not", *CPh* 83, 112–28.
Warren, J. (2002), "Democritus, the Epicureans, Death and Dying", *CQ* 52, 193–206.
Warren, J. (2004a), "Ancient Atomists and the Plurality of Worlds", *CQ* 54, 354–65.
Warren, J. (2004b), *Facing Death: Epicurus and his Critics*, Oxford.
Warren, J. (2006), "Psychic Disharmony: Philoponus and Epicurus on Plato's *Phaedo*", *OSAP* 30, 235–59.
Warren, J. (2007), "Lucretius and Greek Philosophy", in: S. Gillespie/P. Hardie (eds.), *The Cambridge Companion to Lucretius*, Cambridge, 19–33.
Warren, J. (2014), *The Pleasures of Reason in Plato, Aristotle and the Hellenistic Hedonists*, Cambridge.
Waszink, J.H. (1966), "Letum", *Mnemosyne* 19, 249–60.
Waterfield, R. (2008), *Plato: Timaeus and Critias*, Oxford.
Webb, D. (2006), "Michel Serres on Lucretius: Atomism, Science, and Ethics", *Angelaki* 2, 125–36.
Webb, R. (1997), "Imagination and the Arousal of Emotions in Greco-Roman Rhetoric", in: S.M. Braund/C. Gill (eds.), *The Passions in Roman Thought and Literature*, Cambridge, 112–27.
Webster, T.B.L. (1974), *An Introduction to Menander*, Manchester.
Wee, J.Z. (2017), "Earthquake and Epilepsy: The Body Geologic in the Hippocratic Treatise *On the Sacred Disease*", in: J.Z. Wee (ed.), *The Comparable Body: Analogy and Metaphor in Ancient Mesopotamian, Egyptian and Greco-Roman Medicine*, 142–67.
Weidauer, K. (1954), *Thukydides und die hippokratischen Schriften*, Heidelberg.
Wender, D. (1974), "The Will of the Beast: Sexual Imagery in the *Trachiniae*", *Ramus* 3, 1–17.
West, D.A. (1969), *The Imagery and Poetry of Lucretius*, Edinburgh.
West, D.A. (1979), "Two Plagues: Virgil, *Georgics* 3.478–566 and Lucretius 6.1090–1286", in: D.A. West/T. Woodman (eds.), *Creative Imitation and Latin Literature*, Cambridge, 71–88.
Wilamowitz-Moellendorff, U. von (1876), "Der Pessimist des Menandros", *Hermes* 11, 498–506.
Williams, G.D. (2012), *The Cosmic Viewpoint: A Study of Seneca's 'Natural Questions'*, Oxford.

Williams, G.D. (2016), "Minding the Gap: Seneca, the Self, and the Sublime", in: G.D. Williams/ K. Volk (eds.), *Roman reflections: Studies in Latin Philosophy*, Oxford/New York, 172–91.
Wilson, C. (2008), *Epicureanism and the Origins of Modernity*, Oxford.
Winter, K. (2019), "Taking a Stance: Two Vignettes in Lucretius's *De Rerum Natura* and Seneca's *Troades*", *TAPA* 149, 395–417.
Woodman, A. (1988), *Rhetoric in Classical Historiography*, London.
Worman, N. (2000), "Infection in the Sentence: The Discourse of Disease in Sophocles' *Philoctetes*", *Arethusa* 33, 1–36.
Worman, N. (2015), *Spaces of Metaphor in Ancient Literary Theory and Criticism*, Cambridge.
Wright, M.R. (1981), *Empedocles: The Extant Fragments*, New Haven/London.
Zetzel, J. (1983), "Catullus, Ennius and the Poetics of Illusion", *ICS* 8, 251–66.

Index Rerum et Nominum

air / wind
– as a constituent element of the human body 82–83
– as an external force affecting the body 84
– subterranean winds as causes of earthquakes and volcanoes 99, 104–6
analogy, between microcosm and macrocosm 78, 93, 107, 154–56 (*passim*)
anima 1 with n.1, 49, 55 n.64, 95 n.63
animal imagery
– humans and animals 81, 149, 161
– humans as animals 69 n.110, 119
– animalization caused by disease 76, 80–81
– disease as an animal 92–93
– animal substances in therapies of disease 114
– the "animal" within the human body 95–96, 115
animus 1 with nn.1–2, 12 with n.13, 49–50
anthropomorphization, of atoms / atomization, of humans 34–35
antiphrastic allusion 147
Aristotle 28–29, 86, 111, 114, 135, 173
Asclepiades of Bithynia 26–27, 60, 82 n.17
ataraxia 7, 9, 53 n.60, 102
athroisma 27
body parts
– bones 62 n.87, 139, 143, 146
– chest 43–44, 50, 63 n.92, 68 n.107
– eyes 5 n.14, 11 n.2, 17, 49, 58, 64 n.96, 66, 80, 98, 104 n.85, 146 with n.84, 167–68
– feet 17, 49, 147 n.88
– hair 104 n.87, 11 n.99
– head 43 with n.25, 64 n.96, 66, 88–89, 165–66
– heart 27, 168 n.155
– mouth 17, 51, 58, 77 n.4, 79–83 (*passim*), 132, 144, 155–56, 167–68
– skin 49, 63, 66, 96, 110, 146, 154,

– teeth 51, 80, 97, 100
– throat 63 n.92, 68 n.107, 146, 154 n.108
– womb 25, 113 with n.112, 115
bond (*desmos*), Stoic concept of 16–17
Brown, Robert 54, 126, 135
burden / weight imagery 42–47
burial 35, 81, 152, 161
Callimachus 122–47 (*passim*)
Campbell, Gordon 17, 29, 115
chance 14 with n.9, 28–31
chaos 7, 28–29
children 1–2, 15 n.15, 36 n.89, 73, 166
Cicero 14–19, 48–49
clinamen 20–32
closure 37–76
cloud imagery 85–86, 96, 102, 115, 149–54 (*passim*)
comedy / comic representation of disease 44–47
Commager, Steele 67–69
conflagration (*ekpurōsis*), Stoic concept of 17, 171 n.163
contagion imagery 11 n.2, 50 with n.49, 72–73, 151, 167
Conte, Gian Biagio 85
contradictions / contrasting discourses about disease 6
DeLillo, Don 37
Derrida, Jacques 30
design
– of the poem 37–75
– imparted through the function of disease as *fabricator leti* 13–20
disease
– as a force of destruction 11–36
– as a force of (re)creation 11–36
– and poetic design 37–41
– as a closural device 37–76
– as a paradoxical phenomenon / experience 89–98, 108–21
– at the crossroads between medicine and paradoxography 108–21
– as a means of understanding earthquakes and volcanoes 99–108

–as a sublime spectacle 147–60
–as a foreign / alien entity 76–77, 95–96
–sudden occurrence of 31, 79–82 (passim), 89–90, 100–101, 150, 160–62
–literalisation of 39–40, 54–55 with nn.65–66
disgust 42, 51, 119, 138
doctrina 123
dreams 47, 55–56, 62, 145
dysentery 70
earthquakes 99–102, 106–7
ejection / emission, of
–blood 59 with n.81
–semen 54 n.63, 58
–voice (*semina vocis*) 58–59
Empedocles 27, 115, 134, 166–68
enargeia (*ante oculos*) 98
epilepsy 58, 76–121 (*passim*)
–and its medical explanation by Lucretius 78–89
–and its description through metaphorical language 89–98
–and its persisting marvelous properties 89–98, 108–19
–as a metaphor for the earth's ailing body 99–108
Erysichthon 140–47 (*passim*)
erysipelas 63 with n.92 (see also *sacer ignis*)
facies Hippocratica 66
Farrell, Joseph 37–38
fear
–embodiment of 58, 103–5
–of death 66–73 (*passim*)
–and the sublime 103–5, 147–48
female
–excitement during sex 56
–the female body as intrinsically strange 108–19 (*passim*)
–dirt 114, 119
–the "feminine principal" in Lucretius 114–15
–feminization of the earth 116–17
fever 4, 32, 49, 66, 87–89, 104 n.86
filth
–and the female body 114, 117

–and Callimachean aesthetics 132, 139, 143–44
–and the plague 97, 137, 139
fire imagery 62, 97, 101, 107, 151–54 (*passim*), 158
fluids in/of the body
–bile 4, 32, 54 n.63, 92 with n.47
–blood 59 with n.81, 80–84 (*passim*), 113–14 (menstrual), 154 n.108, 162 n.131, 168 n.155
–faeces 92, 117
–phlegm 43 n.25, 80–83 (*passim*)
–spittle 66, 140 n.62
–sweat 58, 66, 97, 105 n.89, 140 n.62
–urine 88–89, 117
–vomit 81, 92, 110
foedera naturae 29
Fowler, Don 9, 21, 37, 115
furor
–distinguished from *insania* 48–49
–and erotic / sexual desire 52, 54, 56
–and *lethargus* 51 with n.53
–in the course of the plague 67, 168
–in Jerome's story about Lucretius' suicide 131, 173–74
Gale, Monica 112
Galen 2, 26, 92, 164–65
Gardner, Hunter 64
gods
–not interfering with our lives 19
–immune to pain and disease 19 with n.30
–'substituted' by disease 18–20
Graver, Margaret 3–4
Greenblatt, Stephen 102
groaning
–caused by a painful disease 58, 79–80
–at the moment of death 81
Hardie, Philip 145–46, 165–66
headache 109–10
Helicon 110, 137
Hellenistic epigram 124
Heracles 6 with n.91, 93
Holmes, Brooke 114
honey 1–6, 72, 109–10, 125–26
Horace 165–68 (*passim*)
horror / *phrikē*

–in association with knowledge 103–5
–in association with *mirum* 103 with n.83
humoural medicine 26, 31 n.72, 54, 82 with n.16, 92, 100
hunger 49, 140–46 (*passim*)
hymns
–Callimachean 132, 135, 140, 143–45
–the hymnic form in the *DRN* 140 n.64
hyperbole 163
immortality, Empedocles' wish for 168
indestructibility
–of matter 12, 33
–of the divine 87 with n.31
insinuare 94
jaundice 5 with n.14, 167
Josephus 162–63
Kennedy, Duncan 131
Kenney, Edward 123–24
Korsmeyer, Carolyn 147–48
lamenting
–for the dead 36, 151
–and its resemblance to a newborn's wailing 36
–as a distortive evocation of bucolic song 137–38
leptotēs 128–29
lethargy 12, 51–52, 63–64, 84
Longinus 129–33, 163–65
magic 111 n.100, 114 nn.113 and 118
magnet 112, 118
Mann, Thomas 11
McCarthy, Cormac 122
medical
–analogy 2–3, 39–40
–idiom in Latin 55–57
–(especially Hippocratic) intertexts 43, 56, 58–59, 66, 78–89, 113
memory
–loss of it as a consequence of disease 52, 63–64
–overpowering disease through memory of past events 70–71
menstruation / menstrual blood 108–19 (*passim*)
metaphors
–description of disease through metaphorical language 89–98

–disease as a metaphor 60, 68, 99–108 (*passim*), 136
mirum / mirari / mirabilia 77, 85–86, 101–4, 120 with n. 136
mortality, of the soul 11–12, 50, 78–79, 106
mother, the earth as a 9 n.25, 59 n.82
mountains 99, 101, 109, 111 n.99, 133, 137, 152, 170
multiple
–voices in the *DRN* 9
–elements contained in the earth and the sky 109, 111 with n.101
–explanations 112 with n.108
–wombs in the earth 115
Nicander 92
Nile 112, 118, 132–33
nimirum, its philosophical and medical background 85–89
nova tempestas 159–60
novi poetae 123–24
Nugent, Georgia 116
ocean 132
Ovid 145–46, 157–58, 165–66
oxymoron
–of disease as a "maker / architect (of death)" 11–12
–of the "dead life" 47
–of the "living tomb" 81 with n.14
pain (*dolor*) 19, 34, 39–40, 49 n.45, 57, 63, 71–72
paradoxography 108–19
pathē ("affections/passions of the soul") 2–3, 39–40
"perceptual relativity" 4–6
personification,
–of disease 12
–feminine personification of Nature 59 with n.82
–Tisiphone as personification of the plague in Vergil 166 n. 144
pessimistic, readings of Lucretius 9–10, 74
Phaethon
–in Lucretius 89–90
–in Ovid 166

Philodemus   24, 28 with n.63, 92 with n.47, 104 with n.85
Pieria / Pierides   1, 138, 149
plague
–Lucretius' debt to Thucydides   139
–as a symbol of human life and suffering   60, 68, 136
–and emphasis on the body   67–74
–as a sublime spectacle   147–60
–and closure   60–67
Plato   14–19, 22–23, 50 n.49, 115
Pliny the Elder   113, 119–21
poison imagery   63 n.31, 77, 79, 91–95 (*passim*), 110, 116, 119, 144, 163
Porter, James   101, 128–30, 153
Posidippus   128–29
providence (divine)
–in Plato and the Stoics   14–17
–absence of it in the *DRN*   18–20, 111
putrefaction   43 with n.25, 95 with n.63, 96, 148
recycling, of matter   20, 136
religion
–Lucretius' religious devotion to Epicurus   127
–implication of religious imagery in Lucretius' depiction of epilepsy   89–98 (*passim*)
–religious language in *DRN* 3.28–30   131
–abandonment of religion in the course of the plague   34
–attacks against religious modes of healing in medical texts   86–87
restlessness
–combined with discontent and boredom   41–43
–erotic   53
sacer ignis   61, 63, 97–98, 100
Sappho   57–58, 164–65
scabies   167
Scarry, Elaine   95
Schiesaro, Alessandro   33, 166
Schrijvers, Pieter   107
Sedley, David   127
Segal, Charles   12, 43, 50, 76–77, 156
semen   54–56 (*passim*)
Seneca the Younger   5, 102, 169–71

senses
–hearing   57–58
–sight   57, 98, 114, 129, 132, 151
–smell   4–5 with n.18, 92, 108–9, 119
–taste   3–6, 94 n.58, 108
–touch   21, 63, 94, 97, 108–9, 153, 166–67
Serres, Michel   11, 27–28
sexual intercourse   21–23, 55–59 (*passim*)
Sharrock, Alison   9
Sicily
–Empedocles' birthplace   134–35
–as a land of wonders   112 n.105
–and the Athenians' defeat by the Syracusans   163
similes   1–3, 83, 91
simulacra   22, 57, 145
sleep   12, 42, 45–47 (*passim*), 51–52, 84, 104, 109, 133, 145, 168
snakes / serpents   77, 81, 91–94, 96, 110, 119
Sontag, Susan   76
Soranus of Ephesus   25–26
sponte sua   21 n.36, 30, 35 with n.86, 70 n.118
stars   116, 133, 149–52
Stoics/Stoicism   2, 16–18 (*passim*), 48 with nn.39–43, 120–21, 169
strangury   70
sublime, the   147–60 (*passim*)
suicide
–of Empedocles (according to Horace)   166–68
–of Lucretius (according to Jerome)   173
surface
–of the body   63
–of the earth   99, 152
swans   133, 166
sympathy and / vs. antipathy   111 with n.100
symptoms, lists of   58, 61, 66, 80–81, 98
teratogenesis   25
thauma / thaumazein
–in Aristotle   86, 111–12
–in the Hippocratic Corpus   86–89

—in the paradoxographical tradition 110–12
threshold (*limen*) imagery 42, 64 with n.94, 71 n.122
Thucydides 60–74 (*passim*), 136–44, 153–55, 160–65
thunderbolts 89–94 (*passim*), 102, 104, 151, 154
tragic, models of suffering 57, 93
Venus
—the opening hymn to 69 with n.110, 137
—and sexual desire / intercourse 21–24, 59 with n.82, 124, 145
vessel, the human body as a 15 n.15, 40
volcanoes / volcanic activity 85–86, 100–101, 107, 131, 148

war imagery
—war between elemental forces 34 n.83, 158, 160 n.24
—combined with famine and plague 141–42, 158
—in the proem of *DRN* 2 157
Wardy, Robert 77–78
water imagery 51, 61–62, 100, 132–33, 138–45 (*passim*), 155–58, 163–64, 170–71
wormwood 1–2 with nn.3–4, 6 with n.20, 109, 126
wound(s) 21, 23–24, 53–54, 56–57, 59, 88, 93 n.54

Index Locorum

Aelian
De natura animalium
1.51   96 n.67
Varia historia
10.6   147 n.88

Aeschylus
Agamemnon
1389–92   59 n.81
[*Prometheus Bound*]
643   94 n.56

Antigonus of Carystus
Mirabilia
89   96 n.67
118   117 n.128

Apollonius Rhodius
Argonautica
2.200–1   143 n.74
3.761–65   55 n.66
4.1278–82   64 n.97

Apuleius
De dogmate Platonis
1.8   15 n.13

Aristotle
De generatione animalium
725b4–8   55 n.67
726b1–13   55 n.67
De insomniis
459b–460a   114
[*De mirabilibus auscultationibus*]
18   110–11
66   110
77   110
78   111 n.99
81   117 n.128
De partibus animalium
645a25–27   103 n.81
Historia animalium
581b1–2   114 n.116

Metaphysics
928b13–15   111 n.103
983a12–21   86 with n.28, 103 n.81, 111–12
Meteorologica
366b16–30   99 n.75
Physics
197a18–33   29
[*Problemata Physica*]
880a22–29   55 n.67
954b35   47 n.38

Athenaeus
Deipnosophistae
12.552B   147 n.88

Caelius Aurelianus
De morbis acutis
2.31.163   27
3.19.188   27 n.57

Callimachus
Aetia
fr.1.3–4 Harder   134
fr.1.9–12 Harder 126
fr.1.25–28 Harder 138
fr.1.33–34   132 n.42
Epigrams
27   126
28   124, 138
31   125 n.8
In Apollinem
105–12   143–44
108–9   132
110   126
111–12   134, 138–39
In Cererem
27–29   145
59–60   141
65–67   140
87–90   142, 142 n.71
88–93   143
114–15   143

In Delum
13–14   135
94   135 n.52

Catullus
Carmina
76.13   46 n.35
76.25   46 n.35

Celsus
De medicina
3.3.3   104 n.86
3.20.1   52 n.53
3.23.1   113 n.109
3.23.7   89 n.37

Chrysippus
SVF
2.719   16 n.20
3.417   3

Cicero
Epistulae ad familiares
7.26.1   72 n.124
De consulatu suo
fr.10.36–46 Courtney 90 n.42
De divinatione
1.19–20   90 n.42
De fato
22   30 n.68, 32 n.74
De finibus
1.19   23 n.38, 30 n.68
3.35   48 n.41
De natura deorum
1.4   18 n.27
1.18   15 n.16
1.20   17 n.23
2.115   16 n.20
2.133   18 n.27
Lucullus
119   18 n.27
Paradoxa Stoicorum
4   48 n.42
[*Rhetorica ad Herennium*]
4.68   98 n.74
Timaeus
6   14

15   16
16–17   18–19
17   135
Tusculanae Disputationes
3.7   39 n.12, 48
3.11   48–49
4.24   56 n.72

Diodorus Siculus
Bibliotheca historica
3.46.4   162 n.133

Diogenes Laertius
Vitae Philosophorum
5.89–90   96 n.67
10.22   70

Diogenes of Oinoanda
3.IV.3–V.8 68 n.108

Dioscorides
De materia medica
3.23   2 n.3

Empedocles
B 121 D–K   49 n.47

Ennius
Annales
67 Skutsch   148 n.94
125–26 Skutsch   81 n.14
483–4 Skutsch   64 n.96

Epicurus
Epistle to Menoeceus
123   87 n.31
125   64 n.98
KD 4   71
SV 18   57 n.76
fr.221 Usener   3

Euripides
Bacchae
666–67   162 n.132
Hercules Furens
861–63   93

Iphigenia at Aulis
839–40   162 n.132
Medea
1200–2   93 n.50

Galen
Ad Glauconem de methodo medendi
1.15 (11.47–48 K.)   25 n.46
De atra bile
4 (5.115 K.)   92
[*Definitiones Medicae*]
19.395 K.   165 and n.141
19.453–54 K.   25
De locis affectis
3.10 (8.189 K.)   92 n.48
3.11 (8.193–6 K.)   92
De placitis Hippocratis et Platonis
5.2.22 (5.437 K.)   3 n.7
De theriaca ad Pisonem
11 (14.250 L.)   26 n.54
De usu partium
14.10 (4.187 K.)   59 n.80

Heraclides of Pontus
fr.16 Wehrli   96 n.67

Hesiod
Opera et dies
243   141

[Hipp.]
Coa praesagia
80 (5.600 L.)   88
189 (5.624 L.)   67 n.104
309 (5.652 L.)   12 n.4
360 (5.660 L.)   96 n.69
De diaeta acutorum (Sp.)
8 (2.426 L.)   88–89
De diebus iudicatoriis
10 (9.306 L.)   43 n.25
De flatibus
3 (6.94 L.)   84 and n.22
14 (6.112–14)   82–85
De genitura
4–5 (7.474–6 L.)   56 n.71
De locis in homine
33 (6.326 L.)   31 n.72

De morbis
1.13 (6 160 L.)   43 n.25
1.29 (6.198 L.)   62 n.87
2.41 (7.58 L.)   62 n.87
2.72–73 (7.108–112 L.)   43 n.25
3.7 (7.124 L.)   43–44
4.15 (7.574 L.)   104 n.86
De morbo sacro
1 (6.352–54 L.)   86–87
4 (6.360 L.)   80 n.12
10 (6.372 L.)   80 and n.11, 82
13 (6.378–80 L.)   80 n.11
De natura pueri
30 (7.530–38 L.)   115 and n.123
De victu
1.24 (6.496 L.)   88
4.86–93 (6.640–42 L.)   56
Epidemiae
3.17(14) (3.140 L.)   43 n.25
6.8.31 (5.356 L.)   92 n.47
Prognosticon
2 (2.114 L.)   66
5 (2.122 L.)   67
6 (2.124 L.)   66
14 (2.144 L.)   66
23 (2.176–8 L.)   63 n.92, 96 n.69
Prorrheticon
2.12 (9.34 L.)   88

Homer
Odyssey
5.44–50   149
8.493–94   14 n.10

Horace
Ars Poetica
416–17   167 n.150
455–66   165–69
Odes
1.1.30–32   167 n.152
1.1.35–36   165
Satires
1.2.105–8   125 n.8
2.3.145   52 n.55

Jerome
Interpretatio chronicae Eusebii Pamphili
PL 27: 523   131, 173

Josephus
Bellum Judaicum
5.177–80   162–63

Longinus
De sublimitate
1.4   130
10.2–3   164
16.2   130
33.2   133 n.44
33.4–5   129 n.28
33.5   130
34.4   130
35.3   131–32
35.4   133
38.3   163–64

Lucan
De bello civili
1.79–80   16 n.19
1.605   135 n.51

Lucretius
De rerum natura
1.1–49   69, 137
1.31–36   23 n.41
1.72–77   166
1.117–18   137
1.262–64   10 n.26, 12–13, 20
1.271–76   84 and n.23
1.340   150 n.98
1.410–17   134
1.412–13   144
1.485–86   12 n.5, 33 n.78
1.714–41   134–35
1.726–30   112 n.105
1.738–39   135 n.52
1.926–30   138–40
1.926–50   1, 76, 126
1.936   144
1.938   72
1.939–42   73, 89 n.39
1.945–46   73

1.954–57   155 n.111
2.1–6   157
2.16–19   49 n.45
2.55–58   73 n.130
2.62–66   33 n.76
2.66   71 n.120
2.67–70   15–16
2.92–93   155 n.111
2.180–81   28 n.64
2.206   150 n.98, 152
2.216–24   20
2.221   29 n.67
2.357–59   81 n.15
2.398–477   109
2.576–77   36 n.89
2.891   71 n.120
2.947   32
2.963–66   49 n.45
2.1002–6   33
2.1058–63   30
2.1090–92   35 n.87
2.1173–74   158 n.121
3.9–13   125–27
3.28–30   103, 131
3.96–97   11 n.2
3.110   49 n.45
3.136–37   11 n.1
3.140   43
3.147–48   49 n.45
3.152–58   58
3.155   73 n.128
3.170–73   105 n.88
3.231–322   82 n.16
3.290–91   104 n.87
3.333–36   32 n.73
3.459–61   30 n.13, 49 n.45
3.463–73   12, 63–64, 80, 84
3.467–68   52
3.470–71   50 n.49
3.484–86   94 n.60
3.487–91   80
3.487–509   78–79
3.489–91   58
3.495–97   58
3.504–9   106
3.580–81   95 n.63
3.593–98   55 n.64

3.652	72 n.126	4.1119–20	53–54
3.654–56	64 n.96	4.1121–22	54 n.61
3.660–63	93 n.54, 95 n.63	4.1174–81	118–19
3.719–21	9 n.25	4.1192–1208	56
3.722–29	13 n.7	4.1209–32	55–56
3.731–32	49	5.94–96	13 n.8, 16, 157–58, 169, 159 n.122
3.828–29	51 n.53		
3.830–37	147 n.90	5.155	37 n.2
3.888	95 n.63	5.156–65	17 n.22
3.982	46 n.34	5.220–21	20 n.33
3.1039–41	70 n.118	5.223–26	36
3.1047–48	52	5.230	73 n.128
3.1053–54	43	5.341–44	170
3.1053–75	41–42	5.345–47	149 n.97
4.31–37	104	5.351–68	24 n.42
4.132–33	150 n.98	5.366–69	34 n.81
4.332–36	5 n.14	5.373–75	156
4.391–94	149 n.96	5.380–84	34 n.83, 158
4.398	155	5.394–95	158
4.409–11	133–34	5.399–405	89–90
4.414–19	132	5.405–97	116
4.417	155	5.406	90 n.40
4.633–35	3 n.10	5.411–12	170
4.643	71 n.120	5.416–31	30 n.70
4.649–57	27	5.436–42	159, 160 n.124
4.663–72	4	5.780	159
4.664–67	32, 52 n.54, 54 n.63	5.795–98	9 n.25
4.672	4 n.13	5.805–20	115
4.677–80	4 n.12	5.840–41	17
4.826	64 n.95	5.958–61	35 n.86
4.943–44	32, 52 n.54	5.960–65	21 n.36
4.1011–36	55	5.990–93	65 n.99, 81
4.1016	95 n.63	5.1191	152
4.1024–25	62 n.89	5.1392–96	137–38
4.1034	54 n.63	5.1398	138 n.57
4.1037–57	54, 58–59	6.79–80	76 n.2
4.1040–44	54 n.63	6.96–98	149
4.1048	60 n.83	6.128–29	115
4.1049–51	59	6.130–31	85–86
4.1058	59 n.82	6.150–55	137 n.55
4.1068–72	21, 52, 53, 56, 63, 124	6.181–82	150
4.1076–78	53	6.185–86	150, 151
4.1097–1100	62, 145	6.189–93	152 n.104
4.1101–11	22	6.202	154
4.1108–11	51	6.219–21	154
4.1113–14	23 n.40, 55 n.64	6.246–47	151
4.1116–17	52	6.250–55	152

6.266–68	151	6.1168	62 n.87, 107
6.277–78	154	6.1168–69	153–54
6.323–28	102	6.1172–75	155, 167–68
6.379–422	90	6.1176–77	62
6.387–95	90	6.1178–79	162 n.131
6.417–20	90 n.42	6.1179	65, 72–73
6.424–25	150	6.1180–84	167–68
6.431–37	150, 102 n.78	6.1182–96	65–67, 70 n.113
6.451–53	150	6.1187	66, 140 n.62
6.489–91	86	6.1189	154 n.108
6.507–9	151 n.102	6.1194	156 n.115
6.543–47	99	6.1195	66
6.555–56	100	6.1202–3	49 n.45
6.570–74	106	6.1208–9	71 n.122
6.592–95	104–5	6.1213–14	64, 71
6.601–7	106	6.1235–36	11 n. 2, 72–73
6.608–15	132	6.1241–42	90
6.639–40	154 n.108	6.1243–46	67, 73
6.647–54	101	6.1247–48	158 n.120
6.655–69	100–101	6.1250–51	65
6.658–61	49, 54 n.63, 96–97	6.1256–58	73–74
6.663–64	19 n.31	6.1262–71	139, 151
6.680–81	107, 154	6.1264–66	62 n.89
6.689	154 n.108	6.1267–71	142
6.690–92	101	6.1276–77	34
6.701–2	154 n.108	6.1278–81	35
6.712–37	132–33	6.1283–86	151–52
6.769–805	108–110		
6.777–78	94	**Macrobius**	
6.786–87	137	*Saturnalia*	
6.791–93	113, 116	2.8.16	59 n.80
6.821–23	119		
6.955	94	**Manilius**	
6.1090–97	31	*Astronomica*	
6.1090–1137	148	2.363	135
6.1106–13	159 n.122	2.807	16 n.19
6.1119–24	96	5.30–31	14 n.10
6.1125	158–59		
6.1138–39	148 n.93	**Menander**	
6.1140	140 n.62	*Phasma*	
6.1141–43	148–49	31–53	45–47
6.1147–48	154 n.108		
6.1151–53	68 n.107, 154 n.108	**Nicander**	
6.1156–57	64 n.94	*Theriaca*	
6.1160–62	168	98	96 n.66
6.1163–77	61, 63	282–85	92
6.1166–67	97		

Ovid
Amores
1.15.23–24   150 n.99, 157
Fasti
1.301   157 n.118
Metamorphoses
1.57   14 n.10
2.252–53   166
7.541   35 n.86
8.796–808   146 and n.84
8.823–27   145
15.389–90   96 n.67
Tristia
2.423–26   157 n.118
5.12.47   14 n.10

Pacuvius
224 R. (*ROL* II 265)   104 n.84

Persius
Satires
3.83–84   131 n.36

Philo of Alexandria
De aeternitate mundi
66–67   115

Philodemus
De ira
col.3.14–15   104 n.84
col.9.18–10.1   92 n.47
De oeconomia
col.24.3–4   104 n.84
De signis
col.36.11–17   28 n.63
col.36.12–13   24

Philostratus
Heroicus
8.5–10   96 n.67

Plato
[*Axiochus*]
365c   96
Gorgias
493a–494c   15 n.15

Leges
644d8–9   120 n.135
Phaedo
67a   50 n.49
Republic
407b4–c6   40 n.15
Sophist
234b   15 n.15
Symposium
181a–b   124 n.7
191a5–8   22–23
Timaeus
28c–29a   14–15
31a–b   17–18
32c   16
41a–b   16
81e–82a   19 n.29
91b–d   115

Plautus
Aulularia
564   143 n.74
Amphitruo
1117–18   104 n.84
Captivi
135   143 n.74
Menaechmi
889–91   52 n.53

Pliny the Elder
Naturalis Historia
7.32   120
7.63–65   113
7.64   114 n.118
8.98   119
10.188   96 n.67
11.6   120 n.133
17.29   120
28.77–84   113
28.82   114 n.118
28.83   113 and n.110

Plutarch
Adversus Colotem
1110b12–c2   5–6
Cleomenes
39   96

De sollertia animalium
964c   28 n.63
[*Placita Philosophorum*]
884d3–8   27

Porphyry
Ad Marcellam
31   3 n.8

Posidippus
Epigrams
AB 15=20 G–P   128

Quintilian
Institutio Oratoria
1.12.18   98 n.74
3.1.3–4   2 n.4
12.10.73   167 n.151

Sappho
fr.31 Voigt   57–58, 164

Seneca the Younger
De tranquillitate animi
1.2   50 n.50
1.14   171 n.162
2.13–15   42 n.21
14.1   50 n.50
Epistulae morales
75.7   74 n.132
75.11   48 n.41
109.7   5
Naturales Quaestiones
3.15.1   99 n.75
3.27–30   169–72
6.4.1   102 n.80
6.4.2   102
Oedipus
188   98 n.72
Troades
104 n.87

Sextus Empiricus
Against the Logicians
2.53–54   5
Outlines of Scepticism
1.213   5 n.18

Sophocles
Ajax
206–7   94 n.56
Philoctetes
259–60   57
313   57
743–44   93
770–71   97 n.70
787–88   93
1018   96 n.64
1030   96 n.64
1207   93
Trachiniae
770–71   97 n.70
1051–54   63 n.91, 97 n.70
1084   93 n.50

Soranus of Ephesus
Gynaecia
1.30   55 n.67
3.50   25

Statius
Achilleid
1.375   103 n.83
Silvae
7.76   131 n.36
Thebaid
8.4   103 n.83

Theocritus
Idylls
1.146–51   126 n.9
2.90   143 n.74
3.17   62 n.87
3.52   110 n.97
11.15   55 n.66
11.70–71   55 n.66

Theophrastus
De causis plantarum
6.4.5–6   2 n.3
De sensibus
63–67   5 n.18

Index Locorum — **211**

Thucydides
Histories
2.47.3	72 n.123
2.48.2	144 n.77
2.49.1	63 n.90
2.49.2	160, 164
2.49.3	68 n.107
2.49.5	62 n.87, 63 n.90, 142, 153–55, 164
2.49.6	63 n.90, 142–43
2.49.8	71 n.119, 71 n.122
2.50.1–2	161–62
2.51.1	160–61
2.51.4	60 n.85
2.51.6	67
2.52.1–2	139 n.59
2.52.2	64 n.96, 141, 164, 165
2.52.4	60 n.85
2.54.2–3	141–42
2.61.3	161–62
7.84	163
7.87.1–2	164

Varro
De re rustica
1.12.2–3	77 n.4

Vergil
Aeneid
2.215	127
2.221	97 n.70
2.264	14 n.10
3.26	103 n.83
3.29–30	104 n.87
3.156–59	148 n.94
11.185–202	152 n.103
12.718	162 n.131

Eclogues
10.75–76	10 n.97

Georgics
2.483–86	168 n.155
3.457–58	127 n.14
3.515–17	81
3.520–24	144–45
3.551–53	97, 166 n.144
3.561–66	97
3.566	63 n.91
4.441–42	103 n.83
4.539	126

Vitruvius
De architectura
1.1.1	13

Xenophon
Memorabilia
3.11	162 n.133

www.ingramcontent.com/pod-product-compliance
Lightning Source LLC
Chambersburg PA
CBHW020838160426
43192CB00007B/702